The Butterflies of West Virginia
and Their Caterpillars

Pitt Series in Nature and Natural History

MARCIA BONTA, EDITOR

The Butterflies of West Virginia and Their Caterpillars

Thomas J. Allen

UNIVERSITY OF PITTSBURGH PRESS

Published by the University of Pittsburgh Press, Pittsburgh, Pa. 15261

Copyright © 1997, University of Pittsburgh Press

Manufactured in the United States of America

Printed on acid-free paper

10 9 8 7 6 5 4 3 2

Library of Congress Cataloging-in-Publication Data

Allen, Thomas J., 1940–

   The butterflies of West Virginia and their caterpillars / Thomas J. Allen.

      p.   cm. — (Pitt series in nature and natural history)

   Includes bibliographical references (p.   ) and index.

   ISBN 0-8229-3973-8 (cloth : acid-free paper). — ISBN 0-8229-5657-8 (pbk. : acid-free paper)

   1. Butterflies—West Virginia.   I. Title.   II. Series.

QL551.W4A44 1997

595.78'9'09754—dc21   97-4637

Contents

Figures and Tables

FIGURES

TABLES

Preface

I began my lifelong interest in butterflies as a small child in Massachusetts. Something about those colorful and graceful creatures made them irresistible. My family lived adjacent to an old field that had become overgrown with weeds and shrubs. My mother recognized my insatiable appetite to chase after and attempt to catch the butterflies that inhabited the field, so she made me a red fabric net—enabling her to keep an eye on me in the tall weeds. My father, through books and contacts he had made, taught me how to handle and mount the butterflies I caught. He bought me a few cases to house my collection and built me a rearing cage, which I still use today, patterned after one at the Children's Museum in Boston.

As time passed my interest continued to grow, as did my collection. At the University of Maine I studied entomology, although my desire to seriously research, rear, and study the life cycle and habits of butterflies didn't really develop until I came to West Virginia in 1970. Following in the footsteps of all those who preceded me in the state, beginning with William H. Edwards in the late nineteenth century through Paul Opler's surveys in the early 1980s, I continued the effort to survey the state's butterfly fauna.

I began the rewarding experience of rearing butterflies as part of my desire to produce a field guide that included larval plates. Rearing and studying food requirements and behavior of caterpillars has aided a great deal to my appreciation and enjoyment of butterflies. Though I still collect when I have the opportunity, I also enjoy watching butterflies simply flying from flower to flower. In this rapidly moving world we live in, what better way is there to relax than to go out on a sunny afternoon and enjoy nature at its best?

I am hopeful that this book will pique your interest in butterflies as well and provide the necessary steps and information for you to learn about and enjoy the fascinating butterflies of West Virginia.

FIG. 1. Map of West Virginia counties.

1

Environment

Land, Water, and Climate

West Virginia lies in the Appalachian Mountains with an average elevation of 1500 feet above sea level, making it the highest state east of the Mississippi River. The lowest point in the state occurs at the confluence of the Potomac and Shenandoah Rivers at Harpers Ferry, Jefferson County (247 feet), and the highest point is 4862 feet at Spruce Knob in Pendleton County.

West Virginia lies within 3 physiographic provinces: the Allegheny Plateau, the Allegheny Mountains, and the Ridge and Valley Province (fig. 2) (Fenneman 1938; Core 1966; Acciavatti et al. 1992). The Allegheny Plateau is an ancient tableland carved into valleys and hills by the action of running water. It is characterized by a gradual relief of rolling hills and wide valleys in the northern portion (ranging in elevation from 500–1500 ft.) and increased uplifts separated by deep, narrow valleys in the southwest. Soils along the Ohio River and its tributaries are deep, well drained, and fertile. To the east the hilly section ends and the mountainous section begins.

The Allegheny Mountains contain the highest mountains and deepest gorges in the state. Rocky cliffs often tower above the gorges through which rushing streams flow. Many of the mountains in this region contain expanses of rolling uplands covered by cool, moist northern forest communities. Much of the eastern boundary of this province is delineated by a massive, steep ridge known as the Allegheny Front. Soils in this region are mainly well drained, rocky, undifferentiated loams of sandstone derivatives.

The Ridge and Valley Province to the east encompasses the Potomac River and Greenbrier River basins. Soils are mainly shale, with wide valleys between low ridges. The extreme eastern region of this province is composed of narrow ridges of very resistant Cambrian sandstone anticlines. Soils over

FIG. 2. Physiographic provinces and geographic regions.

Ohio River Lowlands

Monongahela-Upper Ohio Basin

Cumberland Mountains

Allegheny Mountains

Allegheny Ridge and Valley

Valley of Virginia and Blue Ridge

much of this province are fine silts developed from shales. The region contains the shale barrens within the state. Fertile upland soils containing limestone are found primarily in extreme eastern West Virginia extending south through eastern Greenbrier and Monroe Counties. Limestone outcrops occur elsewhere sporadically throughout the state.

More than 20,600 square miles of West Virginia drain into the Ohio River, 3600 square miles are drained by the Potomac River, and about 80 square miles drain into the James River. Most of the state is characterized by a branched (dendritic) drainage pattern. Approximately 4000 square miles of the eastern portion of the state is characterized by a parallel (trellised) drainage pattern (WVDNR 1973).

West Virginia lies in an area of North America dominated by eddies of air currents that flow in a west-to-east direction. As a result the climate varies, sometimes bringing in cold, dry arctic air currents and at other times warm, humid air masses from the south. As these air masses come together, large-scale storms develop. Storm tracks generally follow the Ohio River Valley and the eastern seaboard from Georgia. At times these storm patterns affect the western portions of the state, and at other times only the eastern portions are affected. In general, though, the area east of the Allegheny Front has moderate temperatures and receives half the amount of rainfall (30–35 in. per year) as the mountain and western counties. The greatest rainfall, nearly 60 inches per year, occurs along the western slopes of the high mountains in Randolph, Webster, and Nicholas Counties.

Cold air masses from Canada are often moderated by the Great Plains before reaching West Virginia; however, occasionally these cold air masses come from the northeast moving overland around Lake Ontario, bringing the state its lowest temperatures. The effect of warm, humid air from the Gulf, which may become stationary over this region in any season, provides many warm days during winter and hot days during summer. The higher elevations of the mountains tend to be cooler during warm weather than the lowlands.

Approximately 8 percent of the annual precipitation occurs as snowfall and varies considerably from 30 inches in the southwestern counties to 150 inches in the mountains (Miller 1977).

Forests

West Virginia is a heavily forested state, with approximately 79 percent of its surface covered by forests. Oak-hickory types, including pine-oak hardwoods, occupy 77 percent (9.2 million acres) of the merchantable forests. Northern forest types of beech-birch-maple occupy 14 percent (1.7 million acres). A small portion, consisting of approximately 430,000 acres, is occupied by coniferous forests (fig. 3) (Gillespie and Murriner 1991).

Because of its physiography and geographic position in the eastern United States, West Virginia has a wider variety of plant and animal communities than many other states in this region. Here, many southern and northern plants come together at the limits of their range. Much of the western mountain slopes of the state are covered by oak-hickory forests. The xeric south and southwest slopes support oak-hickory and oak-pine forests, and the north-facing slopes and deep fertile coves support mixed mesophytic or cove hardwoods. In the southwestern region of the state this changes from xeric to mesic forests. The mountainous region west of the Allegheny Front is occupied by a mesic forest typical of northern states, with the highest elevations of this region predominantly boreal, spruce-fir forests. At lower elevations (below 2500 ft.) in this region the forests become central

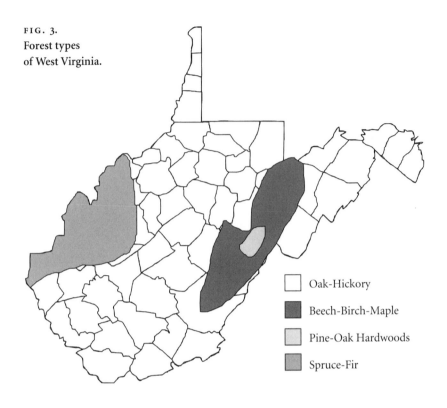

FIG. 3.
Forest types
of West Virginia.

☐ Oak-Hickory

■ Beech-Birch-Maple

▨ Pine-Oak Hardwoods

▨ Spruce-Fir

hardwoods. To the eastern boundary of the state, in the rain shadow of the mountains, the forest type is oak-pine. The oak-pine type of the western counties is an area of higher rainfall than east of the mountains and therefore somewhat different. The eastern oak-pine type is dry.

West Virginia contains portions of 3 national forests and nearly 50 state-owned or managed wildlife management areas. The Monongahela National Forest, by far the largest within the state, encompasses nearly a million acres in the mountainous region west of the Allegheny Front. The George Washington National Forest is found along the eastern border with Virginia and encompasses approximately 105,000 acres. A small amount of the Jefferson National Forest occurs in the extreme southeastern portion of the state in Monroe County and consists of 18,400 acres. State managed lands, distributed throughout West Virginia, vary in size from less than 1000 acres to more than 20,000 acres.

Although forest types vary within the state, the oak-hickory type makes up the largest portion of the state's forests. Within the oak-hickory type, portions of the state are moist (southwestern counties), whereas others are extremely dry (eastern counties). Some species of butterflies prefer certain microclimates and ecosystems within a forest type. The Diana fritillary (*Speyeria diana*), for instance, is found only in the moist oak-hickory forests of southern West Virginia, and although it is often found along ridge tops, it prefers the narrow, moist, and shady coves of this region, where the vegetation is lush and violets (*Viola*) abound. Most woodland species inhabit woodland types, which produce an abundance of their host plants.

Some species of butterflies prefer wetland habitat. These wetlands may be located in lowland meadows or bogs, or as part of open fields or wooded areas. The selection of these sites again depends on the abundance of host plants, as well as the preference of the butterfly for open versus shaded areas. The Silver-bordered Fritillary (*Boloria selene myrina*) prefers open wetland habitats, whereas the Appalachian Brown (*Satyrodes a. appalachia*) prefers shaded habitats.

Much of West Virginia's open land is pastured by livestock. These pastures are home to a few species of butterflies, such as skippers. Other open-area butterflies prefer ungrazed fields. Many of these habitats are maintained for hay production and are mowed 2 to 3 times per year. Such weedy fields provide habitat for many species of butterflies. Abandoned farms and old fields are those that are allowed to undergo succession at least for a few years before being mowed. These areas, which include power- and gas-line right-of-ways, provide some of the best habitats for butterflies in the state. These areas generally produce a diversity of plant species used both as hosts and nectar feeding stations. Some of the rarest species of butterflies found in West Virginia occur in these areas, including the Grizzled Skipper (*Pyrgus centaureae wyandot*), Olympia Marble (*Euchloe olympia*), and Cobweb Skipper (*Hesperia m. metea*).

Many species of butterflies are quite mobile and are associated with urban areas around homes and gardens. Increased interest and awareness of butterflies have resulted in many people developing floral gardens to encourage visitation by butterflies. By learning about habitat and host plant requirements of various butterfly species, one can develop gardens that will provide the necessary plants for many species to complete their life cycles. Chapter 5 details how to develop a butterfly garden.

Because of the diversity of habitat types resulting from such differences in topography, West Virginia features habitats ranging from dry, arid shale barrens to Canadian zone sphagnum bogs and boreal forests. This diversity of habitats expands the potential of the state to support both northern and southern butterfly faunas.

2

Using This Guide

In this guide 128 butterfly species (and 1 subspecies that differs in appearance) are presented. Most of the species covered are resident in West Virginia at some point during the spring, summer, or fall. A few are annual migrants into the state, whereas others remain year round. A few butterflies were reported from West Virginia in historical records, and these were also included. On rare occasions butterflies will be transported out of their native habitats by one means or another and turn up in areas like West Virginia. The only species covered in this guide are those that have been reported at one time or those that have been recently reported from neighboring states close to West Virginia's border (because these species may appear in the state in the near future).

Common names of butterflies used in this guide are those published by the North American Butterfly Association (NABA) 1994, and scientific names are those used by Opler and Krizek (1984) and Opler and Malikul (1992) for each species listed in these accounts. Common names of plants are followed by the scientific name given by Strausbaugh and Core (1977), at their first use in each presentation. Plants listed in this guide represent only those found within the state. Host plants or nectar sources not found in West Virginia have not been included.

Each butterfly species is presented in a biological overview as well as in a color plate. Color plates 1 to 30 show both the upper and lower wing surfaces of each butterfly species. Both sexes are shown when they are noticeably different. Color forms as well as seasonal forms are shown where applicable to aid in field identification. A series of color plates (31–43) follows with photos of full-grown caterpillars of each species to assist with the interpretation of larval descriptions. Seven additional plates (44–50) show the chrysalis of several genera to illustrate differences in size, shape, and color.

Following the chapter on butterfly gardening, a key is presented to guide the user to the proper family and subfamily of the butterfly being identified. The key is based mainly on characteristics that can be observed in many cases without having to capture the butterfly. Learning to use the key will be helpful in locating the proper plates quickly for species identification.

At various points throughout this guide, reference is made to certain areas of the butterfly's wing as well as to some of the veins within the wing. Certain groups of butterflies are distinguished by characteristics of wing venation. In figure 4 a typical Nymphalidae wing is shown with the areas of the wings and margins labeled. This figure will aid in understanding the location of wing features when mentioned in the text. Not all butterflies have the same arrangement of veins; some are lacking and others are branched, but where this occurs in various families or subfamilies a figure is presented in the text to illustrate the feature. Wing venation of a typical Nymphalidae butterfly is presented in figure 5.

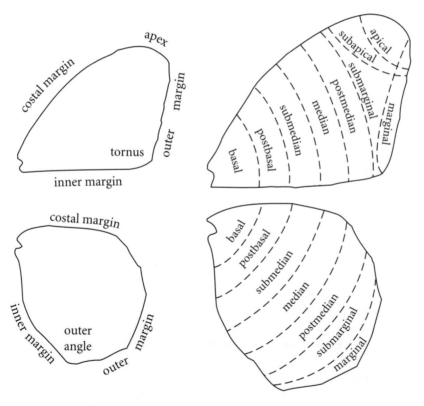

FIG. 4. Typical butterfly wing areas and margins.

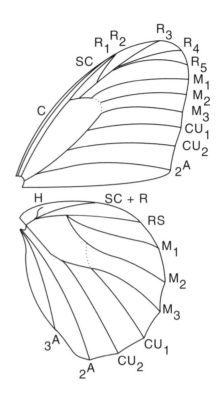

FIG. 5.
Location and
identification of butterfly
wing veins:

C, costal

SC, subcostal

R_1–R_3, radial veins

RS, radial sector

M_1–M_3, medial veins

CU_1–CU_2, cubital veins

2^A–3^A, anal veins

H, humeral vein

Species Account Format

Description
In the species accounts a description is presented of the adult butterfly with
the range in wingspan measurements given in both inches and millimeters.
This is the tip-to-tip distance taken across the forewings, and in most cases it
is based on measurements taken of West Virginia specimens. Differences in
size between sexes will show up in this measurement but may not be
mentioned; however, the color plates show the adult butterflies in actual size
with the exception of Papilionidae, plates 1 to 3, and Nymphalidae, plates 11
to 13, which are shown two-thirds actual size.

Distribution
The total range of each butterfly is presented to give the reader an overview of
how widespread the species is over the continent. Many of the species

presented are more widespread within the state than the maps indicate. When this is true, mention is made in the text. However, the maps reflect only actual sight or collection records made in the various counties from which the species has been reported. The county maps are intended to show the regions of the state where most species will likely be found. County names are not included on individual maps but are listed for reference in figure 1.

Habitat
The habitat description is the key to locating each species of butterfly sought within a county. As nearly as possible the actual locations to search for a butterfly within its favorite habitats are presented. Habitat preference should be used in conjunction with the life history information to enable the enthusiast to locate various butterfly species at the proper times during the flight season.

Life History
The life history section is designed to acquaint the reader with aspects of a butterfly's behavior and biology that will facilitate its location and study. Many species have unique behavior patterns or life cycles, and, therefore, a good knowledge of what to look for and when to look is important in finding and studying each species. The number of broods produced each year as well as the flight dates for each brood are given for West Virginia. Flight dates and broods may vary for other regions within the species' range, but, in general, flight dates do not vary much from more northern habitats. Most flights peak during the midpoint of the dates given, which would be the best time to look for the species. Spring dates of appearance may vary from year to year because of weather conditions. A description of the full-grown larva is also presented in this section and, where possible, depicted in a color plate. This will aid in the interpretation of the description and will facilitate identification of caterpillars found in the wild.

Nectar Sources
Most butterflies nectar at a wide variety of plants that grow within their habitats. Some butterflies restrict their use of nectar plants to favorite colors or the length of the flower tube. For example, many species of gossamer wings (Lycaenidae) have a short proboscis and are unable to reach into deep flowers; these species often prefer composites (Compositae). The plants listed under each species account are a general list at which the butterfly has been observed obtaining nectar. It is by no means an exhaustive list. Some butterflies, such as the anglewings, admirals, tortoiseshells, and satyrs (Nymphalidae), prefer tree

sap, fermenting fruit, or dung to flower nectar. Many species also depend upon soil moisture and salts as part of their diet.

Larval Host Plant

Most butterflies are quite specific in their selection of host plants for the larvae, and most butterflies will not stray far from host plants. In studying butterflies it is essential to know the plant(s) on which the larvae feed in order to know where to search for a species within its habitat. Where possible the host plants used by a species within West Virginia are listed. In cases where that information is not available, host plants that occur in the state and listed by other researchers are presented. These are probably the host plants used in West Virginia as well. Where possible, a full list of acceptable hosts that occur in West Virginia is presented to enable butterfly enthusiasts to search all possible locations for a given species.

3

What Are Butterflies?

Butterflies are insects belonging to the class Insecta. All butterflies have 3 pairs of legs, although in some groups not all are used for walking. Butterflies have 3 body regions: the head, thorax, and abdomen; 2 antennae; and all West Virginia butterflies have 4 scaled wings.

Butterflies and moths belong to the order Lepidoptera, and in a few cases are difficult to separate. However, in this region most butterflies and moths can be separated easily, based on a few characteristics. Butterflies are often brightly colored and fly only in the daytime (diurnal). Butterflies are sun-loving creatures and usually remain inactive on dull, cloudy days. Moths, on the other hand, are primarily nocturnal, although there are species in this region that fly during the day. Butterflies can be distinguished from these day-flying moths simply by examining the antennae. All butterflies have a noticeable club or enlarged tip on the antenna. The antennae of moths are variable, some feathery, some fine and thin, and others, especially the sphinx moths (Sphingidae), have antennae that gradually enlarge to the tip, but none have a pronounced club. Butterflies are usually thin bodied, whereas moths tend to be more robust.

Butterflies can be further divided into 2 groups: the true butterflies (superfamily Papilionoidea) and the skippers (Hesperioidea). Skippers are more robust than true butterflies and have larger heads relative to their body size. They are generally dull colored, being a combination of browns, orange, or black. The antennal club of skippers ends in a hook called an *apiculus*.

From the superfamily, the butterflies can be split into various families, the number depending on the author's preference. In this guide 5 families are found under the true butterflies (Papilionoidea). They are the swallowtails (Papilionidae); whites and sulphurs (Pieridae); harvesters, coppers, hairstreaks, and blues (Lycaenidae); metalmarks (Riodinidae); and the brush-footed butterflies (Nymphalidae). Under the skippers (Hesperioidea) only 1 family is considered, Hesperiidae. Each family contains a number of subfamilies based on similar characteristics. Subfamilies are further subdivided into genera and species based on specific characteristics such as wing patterns, body structures, and habits.

A species includes populations of similar butterflies that breed with one another and produce fertile offspring. Subspecies are geographical populations that have become genetically isolated and over time have become different enough in physical characteristics or habits to be separated. The only subspecies with notable differences in wing color and pattern is included in this guide along with the common species found within the state.

Structure

Adult butterflies have body structures characteristic of most insects, although the presence of scaled wings makes them distinctive (fig. 6).

Head

The head contains 2 segmented antennae, each bearing a club at the end. In skippers the club is drawn out in a narrow extension *(apiculus),* which is often hooked. The antennae are sensory organs used for smell or touch. On the head are 2 large compound eyes made up of thousands of elements, called *ommatidia,* that appear on the eye surface as many small facets. Each one is connected to the optic nerve. The eyes of a butterfly are far more sensitive to ultraviolet light waves than the human eye. On the front of the face are a pair of hairy *labial palpi* that are often pointed and protrude upward along the face. In some species, such as the snouts (Libytheanae), the labial palpi are very long and protrude in front of the head. Their purpose is to clean and house the straw-like feeding tube or *proboscis* that coils up between them, but they also serve as sense organs for smell. The proboscis is made up of 2 halves of a cylinder that fasten together once the butterfly emerges from its pupa. The proboscis can be rolled and unrolled by the action of muscles and is used to draw up nutrients in the form of nectar or those dissolved in water.

Thorax

The thorax comprises 3 segments. Each segment of the thorax bears a pair of segmented legs. Each leg is made up of several segments, each beginning at the body with the *coxa* and moving out to the tip with the *trochanter, femur, tibia,* and 5-segmented *tarsus,* and ending in a *tarsal claw.* The legs are moved

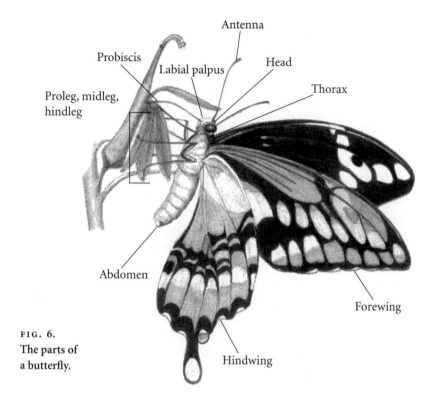

Antenna

Probiscis

Labial palpus

Head

Thorax

Proleg, midleg,
hindleg

Abdomen

Forewing

FIG. 6.
The parts of
a butterfly.

Hindwing

by large muscles attached in the thorax; however, not all 6 legs are necessarily used for walking. Some families, especially the Nymphalidae (brush-footed butterflies), have reduced front legs or *forelegs,* so much so that they cannot be used for walking. Instead they are used as sensory organs and have developed detectors for smell. Many of the Lycaenidae (gossamer wings) also have reduced forelegs, especially in the males; however, they can still be used for walking.

On the thorax are attached the 4 wings (2 forewings and 2 hindwings) used for flight. The wings are operated by large flight muscles in the thorax and are the most visible parts of a butterfly. Small, thin, overlapping scales cover each wing and provide the color and pattern by which most butterflies are identified. Some species have specialized scales *(androconial scales),* especially the males of Hesperiidae and Lycaenidae, that make up the *stigma,* or scent patch, on the forewings. Androconial scales may be located on the hindwings, legs, or bodies of some species. These sex scales release phero-mones, or chemical scents, that attract mates and aid in sex recognition.

The scales of the wings may be pigmented, giving the wing its characteristic color or pattern, but in metallic or iridescent species the scales are faceted to refract and reflect the colors seen. Wings of various species are shaped differently and display different colors and patterns. These patterns, shapes, and colors are recognized by other members of the species and play an important role in recognition, courtship, and mating behavior. Wing colors and patterns also serve as camouflage and protection for a species. Many Nymphalidae, especially the anglewings *(Polygonia)* and tortoiseshells *(Nymphalis),* have cryptic wing patterns, and the butterflies resemble dead leaves or bark when at rest. Others have large eyespots, bright colors, or tails that distract or alarm predators and allow the butterfly to escape. Some species use colors and patterns to mimic other species that feed on toxic plants. This mimicry, called Batesian mimicry (after Henry Bates, who first studied mimicry in *Heliconius* butterflies during the mid-1800s), helps protect the species from predators, especially birds, since they quickly learn that the toxic species are inedible. The distasteful models are generally more abundant than their mimics. A group of species that includes the female Diana *(Speyeria diana),* the female Eastern Tiger Swallowtail *(Papilio glaucus),* the Red-spotted Purple *(Limenitis arthemis astyanax),* and other black swallowtails mimics the inedible Pipevine Swallowtail *(Battus philenor).* The palatable Viceroy *(Limenitis archippus)* mimics the well-known and distasteful Monarch *(Danaus plexippus).*

Abdomen
The abdomen contains most of the respiratory, digestive, and reproductive organs and is also used to store fat body for energy consumption. The *genitalia,* the external portion of the reproductive system, are often used by taxonomists to separate various closely related species of butterflies because their structures usually remain constant within a species. Observation of the genitalia often requires dissection and magnification.

Life Cycle

Butterflies go through 4 stages of development: egg, caterpillar, chrysalis, and adult (fig. 7). Most butterflies will reach the adult stage from the egg in about 4 weeks unless the process is broken by hibernation or diapause.

Depending upon the species, eggs are laid singly, in short stacks or in clusters, usually on or near the host plant. Eggs vary in size, shape, and color from one species to another and may be round, conical, or flattened. Eggs may appear smooth, ribbed, pitted, or have an embossed pattern. In some

FIG. 7.
The
Monarch
butterfly
life cycle.

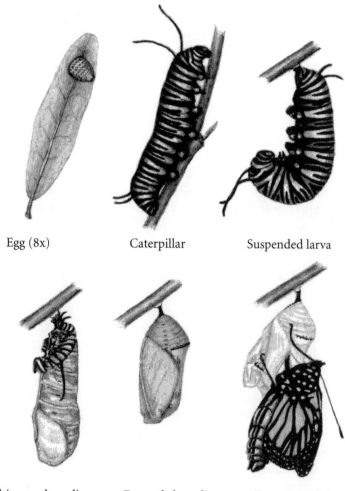

Egg (8x)   Caterpillar   Suspended larva

Molting to chrysalis   Formed chrysalis   Emerging adult

butterflies eggs hatch within a few days (4), but may take as long as 25 to 28 days, as in the fritillaries *(Speyeria)*. Some eggs may overwinter from the summer and fall until the following spring before they hatch.

The newly hatched larva usually consumes its eggshell as its first meal, before feeding on the host plant. Larvae have simple eyes, chewing mouthparts, 3 pairs of segmented legs at the front, and 5 pairs of grasping prolegs toward the rear. The larva is enveloped in the skinlike exoskeleton. The main component of the exoskeleton is an organic compound called *chitin,* which does not stretch or grow. Therefore, larvae must shed this chitin layer once it becomes tight, replacing it with new chitin. This shedding process is called molting, and most butterfly larvae go through 3 to 5 molts, with each stage termed an *instar*. As the larva develops, its appearance also changes, including its color, number of setae and their length, and the length and shape of spines.

After hatching, some larvae—for examples, the fritillaries (*Speyeria*)—hibernate in the leaf litter during fall and winter and await young plant growth in spring before they begin feeding. Other species feed through 2 to 4 instars before diapausing until spring, at which time they feed again, completing their growth. Some species will actually use a different host in the spring. A good example is the Baltimore *(Eupydryas phaeton).* Larvae of other species may complete development and then hibernate for the winter before pupating, such as the duskywing skippers *(Erynnis),* or may pupate and then hibernate, as in the swallowtails (Papilionidae).

Butterfly larvae vary tremendously in size, shape, and color patterns. Many are cryptic (such as the swallowtails) and resemble a bird dropping for protection, whereas others have large eyespots, spines, or setae. Most butterfly larvae use the protection of leaf shelters, which they construct with silk to protect themselves during the day and feed only at night. Those that are visible during the day are usually cryptic or feed on toxic plants that make them unpalatable and less likely to be eaten by predators. Many Lycaenidae larvae have glands on the tenth abdominal segment that secrete a sugary solution milked and fed on by ants. The ants that tend the larvae help protect them from predators and parasites. Hymenoptera parasites take a large toll on butterfly larvae. Larvae serve as food for many groups of mammals, fish, birds, insects, and spiders, and, therefore, being inconspicuous helps ensure survival. Most butterflies deposit several hundred eggs with the possibility of having 1 pair reach maturity for the next generation.

Most larvae feed on parts of plants or trees, including leaves, buds, flowers, or fruit, during development. One species, the Harvester *(Feniseca tarquinius),* is predaceous, and its larvae feed on aphids.

The *pupa,* or *chrysalis,* is the transition stage of the butterfly from larva to the adult. Inside the pupa the larval organs are dissolved or broken down and reassembled into new structures that comprise the adult butterfly, complete with sipping mouthparts, large eyes, and reproductive organs. All this takes place in an average of 10 to 12 days. Once the larva has completed feeding, it finds a suitable place to form its chrysalis (pupa). It may seek shelter on the host plant in rolled leaves, or it may climb down into the leaf litter. The chrysalis itself is made up of a hard chitin shell that protects the soft, fluid parts inside and is produced when the larva molts for the final time. Pupae are vulnerable to predation and parasites, and many are lost to these factors.

Some species of butterflies hibernate in the chrysalis stage during winter and emerge the following spring. In areas of severe drought, as in the southwestern United States, some species may spend 2 years in the chrysalis. Many butterflies that have only 1 flight during the year winter as pupae or eggs.

Within families, pupae are quite similar. Swallowtails (Papilionidae) attach their chrysalis to a substrate by caudal hooks in a pad of silk and hold it in position by a silk girdle. Pieridae are quite similar in their use of a silk girdle. The pupae of Lycaenidae are small and robust and usually formed in the leaf litter, also with a fine silk girdle. The Nymphalidae, however, suspend their chrysalis upside down from a substrate that is often a group of leaves held loosely together by silk. The caudal end of the nymphalid chrysalis has a stiff *cremaster* composed of several hooks at its tip to support it from its silken base.

Once the butterfly emerges from the chrysalis it must immediately pump its blood, *hemolymph,* into the veins of the wings to expand them. Once the wings are expanded they are allowed to dry before the butterfly can take flight. Adults of a species do not all emerge simultaneously, although some species have a short flight period. Most species spread their emergence over a period of 2 to 4 weeks to ensure survival in periods of adversity.

Adult butterflies have varying life spans. Some of the more delicate species, such as the blues (Polymmatinae), live only a few days (3–5) as adults. In that period a mate must be found and eggs must be laid for the next generation. Butterflies that hibernate as adults, such as the Mourning Cloak *(Nymphalis antiopa),* and migratory species, such as the Monarch *(Danaus plexippus),* have extremely long life spans, from 6 to 10 months. These are exceptions; most butterflies live only 2 to 4 weeks as adults. The fritillaries (Nymphalinae) have a differential life span between males and females. Males generally emerge a week or 2 before the females and live long enough to ensure breeding (3–4 weeks). Females, on the other hand, live until fall, often in excess of 8 weeks.

Mating takes place immediately after the female fritillaries emerge, but egg development and ovipositing do not begin for almost 4 weeks. Eggs are deposited by females late in their life and are deposited until they die. Most butterflies are capable of laying 200 to 300 eggs, some species fewer and some more. Each female fritillary, however, is capable of laying from 1000 to 1500 eggs. Once a butterfly emerges from the chrysalis it begins to search for a mate. Males either perch on vegetation and await passing females or patrol their habitat in search of them. Different species have different behavior patterns. Freshly emerged males of some species gather together at wet spots along roads or streams to sip moisture. This activity is called "puddling." Once a receptive female is located, courtship and mating take place.

Butterflies need nourishment during their adult lives, and most species acquire it from flower nectar. However, a few species of Nymphalinae, Satyrinae, and Limenitidinae prefer to acquire nutrients from rotting fruit, tree sap, dung, or carrion rather than from flowers. The Harvester (Miletinae) prefers to feed on the honeydew of aphids. Regardless of what butterflies feed on, they must imbibe the nutrients in a liquid form through their proboscis.

Butterflies are cold-blooded creatures and depend primarily on solar radiation to warm their bodies. This is accomplished through basking. Many species bask on a warm surface such as a leaf or on the ground with their wings outstretched, exposing a large surface area to the warming rays of the sun. Others, such as the hairstreaks, bask with their wings closed, tilting the undersurface in a plane perpendicular to the sun's rays. During periods of little sunlight many species can vibrate the large thoracic muscles to move the wings in a shivering fashion, thus creating heat energy.

Butterflies go to roost once the sun sets and the temperature drops, usually in a protected site on the underside of leaves, in the grass, or on a tree branch or trunk. The *Erynnis* (duskywing skippers) wrap their wings around a twig to roost, resembling a moth.

4

Studying Butterflies

Over the last decade there has been a tremendous increase in butterfly awareness and enjoyment by the American public, leading to a movement toward butterfly conservation by various groups. Garden clubs have supported the planting of flowers along America's highways for their esthetic value as well as to attract butterflies. Many nature-oriented clubs are creating butterfly gardens in private and public facilities purely for their enjoyment.

The enjoyment and study of butterflies does not revolve around collecting as much today as it once did. Many people who are nature lovers and conservationists have taken up butterfly watching much the same as bird watching. Groups now take trips to exotic places to view rare species and photograph butterflies without disturbing them.

Using a pair of low-power binoculars capable of close-up focusing will aid in observing butterflies at a distance while they perch or nectar. Visiting a habitat and simply observing butterflies and their behavior will greatly enhance your knowledge about a species as well as provide pleasure and relaxation.

Many people like to photograph butterflies. To do so requires a certain amount of camera equipment. If you wish to make a collection of butterfly photographs, a single-lens reflex (SLR) camera is a must. This gives you the ability to look directly through the lens at your subject to obtain optimal positioning. A good lens, capable of magnifying your subject, may also be desirable. A 50mm lens will suffice; however, the butterfly will have to be carefully approached, close enough to obtain a good picture. I prefer a larger lens and use a 105mm macro lens for most of my photos. This enables me to obtain the same size photos at twice the distance. Macro lenses enable you to take close-up photos as well, and I use this same lens for larval photos. If you wish to expand your collection of butterfly photos to include caterpillars, then you may find a good flash (I like a ring flash) and a tripod necessary additions. The flash will enable you to obtain good lighting for your photos and increase the depth of field (f-stop) when taking close-up pictures. For small larvae I use extension tubes to increase the magnification. Many of the caterpillar photos depicted in the plates were taken with such equipment.

Depending on the strength of your interest in butterflies, you may wish to go further than mere observation and photography. I find rearing various butterflies from egg to adult a fascinating and rewarding endeavor. Some people rear butterflies to photograph or to study their life cycles and requirements, whereas others rear them for a collection or for specimens to trade with other collectors. There is little doubt that rearing butterflies produces perfect specimens for a collection.

There are several approaches one might take in rearing butterflies. Butterflies can be reared from eggs or from larvae collected in the wild. If rearing is to be done from eggs, there are 2 ways to do it. One way is to follow a female while she oviposits and carefully collect the eggs as she deposits them. This may be difficult because many species lay their eggs on the underside of leaves, often near the base of plants or in grass. You must keep your eye on the leaf while you approach it in order to find the egg. If you become distracted by the female moving to a new site, the egg (or eggs) will be almost impossible to find. Eggs collected should be placed in a small container along with a portion of the host leaf to prevent them from being crushed. Another method of obtaining eggs is to capture a female and put it in a small cage along with a few fresh cuttings from the host plant. Cuttings from a nectar source should also be placed in the cage. The butterfly should be well illuminated, but care should be taken to prevent the plant material from drying out. If a butterfly is to be kept for several days, you may want to supplement its feeding with some sugar water. A weak solution (10 percent) of sugar and water can be provided by saturating a small piece of cotton in a small vial cap or film container lid. The butterfly should be handled only with a pair of forceps, preferably flat-tipped stamp forceps. Pick the butterfly up in the forceps by the strong costal margins of the wings (the closer to the base of the wings the better) and place it on the cotton. Most species will detect the sugar and begin feeding. If you are feeding the butterfly outside the cage place a drinking glass or other container over it until it has finished. Dip the butterfly in a little clean water to remove the sugar from its legs before returning it to its cage. Female butterflies fed twice daily can be kept in captivity for several weeks. Fritillaries (*Speyeria* spp.) do not oviposit early in their adult life and usually have to be kept for a week or 2 before they will begin to lay eggs. Fritillaries will often deposit eggs better if kept in an illuminated paper bag, with a small, damp sponge and an abundance of host leaves (violets). Fritillaries will deposit their eggs on the sides of the paper bag as well as on the host leaves. Once the desired number of eggs are collected for rearing, the adults should be released where they were collected if possible. This will allow them to lay their remaining eggs in their natural habitat.

Caterpillars can be reared using several techniques. By far the easiest method is to place the caterpillar on a host plant and securely fasten a net sleeve over the plant or branch to prevent the larvae from wandering off or from being preyed on or parasitized. Caterpillars reared this way should be tended regularly to move them as they consume their food supply. Small caterpillars are very susceptible to predation by spiders, so care should be taken to ensure the host plant is free of spiders and other predators before sleeving the larvae. Sleeving can be done at home on a potted host plant or in the butterfly's natural habitat. Larvae can also be reared in various containers, jars, or plasticware. When rearing larvae in containers, care should be taken to provide air circulation; a tight container will build up moisture, causing mildew and fungi to develop. Most caterpillars are sensitive to mildew and fungi and will die if left unattended. Containers should be changed or cleaned regularly to remove the droppings, or frass, and provided with dry paper towels and fresh foodplant leaves. Larvae do best if kept in a natural environment, and a small rearing cage placed outside should provide ideal conditions for rearing most native species.

In deciding which butterflies you might like to rear, first examine the life history section under their species account in this book. In some species the larvae do not develop directly from the egg to the adult. Some overwinter before feeding and others feed for awhile and then diapause for a period or hibernate. In general, the easiest species to rear are those that produce more than 1 brood per year.

Pupation takes place shortly after the full-grown larva has completed feeding. Larvae will usually become active, continuously crawling about the container in search of a place to pupate. If the species is a brushfoot (Nymphalidae), the larva will want to suspend its chrysalis from the top or side of the container. Other species may attach their chrysalis to the host plant. In either case, provide space for the larva to complete its development. Pupae are delicate but should eclose (emerge) in 10 to 12 days if provided adequate ventilation and moisture. Some butterflies hibernate in the pupal stage, especially in the late summer brood. If this is the case, wintering the chrysalis in the most natural environment possible will ensure development

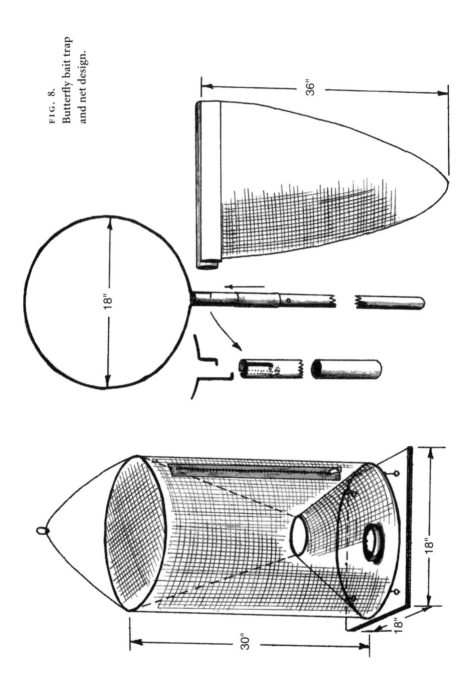

FIG. 8.
Butterfly bait trap and net design.

and emergence of the adult later on. Many researchers winter their pupae in refrigerators. If this is done care must be taken to prevent the pupae from desiccating.

Many butterfly enthusiasts enjoy collecting specimens for study, reference, or just for display. Collecting butterflies can be a rewarding hobby and, if done conscientiously, will not harm the population. Butterflies are used as food by many forms of wildlife, including other insects. Collecting most species of butterflies will have no effect on the population as long as it is done in moderation. However, unlimited collecting of an extremely rare species inhabiting small, defined habitats can have a pronounced effect on the population, especially if females are taken. If we are to be conservationists with a desire to preserve habitats and species for future generations, we need to be careful in our collecting efforts not to jeopardize any butterfly populations. Normally, males are more abundant than females, so when in question as to the status of any given population of rare butterflies, collecting a few males only will not harm the species. Federally threatened or endangered species cannot be collected or disturbed unless it is for specific research purposes with the *appropriate permits*.

In making a butterfly collection, keeping accurate records and labeling specimens are essential if your collection is to have any scientific value. Even if your collection is only to be displayed in your home, good labels containing information as to where the specimen was caught and the date of capture or emergence will help you remember the origin of the specimen. Later on, that information may help you return to those areas at the proper time or season. Should your collection grow to several hundred or even thousands of specimens, at some point in time you may wish to donate it to an institution or museum, and keeping accurate records and labels will make your collection all the more valuable to science. A specimen label should be small, no more than ½ inch by 1 inch, if possible, and should contain at least the following information: state, county, specific locality (town, river, or mountain—if collected on a mountain, elevation should be included), date, and name of collector. Some collectors like to include other information about the catch as well, such as nectar plants or host plant if reared from a larva. For labels use permanent black ink and card stock with at least 25 percent cotton.

Butterflies may be captured in bait traps or with a net (fig. 8). Bait traps work well for attracting and capturing those butterflies that prefer fermenting fruits to flower nectar. The best baits consist of a mixture of ripe fruit, such as banana, beer, brown sugar, and yeast which is allowed to ferment. Butterfly nets can be purchased from any biological supply house or homemade. The net bag should have a diameter of at least 18 inches and should be twice as deep. Sheer polyester fabric makes a good, lightweight net bag for easy swinging.

Some collectors like to dye their net bag green so as not to frighten their quarry. The secret to capturing a butterfly is not the color of the net bag, however, but rather how the butterfly is approached. Approach carefully and slowly, making a quick, deliberate swing when in range. Overswinging will often damage the wings. Once the butterfly is in the net, flip the bag over the hoop to prevent the catch from escaping. If the butterfly is on the ground, quickly flip the net over it, and while holding the net rim against the ground, lift the end of the bag with the opposite hand to allow the butterfly to move up into the net. It doesn't take much of an opening between the net and the ground to permit the quarry to escape. Once the butterfly has been captured, it can be put into a small container, if it is to be kept alive, or in a killing jar.

Various chemicals can be used successfully in a killing jar. Most chemicals are toxic, so extreme care should be used when handling them. A popular chemical for killing jars is ethyl acetate. I prefer to make my own killing jars using cyanide. Many collectors, myself included, prefer to pinch the thorax of specimens. Pinching immobilizes most species, killing several, so that they can be easily removed from the net and placed in a glassine envelope. Small butterflies, such as skippers (Hesperiidae) and Lycaenidae, should be killed in jars rather than pinched, since they are easily damaged. Each butterfly should be placed in a separate glassine envelope (I like stamp envelopes) and immediately labeled with the collecting information. Later, the day's catch can be placed in a freezer to ensure that all specimens have been killed.

Specimens are probably easiest to mount when they are fresh, but not all collectors can prepare their catch immediately. Butterflies may be best stored in a freezer by placing the envelopes in a tightly closed plastic container. Placing butterflies in a freezer will prevent them from being attacked by pests such as dermestid beetles (Dermestidae), which can completely destroy a collection. Specimens can also be allowed to air dry and then stored in a plastic container. Care should be taken to ensure that specimens are dry before tightly closing any container not kept in a freezer because mold will ruin the specimens. Specimens may be stored with a few moth crystals (paradichlorobenzene, PDB) or similar agent to prevent them from being attacked by pests. Repeated breathing of these agents may be harmful to your health, so take care when using them. I prefer to use as little PDB as possible and keep my collection in tightly sealed display cases, which I monitor regularly for the presence of insect pests. This seems to work well without my having to worry about using chemicals that may be a health hazard. Dried specimens to be mounted for display should first be placed in a humidifying

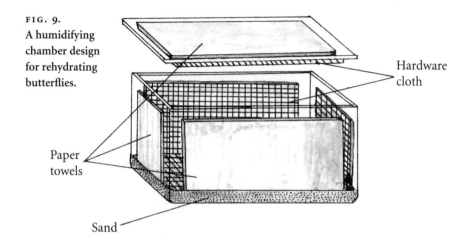

Hardware
cloth

Paper
towels

Sand

chamber. The best chamber to use is one that will provide moisture on all 6 sides. A specimen placed in such a chamber will usually rehydrate and be suitable for mounting in 24 to 36 hours. A plastic container with a tightly fitting lid is best for a humidifying chamber. Place an inch of sand in the bottom. Cut and bend ¼ inch to ½ inch hardware cloth (purchase at any hardware store) to fit loosely across the bottom and up to the 4 sides on the inside of the container. Place folded paper towels down the sides between the hardware cloth and the container. Place paper towels in the lid of the container as well and hold in place with hardware cloth cut to fit. Providing moisture in the lid is important to keeping the moisture content at 100 percent (fig. 9).

An antifungal agent should be used to reduce the possibility of mold forming on the specimens. Agents such as methylparaben (methyl 4-hydroxybenzoate) or Chlorocresol work well and can be purchased from biological supply houses or chemical companies. Household vinegar will also work in preventing mold. Wet the inside of the container completely with water. The specimens can then be placed on the hardware cloth in the bottom and allowed to absorb moisture. You may want to put some type of slotted rack in the container that will allow you to stand the envelopes on end. Make sure that any information written on the envelope is done in indelible ink—the ink will bleed onto the specimens if it is not—or pencil. Once the specimens are rehydrated (1–2 days), they are ready for spreading or mounting.

Figure 10 shows the proper procedure for mounting a butterfly. Mounting boards can be either purchased from biological supply houses or homemade.

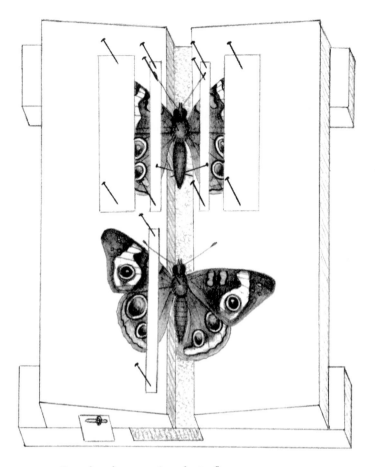

FIG. 10. Procedure for mounting a butterfly.

They can have fixed openings or be adjustable. The opening or slot should be just slightly larger than the body of the specimen to be spread. If a board is made, it should have balsa wood or cork for the bottom of the pinning slot. The flat spreading pieces should be constructed of soft pine or basswood and can be slanted slightly upward away from the slot. Use insect pins for mounting specimens. A number 1, 2, or 3 pin is suitable for mounting all butterflies found in this guide. Push a pin through the thorax to the right of center and stick it into the bottom of the slot. Spread the wings with small strips of tracing or waxed paper starting on 1 side. Pull the wings down flat on the board with a paper strip close to the body and move the wings into position perpendicular to the midline of the body with a pin, using the strong costal margin of the wings for leverage. Once the wings are in place pull the paper strip taught and secure with pins. Use a second, wider strip along the outside edge of the wing and secure it. Wing edges and tails will sometimes curl if not held down. Spread the other set of wings as you did the first. Move the antennae into place and secure with pins, and then support the abdomen from underneath with pins. Lastly, place your label on the board next to the specimen. Allow the specimens to air dry for several days before carefully removing them. Dried specimens are fragile. Place the label on the pin under the butterfly. Your specimen is now ready for storage.

Several types of storage or display cases are available for your collection. Various styles can be purchased from biological supply houses or constructed at home. If you chose to display your specimen in riker mounts, which are thin cases with cotton or fiber backing, then the insect pin through the thorax of the butterfly should be removed as soon as the butterfly is spread. In the riker mounts no pins are used and butterflies are held in place by the cotton or polyester padding. Many serious collectors use museum standard display cases. The 2 most widely used are the California Academy Drawer and the Cornell University Drawer. Unit trays are available for each drawer in which the specimens can be grouped by genera and families. They are convenient since they can be moved around within the drawers without disturbing the spread insects. Whatever means you decide to use for displaying or housing a collection, be sure to provide some type of pest protection as mentioned earlier.

Butterfly collecting is a fascinating hobby and can be extremely educational as well as provide endless hours of enjoyment. Further information on collecting and preserving butterflies can be obtained by writing the West Virginia Division of Natural Resources, Nongame Wildlife and Natural Heritage Program, P.O. Box 67, Elkins, WV 26241.

5

Butterfly Gardening

A backyard butterfly garden can be as simple as planting a single nectar-rich plant or as complex as maintaining patches of wild flowers and host plants. To have an effective butterfly garden, plants that provide both nectar and larval food should be favored.

No matter where you live or how large a yard you may have, whether you live in town or in the country, you can attract various species of butterflies to your garden. Of course, the larger the area and the greater diversity of habitats you have to work with, the greater the number of butterfly species you can attract. But even 1 butterfly bush *(Buddleia* spp.) or 1 lilac tree *(Syringa* spp.) in your yard will attract many butterflies. A butterfly garden does not have to be elaborate to be effective.

In creating a butterfly garden one needs some knowledge of the common butterfly species that might be attracted. A fair knowledge is also required concerning the needs of those species of butterflies for habitat, nectar sources, and larval host plants if you wish to provide for the full life cycle. Attracting butterflies for nectar only is fine, but it is always nice to be able to provide for the full life cycle and see butterflies reared on your property.

The distribution maps in this book will assist you in determining which butterflies are most common in your area. The species accounts will provide the necessary information to help determine which plants will be most attractive to each species.

Many common butterflies that can be attracted to any garden in West Virginia are presented in table 1.

Many more species than the few listed earlier can be attracted to your garden with little effort. This list includes only the most common butterflies statewide that are likely species to be attracted. Many of the butterfly species

TABLE 1

Common butterflies in West Virginia gardens

Butterfly	Scientific Name	Host Plant
Black Swallowtail	*Papilio polyxenes asterius*	carrots, parsley, dill, fennel
E. Tiger Swallowtail	*Papilio glaucus*	cherry, yellow poplar
Cabbage White	*Pieris rapae*	cabbage, broccoli, cauliflower, mustards
Clouded Sulphur	*Colias p. philodice*	clovers
Orange Sulphur	*Colias eurytheme*	clovers
Eastern Tailed-Blue	*Everes c. comyntas*	red clover, legumes
Spring Azure	*Celastrina ladon*	flowers of dogwood, black cherry, wingstem
Great Spangled Fritillary	*Speyeria c. cybele*	violets, pansies
Aphrodite Fritillary	*S. aphrodite*	violets, pansies
Meadow Fritillary	*Boloria b. bellona*	violets, pansies
Pearl Crescent	*Phyciodes tharos*	asters
American Lady	*Vanessa virginiensis*	pussytoes
Painted Lady	*V. cardui*	thistle, pearly everlasting
Silver-spotted Skipper	*Epargyreus clarus*	black locust
Dreamy Duskywing	*Erynnis icelus*	willows
Juvenal's Duskywing	*E. juvenalis*	oaks
Peck's Skipper	*Polites peckius*	grasses
Monarch	*Danaus plexippus*	milkweeds

listed here are inhabitants of open fields, especially ungrazed fields. If you have such a field or live next to one you have a better chance of attracting many of these butterflies to your garden. Fields with native plants, such as milkweeds (*Asclepias* spp.), thistles (*Cirsium* spp.), goldenrods (*Solidago* spp.), asters (*Aster* spp.), daisies (*Chrysanthemum* spp.), and others, provide important nectar sources and host plants for butterflies. A small, unmowed patch or strip along a fence or woodland edge will provide a marvelous addition to your butterfly garden. Remember, the greater diversity or variety of habitats and plants you provide, the more butterflies you will attract.

If you have a natural depression, wet area, or marshy section of a field, you have the possibility of adding several more species of butterflies to your list. Letting this area grow in grasses (Poaceae), sedges (Cyperaceae), ironweed (*Vernonia* spp.), and milkweed will attract many butterflies, especially skippers. Grasses and sedges are the host plants of many of the skippers. A typical American lawn with no shrubs, trees, or flowers is a very sterile environment for butterflies, and most species will move on to better habitats.

In beginning your butterfly garden pick an area or areas you want to set aside for your creation. Decide what portion you might leave natural and whether you want to plant annuals and perennials. There are also several shrubs or trees you might consider planting for butterflies. These can be used as accents to your home. In designing your garden consider its placement relative to the amount of sun it will receive and which parts of the day it will receive sun. Butterflies generally nectar during midmorning and late afternoon more so than at other times during the day. Therefore, a garden placed to receive morning or afternoon sun may be better than placing it where it gets full sun all day long or no sun at all. Full sun all day may cause drying of your garden plants during the hot summer months, depending on where you live. Being sun-loving creatures, no sun at all will deter some butterflies from visiting your garden.

Some knowledge of plant requirements is also necessary to provide proper growth and flowering throughout the seasons. The most effective garden is one that provides a nectar source continuously from spring to fall. Therefore, you should select plants for your garden that bloom in different seasons. Short plants should be planted to the front of your garden, with the taller plants toward the rear. A mixture of nectar plants and host plants is a good idea. Including a small wet area or pool in the garden will provide drinking water for butterflies.

The list of plants in table 2 provides some information on size, season of flowering, and whether they serve as a nectar sources or as larval hosts. This is only a partial list, and many other plants can be used. Several trees can also be planted in your yard or may already be present nearby. Favorable species used for nectar as well as host trees include yellow-poplar *(Liriodendron tulipifera)*, black cherry *(Prunus serotina)*, black locust *(Robinia pseudo-acacia)*, red or white oaks *(Quercus* spp.), flowering dogwood *(Cornus florida)*, redbud *(Cercis canadensis)*, and willows *(Salix* spp.). Your butterfly garden should also provide some perching sites for males, such as nearby shrubs, trees, or even tall grasses. The taller plants in your garden may also serve as perching sites for males of some species.

An assortment of woodland butterflies utilize woodland edges. If such areas are available near your garden, or if you create a garden along a woodland edge, you may encourage its use by several additional butterflies. Many of the woodland butterflies, such as anglewings *(Polygonia* spp.), Mourning Cloak *(Nymphalis antiopa)*, and wood nymphs (Satyrinae), prefer

TABLE 2
Plants Suitable for Gardens in West Virginia and Their Preferred Use by Butterflies

Plant Name	Type	Size	Sun Preference	Flowering Season	Nectar Source	Host
asters (*Aster*)	perennial	med.-tall	sun	summer-fall	X	X
bee balm, oswago tea (*Monarda*)	perennial	tall	partial shade	summer-fall	X	
blazing star (*Liatris*)	perennial	med.-tall	sun	summer	X	
butterfly bush (*Buddleia*)	shrub	tall	sun	summer-fall	X	
butterfly weed (*Asclepias*)	perennial	tall	sun	summer	X	X
cabbage, broccoli, cauliflower, mustards (*Cruciferae*)	annual	med.	sun	spring-summer		X
cardinal flower (*Lobelia*)	perennial	tall	sun	summer-fall	X	
carrots (*Daucus*)	biennial	med.	sun	summer		X
clovers (*Trifolium*)	perennial	low	sun	spring-summer-fall	X	X
common milkweed (*Asclepias*)	perennial	tall	sun	summer	X	X
coneflower (*Rudbeckia*)	perennial	tall	sun	summer	X	
daisies (*Chrysanthemum*)	perennial	med.	sun	summer	X	

continued

TABLE 2
continued

Plant Name	Type	Size	Sun Preference	Flowering Season	Nectar Source	Host
goldenrod (*Solidago*)	perennial	tall	sun	summer-fall	X	
honeysuckle (*Lonicera*)	vine	tall	sun	spring-fall	X	
lilac (*Syringa*)	shrub	tall	sun	spring-summer	X	
marigolds (*Tagetes*)	annual	low	sun	summer-fall	X	
mints (*Mentha*)	perennial	med.	sun	summer-fall	X	
mock orange (*Philadelphus*)	shrub	tall	sun	spring-summer	X	
nettle (*Urtica*)	perennial	tall	shade	spring-fall		X
phlox (*Phlox*)	perennial	low-med.	sun	spring-summer	X	
pussytoe, everlasting (*Antennaria*)	perennial	low-med.	sun	spring-fall	X	
sunflowers (*Helianthus*)	perennial	tall	sun	summer	X	X
thistle (*Cirsium*)	perennial	tall	sun	summer	X	X
vetch (*Vicia*)	perennial	med.-tall	sun	spring-fall	X	X
violets (*Viola*)	perennial	low	shade	spring	X	X
yarrow (*Achillea*)	perennial	med.-tall	sun	summer-fall	X	
zinnias (*Zinnia*)	annual	med.	sun	summer-fall	X	

rotting fruit or tree sap to flowers for nourishment. These species can be attracted to baits or rotting fruit placed on the ground in the shade. In late summer and fall these species will frequently visit rotting fruit under apple trees.

Your butterfly garden can be a rewarding experience by providing a welcomed environment for many local species, as well as providing a pleasant landscape to your home.

6

Key to Families and Subfamilies of West Virginia Butterflies

1a.   Butterfly wingspan variable. Head narrow; less than twice as broad as high. *Antennae close together at base without a curve or hook at distal end.* See 3.

1b.   Butterfly small (¾ in., 19 mm) to medium (2⅜ in., 60 mm). *Antennae widely separated at base with a small curve or hook on the distal end of the club.* Butterfly background color dull brown, black, orange, or yellow. May be marked with black or unmarked checkered with white. On medium individuals a gold band or white spot may be prominent. Head very broad, body robust. Most are rapid fliers. When at rest, wings held partially opened to fully extended horizontally. Males may have an elongated, black velvety patch in upperside of forewing. Family Hesperiidae. See 2.

2a.   Butterflies brown to black with white, gray, or dull gold markings. Size variable. Usually rests with wings open. *Antennal clubs long and sickle-shaped. No visible stigma on forewings.* Subfamily Pyrginae—Open-winged Skippers / Page 182 / Plates 24–26, 30

2b.   Butterflies small; either yellow, orange, brown, or black. *Antennal club short and not strongly hooked.* Butterflies bask with wings partly opened and perch with wings closed or partly opened. *Males usually have black stigma in forewing.* Subfamily Hesperiinae—Branded Skippers / Page 211 / Plates 27–30

3a.   *Front legs in males or in both sexes imperfect, either small and held folded close to body or at least reduced in size.* Butterfly appears to have only 4 walking legs, or butterfly with reduced front legs and prominent white eye ring. If white eye ring present, butterfly is usually small.
See 4.

3b.   *Front legs perfect and used for walking in both sexes.* Eyes *not* ringed with white. If small to medium, color is white, yellow, or orange with or without black. If large, butterfly has prominent tails on hind wings and may be black, black and white, or black (brown) and yellow striped.
See 15.

4a.   Head small and narrow. *Bases of antennae notching the eyes.* Size generally small, not exceeding 1½ inches (38 mm). Color variable but usually black, gray, brown, silvery, green, pale blue, or metallic blue.
See 11.

4b.   Head large, nearly as broad as thorax. *Antennae not notching the eyes.* Forelegs in males and usually females greatly reduced, brushlike, and not used for walking. Size variable—may be small (1 in., 25 mm) to greater than 4⅛ inches (105 mm).
Family Nymphalidae. See 5.

5a.   *Palpi on front of head very much elongated,* more than half the length of the antennae giving the appearance of a long pointed snout. Size 1⅝ to 1⅞ inches (41–48 mm).
Subfamily Libytheinae—Snouts / Page 117 / Plate 23

5b.   Palpi on front of head not elongated.
See 6.

6a.   Large (3½–4 in., 89–102 mm), red-brown to brown butterfly marked with white and black. *Body black, spotted with white. Lacks black band across center of hindwing above. Antennae without scales.*
Subfamily Danainae—Milkweed Butterflies / Page 178 / Plate 23

6b.   Body not spotted with white. *Antennae with scales.*
      See 7.

7a.   Dull to chocolate brown butterfly, usually with
      noticeable eye spots on wings. If lacking spots, size is
      small, less than 1⅜ in. (35 mm). Flight is slow to
      moderate, bouncing through vegetation close to
      ground. *One or more of the veins in the forewing swollen
      or enlarged at base.* No cream or white spots visible outside eyespots.
      **Subfamily Satyrinae—Satyrs and Wood Nymphs / Page 167 / Plates 22–
      23**

7b.   Veins in base of forewings not swollen.
      See 8.

8a.   Underside of hindwings with numerous conspicuous silver or whitish
      spots, triangles, or a submarginal row of fine silver dashes. May be small
      (1 in., 35 mm) to large (4⅛ in., 105 mm). Color orange, orange brown,
      or black, with black, cream, or blue markings.
      Subfamily Heliconiinae—Longwings / Page 119 / Plates 11–14

8b.   Underside of hindwings without numerous silver spots or a fine row of
      silver dashes.
      See 9.

9a.   Underside of hindwings variegated; tan, brown, orange, yellowish, or
      purplish or a combination of these colors. The upperside of wings light
      to medium orange or light brownish with black markings, dashes,
      circles, and a submarginal row of black spots.
      See 10.

9b.   Wing pattern or colors not as in 9a.
      Subfamily Nymphalinae—Brushfoots / Page 132 / Plates 14–21

10a. Butterfly small to medium (1¼–1⅞ in., 32–48 mm). Forewing truncated
      (squared off). Upperside without a black wing margin or border.
      Underside brown with some yellow and purple to lavender toward the
      outer margin.
      **Subfamily Heliconiinae—Longwings / Page 119 / Meadow Fritillary
      (*Boloria bellona*) / Plate 14**

10b. Size medium, 1¾ to 2⅝ inches (44–67 mm), brownish yellow above. Submarginal black spots inside larger, pale spots. Also black-rimmed, pale spots interiorly. Underside yellow to whitish, variegated with brown, forming a pale band across the hindwing.
Subfamily Heliconiinae—Longwings / Page 119 / Variegated Fritillary (*Euptoieta claudia*) / Plate 11

11a. Forelegs of males not greatly reduced. *Conspicuous white ring around the eyes.* Antennae usually ringed with white lines. Wings held vertical or nearly so at rest. Some individuals have small tails on hind wings, and/or may lean to one side when at rest, and/or rub their wings together.
Family Lycaenidae—Harvesters, Coppers, Hairstreaks, Blues. See 12.

11b. Forelegs greatly reduced in males. *No white ring around eyes, but antennae ringed with white.* Wings held horizontal at rest. Small, 1 to 1¼ inches (25–32 mm). Color orange brown with small, black markings above, yellow orange with metallic gray flecking below.
Family Riodinidae, Subfamily Riodininae—Metalmarks / Page 112 / Plate 10

12a. Antennae at least half as long as forewings with segments longer than wide.
See 13.

12b. Antennae less than half as long as forewings, with segments as long as wide. Butterfly orange with brownish black borders and blotches on upperside. Underside brown with rust blotches circled with fine white lines. Species rests with wings closed.
Subfamily Miletinae—Harvesters / Page 72 / Plate 7

13a. Butterflies with conspicuous lobe at outer angle of hindwing or with 2 hairlike tails. Color brown, charcoal gray, or iridescent blue on upper surface. Underside gray, brown, green, or blackish, usually with white lines, stripes, or bands. May have blue, orange, and black spots near outer angle of hindwing. May be rapid, erratic fliers.
Subfamily Theclininae—Hairstreaks / Page 79 / Plates 8–10

13b. Butterflies with rounded hindwings, no conspicuous lobes, tailless or with a single tail.
See 14.

14a. Butterflies orange with black spots above, or brownish-gray with or without purple cast. Underside silvery-white with small black dots. If brownish-gray, butterfly is associated with bog area. *No tails.*
Subfamily Lycaeninae—Coppers / Page 74 / Plates 7–8

14b. Butterflies pale to medium blue with narrow to broad, black borders, or charcoal gray on upper wing surface. Underside silvery white to grayish, with black dots or spots. Tailless or with single tail. If tail present, species has 2 orange spots on outer angle of hindwing.
Subfamily Polyommatinae—Blues / Page 102 / Plate 10

15a. Butterfly large (2⅜–5½ in., 60–140 mm). *Hindwings with conspicuous tails.* Color black, yellow, or whitish, with or without black stripes.
Family Papilionidae, Subfamily Papilioninae—Swallowtails / Page 40 / Plates 1–3

15b. Butterfly small to medium (1–2¾ in., 25–70 mm). Hindwings without tails. Wings white, yellow, or orange, with or without a black border but never striped.
Family Pieridae. See 16.

16a. Butterflies white with some black or greenish markings. May have orange forewing tips. Wings usually lack black borders. If black border present, it *does not* cover entire forewing margin.
Subfamily Pierinae—Whites / Page 53 / Plates 4–5

16b. Butterflies yellow, orange, or white. Outer wing margin black with or without spots. If butterfly white, black forewing margin is entire, spotted with white.
Subfamily Coliadinae—Sulphurs / Page 61 / Plates 5–7

7

Superfamily Papilionoidea

Family Papilionidae—Swallowtails

The swallowtails, which include the largest butterflies and some of the most colorful, number approximately 534 species worldwide. Only 30 species occur in North America, with most found in the South or West. In West Virginia there are 7 species.

The swallowtails can be easily distinguished from other groups by several characteristics. The prothoracic pair of legs is fully developed and used for walking, thus allowing swallowtails 6 walking legs instead of 4. All members of this group have a tibial spur or epiphysis on the front legs. Only 1 anal vein (fig. 11) is present in the hindwing, and all West Virginia swallowtails possess tails on the hindwings. The caterpillars of this group are hairless or possess fine, short hairs, which give them a velvety appearance; if tubercles are present, they are generally fleshy. Swallowtail larvae possess a forked, pungent-smelling, yellow or orange gland, called an *osmeterium*, behind the head

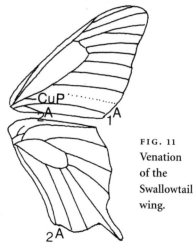

FIG. 11 Venation of the Swallowtail wing.

that can be eversed when disturbed. This is used as a defense mechanism. Caterpillars resemble bird droppings in their early development and feed on various plants belonging to several families of dicotyledons with aromatic leaves.

The chrysalis of the swallowtail is exposed and held fast to its substrate by a silken pad at the caudal end and a silk girdle. The chrysalis is green or brown and is the overwintering stage of the swallowtails.

Mimicry is common in this group, with 3 of the 6 species found in West Virginia mimicking the distasteful *Aristolochia*-feeding Pipevine Swallowtail *(Battus philenor)*. Two butterflies in the family Nymphalidae, the female Diana fritillary *(Speyeria diana)* and the Red-spotted Purple *(Limenitis arthemis astyanax),* also mimic the Pipevine Swallowtail.

The family Papilionidae is divided into 3 subfamilies—Papilioninae, Parnassiinae, and Baroniinae—with the first 2 occurring in North America. All West Virginia swallowtails belong to the Papilioninae subfamily.

Subfamily Papilioninae—Swallowtails

Adults are characterized by a small CuP vein at the base of the forewing (fig. 11); the pupa has 2 short horns at the head. All West Virginia swallowtails have a tail on each of the hindwings. Three genera of this group are found in West Virginia: *Battus, Eurytides,* and *Papilio.*

Battus is an *Aristolochia*-feeding swallowtail genus. These plants, because of their toxins, make the larvae and adults unpalatable and thus protect them against predation. As a result, other members of the Papilioninae, as well as other families, mimic the *Aristolochia*-feeding swallowtails. Members of the *Battus* group can be identified by the deep sensory groove on the antennae and 4 rows of spines on the tarsi not separated into 2 groups by a smooth area as in the *Papilio. Battus* larvae are heavily clothed with fine hairs, which give them a velvety appearance. They have long soft tubercles also covered with fine hairs. When nectaring, adults flutter their wings constantly. Members of this genus generally bask with their wings spread and may puddle, which is characteristic of the swallowtails, with wings either spread or closed.

The second genus, *Eurytides,* is characterized by a fold of scent scales on the lower margin of the hindwing. Adults have long tails and are zebra-striped. Larvae feed on paw paw (Annonaceae).

The genus *Papilio* is represented in West Virginia by 5 species. Papilios are also characterized by fluted antennae with sensory grooves, which are not easily seen. Two vertical rows of spines are present on the tarsi and are clearly separated by a smooth area between. The hindwing margin lacks the scent patches found in *Battus* and *Eurytides.*

Fully grown *Papilio* larvae generally lack tubercles and often display eye spots on the third thoracic segment. Host plants for *Papilio* are not as restricted as in the other 2 genera.

Pipevine Swallowtail

Battus philenor (Linnaeus), 1771

Adult: Plate 1, Rows 1, 2
Larva: Plate 31, Row 1

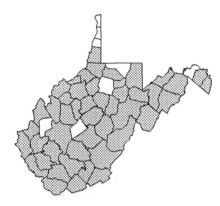

Description: Wingspan is 2½ to 4¼ inches (63–107 mm). The male Pipevine Swallowtail is black to dark gray above, with an iridescent blue-green hindwing. A row of light blue-green spots occurs near the outer margin of the hindwing. In the female only a slight iridescence appears on the hindwing, and the submarginal row of spots is a pale lavender. The underside of the wings is distinctive from other swallowtails in both sexes. There is a curved row of 7 circular orange spots on a background of iridescent blue green on the hindwing. A row of white marginal spots is found on the underside of the hindwing. Several West Virginia butterflies mimic the Pipevine Swallowtail because of its toxicity. This toxicity is derived from the larval foodplant and results in a lower predation rate by birds. These species include the Spicebush Swallowtail *(Papilio troilus),* the dark form of the female Eastern Tiger Swallowtail *(Papilio glaucus),* the female Black Swallowtail *(Papilio polyxenes asterius),* the Diana fritillary female *(Speyeria diana),* and the Red-spotted Purple *(Limenitis arthemis astyanax).*

Distribution: The Pipevine Swallowtail ranges southward from southern New England west through southern Michigan to the Southwest desert region and into Mexico. A small population also occurs in central California. In West Virginia the Pipevine Swallowtail has been recorded from almost every county. It undoubtedly occurs statewide.

Habitat: This species prefers deciduous forests and is often found along woodland roads and streams, road edges, and brushy hillsides. Males and females readily nectar in fields and gardens, and males gather in large numbers at moist sandy spots along gravel or woodland roads or at stream edges.

Life History and Habits: Males of this species patrol for females in a low, rapid flight, stopping periodically to nectar or puddle with other males. Females spend much of the day searching for host plants, egg laying, and nectaring. Nectaring takes place more often during midmorning and late afternoon. When nectaring at flowers or puddling at moist sand, this species flutters its wings, as do some of the other swallowtails. The Pipevine Swallowtail is bivoltine in West Virginia, with the first flight occurring in early spring from April to June. The second flight occurs in July and August and extends into late September and October. On occasion a partial third flight may occur, especially in warmer areas. Females lay eggs in groups on the underside of young host leaves or on the stem at the base of the leaf. If the vine is small, a few eggs are deposited, and if the vine is large, a large number may be deposited. Eggs are round and orange. Young larvae feed in groups on the underside of host leaves. As larvae grow they move to new leaves and feed alone. The caterpillar is dark brown with dark, fleshy tubercles in rows along the body. Those near the head are long, and those along the abdominal segments are short with red bases. The chrysalis is brown or green, with strongly fluted lateral keels along the abdomen and is supported by a silk girdle. The chrysalis is the overwintering stage for this species.

Nectar Sources: The Pipevine Swallowtail nectars at a variety of plants and shrubs in bloom during its flight periods. Pink and purple flowers are among its favorite colors and include phlox *(Phlox),* milkweeds *(Asclepias),* Joe-pye weed *(Eupatorium),* ironweed *(Vernonia),* thistles *(Cirsium),* and turk's cap lilies *(Lilium superburn).*

Larval Host Plant: Dutchman's pipe *(Aristolochia macrophylla)* is the most commonly used host in West Virginia. Other *Aristolochias,* such as Virginia snakeroot *(A. serpentaria),* are also utilized where present.

Zebra Swallowtail

Eurytides marcellus (Cramer), 1777

Adult: Plate 1, Rows 2, 3
Larva: Plate 31, Row 1
Pupa: Plate 44, Row 1

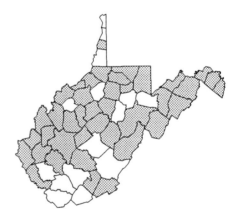

Description: Wingspan is 2¼ to 3½ inches (57–89 mm). The Zebra Swallowtail is a black and greenish white, striped butterfly with triangular wings and long swordlike tails. There are 2 deep blue spots and a bright red spot at the lower edge of the hindwing on the upper surface. On the underside is a red stripe, bordered in black, through the middle of the hindwing. The width of the black stripes and the length of the tails vary with broods. The spring brood is smaller and has shorter tails than the summer brood. The summer form ("lecontei") has white-edged tails that may exceed 1 inch (25 mm) in length.

Distribution: The Zebra Swallowtail ranges from southern New York and New Jersey to Minnesota and south to Florida and the Gulf Coast. It is rare in the northern part of its range. In West Virginia the species has been recorded from many counties and should be found statewide. It is closely associated with its host plant, paw paw *(Asimina triloba)*, and populations are centered around areas where paw paw occurs.

Habitat: The Zebra Swallowtail is found in and about rich woodlands, especially along streams and rivers where its host plant occurs. Males often fly along woodland roads. The species frequently wanders into fields and brushy areas in search of nectar plants.

Life History and Habits: Males of the species patrol a few feet above the ground in a rapid flight along roads, streams, or woodland edges in search of females. In the spring brood especially, males gather at wet, sandy areas along streams or woodland roads and sip moisture and minerals. Females oviposit from midmorning until late afternoon. Females fly rapidly up and down trees and shrubs searching for suitable sites on which to oviposit. Oviposition is done very rapidly on fresh young leaves at the tips of branches on the host plant. The female lays a single egg without stopping and immediately moves on to look for another leaf. The Zebra Swallowtail is bivoltine in West Virginia, with the first brood emerging in April and extending into early June. The second brood emerges from mid-June into August. Larvae of the second brood pupate and then hibernate until the following spring. In some years, especially when spring is late, only a partial second brood may occur, and many pupae from the first brood overwinter. The caterpillar is pale blue green with thin, transverse stripes on each segment: 4 gray or black and 1 yellow. The chrysalis is either green or brown, stout and smooth, and often suspended on the underside of a leaf on the host plant.

Nectar Sources: Males frequently sip moisture and minerals from moist soil; however, shrubs and plants are visited, including blackberry *(Rubus)*, dogbane *(Apocynum)*, redbud *(Cercis canadensis)*, milkweed *(Asclepias)*, and viper's bugloss *(Echium vulgare)*.

Larval Host Plant: In West Virginia, paw paw *(Asimina triloba)* is the only host plant utilized by the Zebra Swallowtail.

Black Swallowtail

Papilio polyxenes asterius(Stoll), 1782

Adult: Plate 2, Row 1
Larva: Plate 31, Row 2

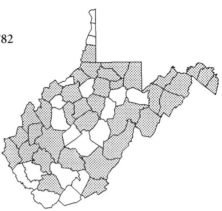

Description: Wingspan is 2⅜ to 3¾ inches (60–95 mm). The Black Swallowtail is a large black butterfly with prominent tails. Males have a band of bright yellow spots across the outer portion of both wings above and a marginal row of smaller, yellow spots and crescents. Females lack the strong submarginal band of yellow spots and may only show a hint of it. A large patch of blue occurs on the hindwing of the female. Both sexes have a bright orange anal spot with a black center in the hindwing. The underside is black with 2 rows of yellow-and-orange spots across both wings.

Distribution: The Black Swallowtail is widespread, ranging from the Maritime Provinces west to the Rocky Mountains and south through the entire eastern United States to New Mexico, Arizona, and California. In West Virginia the species can probably be found in all counties.

Habitat: This species prefers open areas, such as fields, pastures, roadsides, brushy hillsides, wetlands, and gardens and is often found in fields where weeds abound.

Life History and Habits: Males perch and patrol for females in open areas. When perching they land on the tops of tall grass stems or on leaves of shrubs and small trees in open areas. Patrolling and perching are often done on hill tops in fields. Females flutter close to the ground along road edges or through fields in search of host plants on which to oviposit. Once a suitable host plant is found the female will deposit a single egg on the tip of the leaf. She may move around the plant and deposit a few eggs before moving on in search of a new plant. The Black Swallowtail is bivoltine in West Virginia, although a small third brood does occur in some areas. Adults of the first brood, emerging from the overwintering chrysalis, fly in early April and continue into June. A second flight begins in late June and extends into August. Some pupae from the second brood diapause for the winter. However, in warmer areas of the state a partial third flight occurs from late August into September and rarely into October. Young larvae, which are often found on carrots, parsley, or dill (Umbelliferae) in one's garden, are black with a white dorsal saddle resembling a bird dropping. The last instar caterpillar is pale to bright green, with black bands on each segment. A series of yellow to orange spots occurs in each black band. The head is green and striped with black and orange. The chrysalis is green or brown, mottled, and streaked with darker markings. It is attached upright on a stem or branch with a silk girdle. The overwintering chrysalis is brown resulting from the shortening photoperiod (West et al. 1972).

Nectar Sources: Many plants and shrubs are used for nectaring by the Black Swallowtail. Some of these include clovers *(Trifolium),* milkweed *(Asclepias),* thistles *(Cirsium),* ironweed *(Vernonia),* and Joe-pye weed *(Eupatorium).*

Larval Host Plant: Black Swallowtails feed on a number of plants in West Virginia belonging to the carrot family (Umbelliferae). The most often selected hosts include Queen Anne's lace *(Daucus carota),* cultivated carrot *(D. carota* var. *sativa),* dill *(Anethum graveolens),* parsley *(Petroselinum crispum),* fennel *(Foeniculum vulgare),* and common rue *(Ruta graveolens).*

Giant Swallowtail

Papilio cresphontes (Cramer), 1777

Adult: Plate 2, Row 2
Larva: Plate 31, Row 2
Pupa: Plate 44, Row 1

Description: Wingspan is 3⅜ to 5½ inches (86–140 mm). The Giant Swallowtail is a large dark brown butterfly with a band of yellow, connected spots from the tip to the base of the forewing and across the base of the hindwing. There are also a submarginal row of yellow spots on the upper surface of both wings and a yellow spot in each tail. Below is a large amount of pale yellow on a black background, so much so that the wings are predominately yellow. A thin, median band of blue and orange occurs in the hindwing.

Distribution: The Giant Swallowtail ranges southward from Delaware and southern Pennsylvania to southern Florida and west along the Gulf to southern Texas and California. This is basically a southern species and is more common in the southern portions of its range. In West Virginia it is usually encountered in small colonies along the Potomac and Shenandoah Rivers in the eastern counties of Berkeley, Jefferson, and Morgan. However, it has also been found in Mason, Mercer, Mineral, Monongalia, Pendleton, Raleigh, and Summers Counties. It is undoubtedly found in other counties as well.

Habitat: The species prefers brushy, semi-open areas along streams, rivers, and ridge tops. It also uses semi-open wooded areas of limestone origin, particularly woodland roads, and is usually found close to its host plant.

Life History and Habits: Males patrol along woodland roads and edges or ridge tops in search of females. They fly a few feet above the ground and stop periodically to nectar. Like other swallowtails, Giant Swallowtail males also gather at moist areas along streams to sip water and minerals. Females fly lazily along trails or edges in search of host plants. Oviposition occurs from midmorning to midafternoon. The female deposits a single egg on the upper surface of a young host leaf while fluttering her wings and then moves on to another part of the plant or tree. In West Virginia the Giant Swallowtail is bivoltine, with the first flight occurring in May and extending into June. A second flight occurs in late July and extends through August and into September. The caterpillar of this species is a mixture of white, brown, and black, and, combined with its behavior of resting in the center of a leaf, it very much resembles a bird dropping. In fact, all instars resemble a bird dropping in some fashion. The caterpillar is mottled brown to dark brown, with the posterior cream to white. The anterior end has a thin, white lateral band, and the midsection of the larva contains a broad, oblique band of tan to brown. The chrysalis is pale brown and has 2 projections on the rear of the head. It is tied to a branch with a silk girdle like the other swallowtails.

Nectar Sources: Nectar plants recorded for Giant Swallowtails in the East include milkweed *(Asclepias)*, especially the smaller woodland species, goldenrod *(Solidago)*, bouncing bet *(Saponaria officinalis)*, and Japanese honeysuckle *(Lonicera japonica)*.

Larval Host Plant: Prickly ash *(Zanthoxylum americanum)* and wafer ash *(Ptelea trifoliata)* are the most widely used hosts in West Virginia. Hercules' club *(Zanthoxylum clava-herculis)* as well as citrus species are accepted hosts, especially in the South, but do not occur in West Virginia.

Spicebush Swallowtail

Papilio troilus troilus (Linnaeus), 1758

Adult: Plate 2, Row 3
Larva: Plate 31, Row 2
Pupa: Plate 44, Row 2

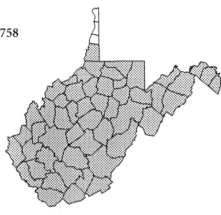

Description: Wingspan is 2½ to 4½ inches (89–114 mm). The Spicebush Swallowtail is a large black butterfly with prominent tails. In both sexes a large orange spot occurs along the upper margin of the hindwing upper surface that is not found in the other black swallowtails. There is also a marginal row of pale yellow spots in the outer forewing and a row of blue-green crescents in the margin of the hindwing of the male. The hindwing is dusted with blue green. The female is similar to the male, except the hindwing is blue. The underside of the hindwing has 2 rows of orange spots separated by a dusting of blue in both sexes.

Distribution: The Spicebush Swallowtail ranges from New England to southern Manitoba and then southward to Florida and Texas. In West Virginia the species is found statewide, and records have been collected from most counties.

Habitat: This swallowtail prefers semi-open woodlands and open fields near woods. It is found along woodland roads and edges where its host generally grows. It flies readily into open fields and pastures in search of nectar.

Life History and Habits: Males gather with other butterflies at moist, sandy areas along roads or streams to sip moisture and minerals. Females are usually observed fluttering about trees and shrubs in search of host plants or visiting flowers for nectar. Oviposition by the female occurs during the warm portion of the day from midmorning throughout much of the afternoon. Eggs are laid singly on young leaves of the host plant. The Spicebush Swallowtail is bivoltine in West Virginia, with the first brood emerging from the overwintering chrysalis in early April. The first flight extends through May and into June. The second flight occurs from July through September. On occasion a few adults will emerge from pupae of the second generation, although most second brood pupae overwinter. Young larvae fold the leaf of the host plant on the top side with silk and live within the fold. As the larva molts and grows, it moves to a new leaf and makes a larger fold. Feeding is done by venturing from the fold at night. The caterpillar is green with 2 black-and-yellow eyespots on the thorax. Behind the eyespots are 2 yellow circles ringed with black and a double row of small blue circles ringed in black down the back. There is a yellowish lateral stripe along the body. Larvae turn bright yellow before pupating. The smooth chrysalis is either green or brown and supported by a silk girdle.

Nectar Sources: The Spicebush Swallowtail uses a variety of plants for nectar, and with its long proboscis it can utilize long tubed flowers. Therefore, plants, such as Japanese honeysuckle *(Lonicera japonica)* and touch-me-not *(Impatiens)* are frequently visited. Milkweeds *(Asclepias),* thistles *(Cirsium),* Joe-pye weed *(Eupatorium),* dogbane *(Apocynum),* azalea *(Rhododendron),* and mimosa *(Albizia julibrissin)* are also favored.

Larval Host Plant: Sassafras sprouts and trees *(Sassafras albidum)* and spicebush *(Lindera benzoin)* are the most widely selected hosts in West Virginia. Reports of yellow-poplar *(Liriodendron tulipifera)* and prickly ash *(Zanthoxylum americanum)* as possible hosts need confirmation.

Eastern Tiger Swallowtail

Papilio glaucus (Linnaeus), 1758

Adult: Plate 3, Rows 1, 2, 3
Larva: Plate 31, Row 3
Pupa: Plate 44, Row 2

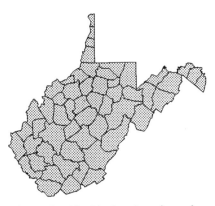

Description: Wingspan is 2½ to 4½ inches (64–115 mm). The Eastern Tiger Swallowtail is a large yellow-and-black striped butterfly. The background color is bright yellow on the upper surface and pale yellow on the underside. Black stripes from the costal margin traverse the forewing or partly so, and a single stripe traverses the hindwing. There is a broad, black border on both wings containing a row of yellow spots and crescents. Males have very little blue scaling on the hindwing, whereas females have much more blue. The underside is marked similar to the upperside except that the spots in the hindwing contain orange, and there is a varying amount of blue-green scaling. Female Eastern Tiger Swallowtails are more frequently black than yellow in West Virginia. Yellow scaling is replaced with charcoal to black scales; however, the darker stripes can still be distinguished, especially on the undersurface. A peppering of black and yellow may occur in some females; these aberrations occur occasionally in the Eastern Tiger Swallowtail. The dark form of the female Eastern Tiger Swallowtail mimics the Pipevine Swallowtail and is, therefore, preyed upon by birds at a lower rate than yellow individuals. The Eastern Tiger Swallowtail is very similar to the Canadian Tiger Swallowtail *(P. canadensis)* found at higher elevations in West Virginia. See that account for differences between the species.

Distribution: The Eastern Tiger Swallowtail ranges throughout the eastern United States from New England south to Florida and west to eastern Colorado and Texas. In West Virginia the species is found statewide and is the most common and widely distributed of all the swallowtails.

Habitat: The Eastern Tiger Swallowtail is associated with deciduous forests and is found in almost all situations from woodlands to open fields, wet meadows, and home gardens.

Life History and Habits: Eastern Tiger Swallowtail males are most often encountered flying along roads, trails, and streams at all levels from a few feet above the ground to the treetops. Males also gather in large numbers during spring at moist, sandy spots along woodland roads or stream edges. Females are usually observed at nectar plants. In West Virginia the Eastern Tiger Swallowtail is bivoltine, with a spring brood emerging as early as mid-March in warmer areas. Emergence of adults is somewhat staggered, with the spring flight extending into June. A second flight begins in July and continues into late September. Individuals from the second brood overwinter as pupae. Eggs are laid singly on leaves of the host plant. First instar caterpillars are black with a white saddle, giving them the appearance of a bird dropping. The fully grown caterpillar is dark green with 2 small eyespots on a swollen thorax. Some larvae, especially from the second brood, are medium brown. The chrysalis is tan, brown, or green. The overwintering chrysalis is usually brown with black mottling and streaks and is attached to its substrate by a silk girdle.

Nectar Sources: Many trees, shrubs, and herbaceous plants are used for nectaring. Some of the favorite species include milkweed *(Asclepias),* thistles *(Cirsium),* ironweed *(Vernonia),* Joe-pye weed *(Eupatorium),* azaleas *(Rhododendron),* dogbane *(Apocynum),* mimosa *(Albizia julibrissin),* various lilies *(Lilium* spp.*),* and red clover *(Trifolium pratense).*

Larval Host Plant: Yellow-poplar *(Liriodendron tulipifera)* and black cherry *(Prunus serotina)* are the most widely selected hosts in West Virginia, although other plants, such as ash *(Fraxinus),* spicebush *(Lindera benzoin),* lilac *(Syringa vulgaris),* and wafer ash *(Ptelea trifoliata),* may also be utilized to some extent.

Canadian Tiger Swallowtail

Papilio canadensis (Rothschild and Jordan), 1906

Adult: Plate 20, Row 1

Description: Wingspan is 2¾ to 3½ inches (70–90 mm). The Canadian Tiger Swallowtail is similar to the Eastern Tiger Swallowtail *(Papilio glaucus).* Three features examined in the males help distinguish the 2 species (Hagen et al. 1991). The Canadian Tiger Swallowtail is smaller than *P. glaucus,* with a forewing measurement of 1⅝ to 2 inches (41–50 mm) from base to tip. The upperside of *P. canadensis* is similar to *P. glaucus* (see *P. glaucus* description). On the underside of the male forewing, the submarginal row of yellow spots forms a continuous band in *P. canadensis,* whereas in *P. glaucus* the spots are separated along the veins by black scaling. The black band along the inner or anal margin of the hindwing on the underside is wider than half the distance from the wing margin to the Cu_2A vein at its juncture with the discal cell. Females have wider black bands than males, but differences between the species still exist. The black-form female that occurs readily in *P. glaucus* does not occur in *P. canadensis.* Females are yellow in this species. Many *P. glaucus* individuals that hibernate through the winter tend to be small, to have wider black inner marginal bands on the hindwings, and, in general, to more closely resemble *P. canadensis* than those that do not hibernate. Therefore, distinguishing these 2 species based on these characteristics should be done with caution. The 2 species hybridize where the populations intermix (Luebke et al. 1988), and most individuals found in West Virginia are probably hybrids.

Distribution: The Canadian Tiger Swallowtail ranges throughout Canada from the Maritime Provinces to Alaska south to the Great Lakes. It occurs in a hybrid zone from New England through the Great Lakes states and then south through the Appalachian Mountains to West Virginia, Virginia, and western North Carolina. Records from the state are most likely those of hybrid *P. canadensis* and *P. glaucus* from the higher mountain regions around Dolly Sods, Lanesville in Tucker County, and Spruce Knob in Randolph County.

Habitat: In the northern part of its range the Canadian Tiger Swallowtail inhabits the boreal coniferous forest, whereas the hybrid zone is a mixture of coniferous and northern deciduous forest types. The species is found along roads, trails, and forest edges in this habitat type at higher elevations.

Life History and Habits: Like the Tiger Swallowtail, males patrol along trails and roads, readily stopping at wet spots to gather with other males. The Canadian Tiger Swallowtail is univoltine throughout its range, with a single flight in June. In West Virginia the flight begins in late May and continues through June into July. Larvae from this brood pupate and diapause until the following spring. Caterpillars are identical to those of *P. glaucus* (see description); however, early instar larvae differ by having 3 white saddles across the back, whereas *P. glaucus* has only 1 in the center of the dorsum.

Nectar Sources: A variety of plants are used for nectar (see Tiger Swallowtail account). Males also visit damp spots for moisture.

Larval Host Plant: Yellow-poplar *(Liriodendron tulipifera),* which is utilized as a host by the Tiger Swallowtail, is toxic to the Canadian Tiger Swallowtail. Hosts for the Canadian Tiger Swallowtail include quaking aspen *(Populus tremuloides),* big-toothed aspen *(P. grandidentata),* and birches *(Betula* spp.), species that are not accepted by *P. glaucus.* The Canadian Tiger Swallowtail readily uses black cherry *(Prunus serotina)* as well, a host commonly used by *P. glaucus.*

8

Superfamily Papilionoidea
Family Pieridae—Whites and Sulphurs

The whites and sulphurs are found worldwide, except in the Antarctic, and are represented by approximately 1000 species. In North America the family is represented by 63 species (Miller and Brown 1981) and in West Virginia by 11 species. The family contains 4 subfamilies worldwide, but only 2 are common in the United States. A third subfamily occurs in Mexico and on occasion may venture into the United States. The 2 subfamilies found in the United States include Pierinae (whites), which are represented by 5 species in West Virginia, and the Coliadinae (sulphurs), represented by 6 species in the state.

The whites and sulphurs are small to medium (1–2¾ in., 25–70 mm) butterflies of various shades of white, yellow, or orange, usually marked with black or green. This group is unique in that the caterpillars possess pteridine pigments that reflect or absorb ultraviolet light, thus creating a pattern, or fluorescence, on the wings. Many pierids recognize the opposite sex by this fluorescence.

The whites and sulphurs are characterized by a few traits worth mentioning here. The group has 6 fully developed walking legs with claws at the tips that are strongly forked. The tibial spur or epiphysis on the front legs, characteristic of the swallowtails, is absent in the whites and sulphurs.

The eggs of this group are long and spindle-shaped and are ribbed vertically. The larvae are slender, usually green, and have thin lateral and dorsal, longitudinal stripes that are often white or yellow. Full-grown larvae are generally covered with small tubercles each bearing a short, fine hair. The larvae feed primarily on dicotyledons in the Cruciferae (mustards) and Fabaceae (legumes) families. Pupae of this group are attached to a substrate by the cremaster, as well as a silk girdle. Often the wing cases are large, forming a deep ventral curve. The head is pointed, often into a cone.

Male Pieridae patrol in a fairly straight, steady, and usually rapid flight in search of females. The West Virginia White *(Pieris virginiensis)* and the Cabbage White *(Pieris rapae)* fly slower than the other members of this group. Many pierids colonize northward, with the southern species migrating into West Virginia in favorable years. Resting is done with the wings closed, although many pierids bask with the wings partially or fully extended. All members of this group visit flowers for nectar, and males frequently puddle and take moisture at wet places along roads and streams.

Most of the multibrooded pierids exhibit seasonal forms resulting from changes in day length. Short-day forms are generally smaller and darker.

Subfamily Pierinae—Whites

This subfamily includes the whites, marbles, and orangetips. The Cabbage White, an introduced species from Europe, is probably West Virginia's most common butterfly.

The Pierinae can be distinguished from the Coliadinae by several characteristics. West Virginia species are white or shades of white, with black markings or greenish mottling (on the undersurface), and in the Falcate Orangetip *(Anthocharis midea),* the male has orange forewing tips. The humeral vein (H) near the base of the hindwing is well developed (fig. 12a).

The larvae feed largely on plants in the mustard family (Cruciferae). The 2 tribes of Pierinae in West Virginia are the Pierini (whites) and the Euchloini (marbles and orangetips). The Pierini are the slowest fliers of the family and are easily captured.

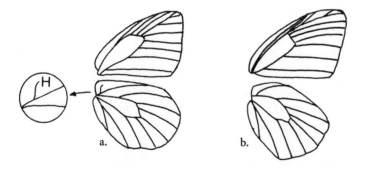

FIG 12. Presence of humeral vein *(H)* in Pieridae: *(a)* Pierinae, *(b)* Coliadinae.

Checkered White

Pontia protodice (Boisduval and LeConte), 1829

Adult: Plate 4, Rows 1, 2
Larva: Plate 31, Row 3
Pupa: Plate 44, Row 3

Description: Wingspan is 1¼ to 1¾ inches (32–44 mm). This is a variable species with both dark and light individuals. Males are white above with 1 to 3 black markings in the forewings. Usually a small amount of charcoal scaling occurs along the margin of the forewing tip. On the hindwing underside of the spring-form male there is strong green veining; summer forms are much lighter. Females are more heavily patterned with black on the upperside than males, especially along the wing margins. On the underside the venation of females is more strongly marked with gray green than in males.

Distribution: The Checkered White is a resident of the southern United States from the Carolinas through the Gulf states to northern Mexico. It regularly colonizes many of the northern states to Canada. In West Virginia the butterfly has only been recorded from 8 counties, although it may show up locally in almost any county in years of abundance. It can be most often found in the counties along the Ohio River.

Habitat: The Checkered White prefers open areas, especially fields (untilled and tilled), pastures, railroad tracks, and disturbed areas where its host plant occurs.

Life History and Habits: Males patrol over open areas in search of females. Their flight is more rapid than that of the Cabbage White *(Pieris rapae),* which it closely resembles. Mating occurs during the morning hours and until 1400 hours (2:00 P.M.) (Rutowski 1980). Females fly about fields and clearings, stopping regularly to nectar and oviposit. Eggs are laid singly on the flower buds of the host plant. They are slender, pointed at the tip, and pale orange. The Checkered White may have as many as 3 broods in West Virginia, with the first adults appearing in May and continuing into June. A second flight appears in July and early August, and a third flight appears in late August and continues into October. The caterpillar is green, alternately striped with yellow and darker green to purple, and is covered with black, setiferous tubercles. The head is bluish gray. The chrysalis is grayish green and speckled with black and has a red-and-yellow dorsal ridge and 2 yellow lateral ridges along the abdomen. The last brood overwinters in the chrysalis stage.

Nectar Sources: Adults visit many species of flowers for nectar, especially hedge mustards *(Sisymbrium)* and winter cress *(Barbarea vulgaris),* as well as other mustards. They also use milkweeds *(Asclepias)* and clovers *(Trifolium).*

Larval Host Plant: Wild peppergrasses *(Lepidium virginicum* and *L. densiflorum)* are the favored hosts for the butterfly in West Virginia. Checkered Whites are also reported to use shepherd's purse *(Capsella bursa-pastoris)* and winter cress *(Barbarea vulgaris),* as well as other mustards.

West Virginia White

Pieris virginiensis (Edwards), 1870
Adult: Plate 4, Row 3
Larva: Plate 31, Row 4
Pupa: Plate 44, Row 3

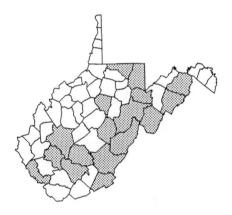

Description: Wingspan is 1⅜ to 1⅝ inches (35–41 mm). The West Virginia White is dusky white with smoky gray scaling along the wing margin and wing base on the upperside. Females have more gray than males. The underside of the hindwings is suffused with brownish gray along the veins. There is considerable variation in the amount of gray along the hindwing veins, but males tend to be darker than females on the underside. Females are generally a softer white.

Distribution: The West Virginia White ranges from Wisconsin east to New England and then southward through the Appalachian Mountains to northern Georgia and Alabama. In West Virginia the butterfly is widely distributed but is most frequently found in wooded areas in the mountains.

Habitat: This butterfly is a woodland species found in or along woodlands, woodland roads, and meadows. It generally does not stray far from its host plant, which is a woodland herb in the genus *Dentaria,* and is reluctant to cross large openings or pioneer new areas for colonization.

Life History and Habits: The West Virginia White is a slow-flying butterfly generally seen flying among the forest floor vegetation. Males actively fly close to the ground in search of females and will frequently puddle at wet areas along woodland roads or stream edges. The butterfly is active only in early spring, with 1 flight beginning in March and extending into late May. The host plant, toothworts *(Dentaria* spp.), is found through April and May. By the first of June the plant has begun to die back, and larvae from eggs produced by late-flying adults do not survive to pupation on *Dentaria.* Females search out host plants and lay a single egg on the underside of a leaf. Oviposition occurs from midmorning until late afternoon. The larvae of this species develop rapidly, and pupation occurs within 4 weeks. The caterpillar is green and covered with short white hairs each arising from a small tubercle. There is a fine, pale lateral stripe on each side that is not very prominent. The chrysalis may be green, yellow, or tan and is closely attached to the substrate with a silk girdle. The front end of the chrysalis is pointed, with 2 dorso-lateral projections. The West Virginia White overwinters in the chrysalis stage.

Nectar Sources: The West Virginia White visits a variety of early spring wild flowers for nectar. These include spring beauty *(Claytonia),* toothwort *(Dentaria),* stonecrop *(Sedum),* and violets *(Viola).*

Larval Host Plant: In West Virginia various species of toothwort *(Dentaria* spp.) are the favored host of the West Virginia White. The cutleaf toothwort *(D. laciniata)* and the two-leaved toothwort *(D. diphylla)* are the most commonly used species in the state. The West Virginia White will also feed on various rockcresses *(Arabis* spp.) and garlic mustard *(Alliaria officinalis)* when *Dentaria* is in short supply. Late-flying individuals will select shale barren rockcress *(Arabis serotina),* which blooms later than *Dentaria* or the other rockcresses. Various bittercresses *(Cardamine* spp.), especially *C. hirsuta* (hairy bittercress), may also be selected by females for ovipositing. Larvae reared on *Cardamine* reach pupation within 2 to 4 days of those reared on *Dentaria.* None of the alternative hosts, however, are selected as readily as *Dentaria.* In central Ohio some populations utilize smooth rockcress *(A. laevigata)* as their primary host (Shuey and Peacock 1989).

Cabbage White

Pieris rapae (Linnaeus), 1758

Adult: Plate 4, Rows 4, 5
Larva: Plate 31, Row 4

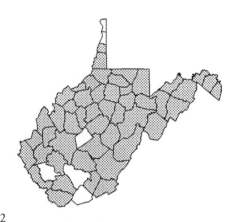

Description: Wingspan is 1¼ to 1¾ inches (32–48 mm). The Cabbage White is a white butterfly with charcoal forewing tips and a charcoal or black spot in the forewing and on the costa of the hindwing in males. The female has 2 black forewing spots. The underside of the hindwing is pale yellow in both sexes. In the spring brood, however, the black spots in the wings may be so faded as to be difficult to see. Similar species are the male Checkered White *(Pontia protodice)*, which has more charcoal spotting on the wings and is a more rapid flier, and the West Virginia White *(Pieris virginiensis)*, which lacks the submarginal wing spots and the yellow hindwing underside.

Distribution: This species was introduced from Europe and now occurs in North America from coast to coast and from Canada to northern Mexico. It is rare, however, along the southern edge of its range. In West Virginia records show the species in almost all counties. The Cabbage White occurs statewide and is probably our most common butterfly.

Habitat: This species utilizes a wide variety of habitats but is most frequently found in open areas, such as fields, meadows, pastures, yards, and gardens. In the spring the species is common in dense woods but can be found in open woods at any time. Virtually any habitat that supports various members of the mustard family (Crucifers) is suitable for the Cabbage White.

Life History and Habits: Males patrol in a slow flight close to the ground along trails and open areas, stopping frequently to nectar. Mating may occur at anytime during the day but frequently occurs around midday. Eggs are deposited singly on young host leaves. Although 3 to 4 broods usually occur in West Virginia, they are difficult to separate because staggered emergence results in individuals flying throughout the spring, summer, and fall. Butterflies may be seen from March through November in many areas of the state. The caterpillar is apple green and covered with fine, short white hairs, giving it a softened appearance. There is a fine, yellow dorsal stripe and a similar lateral stripe along the spiracles. The chrysalis is green or tan and is pointed at the front, with medial and lateral projections, and is the overwintering stage of the species.

Nectar Sources: The Cabbage White visits a wide variety of flowering plants for nectar throughout the season. Dandelions *(Taraxacum)* and various mustards *(Lepidium, Brassica)* are favored by the species in spring, and clovers *(Trifolium)*, mints *(Mentha)*, and asters *(Aster)* are visited later on. Some species of flowers widely used by other butterfly species are rarely visited. Such species include milkweeds *(Asclepias)*, Joe-pye weed *(Eupatorium)*, and other large composites.

Larval Host Plant: The Cabbage White utilizes a wide range of crucifers, especially those with mustard oils (glucosinolates). Common hosts in West Virginia include winter cress *(Barbarea vulgaris)*, mustards *(Brassica* spp.), and various cultivated crucifers, such as broccoli, cauliflower, and cabbage. The species also utilizes garlic mustard *(Alliaria officinalis)* during spring, especially in wooded areas.

Olympia Marble

Euchloe olympia (Edward), 1871
Adult: Plate 5, Row 1
Larva: Plate 32, Row 1
Pupa: Plate 44, Row 3

Description: Wingspan is 1¼ to 1¾ inches (32–44 mm). This is a small to medium, white butterfly with charcoal gray to black forewing tips and a black dash in the midforewing. The underside of the hindwing is patterned with yellow-green marbling. A pink flush usually occurs at the base of the hindwing underside.

Distribution: The Olympia Marble ranges from the mountains of Virginia, Maryland, Pennsylvania, and West Virginia in isolated populations south to Kentucky, Arkansas, and central Texas. Another population occurs through southern Ontario and Minnesota and west to Montana and Colorado. In West Virginia the Olympia Marble has been reported mainly from the drier regions of the state. It particularly favors the shale barren areas of the eastern counties where populations are fairly common. It also occurs at a few sites in southwestern West Virginia.

Habitat: The Olympia Marble is frequently found in semi-open, scrub oak-pine habitats of the eastern counties where exposed shale slopes occur. It will also use semi-open wooded areas in this same region. The species also occurs sporadically in the oak-pine region of the western counties.

Life History and Habits: This butterfly is a rapid flier, flying within a few feet of the ground. Males patrol in search of females in a direct, rapid flight. Females search out host plants *(Arabis)* and deposit a single white egg on a leaf or flower bud before flying on to another. The egg turns red shortly after being deposited and then gray before hatching. The Olympia Marble is univoltine, with its only flight occurring during April and extending into late May. The caterpillar is gray with a yellow dorsal stripe and a yellow-and-white lateral stripe. It is finely spotted with black throughout. Larvae feed on both leaves and flower buds of the host plant. The chrysalis is pale brown and pointed, with fine, dark longitudinal striations, and is supported by a silk girdle.

Nectar Sources: The Olympia Marble visits several of the early spring wild flowers to obtain nectar. These include spring beauty *(Claytonia),* bird's-foot violet *(Viola pedata),* phlox *(Phlox),* bluets *(Houstonia),* chickweed *(Stellaria),* and rockcresses *(Arabis),* as well as other woodland plants.

Larval Host Plant: The rockcresses are selected as the preferred host for the species in West Virginia. They include smooth rockcress *(Arabis laevigata),* shale barren rockcress *(A. serotina),* and other rockcresses. The Olympia Marble will also utilize hairy bittercress *(Cardamine hirsuta)* to a lesser degree.

Falcate Orangetip

Anthocharis midea annickae (dos Passos and Klots), 1969

Adult: Plate 5, Row 2
Larva: Plate 32, Row 1
Pupa: Plate 44, Row 4

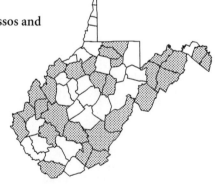

Description: Wingspan is 1¼ to 1¾ inches (32–44 mm). This small white butterfly can be easily distinguished by its hooked, or falcate, forewing tips. Both sexes have a small black dot on the upper surface of the forewing and black border on the forewing tip. They are heavily marbled with a fine pattern of gray green on the underside of the hindwing. The outer portion of the forewing tip is orange in the male and white in the female. On occasion the female may show a hint of yellow on the forewing tip.

Distribution: The Falcate Orangetip ranges from southern New England west to Wisconsin and Missouri and south in the East to Georgia and across the northern Gulf states to Texas. In West Virginia the species is widespread, being reported from many counties around the state. It has not been found at high elevations in the mountains of north-central West Virginia but may be found at lower elevations in these counties in suitable habitat.

Habitat: The Falcate Orangetip is a species of open, deciduous woodlands that vary from lowland wooded meadows and riparian habitat to dry oak-pine ridges on shale soils of the eastern counties.

Life History and Habits: Males are often encountered flying rapidly through wooded areas close to the ground. They are often difficult to net because of their rapid flight among trees and thickets; however, they do not fly as fast as the Olympia Marble *(Euchloe olympia)*. Females are also frequently encountered flying rapidly through wooded areas, stopping only occasionally to nectar or oviposit. This butterfly is active throughout much of the day when sunshine persists. Although activity diminishes in late afternoon, individuals will fly until 1800 hours (6:00 P.M.). Mating usually occurs during the morning. Egg laying by females has been observed from midmorning until 1645 (4:45 P.M.). During periods when females are ovipositing, they slowly flutter about the shrubs and vegetation in search of host plants. Eggs are deposited singly on the leaves, stem, or bud of a host. The egg is spindle-shaped and orange when laid. In West Virginia, the Falcate Orangetip is univoltine, with its single flight in late March to early April and extending into late May. By the end of June the larvae have pupated. The chrysalis, which is mottled brown, is slender, has a long conical head, and is attached to a stem close to the ground by a silk girdle and cremaster. The species overwinters in the pupal stage; however, emergence of some individuals may not occur for 2 years (dos Passos and Klots 1969).

Nectar Sources: The Falcate Orangetip nectars at a variety of low-growing spring flowers. Some of these include spring beauty *(Claytonia)*, bird's-foot violet *(Viola pedata)*, bittercress *(Cardamine hirsuta)*, peppergrass *(Lepidium)*, toothworts *(Dentaria)*, and rockcresses *(Arabis)*.

Larval Host Plant: The species favors plants of the mustard family. West Virginia hosts include bittercresses *(Cardamine* spp.), rockcresses *(Arabis laevigata, A. serotina, A. glabra)*, garlic mustard *(Alliaria officinalis)*, field cress *(Lepidium campestre)*, and cut-leaf toothwort *(Dentaria laciniata)*, as well as other members of the family.

Subfamily Coliadinae—Sulphurs

This subfamily comprises the sulphurs, which are small to medium (1–2¾ in., 25–70 mm) butterflies whose wings are either white, yellow, or orange in varying amounts, with some black usually along margins and as spots. This group can be further separated from the Pierinae by the lack of a well-developed humeral vein (H) at the base of the hindwing (fig. 12b). The sulphurs also have somewhat shorter antennae than the whites, although this trait is difficult to determine without measurement. Larvae of the sulphurs are largely legume feeders (Fabaceae), except the Pink-edged Sulphur *(Colias interior),* which is a heath feeder (Ericaceae). The larvae are slender, green with white or yellow lateral stripes, and covered with short white setiferous hairs. The flight of the sulphurs is generally rapid and straight. Some members of this group migrate northward and colonize West Virginia in favorable years.

Clouded Sulphur

Colias philodice philodice (Godart), 1819
Adult: Plate 5, Rows 3, 4
Larva: Plate 32, Row 1

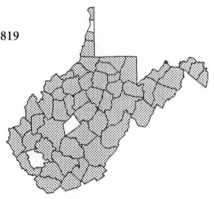

Description: Wingspan is 1⅜ to 2 inches (35–51 mm). Both sexes of this species have bright yellow wings with black borders on the upper surface. The black border on the male is solid, whereas on the female it is slightly wider and interspersed with a row of yellow spots. There is a black spot in the upper center of the forewing in both sexes. The underside of the hindwing may be greenish or yellow with a double, red-rimmed, silvery spot in the center and a submarginal row of small dark spots. About one-third of females of this species occurs as a white form ("alba") instead of yellow (Opler and Krizek 1984). The white females of the Clouded Sulphur are difficult to distinguish from those of the Orange Sulphur *(Colias eurytheme)*, although females of *C. philodice* tend to have a narrower black margin than those of *C. eurytheme.*

Distribution: The Clouded Sulphur ranges over most of the United States to Alaska but is lacking, or at least rare, in the Deep South along the Gulf and in Florida. In West Virginia the species can be found statewide.

Habitat: This sulphur prefers open areas, such as fields, pastures, lawns, and moist meadows. It can be found in almost any open area, including rights-of way, railroad grades, and waste places.

Life History and Habits: Males patrol in a low flight through fields in search of females. They frequently stop to nectar. Males also gather at puddles or stream edges to sip moisture. Mating generally takes place during mid- to late morning, and egg laying by the female extends from midmorning until midafternoon. Females lay their eggs singly on host leaves, usually clovers *(Trifolium)*. There are at least 3 broods in West Virginia, with the first butterflies appearing in late March and April. Flights extend well into the fall, with individuals observed on warm days into December. The caterpillar is yellow green to dark green, with a white lateral stripe that is dark on the lower edge and contains a line of broken, red dashes. The body is covered with short white hairs arising from small dark green tubercles. The chrysalis is green and is the overwintering stage.

Nectar Sources: The Clouded Sulphur visits a wide variety of flowers for nectar throughout the year, beginning with dandelions *(Taraxacum)* in the spring. Clovers *(Trifolium)*, goldenrods *(Solidago)*, ironweed *(Vernonia)*, Joe-pye weed *(Eupatorium)*, asters *(Aster)*, marigolds *(Tagetes)*, and ox-eye daisy and garden mums *(Chrysanthemum)* are among the many favorite nectar plants.

Larval Host Plant: Clovers are preferred as hosts, with white clover *(Trifolium repens)* and red clover *(Trifolium pratense)* being the most commonly used in West Virginia. Other legumes are probably also used.

Orange Sulphur

Colias eurytheme (Boisduval), 1852

Adult: Plate 5, Rows 4, 5
Larva: Plate 32, Row 2
Pupa: Plate 44, Row 4

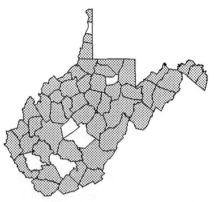

Description: Wingspan is 1½–2⅜ inches (38–60 mm). This species is very similar to the Clouded Sulphur *(Colias philodice)* except that the yellow is replaced by varying amounts of bright orange. Both males and females have orange wings on the upperside, with black borders and a black spot in the forewing cell. The black border of the female is broken with yellow to orange spots. The underside of both sexes is yellow or yellow green to orange, with either a single or double silvery spot rimmed with red in the center of the hindwing. A submarginal row of black spots occurs on the underside of the hindwing. The wing fringes are pink. As in the Clouded Sulphur, there is a white ("alba") form of the female Orange Sulphur, although its wing borders tend to be wider than that of the Clouded Sulphur. Late fall and early spring forms of the sulphur are generally smaller and darker. The Orange Sulphur and the Clouded Sulphur occasionally hybridize, although it was found that male Orange Sulphurs reflect ultraviolet from their wing surfaces, whereas the Clouded Sulphur males absorb ultraviolet (Silberglied and Taylor 1973). The difference in the ultraviolet pattern helps females distinguish between males. Hybrid forms display a varying amount of orange.

Distribution: The Orange Sulphur ranges from the East Coast to the West Coast in North America and from central Canada south to southern Mexico. In West Virginia, the species is found statewide and undoubtedly in every county.

Habitat: Similar to the Clouded Sulphur, this species is found in open fields, such as hayfields, pastures, lawns, and cultivated fields of clover or alfalfa. It also frequents waste places and vacant lots.

Life History and Habits: Males patrol weedy fields in a low, rapid flight searching for females and stop frequently to nectar. Males also gather at wet places or puddles along dirt or gravel roads in a typical puddling behavior. Females lay a single egg on a young host leaf as they encounter the plants in fields. Oviposition occurs intermittently throughout much of the day, with the peak of ovipositing around midday or shortly afterward. In West Virginia there are at least 3 broods and possibly 4 or 5 in some areas. Adults begin to fly in March and continue into November and even December on warm days. Spring forms are smaller and duller than the large brightly colored summer broods. The egg is spindle-shaped and white when laid but turns red and then steel gray before hatching. The caterpillar closely resembles the Clouded Sulphur, being yellow green to dark green, with a white lateral line containing red or orange dashes and a faint yellow, longitudinal stripe toward the dorsal surface. The body is covered with short white hairs arising from small dark green tubercles. The chrysalis is green and is the overwintering stage.

Nectar Sources: This species will nectar at almost any nectar-producing plant that does not have a deep tube, beginning with dandelions *(Taraxacum)* in early spring and ending with asters *(Aster)* in late fall. Clovers *(Trifolium)*, mints *(Mentha)*, ox-eyed daises *(Chrysanthemum)*, teasel *(Dipsacus)*, goldenrods *(Solidago)*, thistles *(Cirsium)*, and ironweed *(Vernonia)* are among the favored nectar sources.

Larval Host Plant: Alfalfa *(Medicago sativa)* is the favorite host of the Orange Sulphur. However, white clover *(Trifolium repens)*, which is more common, is the most frequently selected host in West Virginia. Other clovers *(Trifolium* spp.), white sweet clover *(Melilotus alba)*, wild indigos *(Baptisia* spp.), crown vetch *(Coronilla varia)*, vetches *(Vicia* spp.), and other legumes are also used on occasion.

Pink-edged Sulphur

Colias interior (Scudder), 1862

Adult: Plate 6, Rows 1, 2
Larva: Plate 32, Row 2
Pupa: Plate 45, Row 1

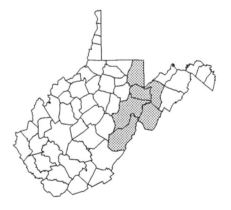

Description: Wingspan is 1½ to 2 inches (38–51 mm). The Pink-edged Sulphur closely resembles the Clouded Sulphur *(Colias philodice)* but can be easily distinguished based on the following characteristics. Males are yellow with black wing margins. The forewing spot in both sexes is reduced to a weak spot, often with yellow in the center. The hindwing spot on the upperside is orange. On the underside, both wing fringes are pink, with a single silver-rimmed central spot in the hindwing. The female is pale yellow with black fading to gray on the outer forewing. The black does not extend to the hindwing as it does in the Clouded Sulphur.

Distribution: The Pink-edged Sulphur is a northern species ranging from Labrador to southern Maine westward across southern Canada to British Columbia and eastern Oregon. In the East, the sulphur occurs in disjunct populations in Pennsylvania, western Maryland, Virginia, and West Virginia. In West Virginia it is found at the higher elevations of Grant, Pendleton, Pocahontas, Preston, Randolph, and Tucker Counties. These areas include Dolly Sods, Canaan Valley, and Blackwater Falls State Park in Tucker County, as well as the Spruce Knob area of Randolph, Pendleton, and Pocahontas Counties.

Habitat: The Pink-edged Sulphur is commonly found in fields and along road banks where it nectars on a variety of weedy species. At higher elevations, such as Spruce Knob and Dolly Sods, the species is often associated with rocky balds, bogs, and barrens where its host plant, blueberry *(Vaccinium* spp.), occurs.

Life History and Habits: Unlike its close relatives the Clouded Sulphur and the Orange Sulphur *(C. eurytheme),* the Pink-edged Sulphur is a weak flier and easily captured. Males and females spend much of the day nectaring on weedy plants and resting on low vegetation. The species also puddles, but this is rarely seen in West Virginia habitats. Females oviposit throughout the day beginning as early as 1100 hours (11:00 A.M.) when the butterflies become active and continuing as late as 1800 hours (6:00 P.M.). A single egg is deposited on the upperside of the host leaf. Eggs are white at first but turn red within a day or 2 and then gray before hatching. The young larvae feed on the host leaf by skeletonizing it until the third instar and then diapause for the winter. In late spring they begin feeding again on the new growth and complete development by July. The caterpillar is dark yellow green with a red-and-white lateral stripe and dark-and-light dorsal stripes. The species is univoltine, with a single flight occurring from mid-June, peaking in July, and extending into August. The chrysalis is green and is held to its substrate by a silk girdle.

Nectar Sources: The Pink-edged Sulphur visits a variety of low-growing plants for nectar. Red and blue flowers appear to be preferred and include red clover *(Trifolium pratense),* heal-all *(Prunella vulgaris),* and field basil *(Satureja vulgaris).* Yellow flowers are also selected, including dandelion *(Taraxacum officinale)* and bird's-foot-trefoil *(Lotus corniculatus).* White flowers are the least favored and include ox-eye daisy *(Chrysanthemum leucanthemum)* and bristly sarsaparilla *(Aralia hispida).*

Larval Host Plant: The larval host most often selected by the Pink-edged Sulphur in West Virginia is lowbush blueberry *(Vaccinium angustifolium);* however, other blueberries occurring in the same area may also be used.

Cloudless Sulphur

Phoebis sennae eubule (Linnaeus), 1767

Adult: Plate 6, Rows 2, 3
Larva: Plate 32, Row 3

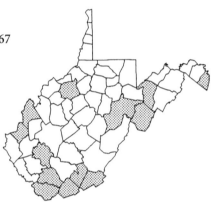

Description: Wingspan is 2⅛ to 2¾ inches (54–70 mm). The Cloudless Sulphur is a large yellow butterfly with somewhat pointed wings. Males are yellow on both surfaces without obvious markings. The underside of the hindwing may contain small rust markings or spots in the fall brood. The female is lemon yellow to bright yellow on the upper surface. There is a row of black marginal spots on the upper surface of the forewing and a hollow blackish spot at the end of the discal cell (near the center of the forewing). Small black to rust markings occur on the under surface of the hindwing.

Distribution: This species is common throughout the southern states from Georgia and Florida west to Texas, Mexico, and then south to Argentina. In the East the species readily migrates northward in favorable years. It does not colonize in West Virginia very often but has been found in the state more in recent years. In West Virginia it has only been reported from 10 counties but has been found both in warmer regions and on top of Cheat Mountain in Randolph County. Therefore, the species may be found at any location from time to time.

Habitat: The Cloudless Sulphur is a species that prefers open areas, such as fields, agricultural land, pastures, roadsides, railroad grades, power- or gas-line right-of-ways, and river banks. This species prefers disturbed sites where its host plant may be abundant, as does the Sleepy Orange *(Eurema nicippe).*

Life History and Habits: The Cloudless Sulphur is a rapid, direct flier seldom stopping to nectar. As a result, it is very difficult to capture. Males generally fly within several feet of the ground in search of females. The species may move into the state as early as May and produce 2 broods by fall. A summer brood appears in late June and July, and a fall brood appears in September. No county records for this species were available before 1987, when a large flight moved northward into several states including Ohio and West Virginia (Calhoun et al. 1989). That year 2 subsequent broods were produced in West Virginia. Eggs are deposited singly on young host leaves, and larvae feed from the midrib of the leaf. The caterpillar is yellow green to dark green and covered with small black tubercles, each bearing a short hair. There is a yellow lateral stripe, and several short rows of black transverse stripes bordered with blue arise from the lateral stripe. The chrysalis is green to pink, with a yellow lateral stripe.

Nectar Sources: The Cloudless Sulphur prefers long-tubed flowers for nectar and will visit a number of plants in West Virginia. A few of the plants include honeysuckle *(Lonicera)*, cardinal flower *(Lobelia cardinalis)*, Rose-of-Sharon *(Hibiscus syriacus)*, thistle *(Cirsium)*, and sennas *(Cassia)*.

Larval Host Plant: The Cloudless Sulphur prefers sennas as hosts. In West Virginia, the species has been found on partridge pea *(Cassia fasciculata)* and wild senna *(C. hebecarpa)* but will probably use senna *(C. marilandica)* and wild sensitive plant *(C. nictitans)* as well.

Little Yellow

Eurema lisa (Boisduval and LeConte), 1829

Adult: Plate 6, Row 4
Larva: Plate 32, Row 3

Description: Wingspan is 1 to 1½ inches (25–38 mm). This small bright yellow butterfly has black forewing tips and a black outer border on the upperside of the wings. In the female the black border on the hindwing is reduced to the upper portion of the wing only and may be followed by a short series of marginal, black spots. Forms are variable, with some being pale yellow to whitish. The underside is pale yellow with small black to gray blotches and a rust spot along the upper margin of the hindwing.

Distribution: The Little Yellow is a resident of the southeastern states and ranges further south into Mexico, Central America, and Costa Rica. During the summer, however, this species ranges northward as far as Canada. In West Virginia the Little Yellow may be found in any county, and records are scattered. However, it is most frequently encountered in the southern counties and in counties along the Ohio River where its host plant is most abundant. The species colonizes for the summer but cannot survive the winters.

Habitat: The Little Yellow prefers open areas, such as disturbed sites, fields, roadsides, and railroad grades.

Life History and Habits: Males patrol along fields and roadsides in a rapid, erratic flight searching for females, stopping periodically to nectar. Males also gather at wet spots, puddles, or stream edges to sip moisture. Females fly along open areas or disturbed sites in search of host plants on which to oviposit. West Virginia records for the species occur from early July into October. The species probably produces 2 and possibly 3 broods during the season. The Little Yellow cannot survive the winters in West Virginia, and the species must immigrate each year. The caterpillar is slender and green with a thin, white or pale yellow lateral stripe.

Nectar Sources: A variety of low-growing plants that bloom during the summer are visited for nectar. Some of these include aster *(Aster)*, goldenrod *(Solidago)*, and clovers *(Trifolium)*. Selfheal *(Prunella)* and blazing star *(Liatris)* are also reported nectar plants for the species (Iftner et al. 1992). Other flowering plants are undoubtedly used as well.

Larval Host Plant: The sennas in the genus *Cassia* are the preferred hosts. Partridge pea *(Cassia fasciculata)* and wild sensitive plant *(C. nictitans)* are the sennas most often selected in West Virginia. The larger leafed sennas are usually avoided.

Sleepy Orange

Eurema nicippe (Cramer), 1779

Adult: Plate 7, Rows 1, 2
Larva: Plate 32, Row 4
Pupa: Plate 45, Row 1

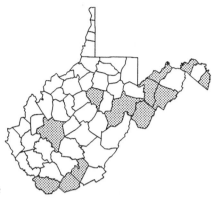

Description: Wingspan is 1⅜ to 1⅞ inches (35–48 mm). Males are bright golden orange, with an irregular, wide, black border on both wings and a small black dash near the tip of the forewing on the upperside. Females are more yellow than orange, with the black border limited to the upper half of the hindwing. On the underside both sexes have a tan to yellow hindwing with small brown blotches. Summer forms are generally yellow on the hindwing, whereas winter forms are tan to brown.

Distribution: The Sleepy Orange ranges throughout the southern and southwestern United States into Mexico and northern Central America. In the East the species migrates northward during the summer to the central states. It rarely reaches New England, Wisconsin, and southern Ontario. In West Virginia it may occur in any county, but records are mainly from the dry eastern counties or the southern counties. The species cannot survive cold winter weather.

Habitat: The Sleepy Orange prefers open areas, such as old fields, pastures, road edges, open pine-oak hillsides, and wet meadows. It particularly prefers disturbed areas where its host plant may be abundant.

Life History and Habits: This is a fast-flying butterfly and difficult to pursue. Males fly close to the ground in search of females and often gather at wet areas to puddle. Individuals nectar readily and are easily captured at flowers. The species seldom survives the winter months in West Virginia and usually depends on immigration from the south to repopulate each year. There may be 2 to 3 broods in the state each year. Migrating individuals may be seen as early as late April or early May, but they are more abundant during the summer months. The species persists until October or even early November. Females lay their eggs singly on young host leaves. Larvae rest along the midrib of the leaf on the upper surface. Pupation often occurs on the stem of the host. The caterpillar is green and slender and is covered with fine short hairs, giving it a velvety appearance. It has a white lateral stripe that is dark on the lower edge. The chrysalis is green or brown, pointed at the front, and suspended by a silk girdle. The fall chrysalis is often heavily mottled.

Nectar Sources: The Sleepy Orange visits a wide variety of plants for nectar. These include clovers *(Trifolium),* white sweet clover *(Melilotus alba),* viper's bugloss *(Echium vulgare),* asters *(Aster),* and ironweed *(Vernonia).*

Larval Host Plant: Larvae prefer the wild sennas *(Cassia hebecarpa* and *C. marilandica),* as well as partridge pea *(C. fasciculata)* and wild sensitive plant *(C. nictitans).* All of these are used in West Virginia.

9

Superfamily Papilionoidea

Family Lycaenidae—Harvesters, Coppers, Hairstreaks, and Blues

The Lycaenidae, or gossamer-winged butterflies include the Harvesters, Coppers, Hairstreaks, and Blues and are distributed worldwide, with approximately 4700 described species. Most are tropical inhabitants, with the majority of the hairstreaks (subfamily Theclinae) found in the New World tropics. In North America there are about 135 species representing 4 subfamilies. Most of the hairstreaks occur in the southern states, while the blues (subfamily Polyommatinae) and coppers (subfamily Lycaeninae) are better represented in the more northern temperate regions. Only a single species of the harvesters (subfamily Miletinae) occurs in North America. In West Virginia, the family Lycaenidae is represented by 25 regular inhabitants and 1 species that is very rare or of historical significance.

The Lycaenidae are a diverse group of butterflies ranging in size from very small to medium. Many characteristics define this group. In the adults the eyes are indented near the antennae, and the face is narrow. The forelegs of males are reduced in size but are still used in walking. The forelegs of females are fully developed. Many of the Lycaenidae are brightly colored and have tails and eyespots that together may appear as the head and antennae of the butterfly to a predator, especially when the wings are rubbed together in the typical hairstreak fashion. Lycaenidae males typically perch as their method of female location, except for the blues, which patrol. For the most part, the Lycaenidae are strong, erratic fliers.

Lycaenidae use flower nectar as a source of energy, although Harvesters (*Feniseca tarquinius*) feed on aphid honeydew secretions. Some Lycaenidae imbibe soil moisture as well.

The venation in the wings is also diagnostic. The radial (R) veins in the forewing are simple, resulting in no more than 1 to 2 branches. In the

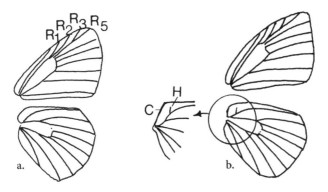

FIG. 13 Wing venation of *(a)* Lycaenidae *(Everes); (b)* Riodinidae *(Calephelis)*

hindwing of North American Lycaenidae there is no costal (C) or humeral (H) vein (fig. 13a).

Larvae of this group use a variety of plants as hosts and usually feed on flowers, buds, or fruit. The Harvester is the only butterfly in this region that is exclusively predaceous, feeding on woolly aphids (Homoptera). Lycaenidae larvae are sluglike, with retractable heads, and are usually covered with short hairs. Many have glands that secrete a sugary solution, and as a result are attended and protected by ants that milk these secretions.

The pupae of this group are rounded and robust, lacking a cremaster, but still have caudal hooks. The pupa is also attached to its substrate by a fine silk girdle. Pupation usually occurs in the leaf litter. Most Lycaenidae overwinter as pupae or eggs but a few do so as larvae.

Subfamily Miletinae—Harvesters

The harvesters are a small group of about 50 species found mostly in the Asian and African tropics, with a few species occurring in Eurasia and a single species in the southern half of North America.

The harvesters are an interesting group whose larvae are mainly predaceous on Homoptera (aphids, leaf and tree hoppers, and mealy bugs). A few feed on ant larvae in ant nests. Larvae are more cylindrical than other Lycaenidae and are often attended by ants. The North American species, *Feniseca tarquinius,* is associated with woolly aphids found on several species of trees.

Adults are very sedentary, seldom straying far from their host, and are characterized by their lack of spurs on the end of the tibiae of the rear 4 legs (as found in other Lycaenidae). They are weaker fliers than most Lycaenidae and quite erratic. Adults rest with wings closed and never rub the hindwings together as do the hairstreaks. They do not visit flowers but feed mainly on aphid honeydew secretions or imbibe moisture and minerals from soil.

Harvester

Feniseca tarquinius (Fabricius), 1793

Adult: Plate 7, Row 3
Larva: Plate 32, Row 4
Pupa: Plate 45, Row 2

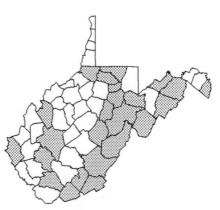

Description: Wingspan is 1⅛ to 1⅜ inches (28–35 mm). The Harvester is a small yellow-orange butterfly with brownish black wing borders and blotches on the upper surface. A submarginal row of black spots occurs on the hindwing. The underside is brownish with rust blotches circled with white on the hindwing. The forewing is pale yellow orange with dark brown blotches and white scaling near the tip.

Distribution: The Harvester is found from Nova Scotia across southern Canada to Minnesota and then south to central Florida, the Gulf states, and central Texas. In West Virginia the species should be found statewide; however, populations are very local, with most records from the eastern half of the state.

Habitat: The Harvester prefers woodland habitats, especially along streams. It is most often found perched along gravel or sandy woodland roads near streams.

Life History and Habits: Freshly emerged males are often found sipping moisture from wet spots or puddles in roads or along streams. Males also perch on the edge of tree leaves and await females. They are fast, erratic fliers, and once disturbed, fly back and forth over a small area before landing again. Their flight is difficult to follow. The Harvester is a predacious species, feeding exclusively on aphids, usually tree-feeding aphids. The flattened, pale green eggs are deposited singly among the aphids or on the twig bark nearby. Larvae feed from a silken web usually under the aphids. They grow rapidly and complete 4 instars in 7 to 11 days (Clark 1926). The pupal stage is also short (8–11 days), which allows the species to complete a generation in about 3 weeks. Two flights are reported in the northern portion of the range, and many broods may occur southward. There may be as many as 6 or more flights in West Virginia, with the first flight occurring in early April. Fresh individuals appear 3 to 4 weeks apart throughout the season into September. The caterpillar is light to dark gray, with brick red on the lower part of the body. There is a dorso-lateral row of white patches containing tufts of grayish hairs emanating from yellow tubercles. The white patches are bordered with chocolate brown on the lower side. On the dorsal surface the larva is marked with black, white, gray, and bluish gray. There are several rows of gray hair tufts along the body. When the larva is feeding under a colony of aphids it becomes covered with white dust and appears whitish or pinkish. The chrysalis is whitish to greenish brown, mottled with dark brown, and resembles a monkey's face. The species overwinters as a chrysalis.

Nectar Sources: The Harvester, which has a short proboscis, feeds mainly on the honeydew secretions of aphids. Adults also sip moisture and minerals from sand or soil, as well as from animal dung.

Larval Host Plant: The hosts for this species are various woolly aphids in the genera *Prociphilus, Meliarhizophagus, Neoprociphilus, Schizoneura,* and *Pemphigus.* These aphid species feed mainly on alder *(Alnus* spp.), witch hazel *(Hamamelis virginiana),* beech *(Fagus* spp.), ash *(Fraxinus* spp.), hawthorn *(Crataegus* spp.), silver maple *(Acer saccharinum),* and greenbrier or carrion flower *(Smilax* spp.) (Opler and Krizek 1984; Scott 1986).

Subfamily Lycaeninae—Coppers

The coppers are small to medium butterflies represented in the temperate portions of Eurasia and North America by approximately 50 species. A few species occur in the Ethiopian and Indo-Australian regions, as well as 1 in Guatemala. In North America 15 species are recognized, and in West Virginia there are 3 species. Coppers, like the blues (Polyommatinae), prefer the more temperate regions, and in North America most occur from the central United States north to the Arctic. The coppers are a sexually dimorphic group, with males displaying many coppery colors from red and orange to iridescent purple and blue, although some are brown. Females, on the other hand, are usually duller, displaying more browns and grays. Males lack the forewing scent patch found in the hairstreaks (Theclinae) and have 4 radial veins in the forewing.

Coppers generally perch with their wings at least partially opened, and males of most species perch to await females. At least 1 North American species does patrol, but none do in this region. Coppers feed on nectar and rarely, if ever, gather at wet spots to sip moisture. The stout-bodied coppers are strong fliers but usually fly slower and are less erratic than the hairstreaks. They do not migrate and generally establish local colonies.

Larvae of this group resemble other Lycaenidae in being somewhat sluglike. They select hosts from a variety of plant families, but the most widely used families are the buckwheats (Polygonaceae) and the roses (Rosaceae). Eggs are usually laid singly on the underside of host leaves, and larvae overwinter in the egg capsule. A few species hibernate as larvae.

American Copper

Lycaena phlaeas americana (Harris), 1862

Adult: Plate 7, Row 4
Larva: Plate 33, Row 1
Pupa: Plate 45, Row 3

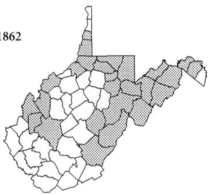

Description: Wingspan is ⅞ to 1⅛ inches (22–28 mm). On the upper surface, the American Copper has a bright, golden-orange forewing with black spots and a gray-brown margin. The hindwing is gray brown with an orange band along the outer margin that contains a row of black spots. The female is similar to the male except that the spots are larger in the forewing. The underside is silvery gray with small black spots and a red-orange irregular line in the outer margin of the hindwing.

Distribution: This species occurs from Nova Scotia west across southern Canada to west central Ontario and Minnesota and then south to northern Georgia, Tennessee, and Arkansas. It also occurs in the Arctic and western alpine habitats. In West Virginia the American Copper is widespread, occurring mainly in nonlimestone areas where its host plant abounds. Records are lacking for the west central and southern counties, but the species can be expected to occur in many of these areas.

Habitat: The American Copper prefers open, disturbed habitats, such as fields, pastures, power- and gas-line right-of-ways, landfills, and vacant lots.

Life History and Habits: Males perch on grass or on top of low vegetation in open areas and are aggressive toward other intruding insects. Mating and egg laying continue throughout much of the day. Females lay a single egg on a host leaf or stem. The larva feeds on the underside of the leaf, chewing grooves or slots in it. As the larvae grow they rest at the base of the plant, crawling up to the leaves to feed. The American Copper has 3 flights in West Virginia, with the first adults appearing in May. A second flight appears in late June or early July, and a third flight occurs in August and September. The species has been seen on the wing in mid-October, but these individuals are worn, resulting from the late summer-fall brood. The caterpillar is bright green and is covered with short white hairs. The chrysalis is pale brown to greenish and spotted with black. American Coppers probably overwinter in the egg stage.

Nectar Sources: The American Copper visits a wide variety of field plants for nectar, some of which include buttercups *(Ranunculus)*, Canada cinquefoil *(Potentilla canadensis)*, ox-eye daisy *(Chrysanthemum leucanthemum)*, clovers *(Trifolium)*, yarrow *(Achillea)*, butterfly weed *(Asclepias)*, and asters *(Aster)*.

Larval Host Plant: The primary host for this species in West Virginia is sheep sorrel *(Rumex acetosella)*, a weed species in most disturbed habitats. Curly dock *(R. crispus)* is also used occasionally as a host.

Bronze Copper

Lycaena hyllus (Cramer), 1775

Adult: Plate 7, Row 5
Larva: Plate 33, Row 1
Pupa: Plate 45, Row 3

Description: Wingspan is 1¼ to 1⅝ inches (32–42 mm). The Bronze Copper is sexually dimorphic. Males are bronze, often with a violet sheen, on the upper surface. The hindwings have an orange marginal band containing a row of black dots. Females have an orange forewing containing several black spots and a brownish black border. The hindwing is brownish black with an orange marginal band containing black dots. The hindwing underside of both sexes is almost white with many small black dots and an orange marginal band bordered by black dots. The forewing is pale orange, except for the tips, and also contains several black dots.

Distribution: The Bronze Copper is found from Maine west across southern Canada to central Manitoba, south to Colorado, and then east to Maryland. In West Virginia the species occurs in local populations. Although it is not necessarily confined to the mountains, it has been found there more often than in other locales. Colonies have been reported from 6 counties: Brooke, Cabell, Marion, Monongalia, Pocahontas, and Randolph. Specific locations within these counties include Pig's Ear in Pocahontas County, Sinks of Gandy in Randolph County, and Greenbottom Wildlife Management Area in Cabell County.

Habitat: The Bronze Copper prefers wet areas in West Virginia, being found in moist to wet lowland meadows and fields, usually near streams, rivers, or ponds.

Life History and Habits: Males perch on top of tall grasses or on low vegetation awaiting females. They generally perch with wings partially opened. Females are usually found nectaring. There are 2 broods in West Virginia, with a partial third brood in the warmer habitats. The first flight appears in May and continues through June into early July. A second flight occurs in late July and August into early September. Individuals have been found in late September through mid-October and probably result from a partial third brood. The flights of the Bronze Copper tend to be delayed at higher elevations, with the first flight appearing in mid-June to early July. Eggs are laid singly on host leaves or stems; the larvae feed on leaves. The caterpillar is velvety yellow green with a dark green dorsal stripe. The chrysalis is variable, but usually yellow brown with brown blotches. The species hibernates in the egg stage.

Nectar Sources: Males do not nectar as readily as females; the species may be found at clovers *(Trifolium)*, blackberry *(Rubus)*, ox-eye daisy *(Chrysanthemum leucanthemum)*, boneset *(Eupatorium)*, dogbane *(Apocynum)*, knotweed *(Polygonum)*, and asters *(Aster)*, as well as other plants.

Larval Host Plant: The Bronze Copper prefers water dock *(Rumex verticillatus)* or curly dock *(R. crispus)* as its primary host. It will also use knotweeds *(Polygonum* spp.) if available (Iftner et al. 1992).

Bog Copper

Lycaena epixanthe epixanthe (Boisduval and Leconte), 1833

Adult: Plate 8, Row 1
Larva: Plate 33, Row 1

Description: Wingspan is ⅞ to 1 inch (22–25 mm). The Bog Copper is a small purplish (males) or brown (females) butterfly with several black spots on the upper wing surfaces. There is a small wavy orange line along the outer margin of the hindwing. On the underside the species is silvery with a strong yellow cast and has several black spots on both wings. The spots in the hindwings are reduced to fine dots. A series of orange-red connected crescents occur along the margin of the hindwing.

Distribution: The Bog Copper is a northern species ranging from the Maritime Provinces west to Minnesota. The range extends southward into New Jersey and from northern Pennsylvania west to southern Michigan. The species occurs in a disjunct population in West Virginia and western Maryland at Crainesville Swamp in Preston County.

Habitat: The Bog Copper is confined to acid bog habitats where there is an abundance of cranberry *(Vaccinium).*

Life History and Habits: The Bog Copper has a relatively slow flight and generally stays within 1 to 3 feet of the ground. They tend to fly short distances, perching on *Vaccinium* or other shrubs. Because of their slow, nonaggressive flight, they are unable to pioneer to other nearby bogs to establish new colonies. No populations have been found to date in Canaan Valley, Tucker County, where cranberry is abundant. The Preston County population was probably established during the latest glacial period. Females lay their eggs singly on the underside of leaves or on host stems. Eggs overwinter, and larvae feed during spring. The Bog Copper is univoltine. Its single flight in West Virginia varies slightly from year to year based on the onset of spring but generally begins in early July and continues into late July or early August. The caterpillar is green, sluglike, and covered with short white hairs.

Nectar Sources: The favored nectar source for the Bog Copper are the flowers of the cranberry plants.

Larval Host Plant: Cranberries are the only host of the Bog Copper. The 2 cranberries found at the site in West Virginia are small cranberry *(Vaccinium oxycoccos)* and large cranberry *(V. macrocarpon)*; and both species probably serve as hosts.

Subfamily Theclinae—Hairstreaks

The hairstreak subfamily is represented by approximately 2000 species worldwide, most of which are found in the tropics. The New World tropics support about 1000 of these. In North America most of the Theclinae are found in the South and are represented by some 86 species. In West Virginia 16 species are recorded, plus a possible occurrence of 1 additional species.

Many of the tropical hairstreaks are brightly colored with iridescent blue, caused by specialized wing scales that reflect light, producing the colors seen. In North America only a few species are brightly colored; most are various shades of brown. North American Theclinae in this region can be identified by having only 10 veins in the forewings, including 3 unbranched radial veins. Hairstreaks generally have tails, and many have an orange-and-black eyespot (often referred to as a "thecla spot") in the distal end of the hindwing near the tails. Males of many species have a stigma, or scent patch, along the coastal margin of the forewing. Hairstreaks perch with their wings closed, frequently rubbing their hindwings together. They commonly bask by tilting toward the sun, exposing the underwing surface. Hairstreaks are rapid, erratic fliers. Mating usually occurs in late afternoon or evening, and eggs are generally laid singly.

Many of the sluglike larvae of this subfamily feed on various hardwood tree species, and they spend the winter in the egg stage. Those that feed on other dicotyledons usually winter as pupae. Hairstreak larvae feed on flowers and fruit by boring into them but will also feed on leaves. One species in this region, the Red-banded Hairstreak *(Calycopis cecrops)*, prefers detritus as a food source.

Pupae of this group are rounded at both ends and lack flexibility in the abdominal segments. The structure of the abdominal sutures often produces a sound when the segments are rubbed together.

Great Purple Hairstreak

Atlides halesus (Cramer), 1777

Adult: Plate 8, Row 2
Larva: Plate 33, Row 2

Description: Wingspan is 1¼ to 1½
inches (32–38 mm). The Great
Purple Hairstreak is the largest of
West Virginia's hairstreaks. The
males are a deep metallic blue on the
upperside, with black wing borders
and a black stigma in the forewing. The female is a pale metallic blue, with
broad, black wing borders. Both sexes are doubly tailed. The underside is
black, with a metallic blue dash in the forewing of the male (the female lacks
this), and a mixture of metallic blue, bronze, and violet blotches in the lower
hindwing. The abdomen is bright red.

Distribution: This is a southern species that ranges along the East Coast from
New Jersey south to central Florida and west through southern Virginia,
North Carolina, and Tennessee to California. It also extends south to Central
America. In West Virginia the Great Purple Hairstreak has been recorded from
2 counties, Boone and Jackson, but it might be found occasionally in any
county where mistletoe *(Phoradendron flavescens)* occurs. Mistletoe is most
prevalent along the Potomac River drainage, as well as the New-Kanawha
River system.

Habitat: The Great Purple Hairstreak is associated with mixed deciduous
woodlands. In West Virginia it will be found in wooded areas, along roads,
and along streams where mistletoe grows.

Life History and Habits: Since mistletoe is generally found in the tops of trees
in West Virginia, the Great Purple Hairstreak confines much of its activity to
high in the trees. Males perch on tree leaves, often at the tops of trees, to await
females. This species is a rapid, erratic flier. When at rest males rub their
wings together. The Great Purple Hairstreak does come down to the ground
to nectar, and often males will land on large rocks in the sun or on dirt roads.
The species is multibrooded in the south, with at least 3 generations. The
species probably does not winter anywhere in West Virginia in most years and,
therefore, does not usually appear before July to mid-August. There may be a
brood at that time with resulting adults flying into late fall. The caterpillar is
green, often striped with yellow laterally, and covered with small yellow

tubercles emitting short orange hairs. A bluish white diamond spot occurs behind the head. The robust chrysalis is brown, mottled with black, and is also covered with short orange hairs. Pupation occurs under loose bark, usually at the base of the tree. The species hibernates in the pupal stage.

Nectar Sources: Nectar plants for the Great Purple Hairstreak include goldenrod *(Solidago),* sweet pepperbush *(Clethra acuminata),* and Hercules' club *(Aralia spinosa).*

Larval Host Plant: The Great Purple Hairstreak uses mistletoe *(Phoradendron flavescens)* as its host, feeding on the male flowers and leaves.

Coral Hairstreak

Satyrium titus mopsus (Hübner), 1818
Adult: Plate 8, Row 3
Larva: Plate 33, Row 2

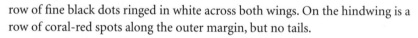

Description: Wingspan is ⅞ to 1¼ inches (23–32 mm). The Coral Hairstreak is uniform brown on the upper wing surface. Males have a dull scent patch near the costal margin of the forewing. The underside is also brown, with a row of fine black dots ringed in white across both wings. On the hindwing is a row of coral-red spots along the outer margin, but no tails.

Distribution: The Coral Hairstreak is widespread, ranging from Maine across southern Canada to British Columbia in the north, and then south to the northern Gulf states, and west to Texas and New Mexico. In West Virginia the species undoubtedly occurs statewide, although it is not abundant, and records are scattered.

Habitat: The Coral Hairstreak prefers unmowed fields near woodland edges or unmanaged grassy, weedy, or brushy woodland openings.

Life History and Habits: Males perch on leaves of trees or shrubs awaiting females. They are rapid, erratic fliers. Males are quite aggressive toward one another, and confrontations occur regularly between individuals. Males and females readily visit flowers for nectar. The Coral Hairstreak is univoltine throughout its range, with a single flight in June and July. Adults are sometimes found in August, but these are generally worn. The grayish white eggs are usually deposited in the rough bark at the base of small host trees within an inch of the ground. Some eggs may be deposited on the leaf litter. There are reports of captive females depositing eggs on twigs, which may also occur in the wild on occasion. The eggs overwinter and the young larvae feed in the spring. Larvae feed at night and spend the day at or close to the base of the tree. They are attended by ants that seek the sugar secretions of the larvae. The caterpillar is yellow green to green, with 1 to 3 bright pink patches on the back and at each end. The head is black. The chrysalis is brown, speckled with black, and covered with short brown hairs.

Nectar Sources: Milkweeds *(Asclepias)* are the favorite nectar plants for the species, especially butterflyweed *(A. tuberosa).* Other plants visited include dogbane *(Apocynum),* New Jersey tea *(Ceanothus americanus),* white sweet clover *(Melilotus alba),* and yarrow *(Achillea).*

Larval Host Plant: The preferred host in West Virginia is black cherry *(Prunus serotina)* where larvae feed on young leaves, flowers, and fruit. Choke cherry *(P. virginiana)* is also used, but is rare in most areas of the state. Other *Rosaceae* species may also be used on occasion.

Edwards' Hairstreak

Satyrium edwardsii (Grote and Robinson), 1867

Adult: Plate 8, Rows 3, 4
Larva: Plate 33, Row 3
Pupa: Plate 45, Row 4

Description: Wingspan is 1 to 1¼ inches (25–32 mm). Edwards' Hairstreak is brown on the upper surface. Males have a scent patch along the costal margin of the forewing. The underside is brownish gray and can be distinguished from other *Satyrium* by the postmedian band that is broken into a series of dark ovals, each ringed by a fine white line. Along the lower margin of the hindwing is a pale blue patch and a short series of orange-red crescents. A fine short tail is present on the hindwings.

Distribution: In the East, Edwards' Hairstreak ranges from southern Maine south to northern Georgia. Populations are scattered and less common south of Pennsylvania. The species also occurs in the Midwest from southern Ontario and southeastern Saskatchewan to Missouri and northern Texas in scattered populations. In West Virginia it has been found only in the eastern region.

Habitat: Edwards' Hairstreaks are found in scrub oak thickets or oak-pine shale barren habitats of the eastern region. The species prefers dry, acidic sites in oak woodlands and is often found along roads, trails, or woodland edges. It prefers habitats with short stunted oaks, such as scrub oak *(Quercus ilicifolia).*

Life History and Habits: Males perch throughout the day on twigs or leaves of host trees or nearby trees. They are aggressive toward other males, and chase flights are frequent. Eggs are deposited singly in the bud axils on host trees. The eggs overwinter, and in the spring larvae feed on buds and young leaves. They live in silken nests at the base of young host trees and feed on the leaves at night. They are also attended by ants, which feed on their honeydew secretions. Edwards' Hairstreak is univoltine and flies from mid-June into late July. The flight period is fairly short and may vary from year to year by a week or so, depending on the weather. The caterpillar is brown to reddish brown and has a series of light dashes along a lateral line. There are pale, oblique dashes along the body, which is covered with short brown hairs. The chrysalis is yellow brown and mottled with dark blotches.

Nectar Sources: Edwards' Hairstreaks readily visit milkweeds *(Asclepias),* dogbane *(Apocynum),* New Jersey tea *(Ceanothus americanus),* staghorn sumac *(Rhus typhina),* goldenrod *(Solidago),* and white sweet clover *(Melilotus alba)* for nectar.

Larval Host Plant: Scrub oak *(Quercus ilicifolia)* is the preferred host for the Edwards' Hairstreak, but it also uses blackjack oak *(Q. marilandica).* The species will also feed on black oak *(Q. velutina)* in captivity.

Banded Hairstreak

Satyrium calanus falacer (Godart), 1824

Adult: Plate 8, Rows 4, 5
Larva: Plate 33, Rows 3, 4
Pupa: Plate 45, Row 4

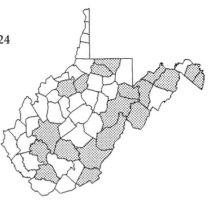

Description: Wingspan is 1 to 1¼ inches (25–32 mm). The Banded Hairstreak is dark brownish black on the upper surface. Males have a scent patch along the costal margin of the forewing. This species is very difficult to distinguish from the Hickory Hairstreak *(Satyrium caryaevorum)* in the field; however, the undersurface generally shows a couple of characteristic differences. Fresh Banded Hairstreaks are dark gray, almost black, on the undersurface. A postmedial dark band and a partial band cross both wings. In both species the bands are outlined in white at least on the outer side. In *S. calanus* the band in the forewing is fairly continuous. If the band is offset at the midpoint, the offset is slight. In *S. caryaevorum* the offset is more pronounced. In the hindwing the bands are usually even and do not expand or spread at the costal margin as they do in *S. caryaevorum*. Because of considerable variation between individuals, the most reliable way to separate the 2 species is by examination of the male and female genitalia.

Distribution: This hairstreak is widespread and the most common. It ranges from Nova Scotia west across southern Canada to southeastern Saskatchewan. In the United States it ranges south to central Florida and west to Texas. In West Virginia the Banded Hairstreak is found statewide. Although records don't indicate its abundance, it probably occurs in all counties.

Habitat: The Banded Hairstreak is associated with mixed deciduous forests and is often found along forest edges, clearings, clearcuts, roads, and trails where sunlight penetrates the canopy and creates sunlit openings. It is also associated with dry, shaley sites. The Banded Hairstreak is frequently found perched on tree leaves or on the ground.

Life History and Habits: Males perch on leaves of trees usually within 4 to 12 feet of the ground. They are very aggressive toward other males, and chases occur frequently. In sunlit openings males are easily seen circling with 1 or 2 other males before disappearing into the tree tops. Males usually return to their perch after the chase. The pale pinkish eggs are laid in the buds on twigs of host trees where they winter until the following spring. Larvae feed on catkins and young leaves. The Banded Hairstreak is univoltine, with its flight occurring from mid-June into mid-July. The caterpillar is variable. It may be whitish with a green dorsal stripe and green blotches, or green with a dark brown dorsal stripe and yellow lines, or brown with or without yellow stripes and oblique dashes (Saunders 1870). The caterpillar is covered with a fine pubescence. The chrysalis is brown and mottled with darker brown.

Nectar Sources: A variety of plants are visited for nectar, some of which include milkweeds *(Asclepias),* dogbane *(Apocynum),* New Jersey tea *(Ceanothus americanus),* yarrow *(Achillea),* staghorn sumac *(Rhus typhina),* white sweet clover *(Melilotus alba),* and elderberry *(Sambucus canadensis).*

Larval Host Plant: Host plants of the Banded Hairstreak include white oak *(Quercus alba),* chestnut oak *(Q. prinus),* black walnut *(Juglans nigra),* butternut *(J. cinerea),* and hickories *(Carya* spp.) (Opler and Krizek 1984). White oak is a known host in West Virginia.

Hickory Hairstreak

Satyrium caryaevorum (McDunnough), 1942

Adult: Plate 8, Row 5

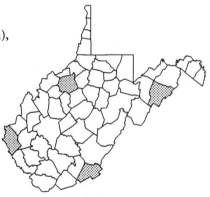

Description: Wingspan is 1 to 1¼ inches (25–32 mm). The Hickory Hairstreak is uniform brown on the upper surface. Males have a dull scent patch along the costal margin of the forewing. This butterfly is difficult to distinguish from its close relative, the Banded Hairstreak *(Satyrium calanus),* but 2 characteristics on the underside help separate them. The Hickory Hairstreak is brown on the underside, usually lighter than *S. calanus,* and has a dark postmedian band outlined in white, at least toward the outside. In the forewing the band is broken and offset, more so in the Hickory Hairstreak than in *S. calanus.* On the hindwing are 2 dark bands, or partial bands, outlined in white; in the Hickory Hairstreak the band expands toward the costal margin of the hindwing. In *S. calanus* the hindwing bands remain the same size or nearly so. Examination of the male and female genitalia should also be used to separate the 2 species when in question.

Distribution: The Hickory Hairstreak is found in spotty populations from New England west to Minnesota and south to Arkansas and northern Georgia. In West Virginia the species is found sporadically. Records exist from only 4 counties: Hardy, Monroe, Ritchie, and Wayne; but because of the difficulty in identifying this species, other county records may have gone unnoticed. The Hickory Hairstreak undoubtedly occurs in other counties.

Habitat: The butterfly is found in second growth deciduous woodlands with a strong hickory component. It is usually found in semi-open areas and along small clearings or roads where sunlight reaches the ground. It prefers sites with richer soils than its counterpart, the Banded Hairstreak.

Life History and Habits: Males perch on tree leaves usually higher up than *S. calanus*. Aggression toward other males is common, and males can be seen chasing one another in towering, spiral flights. As with other hairstreaks, this species is a rapid, erratic flier. The Hickory Hairstreak is univoltine, with its flight beginning in mid-June and continuing through July. Eggs are laid on the twigs of the host tree and winter until spring. The caterpillar is usually green with a dark dorsal band, a series of dark, diagonal subdorsal dashes, often edged in white, and a white or yellow lateral line. The chrysalis is brown, mottled with darker brown.

Nectar Sources: Various plants are visited for nectar, which include milkweed *(Asclepias),* dogbane *(Apocynum),* thistle *(Cirsium),* Queen Anne's lace *(Daucus carota),* staghorn sumac *(Rhus typhina),* white sweet clover *(Melilotus alba),* and New Jersey tea *(Ceanothus americanus).*

Larval Host Plant: Hickory is the primary host for the Hairstreak. Larvae have been collected in the wild from bitternut hickory *(Carya cordiformis)* (Lawrence Gall, personal communication). Other hickories used as hosts in laboratory rearing include pignut hickory *(C. glabra)* and shagbark hickory *(C. ovata)* (Opler and Krizek 1984).

Striped Hairstreak

Satyrium liparops strigosum (Harris), 1862

Adult: Plate 8, Row 6
Larva: Plate 33, Row 4

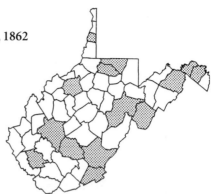

Description: Wingspan is 1 to 1⅜ inches (25–35 mm). This brownish black butterfly can be distinguished from the other *Satyrium* by the broad bands, lined in white, across the underside of the wings that are twice as wide as on the other *Satyrium.* There is a blue and a black-and-orange spot near the 2 short tails on the underside of the hindwing. Males have a dull scent patch on the upper forewings.

Distribution: The Striped Hairstreak is wide ranging, occurring from the Maritime Provinces west across southern Canada to Manitoba and south to Florida, Texas, and southern Colorado. In West Virginia populations are scattered around the state. The species probably occurs in more counties in suitable habitats than records indicate.

Habitat: The Striped Hairstreak is an inhabitant of second growth deciduous woodlands. It may be found along woodland edges, openings, and roadsides. It is also found along shady swamps and bogs.

Life History and Habits: Males perch on tree leaves at varying heights (from a few feet to 20 feet) awaiting females. During early morning hours they often perch on the ground. The Striped Hairstreak is univoltine, with its flight beginning in early June and continuing into mid-July. Eggs are laid on host twigs at buds and overwinter until the following spring. Larvae feed on buds, young leaves, and fruit. The caterpillar is yellow green with pale or yellow-green oblique dashes along the sides and a dark dorsal stripe on the abdomen. The chrysalis is brown, mottled with reddish brown.

Nectar Sources: Striped Hairstreaks readily nectar at such plants as milkweed *(Asclepias),* dogbane *(Apocynum),* staghorn sumac *(Rhus typhina),* New Jersey tea *(Ceanothus americanus),* viburnum *(Viburnum),* and goldenrod *(Solidago).*

Larval Host Plant: The Striped Hairstreak utilizes plants in the families Ericaceae and Rosaceae as its primary hosts. Plants in the heath family (Ericaceae) include blueberries *(Vaccinium* spp.) and flame azalea *(Rhododen-*

dron calendulaceum). Plants in the rose family (Rosaceae) include black cherry *(Prunus serotina)*, hawthorn *(Crataegus* spp.), serviceberry *(Amelanchier* spp.), blackberry *(Rubus* spp.), chokeberry *(Pyrus* spp.), and apple *(Malus* spp.) (Opler and Krizek 1984). American hornbeam *(Carpinus caroliniana)* is also reported as a host in New England (Dale Schweitzer, personal communication). Only black cherry has been confirmed as a host in West Virginia.

Red-banded Hairstreak

Calycopis cecrops (Fabricius), 1793
Adult: Plate 9, Row 1
Larva: Plate 34, Row 1

Description: Wingspan is ¾ to 1 inch (19–25 mm). Males are charcoal gray with a pale blue iridescence in the hindwing and along the base of the forewing on the upper surface. Females lack the blue iridescence. The underside is gray with a zigzag red band crossing the midportion of the wings. The red band is bordered with fine lines of black and white toward the outside. The species has fine tails.

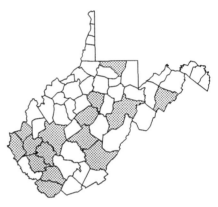

Distribution: The Red-banded Hairstreak ranges from coastal New Jersey south through Florida and west through West Virginia and southern Ohio to Missouri, Kansas, and Texas. In West Virginia reports are scattered, and although the Red-banded Hairstreak is most abundant in the southern counties, it has been found at the highest elevations at Spruce Knob in Randolph County as well.

Habitat: The Red-banded Hairstreak prefers semi-open brushy habitats, which include forest edges, abandoned farms, hedgerows, and clearings.

Life History and Habits: Males perch on leaves of shrubs or trees a few feet above the ground or on tree trunks in shade during hot afternoons awaiting females. They also gather at wet spots or puddles along dirt roads or trails to sip moisture. In West Virginia the species is triple-brooded, especially in the south. The first flight appears in late April and May, and the second flight appears in late June and July. A third flight appears in August and continues into September. Eggs (white) are laid singly on young host leaves or stems or on dead leaves on the ground. Larvae from the eggs laid on the host plants feed on young leaves, and those from eggs laid in the leaf litter feed on detritus. The caterpillar is gray brown and covered with fine short hairs. The chrysalis is pale brown and marked with black blotches, especially along the dorsal surface. The species pupates in the leaf litter. Larvae hibernate in the fourth instar.

Nectar Sources: Red-banded Hairstreaks visit a variety of plants for nectar, including sumac *(Rhus),* dogbane *(Apocynum),* black cherry *(Prunus serotina),* blackberry *(Rubus),* milkweeds *(Asclepias),* autumn olive *(Elaeagnus umbellata),* New Jersey tea *(Ceanothus americanus),* and yarrow *(Achillea).*

Larval Host Plant: In West Virginia the Red-banded Hairstreak utilizes staghorn sumac *(Rhus typhina)* and dwarf sumac *(R. copallina)* as its hosts, although many larvae feed only on detritus found in the leaf litter. In the laboratory, larvae prefer a diet of detritus and grow rapidly on it (about 4 weeks), especially in a moist environment. They show a preference for rotting lettuce leaves *(Lactuca sativa* var: *crispa)* in captivity.

(Olive) Juniper Hairstreak

Mitoura grynea grynea (Hübner), 1819
Adult: Plate 9, Row 2
Larva: Plate 34, Row 1

Description: Wingspan is ⅞ to 1 inch (22–25 mm). The Juniper Hairstreak is a small colorful butterfly with 2 color forms. In the spring the upper surface is tawny orange (females) to bronze (males), with dark brown borders, wing bases, and veins. Males have a scent patch along the costal margin of the forewing. In the summer form, males are more tawny orange than bronze above and females are dark brownish black. The underside is similar in both forms and is bright green, with a zigzag brown-and-white line across the hindwing. In the forewing there is a fairly straight white-and-brown line crossing the wing. The outer margin of the hindwing is gray with black dots. Short tails are present on the hindwings.

Distribution: The Juniper Hairstreak occurs sporadically from New England west through the southern portions of the Great Lakes states to southern British Columbia. It occurs southward in the East to Florida, the Gulf states, and to Texas. In West Virginia the species appears limited to the Eastern Panhandle counties and has been found in Berkeley, Grant, Jefferson, Hampshire, Hardy, Mineral, and Pendleton Counties thus far. However, the host tree, eastern red cedar *(Juniperus virginiana),* is widespread through the drier portions of the state. The Juniper Hairstreak may occur in some of these areas as well.

Habitat: The species is closely associated with cedar trees and is found in fields or dry hillsides amongst cedars. Hillsides with abundant cedars 10 to 20 feet high are good sites for the hairstreak, which usually stays near the tops of the trees.

Life History and Habits: Males perch on the tips of cedar tree branches. Usually small to medium (6–20 ft.) trees are selected. Males walk around stems rubbing their wings together. They frequently fly off the tree and circle a few times before landing again on the same or adjacent tree. Males are aggressive toward one another. Flowers are visited periodically throughout the day. Oviposition by the female occurs from late morning until late afternoon. The pale green eggs are deposited on the needles of the host. The species is bivoltine in West Virginia, with the first brood appearing in mid-April and flying into mid-May. A second brood appears in July and early August. The caterpillar is bright green with white oblique bars on each segment and a white sublateral line. The body is covered with fine, short, brownish hairs. The chrysalis is dark brown and is the overwintering stage.

Nectar Sources: Spring flowers found in fields around cedar trees are used for nectar. These include spring beauty *(Claytonia),* phlox *(Phlox),* bird's-foot violet *(Viola pedata),* field cress *(Lepidium campestre),* winter cress *(Barbarea vulgaris),* and redbud *(Cercis canadensis).* Summer flowers include milkweeds *(Asclepias),* dogbane *(Apocynum),* and white sweet clover *(Melilotus alba).*

Larval Host Plant: In West Virginia the only host for the Juniper Hairstreak is eastern red cedar *(Juniperus virginiana).*

Brown Elfin

Incisalia augustinus croesoides (Scudder), 1876

Adult: Plate 9, Row 3
Larva: Plate 34, Row 2

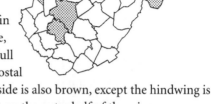

Description: Wingspan is ¾ to 1⅛ inches (19–28 mm). The Brown Elfin lacks markings on the upper surface, which is soft brown. Males have a dull gray-brown scent patch along the costal margin of the forewing. The underside is also brown, except the hindwing is mahogany toward the base and rust on the outer half of the wing.

Distribution: The Brown Elfin occurs from Newfoundland west to Alaska, and south to Minnesota, Michigan, New Mexico, and southern California in scattered populations. In the East it extends through the Appalachians south to northern Georgia. In West Virginia the Brown Elfin is found in both the eastern panhandle and western counties. The species has not been reported from the central mountainous region.

Habitat: The Brown Elfin is found mainly in pine-oak-heath barrens, where soils are usually acidic. The butterfly may be found in openings, such as power- or gas-line right-of-ways, woodland clearings such as clearcuts, and along trails or roads in woodland habitats where there are an abundance of heaths, such as blueberries *(Vaccinium)*.

Life History and Habits: Males perch with wings closed on twig ends or leaves of shrubs and low trees. They also perch on the ground and are often found on dirt roads or along trails. Oviposition continues throughout much of the day. The species is univoltine, with a single flight appearing from mid-April into late May or early June. Eggs are laid on the flower buds of the host plant. Larvae feed on young leaves, flower buds, and fruit. They go through 3 molts and are fully grown in about 3 weeks. The caterpillar is yellow green with faint yellow stripes, oblique on the dorsum and longitudinal on the sides. The head is brown. The chrysalis is light brown and covered with short hairs.

Nectar Sources: The Brown Elfin visits several spring plants to obtain nectar. These include redbud *(Cercis canadensis)*, blueberry *(Vaccinium)*, autumn olive *(Elaeagnus umbellata)*, huckleberry *(Gaylussacia)*, phlox *(Phlox)*, and winter cress *(Barbarea vulgaris)*.

Larval Host Plant: The Brown Elfin uses heaths as host plants. These include blueberries *(Vaccinium* spp.) and box huckleberry *(Gaylussacia brachycera)* in West Virginia.

Hoary Elfin

Incisalia polia (Cook and Watson), 1907

Adult: Plate 9, Rows 3, 4

Description: Wingspan is ¾ to 1 inch (19–25 mm). The Hoary Elfin is a small brown butterfly. A scent patch occurs along the costal margin of the forewing upper surface in males. The underside is also brown with a narrow, white postmedian line in the forewing and a broad, whitish gray border on the hindwing. The forewing has a narrow, gray margin.

Distribution: The Hoary Elfin ranges from Nova Scotia and Maine across southern Canada to Alaska and south into the Great Lakes states, and in the Rockies to northern New Mexico. In the East it ranges into Maryland and Virginia in scattered populations. In West Virginia the species is represented only by a single record from Kanawha County taken in May 1881 by W. H. Edwards (1868, 1884, 1897). The scarcity of the species results from the absence of its preferred host, bearberry *(Arctostaphylos uvaursi),* in West Virginia. The nearby population of *I. polios* in Maryland feeds on trailing arbutus *(Epigaea repens),* and, therefore, populations may also exist in West Virginia on the same host. Populations may exist in Preston and Tucker Counties where *E. repens* occurs.

Habitat: The preferred habitat for the Hoary Elfin is dry, sandy areas or perhaps shaley areas along woodland edges, clearings, rocky slopes, and ridges. Open areas with shrubs and *Vaccinium* are also suitable for the elfin.

Life History and Habits: Males perch on leaves of low shrubs or bushes to await females. They generally stay close to the ground and often land on the ground. The Hoary Elfin is univoltine, with a single flight in early spring, beginning in late April and extending into late May. Eggs are laid on flower buds of the host, and larvae feed on both flowers and young leaves. The caterpillar is green with a light middorsal and lateral stripe and oblique dashes along the sides. The chrysalis is brown to dark brown and is the overwintering stage.

Nectar Sources: Hoary Elfins visit various spring flowers for nectar, including blueberry *(Vaccinium)* and willow *(Salix)*, as well as others.

Larval Host Plant: The preferred host for the species is bearberry *(Arctostaphylos uvaursi)*, which is not reported from West Virginia; however, the Hoary Elfin is also associated with trailing arbutus *(Epigaea repens)* (Opler and Krizek 1984; Scott 1986). Trailing arbutus is locally common in West Virginia.

Frosted Elfin

Incisalia irus irus (Gordart), 1824
Adult: Plate 9, Rows 4, 5
Larva: Plate 34, Row 2
Pupa: Plate 45, Row 4

Description: Wingspan is ⅞ to 1⅛ inches (22–35 mm). Males of this brown butterfly have a long, narrow scent patch along the costal margin of the forewing on the upper surface. The underside is gray brown with less contrasting markings than the Hoary Elfin *(Incisalia polia)*. There is whitish gray scaling along the outer margin of the hindwing containing a dark spot and an irregular dark line, often bordered in white, crossing the midwing. The basal area of the hindwing is usually darker than the outer half.

Distribution: The Frosted Elfin occurs from New England west to central Wisconsin and south to Illinois. In the East, it occurs in local populations to northern Georgia, the northern portions of the Gulf states, eastern Texas, and to northwest Louisiana and southwest Arkansas. In West Virginia the butterfly is only known from 2 small populations in Randolph County. It probably occurs in other counties as well where its host plant is abundant.

Habitat: The Frosted Elfin is found in open areas along woodland edges and roads, brushy fields, and in open oak-pine habitats.

Life History and Habits: The Frosted Elfin is a fairly rapid flier and a good colonizer. Colonies are usually small, comprised of a few individuals. The species is univoltine, with a single spring flight. The flight generally begins a week or so after the other elfins, with adults appearing in late May and flying into mid-June. Larvae feed on the flower heads and small terminal leaves of the host. Pupation occurs in the leaf litter at the base of the plant. The caterpillar is pale greenish white, with a pale lateral line and oblique dashes along the sides. The larva is covered with short whitish hairs. The chrysalis is dark brown with short brownish orange hairs and is the overwintering stage.

Nectar Sources: In Ohio, lupines *(Lupinus)* are reported as a nectar source (Iftner et al. 1992). In West Virginia the butterfly has been observed nectaring on dewberry and blackberry flowers *(Rubus).*

Larval Host Plant: Lupine *(Lupinus perennis)* and wild indigo *(Baptisia tinctoria)* are the primary host over much of the range of this species. In West Virginia, wild indigo *(B. tinctoria)* is the selected host.

Henry's Elfin

Incisalia henrici henrici (Grote and Robinson), 1867

Adult: Plate 9, Row 5
Larva: Plate 34, Row 2

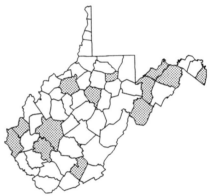

Description: Wingspan is ⅞ to 1⅛ inches (22–28 mm). Henry's Elfin is a small dark brown butterfly, with rust brown toward the center of the wings on the upper surface, especially in females. The underside of the forewing is brown basally and greenish toward the tips. The hindwing is dark mahogany basally and lighter toward the outer margin, which contains a large violet-gray patch. There are rudimentary tails on the hindwing. This species lacks the scent patch on the males.

Distribution: Henry's Elfin ranges from coastal New England west across southern Canada to southeastern Manitoba and south to Florida, the Gulf Coast, and Texas. In West Virginia Henry's Elfin occurs in scattered populations but is most common where an abundance of redbud *(Cercis canadensis)* occurs.

Habitat: This species utilizes a variety of habitats but is usually found in young, deciduous woodlands, pine-oak shale barrens, or old fields and hillsides where redbud occurs. Henry's Elfin is also found along roadsides or power- and gas-line right-of-ways and through wooded areas where redbud is a common component.

Life History and Habits: Males perch on twigs of trees and readily interact with other males. Females tend to perch on low shrubs or grass, whereas males tend to perch higher in trees, from 6 to 20 feet. Males also visit damp soil and mud puddles to imbibe moisture. Henry's Elfin is univoltine, with a single flight throughout its range. In West Virginia adults appear in early April and fly into the latter part of May. The small whitish eggs, flattened dorsoventrally, are laid on the flowers' buds or on a twig at a bud. Young larvae feed on flowers by boring into them. As flowers drop off, larvae move to young leaves where they finish their growth. The caterpillar is pale to dark green, with pale green, yellow-green, or red-green oblique dashes on the dorsal surface and a yellow or reddish lateral stripe. The chrysalis is brown to greenish brown and is the overwintering stage.

Nectar Sources: Henry's Elfins nectar at redbud *(Cercis canadensis)*, fleabane *(Erigeron)*, and phlox *(Phlox)* and imbibe moisture at mud puddles. Other nectar sources are probably also used.

Larval Host Plant: While different populations of Henry's Elfin utilize different host plants, those in West Virginia use redbud *(Cercis canadensis)* as the primary host. At other locations, American holly *(Ilex opaca)*, blueberry *(Vaccinium* spp.), and huckleberry *(Gaylussacia* spp.) are used as hosts. These may also serve as occasional hosts in West Virginia where redbud does not occur (Edwards 1866; Opler and Krizek 1984.)

Eastern Pine Elfin

Incisalia niphon niphon (Hübner), 1823

Adult: Plate 9, Row 6
Larva: Plate 34, Row 3
Pupa: Plate 46, Row 1

Description: Wingspan is 1 to 1¼ inches (25–32 mm). The Eastern Pine Elfin is a small rust-brown butterfly with dark wing borders on the upper surface. Males have a dull gray-brown scent patch near the costal margin of the forewing. Wing fringes are checkered white and black. The hindwing underside is strongly banded with gray, violet, and mahogany brown in an irregular pattern. The forewing is brown with a mahogany band, dashes, and crescents.

Distribution: The Eastern Pine Elfin occurs from Nova Scotia to eastern Alberta and south to Florida, the Gulf states, and Texas. Populations are more scattered south of New Jersey. In West Virginia the species occurs mainly in the Eastern Panhandle counties. It occurs sporadically in a few other counties but probably not in the mountainous region of east-central West Virginia.

Habitat: The Eastern Pine Elfin prefers semi-open to open areas where scrub or Virginia pine *(Pinus virginiana)* and oak predominate. These sites are generally found in dry, shaley regions and may be old fields, forest edges, gas- and power-line right-of-ways, and shale barrens.

Life History and Habits: Males perch on tips of pine branches with wings closed, often near the tops of trees. They are very aggressive toward other males, and chase flights are common. Males frequently gather at wet spots on sand or gravel to imbibe moisture. The Eastern Pine Elfin is univoltine in West Virginia, with a single flight in mid-April that continues into late May and possibly early June. The pale green eggs are laid at the base of young needles on the current year's growth, on which the larvae also feed. Pupation occurs in midsummer and is the hibernating stage. The caterpillar is green with a pair of heavy, longitudinal, cream stripes on the dorsum. The chrysalis is dark red brown and covered with fine, short, brownish hairs.

Nectar Sources: Eastern Pine Elfins nectar at various spring plants, shrubs, and trees. These include phlox *(Phlox),* dandelion *(Taraxacum),* cinquefoil *(Potentilla canadensis),* bastard toadflax *(Comandra umbellata),* blueberry *(Vaccinium),* blackberry *(Rubus),* and redbud *(Cercis canadensis).*

Larval Host Plant: In West Virginia the favorite host for the Eastern Pine Elfin is Virginia pine *(Pinus virginiana).* Young trees up to 20 feet are most often selected. The Eastern Pine Elfin will use other species of hard pines as well, including pitch pine *(P. rigida)* and shortleaf pine *(P. echinata).* The species has also been reared on scotch pine *(P. sylvestris).*

White M Hairstreak

Parrhasius m-album (Boisduval and
LeConte), 1833

Adult: Plate 9, Row 7
Larva: Plate 34, Row 3

Description: Wingspan is 1⅛ to 1¼
inches (28–32 mm). The White M
Hairstreak is bright iridescent blue
with black borders on the upper
surface. Males have a black stigma, or
scent patch, in the forewing. Females have broader black wing borders than
males. The underside is gray with a thin, white-and-black postmedian line
crossing the wings. The line in the hindwing forms a distinct "M" at the lower
margin. Prominent orange-and-blue spots occur near the long tails in the
hindwing.

Distribution: The White M Hairstreak occurs from southern New England
west to Iowa and Missouri, and then south to Florida, the Gulf states, and
Texas. This species is commonly found throughout the Appalachian
Mountains in the East. In West Virginia populations turn up sporadically. The
hairstreak is seldom abundant but is probably more widely distributed in the
state than records indicate.

Habitat: This butterfly is associated with oak forests and is usually found
along woodland edges, clearings, roadways, and trails. Adults often stray into
open fields to nectar.

Life History and Habits: Males perch on leaves of trees or tall shrubs. Males
and females may perch on the ground during early morning hours to absorb
heat. The pale green eggs are laid singly on young leaves or buds of the host.
This hairstreak is multibrooded and has 2 to 3 generations per year. The first
flight appears in late April or early May and continues through May. A second
flight appears in late June and flies until early August, and a third flight or
partial flight appears in September and flies into October. The species
probably winters in the pupal stage, with some of the pupae from the second
brood hibernating until spring. The caterpillar is olive green to yellow green,
with a dark rust-brown spot on the anterior and posterior dorsum. Dark,
oblique dashes may also be present. The larva is covered with fine short hairs.
The chrysalis is brown, with darker blotches on the abdomen.

Nectar Sources: White M Hairstreaks nectar at a variety of plants, including milkweeds *(Asclepias),* boneset *(Eupatorium),* Joe-pye weed *(Eupatorium),* dogwood *(Cornus),* viburnum *(Viburnum),* sumac *(Rhus),* sourwood *(Oxydendrum arboreum),* black cherry *(Prunus serotina),* goldenrod *(Solidago),* dogbane *(Apocynum),* and blackberry *(Rubus).*

Larval Host Plant: The White M Hairstreak selects mainly oaks as its host. In West Virginia, white oak *(Quercus alba)* is commonly used, although other oaks are probably also selected. In Ohio the species feeds on basswood *(Tilia* spp.) (Iftner et al. 1992), which may be a host as well in West Virginia.

(Northern) Southern Hairstreak

Fixsenia favonius ontario (Edwards), 1868

Adult: Plate 10, Row 1

Description: Wingspan is 1 to 1¼ inches (25–32 mm). Males of this small brownish black butterfly have a pronounced scent patch surrounded with black on the upper forewing surface. A variable orange spot occurs in the outer forewing and near the tip of the hindwing that is not seen in the other West Virginia hairstreaks. The underside is grayish brown with a thin postmedian band of white and black crossing both wings. The band in the hindwing forms a "W" near the tails. There are also a blue patch and a series of orange crescents along the margin of the hindwing. The first crescent (next to the blue) is the largest and contains a black spot.

Distribution: The Southern Hairstreak ranges from New England west to Illinois and Colorado. It occurs south to southern Florida and along the Gulf Coast to southern Texas. Populations are very spotty throughout the species' range. In West Virginia the Southern Hairstreak has been recorded from the 4 eastern counties.

Habitat: The Southern Hairstreak is found in dry, oak woodlands, woodland edges and openings, and on shale barrens.

Life History and Habits: Males perch on leaves in oak woodlands awaiting females. Both sexes readily visit flowers along roads and trails, especially during the afternoon. The species is univoltine, with its single flight occurring from late May through June. Eggs are laid on host twigs at buds; this is the overwintering stage. In the spring the larvae develop on buds and flowers, feeding on pollen and switching to young leaves as they grow. The caterpillar is green, with several pale green dashes and a yellow lateral stripe. The chrysalis is brown, mottled with black, and contains a lateral row of black dots.

Nectar Sources: The favorite nectar plants for the Southern Hairstreak are milkweeds *(Asclepias),* dogbane *(Apocynum),* New Jersey tea *(Ceanothus americanus),* and blueberry *(Vaccinium).*

Larval Host Plant: Oaks comprise the only known hosts for this species. They include white oak *(Quercus alba),* post oak *(Q. stellata),* black oak *(Q. velutina),* red oak *(Q. rubra),* and possibly scrub oak *(Q. ilicifolia)* (Opler and Krizek 1984; Iftner et al. 1992).

Gray Hairstreak

Strymon melinus humuli (Harris), 1841

Adult: Plate 10, Rows 1, 2
Larva: Plate 34, Row 4
Pupa: Plate 46, Row 1

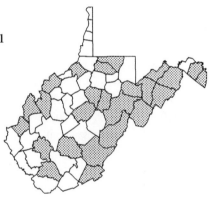

Description: Wingspan is ⅞ to 1¼ inches (23–32 mm). The Gray Hairstreak is charcoal gray on the upper surface, with a prominent orange-and-black spot near the long tail on the hindwing. The underside is steel gray, with a slightly irregular postmedian line of black, red, and white crossing the wings. Two orange-and-black spots occur along the lower margin of the hindwings.

Distribution: The Gray Hairstreak ranges through the entire United States from the Maritime Provinces west to British Columbia, south to southern Florida, and west to California. It also occurs from Mexico to South America. The species is rare in the northern portions of its range. In West Virginia, however, it probably occurs in every county.

Habitat: The Gray Hairstreak is found in a variety of habitats but is most often encountered in old fields, clearings, woodland edges, as well as along roads, power- and gas-line right-of-ways, reclaimed mine areas, and in brushy habitats along wetlands.

Life History and Habits: Males perch on leaves of low shrubs and trees awaiting females. They are aggressive toward other males, and chase flights are frequent. Males usually return to the same perch or one close by. Females lay their eggs singly on the young leaves or flower buds of the host plant, and larvae feed on both. Larvae are attended by ants, which feed on their honeydew secretions. The Gray Hairstreak is multibrooded in West Virginia, with 3 flights. The first flight appears in mid-April and extends into late May. A second flight appears in late June and continues through July, with a few individuals found in early August. A third flight occurs from mid-August through September and into October. The caterpillar varies from yellow green to reddish green, with a series of light-and-dark oblique dashes dorsolaterally and a white to yellow sublateral, longitudinal stripe; or the markings may be very obscured. The larva is covered with fine short hairs. The chrysalis is pale brown, speckled with darker brown, and is the overwintering stage.

Nectar Sources: The Gray Hairstreak visits a variety of plants for nectar, including milkweeds *(Asclepias)*, dogbane *(Apocynum)*, winter cress *(Barbarea vulgaris)*, redbud *(Cercis canadensis)*, thistle *(Cirsium)*, goldenrod *(Solidago)*, mints *(Mentha)*, white sweet clover *(Melilotus alba)*, and clovers *(Trifolium)*.

Larval Host Plant: The Gray Hairstreak uses legumes (Fabaceae) and mallows (Malvaceae) as hosts in West Virginia, including bush clovers *(Lespedeza* spp.), tick-trefoil *(Desmodium* spp.), vetches *(Vicia* spp.), clovers *(Trifolium* spp.), and mallow *(Malva* spp.). They will also feed on beans *(Phaseolus* spp.) and probably other legumes as well.

Early Hairstreak

Erora laeta (Edwards), 1862
Adult: Plate 10, Row 2
Larva: Plate 34, Row 4

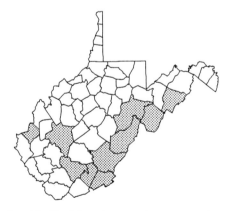

Description: Wingspan is ¾ to 1 inch (25–35 mm). Male Early Hairstreaks are charcoal gray above, with a blue band along the outer margin of the hindwing. Females are iridescent blue on the upper surface, especially toward the basal half of the wings, and on most of the hindwing. The underside is greenish gray, with broken bands of rust, edged in white, across the wings.

Distribution: The Early Hairstreak occurs from the Maritime Provinces across southern Canada to Michigan and Wisconsin, and then south through the Appalachian Mountains to northern Georgia. The species is considered rare over most of its range. In West Virginia the Early Hairstreak has been found in a number of counties, usually represented by 1 or 2 individuals. Only rarely is it found in larger numbers.

Habitat: The Early Hairstreak prefers mixed hardwood habitats and is usually found in openings along roads, trails, and clearings. It may be found along gravel or dirt roads on ridge tops or in lowlands along streams.

Life History and Habits: Males perch on leaves of low trees and shrubs or tall plants and sometimes on the ground. Females frequently come down from tree tops to perch on the ground during hot days, where they imbibe moisture. Males and females readily visit flowers for nectar. The small pale green eggs are laid singly on fruit, catkins, or buds of host trees, and caterpillars feed mainly on young fruit during the spring. The caterpillar develops through 7 instars over a period of 40 days. The Early Hairstreak is bivoltine, with 2 flights in West Virginia. The first flight occurs in April and extends into mid-May. The second flight occurs in July and extends into mid-August. The caterpillar is green to rust brown, with dark reddish blotches on the body. The chrysalis is rust brown and speckled with darker brown, becoming more uniform with age (Scott 1986). The chrysalis is the overwintering stage.

Nectar Sources: A variety of plants are visited for nectar, including spring beauty *(Claytonia)*, fleabane *(Erigeron)*, yarrow *(Achillea)*, ox-eye daisy *(Chrysanthemum leucanthemum)*, Queen Anne's lace *(Daucus carota)*, dogbane *(Apocynum)*, New Jersey tea *(Ceanothus americanus)*, and butterfly weed *(Asclepias tuberosa)*. Females also imbibe liquids at puddles.

Larval Host Plant: Fruits of American beech *(Fagus grandifolia)* and hazelnut *(Corylus* spp.) are the preferred hosts, although the butterfly may use birch catkins *(Betula* spp.) and galls in the second brood (R. P. Webster, personal communication). In captivity the Early Hairstreak can be easily reared on willows *(Salix* spp.), but it is not known if this is a selected host in the wild (Wright 1981).

Subfamily Polyommatinae—Blues

The blues are small butterflies, with approximately 1100 species found mainly in the temperate regions of the world. They are more abundant in the Old World than in the New World but are found in both hemispheres. Very few species occur in the tropics. In North America there are 32 described species that range from the treeline in the north to the tropics. Five species occur in West Virginia.

The blues are dimorphic butterflies, with males usually showing a great deal of iridescent to pale blue coloration, whereas females are mostly brown to gray, with limited blue patches. Some of the blues, especially in the Old World, migrate to establish new colonies; few species migrate in the New World. These fragile butterflies are generally considered slow, weak fliers; however, when disturbed, they are capable of rapid, more powerful flight, and many often fly above the tree tops.

The blues visit a variety of flowers for nectar. Freshly emerged males puddle in large numbers at wet spots to sip moisture and minerals. Male blues patrol for females rather than perch. Blues generally rest with their wings closed but bask with their wings at least partially open. Some, especially *Everes* (tailed blues), rub their hindwings together when at rest, as do many hairstreaks (Theclinae).

The turban-shaped eggs are laid on the flower buds or young leaves of the host plants on which the larvae feed. A variety of plant families are selected as hosts by this group, although legumes (Fabaceae) are chosen most often.

Larvae are sluglike, most often green with various markings, and covered with fine short hairs. They blend perfectly with their host plants in color and pattern. Larvae are also attended by ants, which feed on their honeydew secretions produced from glands on the dorsum of the tenth abdominal segment. In return the larvae are protected from predators and parasites. Most of the blues hibernate as pupae, although some of the more tropical species may diapause as adults or larvae. The chrysalis is rounded, larger toward the abdomen, and is attached to its substrate, generally leaf litter, by a silk girdle. A rasp or file-like structure on one of the sutures of the abdominal segments produces a noise as the abdomen moves or twitches.

Eastern Tailed-Blue

Everes comyntas comyntas (Godart), 1824

Adult: Plate 10, Row 3
Larva: Plate 35, Row 1

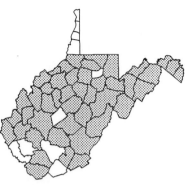

Description: Wingspan is ¾ to 1 inch
(19–25 mm). This small butterfly is the
only blue in West Virginia with tails.
Spring and summer males are purplish
blue on the upper surface. Spring
females are brownish black with patches of purple blue toward the base of the
forewings and toward the outer portion of the hindwing. One or 2 black-
centered, orange spots are present along the hindwing margin. The summer-
form female is a dark charcoal gray, lacking the purple blue. The underside of
both sexes is silvery gray, with numerous black dots and 2 orange spots
containing a black dot along the hindwing margin.

Distribution: The Eastern Tailed-Blue ranges over most of the area east of the
Rocky Mountains from southern Canada to Colorado and Texas, but in the
East it ranges south only to northern Florida. A few isolated populations
occur west of the Rockies. The species also ranges through Mexico and
Central America to Costa Rica. In West Virginia the blue should be found
statewide.

Habitat: This blue is found in open areas, such as fields, pastures, power-and
gas-line right-of-ways, roadsides, and woodland clearings.

Life History and Habits: Males patrol open areas, flying close to the ground in
search of females. They perch readily on grass stems and low vegetation,
rubbing their wings together at rest. They bask with wings partially open.
Males also visit wet spots or puddles along roads and streams for moisture.
Females oviposit between the flower buds or on young leaves of the host
plants usually during the afternoon. Eggs are laid singly and larvae feed
primarily on the buds but will eat young leaves as well. They are attended by
ants that seek their honeydew secretions. The Eastern Tailed-Blue is
multibrooded in West Virginia, with the first adults appearing in April and
May. A second brood appears in late June and July, and a third brood appears
in September and flies through early October. The caterpillar is variable but is
usually green with pale green, oblique lateral stripes, a dark dorsal line, and a
yellow sublateral line. It is covered with fine whitish hairs. The chrysalis is pale
to dark green or brownish yellow and is also variable. Caterpillars hibernate,
often in seed pods, and pupate in spring.

Nectar Sources: With its short proboscis, the Eastern Tailed-Blue seeks plants with short corollas for nectar. Some of these include cinquefoil *(Potentilla)*, winter cress *(Barbarea vulgaris)*, white sweet clover *(Melilotus alba)*, red and white clover *(Trifolium)*, dogbane *(Apocynum)*, peppermint *(Mentha)*, and asters *(Aster)*.

Larval Host Plant: The Eastern Tailed-Blue uses legumes (Fabaceae) as hosts. In West Virginia bush clovers *(Lespedeza* spp.) are a favorite host as well as red clover *(Trifolium pratense)*. They also use alfalfa *(Medicago sativa)* and rabbitfoot clover *(T. arvense)* on shale barren sites. Other legumes also reported include vetches *(Vicia* spp.), beggar's tick *(Desmodium* spp.), and yellow sweet clover *(Melilotus officinalis)* (Opler and Krizek 1984).

Spring Azure

Celastrina ladon ladon* (Cramer), 1780

Adult: Plate 10, Rows 4, 5
Larva: Plate 35, Rows 1, 2

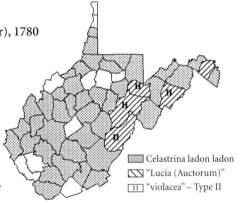

	Celastrina ladon ladon
	"Lucia (Auctorum)"
	"violacea" – Type II

Description: Wingspan is ¾ to 1¼ inches (19–32 mm). The Spring Azure is a small delicate butterfly, with pale blue to violet blue coloration on the upper surface. Spring males have fine, black dorsal wing margins. Females of the spring brood are also blue with broad, black forewing borders. The underside of the common early spring brood in lower elevations, referred to as subspecies *ladon* race "violacea" Type I, is dull to dark gray, with small black spots on the hindwing and a row of spots on the forewing. This butterfly was originally described by Edwards (1866). From high elevations there are spring individuals that have a brown to black margin on the outer portion of the hindwing underside (form "marginata") or a dark black patch in the center of the hindwing beneath (form "lucia"), which are assigned to

---

* In the past this species was referred to as *Celastrina argiolus* L. Because of the complexity of the species, some taxonomists disagree on the assigned name; however, current thinking tends to assign *C. argiolus* to European populations and *C. ladon* to North American populations.

subspecies *lucia Auctorum* (Pratt et al. 1994). Dorsal scales of males of these 2 early spring entities differ (D. Wright, personal communication). In the summer brood, subspecies *ladon* race "neglecta," which does not necessarily result from the spring brood, males and females tend to be larger and have more white on the upper surface, especially on the hindwing. Some females may have almost white hindwings above. Similar to the spring brood, males have a narrow, black wing margin on the upper surface, whereas females have broad, black margins. The underside of the summer brood is silvery gray to white, with contrasting black spotting. "Neglecta" produces flights during summer and additional partial flights in early fall. A separate sibling flight of blues appears between the flights of subspecies *lucia Auct.* and "neglecta" at higher elevations and is referred to as "violacea" Type II (Pratt et al. 1994). This butterfly is dark blue above and silvery gray beneath, with dark black spotting on the hindwing and a row of black spots on the forewing. The "violacea" Type II sibling flight parallels that of the Appalachian Blue (*Celastrina neglectamajor*). The *ladon* races discussed here may eventually be considered full species. Individuals of forms "marginata" and "lucia" are frequently flying at the beginning of the "violacea" Type II flight.

Distribution: The Spring Azure in its several forms and sibling populations ranges throughout the United States and Canada from Labrador west to the Pacific coast and Alaska, and then south to northern Florida, west to the Texas coast, Mexico, and Central America. The complex can be found wherever suitable hosts and habitat permit. In West Virginia the Spring Azure should be found statewide. "Violacea" Type I and "neglecta" occur in large populations, sometimes numbering thousands of individuals in the southern counties, but are found everywhere else in smaller numbers. *Lucia Auct.* and "violacea" Type II are generally found in the higher elevations of the mountain counties of north-central West Virginia.

Habitat: A variety of habitats are utilized by the Spring Azure, although it is most often found in or around woodlands, woodland openings, roads, trails, and edges. It is also found in wet meadows, wooded marshes, and swamps.

Life History and Habits: Males ("violacea" Type I) patrol within a few feet of the ground, in a rather slow flight, searching for females. They perch on occasion on the leaves of herbaceous plants, trees, or shrubs but frequently gather in large numbers at wet areas along gravel or sandy roads or at stream edges. Females oviposit from midmorning until dusk and are often encountered flying high amongst tree branches in search of suitable sites. Females may also be encountered nectaring at flowers throughout the day but are almost never found gathered on the ground as are males. *Lucia Auct.* is univoltine and flies in the mountains from late April to mid-May. *Ladon* races "violacea" Type I and "violacea" Type II are also univoltine in West Virginia, with single flights occurring from March into May for Type I, and from mid- to late April into early June for Type II. "Neglecta," which is multibrooded, flies from late May through June and again in July and August. Some individuals may be found into September and even October. Eggs are pale green to white, flattened dorsoventrally, ribbed, and pitted. Eggs are deposited singly under flower buds. Larvae feed on the buds and are often tended by ants. The caterpillar is green or brown to whitish with a dark dorsal stripe and pale, often cream lateral bands on each segment extending across the back. The head is brown. The chrysalis is light brown and is the overwintering stage.

Nectar Sources: Several species of trees and shrubs are selected as nectar sources. These include apple *(Malus),* wild plum *(Prunus),* black cherry *(Prunus serotina),* serviceberry *(Amelanchier),* redbud *(Cercis canadensis),* viburnum *(Viburnum),* spicebush *(Lindera benzoin),* and blackberry *(Rubus).* Late spring and summer nectar sources include dogbane *(Apocynum),* New Jersey tea *(Ceanothus americanus),* privet *(Ligustrum),* milkweed *(Asclepias),* yellow sweet clover *(Melilotus officinalis),* and white sweet clover *(M. alba),* as well as other plants. Males also gather at wet spots to imbibe moisture and minerals and are also attracted to carrion for nutrients.

Larval Host Plant: Each generation or sibling race selects different flowering hosts. Races "violacea"—Type I and "*lucia* Auctorum," which fly early in spring, utilize dogwood flowers *(Cornus florida)* and black cherry flowers and fruit, respectively, as their host. "Violacea"—Type II, which flies during May, utilizes the leaf galls of black cherry *(Prunus serotina),* formed by eriophyid mites, as their primary host. "Neglecta" and its subsequent broods utilize the flower buds of New Jersey tea *(Ceanothus americana),* black cohosh *(Cimicifuga racemosa),* smooth sumac *(Rhus glabra),* meadowsweet *(Spiraea spp.),* and wing-stem *(Actinomeris alternifolia),* as well as others. Females will oviposit on some plant buds on which the larvae cannot survive. Such plants include wild hydrangea *(Hydrangea arborescens),* elderberry *(Sambucus* spp.), and certain viburnums *(Viburnum* spp.).

Appalachian Azure

Celastrina neglectamajor (Opler and Krizek), 1984

Adult: Plate 10, Row 6
Larva: Plate 35, Row 2

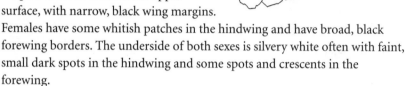

Description: Wingspan is 1⅛ to 1⅜ inches (30–36 mm). The Appalachian Azure is the largest of the blues. Males are pale to violet blue on the upper surface, with narrow, black wing margins. Females have some whitish patches in the hindwing and have broad, black forewing borders. The underside of both sexes is silvery white often with faint, small dark spots in the hindwing and some spots and crescents in the forewing.

Distribution: The Appalachian Azure ranges from southwestern New England and New York southwestward to Virginia, Kentucky, and northern Tennessee. In West Virginia this blue is most common in the eastern and southern portion of the state; however, it should be found in most of the counties. It is particularly common at Fork Creek Wildlife Management Area in Boone County, as well as in the Monongahela National Forest in Randolph County.

Habitat: Like the Spring Azure *(Celastrina ladon),* the Appalachian Azure prefers woodland habitats. It is often found along streams, woodland roads, and shaded road banks where its host plant occurs.

Life History and Habits: Appalachian Azures behave much like the Spring Azure. Males gather, often in large numbers, at puddles along woodland roads or on sandy soil at stream edges. Males patrol along woodland roads and edges in search of females. Females actively oviposit throughout the day beginning in late morning and have been observed egg laying late into the afternoon (1630 hours, 4:30 P.M.). They are often encountered while flying in search of host plants. Once a suitable host is located, the female quickly lands on the flower spike and walks around it depositing 2 to 4 eggs, each at a different point between the buds, before moving on to another plant. They stop regularly to nectar. The species is univoltine, with a single flight occurring during May and early June. A few individuals have been taken as early as April 20, but this is rare. Most Appalachian Azures do not begin flying until mid-May. The egg is pale greenish. The caterpillar of this blue may be yellowish green or brown. The light-and-dark colored bands on the dorsal surface are often missing or very faint. Development is complete by the end of July, and the chrysalis overwinters.

Nectar Sources: A variety of plants, including trees, shrubs, and herbaceous species, are used for nectaring. A commonly used species is blackberry *(Rubus)*, but viburnums *(Viburnum)* are also used. Males sip minerals from damp soil or sand as well.

Larval Host Plant: In West Virginia, as well as throughout its range, black cohosh *(Cimicifuga racemosa)* is the only selected host.

Dusky Azure

Celastrina nigra (Forbes), 1960

Adult: Plate 10, Row 7
Larva: Plate 35, Row 3
Pupa: Plate 46, Row 2

Description: Wingspan is ¾ to 1¼ inches (19–32 mm). The upper surface of the male is uniform charcoal gray. The female is pale whitish blue with broad, black borders on both wings. The underside of the Dusky Azure is silvery gray with small black spots and crescents on both wings.

Distribution: The Dusky Azure ranges in the central Appalachians from Pennsylvania and Maryland southwestward to western North Carolina, Kentucky, and eastern Tennessee. It also occurs in west-central Illinois, eastern Missouri, and northwestern Arkansas (Clench 1972). In West Virginia the Dusky Azure is found in small populations where its host plant abounds. The species is most frequently encountered in southern West Virginia. A good site for this blue is Fork Creek Wildlife Management Area in Boone County, but it is also found in other similar areas in the southern region.

Habitat: The Dusky Azure is found in association with the Spring Azure *(Celastrina ladon,* race "violacea" Type I). It prefers shaded, rich, deciduous hardwood forests; cool, shaded woodland roads; and edges. It is more frequently associated with cove hardwood forest types in West Virginia. In southern West Virginia it is found in narrow hollows near streams or along steep banks where its host occurs.

Life History and Habits: Like the Spring Azure, males patrol along woodland edges in search of females. They readily join congregations of Spring Azure males gathered at wet areas, puddles, or stream edges in forest openings. Male Dusky Azures can only be distinguished from Spring Azures by disturbing a congregation into flight. The gray color of the Dusky Azure can be easily distinguished from the pale blue of the Spring Azure in flight. Females rarely visit puddling males. They are usually found flying slowly through wooded areas or along edges close to the ground in search of suitable plants on which to oviposit. Females stop regularly on tree leaves to rest or at flowers to nectar. Oviposition by females occurs from midmorning until late afternoon. Early in the season, when the host plant is young and only a few inches above the ground, eggs are laid singly on young shoots and leaves. Later in the season, once flower buds appear, eggs are deposited directly on the flower buds. Early larvae feed on young leaves, but as the season progresses they switch to the flower buds. If the larvae consume the entire flower head before reaching full growth, they complete their feeding on the leaves. Larvae are attended by ants and are easily found by watching for ants on the host plant. The Dusky Azure is univoltine throughout its range, with a single spring brood that flies from the latter part of March through April and into May. Worn females may be found into late May, but larvae from eggs laid at that time are not likely to complete development. The peak of the flight is in April. Caterpillars are pale yellow green, with pale lateral stripes. The head is brown. Once the larvae complete development, usually in early June, they diapause in the pupal stage. The chrysalis is pale to medium brown, with greenish or brown wing cases.

Nectar Sources: The Dusky Azure visits a variety of trees, shrubs, and woodland flowers for nectar. Females visit nectar plants more readily than males. Males appear satisfied by sipping nutrients from moist soil or sand. Nectar plants visited by females include redbud *(Cercis canadensis),* wild geranium *(Geranium),* toothwort *(Dentaria),* and spring beauty *(Claytonia).*

Larval Host Plant: The only known host for the Dusky Azure is goatsbeard *(Aruncus dioicus).*

Silvery Blue

Glaucopsyche lygdamus lygdamus
(Doubleday), 1841

Adult: Plate 10, Rows 7, 8
Larva: Plate 35, Row 3

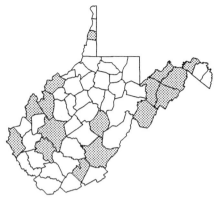

Description: Wingspan is 1 to 1¼
inches (25–32 mm). Males are
silvery blue on the upper surface,
with narrow, black wing margins.
Females are a deeper metallic blue
with broad, black wing margins. The underside of both sexes is uniformly
gray with round, black spots, ringed in white, that form a row across the
wings. There are 2 black dots and a dash near the base of the hindwing and a
dash in the forewing.

Distribution: The various subspecies of the Silvery Blue range from Nova
Scotia west to British Columbia, Alaska, and the Pacific coast, and south to
Baja, California, and Mexico. In the East the Silvery Blue occurs in the
Appalachian Mountains in scattered populations from southern New York to
northern Georgia, Alabama, and Arkansas. In West Virginia the Silvery Blue
probably occurs in most counties, although records of its occurrence are
scattered sporadically throughout the state. Fork Creek Wildlife Management
Area is a particularly good area for the blue where it flies with the Dusky
Azure *(Celastrina nigra)* and the Spring Azure *(C. ladon).*

Habitat: Damp woodland openings are preferred, but the species is also found
in brushy openings and fields in close proximity to woodlands. Sandy or
gravel woodland roads are also used by the blue. Males frequently gather at
wet areas, puddles, or stream edges to sip moisture from sandy soil.

Life History and Habits: Males of the Silvery Blue patrol in a slow flight close
to the ground in search of females. They also gather with other blues at wet
areas. Females are generally found flying along woodland edges in search of
host plants. The Silvery Blue is univoltine in West Virginia, with its flight from
early April into mid-June. Eggs are deposited singly on young leaves, shoots,
or flower buds of the host plant. Larvae feed primarily on the flower buds but
will feed on the leaves as well. They are attended by ants, which "milk" the
larvae for their honeydew secretions. The caterpillar is dull green, with
oblique, white dashes on the dorsum, a dark dorsal stripe and a white lateral
line. The head is brown. The larvae turn reddish before pupating. The

chrysalis is light brown, generally attached to debris near the base of the host plant, and is the overwintering stage.

Nectar Sources: Various spring plants and trees are visited for nectar, including redbud *(Cercis canadensis),* wild vetch *(Vicia caroliniana),* spring beauty *(Claytonia),* and cinquefoil *(Potentilla),* as well as composites.

Larval Host Plant: In West Virginia wild vetch *(Vicia caroliniana)* is the commonly selected host for the Silvery Blue, but it will also use veiny peavine *(Lathyrus venosus).* Other vetches may also be used.

10

Superfamily Papilionoidea
Family Riodinidae—Metalmarks

The Metalmarks are a small family of tropical butterflies with their stronghold in the New World tropics. They number about 1300 species with most living in the tropics of Central or South America. Members of this group barely reach the temperate zone, although 24 species are found in North America. Most are found in the southern United States, and only one species, the most northern inhabitant of the family, occurs in West Virginia.

Riodinidae are small to medium butterflies, and most are brightly colored in metallic hues, hence their name. The more temperate species are not as brightly marked and are usually a combination of browns, orange, black, and white, and have small metallic markings. The family is represented by only one subfamily, Riodininae.

Subfamily Riodininae—Metalmarks

Several characteristics distinguish this subfamily. The front legs of males are reduced in size to half the length of the other pairs and are not used for walking. The first joint (coxa) of the leg at the body extends below the joint with the femur like a long spur. In females the front legs are only reduced about one-third normal size and are functional. Females tend to be larger than males and have broader wings. The hindwings of the species *Calephelis borealis* (found in West Virginia) have a humeral vein and a noticeable costal vein present (fig. 13b). The antennae of metalmarks are elongated, usually more than half the length of the forewings.

The metalmarks are perching butterflies, and most perch with their wings outstretched. When disturbed or when resting, most species perch on the underside of large leaves with their wings outstretched similar to geometrid moths (Geometridae). Most are swift, erratic fliers, although species in the genus *Calephelis* are slow and weak.

The larvae of this group are similar to Lycaenidae larvae, except that metalmarks have broader heads and are covered with long, fine hairs instead of short ones. The North American species hibernate as larvae. Pupae are generally more robust than those of Lycaenidae and occur at the base of plants or in the leaf litter. The pupa is attached at the caudal, or tail end and held by a fine silk girdle.

Northern Metalmark

Calephelis borealis (Grote and Robinson), 1866

Adult: Plate 10, Row 8
Larva: Plate 35, Row 4

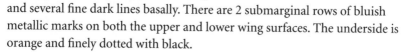

Description: Wingspan is ⅞ to 1⅛ inches (23–29 mm). The Northern Metalmark is a small dark orange-brown butterfly, with a dark band crossing the center portion of the wings and several fine dark lines basally. There are 2 submarginal rows of bluish metallic marks on both the upper and lower wing surfaces. The underside is orange and finely dotted with black.

Distribution: The Northern Metalmark occurs in isolated populations, 1 of which extends from Connecticut through New Jersey, and another occurs from Pennsylvania through the Appalachian Mountains to Virginia, West Virginia, Kentucky, and west to Illinois. Other isolated populations occur in Missouri and Oklahoma. In West Virginia the species is widespread, although it is always scarce and difficult to find. The Northern Metalmark probably occurs in more counties than records indicate.

Habitat: The Northern Metalmark is usually found along wooded areas close to streams, ponds, or lakes and is often associated with limestone or shale barren areas. It is most often encountered in openings along roads passing through woodlands, which may be mixed deciduous forests or scrub oak-pine shale barren habitats.

Life History and Habits: Male metalmarks perch on broad leaves with wings outstretched awaiting females. In inclement weather they rest with wings outstretched on the underside of large leaves, usually within a few feet of the ground. Males sometimes perch on the ground at wet spots where they imbibe moisture. Eggs are laid singly on the underside of host leaves on which the larvae feed. The Northern Metalmark is univoltine, with a single flight that occurs in June and extends through July. Larvae feed on host leaves until the sixth instar and then diapause in the thick rosette of leaves at the base of the host plant or in the leaf litter until spring, at which time they complete development. There are a total of 8 instars (Opler and Krizek 1984). The caterpillar is greenish with a dorsal row of black spots and is covered with long, soft, white hairs. The chrysalis is light brown with a yellowish abdomen and has rows of black dorsal and lateral spots. It also has many long white hairs and is attached to its substrate by a frail silk girdle (Howe 1975, Scott 1986).

Nectar Sources: The Northern Metalmark visits a variety of flowers for nectar that include several composites: yarrow *(Achillea),* ox-eye daisy *(Chrysanthemum leucanthemum),* black-eyed Susan *(Rudbeckia hirta),* goldenrod *(Solidago),* and fleabane *(Erigeron).* They also readily visit butterflyweed *(Asclepias tuberosa).*

Larval Host Plant: In West Virginia the Northern Metalmark utilizes squaw-weed *(Senecio obovatus)* as its primary host. Other ragworts may be used as well.

11

Superfamily Papilionoidea
Family Nymphalidae—Brush-footed Butterflies

The Nymphalidae, or Brush-footed Butterflies, is the largest family of true
butterflies, with nearly 4500 species worldwide and approximately 200 species
in North America. In West Virginia 39 species plus 1 additional subspecies are
represented. Of these 40 species or subspecies, 34 are regular inhabitants of
the state either as residents or migrants, and 6 are either rare or represented
only by historical records.

The family comprises butterflies with many varied characteristics, and as a
result some authors prefer to split these groups into several families, whereas
others lump the groups together. The brush-footed butterflies are all
characterized by having the front pair of legs reduced to short hairy
appendages that are used for smelling rather than walking. It is this feature
that has given rise to the common name for the family. With that particular
characteristic in mind, I shall consider all the brush-footed butterflies in 1
large family, Nymphalidae, comprising several subfamilies. Here, the family
Nymphalidae includes the following subfamilies: Heliconiinae, the longwings;
Nymphalinae, the fritillaries and brushfoots; Limenitidinae, the admirals;
Aparturinae, the hackberry butterflies; Satyrinae, the satyrs, eyed browns, and
wood nymphs; Danainae, the milkweed butterflies; and Libytheinae, the snout
butterflies. These subfamilies all exhibit reduced front legs.

Characteristics that distinguish this large family (as a whole) are many,
and they need to be considered when attempting to describe it. Features that
distinguish the individual subfamilies are discussed under those headings. In
general, the brush-footed butterflies have large hairy palpi, the most notable
being in the Libytheinae. Brush-footed butterflies have only moderately long
antennae, which are scaled and have a pronounced club. Most of the
Nymphalids are strong fliers, although the Satyrinae are fairly weak fliers.

Wing venation varies considerably between groups; however, there are a

FIG. 14.
Wing venation
of Nymphalidae:
(*a*) *Speyeria*
(Nymphalinae);
(*b*) *Hermeuptychia*
(Satyrinae).

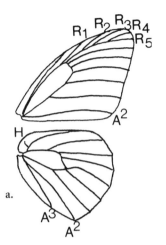
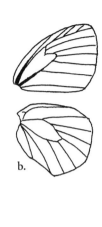

few characteristics worth mentioning. At least 3 of the radial (R) veins in the forewing branch off from a single stem that arises from the discal cell. There is only 1 anal vein (A2) in the forewing, which never divides, and there are 2 anal veins (A2, A3) in the hindwing. There is also a well-developed humoral vein (H) (fig. 14a).

Many Nymphalids are beautifully colored butterflies; the Nymphalinae and Limenitidinae are examples. Others are well camouflaged, resembling dead leaves, especially the angle wings *(Polygonia)* and tortoiseshells *(Nymphalis)*, and others rely upon deceptive color patterns or eye spots for protection. A few of the Nymphalids mimic other species in their color and wing patterns. Examples include the Viceroy *(Limenitis archippus)*, Red-spotted Purple *(L. arthemis astyanax)*, and the female Diana fritillary *(Speyeria diana)*. Butterflies in this family range from small to large.

The majority of Nymphalids spend the winter as larvae in some stage of development. However, a few immigrate from southern zones in the spring, and still others migrate in both directions. A classic example is the Monarch *(Danaus plexippus)*. Other Nymphalids hibernate as adults during winter. Eggs, larvae, and pupa also show a great deal of variation, but, in general, many Nymphalid larvae are spiny, and all suspend their pupa from a cremaster without a silk girdle.

Subfamily Libytheinae—Snouts

The snout butterflies comprise a small group of relic species, with about 10 representatives worldwide. Fossil records of snouts in shale deposits date back 30 million years (Pyle 1981). The snouts are widespread, occurring on all continents. In the Americas there are 3 species, with only 1 common to North America. The snouts are generally brown-and-orange butterflies with white spots; however, males of some Asiatic species are blue.

Characteristics that separate this group include elongated labial palpi, which, in North American species, are longer than the thorax. The snouts also have reduced front legs. In males the legs are greatly shortened with fused tarsae that lack claws, whereas in females the forelegs are reduced only about two-thirds the size of the other 4, and claws are present. The snouts all have long forewings that are squared at the tips. They are cryptic underneath, and when they perch on a twig and point their palpi toward it, they resemble an attached dead leaf. The snouts are erratic, strong fliers and often migrate, sometimes in masses. Most males perch awaiting females. Both sexes rest with their wings closed and bask with wings open.

The larvae of this group are cylindrical and lack spines and horns. The last abdominal segment is somewhat rounded but never forked as in Satyrinae or Apaturinae. The North American genus feeds on *Celtis* (family Ulmaceae). The chrysalis is green and has a dorsal crest formed by the wing cases. It is suspended from the underside of the host leaf.

American Snout

Libytheana carinenta bachmanii
(Kirtland), 1852

Adult: Plate 23, Row 4
Larva: Plate 35, Row 4
Pupa: Plate 46, Row 2

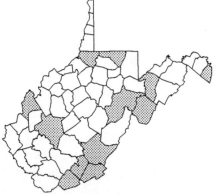

Description: Wingspan is 1⅝ to 1⅞ inches (41–48 mm). The American Snout is a small dark brown butterfly with orange patches on both wings and a few white spots near the tip of the forewing on the upperside. The forewings are sharply truncate (squared off) at the tips. The underside has 2 color forms: uniform brown hindwings or light brown hindwings finely striated with dark-and-light patches. There is often a violet sheen to the hindwings. This butterfly has elongated palpi that resemble a long snout.

Distribution: The American Snout is a southern species ranging across the southern states, into Mexico, and south to Argentina. The species colonizes northward during summer into southern New England and Pennsylvania west to the Rocky Mountains. The species cannot survive winter weather in the north and, therefore, only establishes temporary populations. In West Virginia the species occurs sporadically, usually in the warmer portions of the state. It has been recorded from 12 counties.

Habitat: The American Snout prefers woodland or brushy areas and is most often found along streams, woodland edges and clearings, brushy fields, and roadsides close to its host plant.

Life History and Habits: Male American Snouts perch on leaves of shrubs or small trees awaiting females. They are often seen flying around host trees. They readily visit puddles to sip moisture. Snout butterflies are migratory and on occasion make mass migrations. American Snouts immigrate into West Virginia during the spring or summer months. The species does not overwinter in West Virginia. Adults are generally not seen much before early June. Probably 1 to 2 generations occur between June and September, with many fresh individuals found into late September. The species is at least bivoltine over much of its range. In the southern portions of its range the species diapauses as adults during winter months. The caterpillar is yellow green with a yellow dorsal and lateral longitudinal stripe. The thorax is swollen, giving the larva a humped appearance. Numerous small pale tubercles cover the body. The head is green with 2 black lateral dots. The chrysalis is green and is usually suspended from the underside of a leaf.

Nectar Sources: American Snouts are frequently found at wet spots where they like to sip moisture and minerals. They also visit a variety of flowers, including dogbane *(Apocynum),* goldenrod *(Solidago),* aster *(Aster),* Queen Anne's lace *(Daucus carota),* blackberry *(Rubus),* milkweeds *(Asclepias),* and Joe-pye weed *(Eupatorium).*

Larval Host Plant: American Snouts are closely associated with hackberries *(Celtis* spp.), using these as their only host. In West Virginia 2 hackberries are readily used: the large or common hackberry *(Celtis occidentalis)* and dwarf hackberry *(C. tenuifolia).*

Subfamily Heliconiinae—Longwings

The Heliconiinae are medium-sized butterflies that inhabit the tropical regions of North and South America and Asia and the temperate regions of the Northern Hemisphere. Although the subfamily is richest in the tropics, 30 species occur in North America.

Many of the Heliconiinae are long-lived butterflies, up to 6 months, and several genera are distasteful. As a result, other butterflies mimic the Heliconiinae.

Males have androconial scales on the wing veins. Females have glands on the abdomen tip that produce a scent attraction for males.

Heliconiinae rest with their wings closed and bask with wings outspread, especially in mountain species where absorbing the sun's rays is important for warming.

Temperate species lay their eggs haphazardly, usually near the host, but often not directly on it as most butterflies do. The eggs of fritillaries *(Speyeria)* do not mature until late in the season; therefore, females often lay their eggs in the vicinity of dried violet *(Viola)* leaves. Many temperate species hibernate as first instar larvae, although most *Boloria* hibernate in the fourth instar. *Euptorieta* may not have a true diapause. Larvae bear many branching spines and lack a middorsal row of spines.

Temperate species use dicotyledons as hosts, especially violets, and tropical Heliconiinae feed mainly on passion vines *(Passaflora)*.

Variegated Fritillary

Euptoieta claudia (Cramer), 1775

Adult: Plate 11, Row 1
Larva: Plate 36, Row 1
Pupa: Plate 46, Row 3

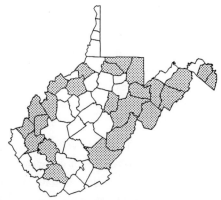

Description: Wingspan is 1¾ to 2⅝ inches (44–67 mm). The Variegated Fritillary is a medium tawny-orange butterfly with zigzag black bands, black dots, circles, and crescents on the upper wing surface. There are 2 black bands running along the outer margin of the wings. This species lacks silver spots on the underside found in other fritillaries. The undersides of the wings are cream to brown, slightly patterned, and mottled. The hindwing is lighter in color along the outer margin, with a row of submarginal spots.

Distribution: The Variegated Fritillary is a regular inhabitant of the southern states from coastal North Carolina through Florida, the Gulf states, to California. It ranges south to Argentina through the higher elevations. In the East it migrates northward into Canada and southern New England. In West Virginia records are sporadic; however, the species will likely be found in all counties. It can be quite abundant by late summer.

Habitat: This species prefers open field habitats, pastures, and mountain meadows. It is often encountered along roadsides and in open waste places.

Life History and Habits: Males patrol open fields in a low, continuous flight searching for females. Females are usually found nectaring on various field plants or actively looking for plants on which to oviposit. Egg laying usually takes place from late morning until late afternoon. Females flutter close to the ground looking for violets on which to lay their eggs. Once a suitable plant is found they stop and walk around on the plants, depositing a single egg on the underside of a leaf. Although the Variegated Fritillary breeds year round in its southern range, there are generally 1 to 2 broods in parts of West Virginia. If individuals appear by late spring, 2 broods will result before winter. Those that reach West Virginia in July probably only produce a single brood by fall. It is unlikely that the Variegated Fritillary is able to overwinter anywhere in the state. The caterpillar is red with black longitudinal stripes containing a series of white dots. The spines along the body are black, and there are 2 long black spines arising from behind the head. The chrysalis is white and marked with brown-and-black patches.

Nectar Sources: The Variegated Fritillary visits a wide variety of field plants for nectar, especially milkweeds *(Asclepias),* thistles *(Cirsium),* dogbane *(Apocynum),* ironweed *(Vernonia),* Joe-pye weed *(Eupatorium),* asters *(Aster),* and red and white clovers *(Trifolium).* They will also use mints *(Mentha)* and viper's bugloss *(Echium vulgare),* as well as several other plants, including garden flowers.

Larval Host Plant: In West Virginia the Variegated Fritillary uses mainly violets *(Viola* spp.) but often selects cultivated pansies *(Viola* spp.) around home gardens. The species is reported to feed on other plants, such as may-apple *(Podophyllum peltatum),* stonecrop *(Sedum* spp.), purslane *(Portulaca* spp.), moonseed *(Menispermum* spp.), and beggar's ticks *(Desmodium* spp.) (Howe 1975; Opler and Krizek 1984).

Diana

Speyeria diana (Cramer), 1775

Adult: Plate 11, Rows 2, 3
Larva: Plate 36, Row 1
Pupa: Plate 46, Row 3

Description: Wingspan is 3 to 4⅛ inches (76–105 mm). The Diana is a large butterfly with rounded wings and is considered to be one of the most beautiful of the fritillaries. It is sought avidly by collectors. The male is deep brown above, almost black, on the basal two-thirds of the wings. The outer third is bright orange, with a few dark brown spots. The underside of the male's wing is tan orange with the basal two-thirds of the forewing marked with black. A row of silver dashes occurs on the hindwing along the outer margin. The female is black above, with the outer third of the hindwing pale blue. The forewing contains several bluish white spots. A row of white spots occurs along the outer margin of the forewing. The underside of the forewing is gray black with bluish white and black spots. The hindwing is brownish black, with white postmedian and marginal lines. The female Diana mimics the Pipevine Swallowtail *(Battus philenor)*. On rare occasions the Diana may occur in a genetic mutation called a bilateral gynandromorph. The mutant butterfly is split longitudinally into female on one side and male on the other. In a dimorphic species like the Diana, the butterfly will be brown and orange on one half and black and blue on the other. One such specimen was field captured in Wyoming County, W. Va., in 1978.

Distribution: The Diana is a southern Appalachian species that ranges from Virginia and West Virginia south to northern Georgia and Alabama. Another small population persists in the Ozark Mountains of Arkansas and Missouri. The Diana is found in West Virginia in the southern third of the state, south from lower Pocahontas County, and west to Kanawha and Lincoln Counties. The species may also occur occasionally in other surrounding counties, as well as the southern counties, with no records to date. Dianas can usually be found in Potts Creek Wildlife Management Area in the Jefferson National Forest in Monroe County, around Babcock State Park in Fayette County, and around Fork Creek Wildlife Management Area in Boone County.

Habitat: The Diana fritillary is a forest species inhabiting mountainous areas in West Virginia. It prefers moist and well-shaded forest covers with rich soils.

The butterfly utilizes small openings and roadsides in search of nectar plants but will not stray far from the woods. Dianas are usually found nectaring along woodland edges.

Life History and Habits: Male Dianas patrol their woodland habitat in a gliding flight several meters above the ground. Mating occurs shortly after emergence of the female. Males emerge a few to several days before females, which ensures a good supply of males for mating. Egg laying occurs in a random fashion on objects along the forest floor as the butterfly walks with wings partially outspread. Generally, when violets are present, oviposition occurs on or near the plants. The female glides around before landing again to repeat the process. Similar behavior by females was reported by Harris (1972). Egg laying observed in captive Dianas takes place from midday to late afternoon. Egg laying may begin in late July and continue into September if weather is favorable, since females are long lived. A female Diana is capable of laying well over 1000 eggs during that period. Dianas, as with all *Speyeria,* are univoltine. The males begin flying as early as late June, reaching their peak in mid-July in West Virginia. Females begin to emerge the first week of July and fly into September. Most males have disappeared by August. Eggs are cream when laid but begin to turn pink and then steel gray within a few days if fertile. Once the eggs hatch, about 4 weeks later, the tiny larvae crawl to a secure place and remain dormant for the winter. In spring with warming weather, larvae seek out young violet leaves *(Viola)* and begin feeding. Caterpillars are velvet black, with 6 rows of black tipped, setose spines that are deep orange or red at the base. The 2 dorsal spines immediately behind the head are entirely black and lean forward over the head. The head is black anteriorly, doubly pointed, and is orange brown on the back side. The brown chrysalis is hung upside down in a loosely woven tent of silk. The chrysalis has a slightly raised pronotum dorsally, followed by a depressed area toward the abdomen. There are 2 dorsolateral rows of short spikes on the abdomen that are more pronounced toward the anterior end. Adults emerge 2 to 3 weeks following pupation.

Nectar Sources: Milkweeds *(Asclepias)* and thistles *(Cirsium)* are the preferred nectar plants of Dianas. Common milkweed *(Asclepias syriaca),* because it grows near woodland areas where Dianas fly, is probably the most commonly used milkweed. Dianas will also use butterfly weed *(A. tuberosa)* and swamp milkweed *(A. incarnata).* Later in the season wild bergamot *(Monardia fistulosa),* Joe-pye weed *(Eupatorium),* and ironweed *(Vernonia)* are the common plants selected. Dianas tend to nectar during midmorning and late afternoon, spending the heat of the day in the woods. Females can be frequently found nectaring until nearly dusk.

Larval Host Plants: As with the other *Speyeria,* woodland violets *(Viola* spp.) serve as host plants for Dianas in West Virginia.

Great Spangled Fritillary

Speyeria cybele cybele (Fabricius), 1775

Adult: Plate 11, Row 4; Plate 12, Row 1
Larva: Plate 36, Row 2
Pupa: Plate 46, Row 3

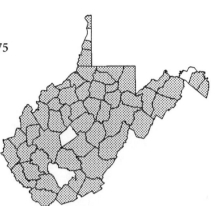

Description: Wingspan is 2⅛ to 3 inches (54–76 mm). The Great Spangled Fritillary is a large bright orange butterfly. On the upper surface of the male the orange is marked with black spots, dashes, and crescents. The female is brownish black on the basal two-thirds of the upper forewing surface. The underside of the hindwing varies from cinnamon brown (male) to dark orange brown (female) toward the base and is strongly marked with silver dots. The best criteria for separating the Great Spangled Fritillary from its close relative, the Aphrodite Fritillary *(S. aphrodite),* is found on the underside of the hindwing. On the Great Spangled Fritillary a broad, submarginal band of yellow brown occurs; on the Aphrodite Fritillary only a narrow band or small yellow-brown patches occur.

Distribution: The Great Spangled Fritillary is found throughout much of the United States from Canada south to the northern portion of the Gulf states. In West Virginia the species can be found statewide, with only 4 counties lacking records to date.

Habitat: This species is generally found in open areas, such as fields, abandoned farms, roadsides, wet meadows, and yards, often in close proximity to wooded areas. The species wanders considerable distances from its breeding habitat.

Life History and Habits: As with other fritillaries, males patrol in search of females and can be found flying back and forth across open fields a few feet above the ground. The Great Spangled Fritillary is univoltine over its range, with a single flight that begins as early as late May. Males emerge first, 2 to 3 weeks before females, and continue to fly through July into early August. Females begin flying in June and continue as late as October. Oviposition by females usually begins in August and continues until the individual dies. Eggs are deposited singly on or near violet plants. Once the larvae hatch, about 4 weeks later, they crawl to a protected site in the leaf litter and diapause until spring. The larvae feed on the young violet leaves in spring. The caterpillar is velvety black, with several rows of black spines, red or brownish orange at their base. The head is bifurcated (doubly pointed), with black on the face and brown to orange over the top and sides. The chrysalis is brown and suspended upside down from its substrate in a loose tent of silk.

Nectar Sources: The Great Spangled Fritillary visits a wide variety of summer plants for nectar, preferring taller plants. Some of its favorite plants include milkweeds *(Asclepias),* thistles *(Cirsium),* Joe-pye weed *(Eupatorium),* ironweed *(Vernonia),* dogbane *(Apocynum),* narrowleaf mountain-mint *(Pycnanthemum flexuosum),* and various composites. They also readily visit clovers *(Trifolium)* and viper's bugloss *(Echium vulgare).*

Larval Host Plant: Various species of violets *(Viola* spp.) are the host for the larvae. Twenty-seven species of violets are known to occur in West Virginia, the most common of which includes common blue violet *(Viola papilionacea),* marsh blue violet *(V. cucullata),* and downy wood violet *(V. soraria).* All are probably used by the Great Spangled Fritillary. *Viola striata* (striped violet), also common throughout the state, has been used as a host plant for larvae reared in captivity. It, too, is a likely host for the species.

Aphrodite Fritillary

Speyeria aphrodite aphrodite
(Fabricius), 1787

Adult: Plate 12, Rows 2, 3
Larva: Plate 36, Row 1
Pupa: Plate 46, Row 4

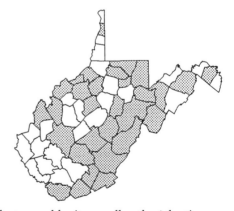

Description: Wingspan is 2 to 2⅞ inches (51–73 mm). The Aphrodite Fritillary is a medium to large butterfly, slightly smaller than the Great Spangled Fritillary *(S. cybele)* but resembles it, as well as the Atlantis Fritillary *(S. atlantis),* in its markings on the upper wing surface. Often a black dot in the cell near the base of the forewing occurs, which is absent in the Great Spangled Fritillary. The outer margin of the forewing contains orange more so in males than in females and is not solid black as in the Atlantis Fritillary. The underside of the hindwings ranges from a light cinnamon brown (male) to a deep red brown (female), with silver spots throughout. The submarginal band of pale yellow brown is reduced in this species to a thin or intermittent band. In females the band tends to be intermittent.

Distribution: The Aphrodite Fritillary ranges from New England west across southern Canada to the Rocky Mountains and then south through the Appalachian Mountains to northern Georgia. This species probably occurs statewide in West Virginia. In many counties it is more abundant than the Great Spangled Fritillary; however, it has not been reported from as many localities, especially in the west and southwestern counties.

Habitat: The Aphrodite Fritillary prefers fields, pastures, open woods, and dry shale barren habitats. It favors mountainous areas of acid soils, which makes West Virginia prime habitat for the species. It is also found in wet meadows and bogs.

Life History and Habits: Males patrol for females in a similar manner as the Great Spangled Fritillary. During morning and late afternoon, males and females can be readily found nectaring on field plants or plants along roadsides and woodland edges. The Aphrodite Fritillary is single-brooded, with its flight beginning in early June and extending into October. Males fly earlier than females by as much as 2 to 3 weeks. Females are common in July and extend their flight well into September after males have disappeared. Egg laying by females occurs late in the season, probably late July through September. The caterpillar is velvety black with 1 to 2 rows of chestnut to orange lateral spines with black tips. The 2 rows of dorsal spines are black. A small band of chestnut occurs on the back of the head. The chrysalis is brown marked with black. Newly hatched larvae hibernate in the leaf litter or at the base of violet plants until spring.

Nectar Sources: The Aphrodite Fritillary visits a number of summer plants for nectar. Some of the favorite plants include milkweeds *(Asclepias),* burdock *(Arctium),* Joe-pye weed *(Eupatorium),* ironweed *(Vernonia),* dogbane *(Apocynum),* thistles *(Cirsium),* viper's bugloss *(Echium vulgare),* ox-eye daisies *(Chrysanthemum),* and narrowleaf mountain-mint *(Pycnanthemum flexuosum).*

Larval Host Plant: Various violets are selected as hosts. The more common blue violet *(Viola papilionacea),* marsh blue violet *(V. cucullata),* downy wood violet *(V. soraria),* and striped violet *(V. striata)* are probably the most widely used species in West Virginia.

Atlantis Fritillary

Speyeria atlantis atlantis (Edwards),
1862

Adult: Plate 12, Row 4; Plate 13, Row 1
Larva: Plate 36, Row 2

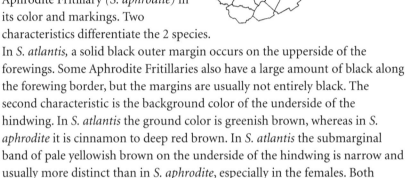

Description: Wingspan is 1¾ to 2⅝
inches (44–67 mm). The Atlantis
Fritillary closely resembles the
Aphrodite Fritillary *(S. aphrodite)* in
its color and markings. Two
characteristics differentiate the 2 species.
In *S. atlantis,* a solid black outer margin occurs on the upperside of the
forewings. Some Aphrodite Fritillaries also have a large amount of black along
the forewing border, but the margins are usually not entirely black. The
second characteristic is the background color of the underside of the
hindwing. In *S. atlantis* the ground color is greenish brown, whereas in *S.
aphrodite* it is cinnamon to deep red brown. In *S. atlantis* the submarginal
band of pale yellowish brown on the underside of the hindwing is narrow and
usually more distinct than in *S. aphrodite*, especially in the females. Both
characteristics should be examined.

Distribution: The Atlantis Fritillary occurs across the northern United States
from the Maritime Provinces of Canada west across the Great Lakes region. It
occurs southward in the Appalachians to West Virginia. A population also
occurs in the western mountains to British Columbia. In West Virginia the
species is disjunct from northern populations and occurs only in the higher
mountains of the north-central counties. Records from Grant, Mineral,
Marion, and possibly Monongalia counties are those of strays and not
breeding populations. The remaining 6 counties hold the breeding
populations for the state.

Habitat: The species favors high mountain pastures, fields, bogs, meadows,
roadsides, and woodland edges. In the peak of their flight, Atlantis Fritillaries
may be found by the hundreds nectaring along road banks adjacent to
wooded areas. This is especially true for Canaan Valley and Dolly Sods in
Tucker County and the Spruce Knob area in Randolph, Pendleton, and
Pocahontas Counties.

Life History and Habits: Males patrol along roadways in search of females but
are frequently found nectaring on roadside plants. Oviposition by females

occurs late in the season and continues until death. The single brood appears in June and extends through August into September. By September individuals are difficult to find. The flight peaks in July when both sexes are common. Mating takes place shortly after the butterfly emerges from the chrysalis. Egg laying probably begins in late July and extends through August. In captivity females refuse to oviposit until mid-August. The caterpillar is chocolate brown, finely striated, and marked with black blotches. There is a double, pale yellow dorsal stripe lined with black. The spines are orange brown and tipped with black, and the head is black with brown toward the rear.

Nectar Sources: The Atlantis Fritillary visits a variety of plants for nectar, including milkweed *(Asclepias)*, dogbane *(Apocynum)*, spiraea *(Spiraea)*, burdock *(Arctium)*, ox-eye daisy *(Chrysanthemum leucanthemum)*, yarrow *(Achillea millefolium)*, daisy fleabane *(Erigeron)*, red clover *(Trifolium pratense)*, mints *(Mentha)*, heal-all *(Prunella vulgaris)*, and basal balm *(Monarda clinopodia)*.

Larval Host Plant: Violets are selected as host plants by the Atlantis Fritillary. Species common to the Atlantis Fritillary's habitat in West Virginia include common wood violet *(Viola papilionacea)*, downy wood violet *(V. soraria)*, sweet white violet *(V. blanda)*, smooth yellow violet *(V. pennsylvanica)*, Canada violet *(V. canadensis)*, striped violet *(V. striata)*, and marsh blue violet *(V. cucullata)*.

Regal Fritillary

Speyeria idalia (Drury), 1773
Adult: Plate 13, Rows 2, 3
Larva: Plate 36, Row 3

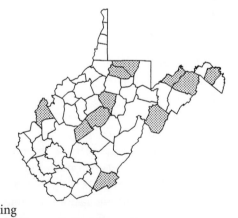

Description: Wingspan is 2⅝ to 3⅝ inches (66–92 mm). The Regal Fritillary is a large spectacular butterfly, as beautiful and different as the Diana *(Speyeria diana)*. It is the only fritillary in West Virginia with a largely reddish orange forewing and mostly black hindwing. The orange forewing contains numerous black spots and a black margin dotted with white on the upper surface. The hindwing of the male is not as black as that of the female; it is more orange basally and has 2 rows of spots. The inner row is white, and the marginal row is orange. The hindwing of the female has 2 rows of creamy white spots on black and can be distinguished from the male on that basis alone. Below, the forewing is similar to the upperside; however, the hindwing is deep olive brown, with many oblong or triangular, silvery white spots. The female is larger and darker than the male.

Distribution: The Regal Fritillary has been rapidly disappearing from its eastern range. Populations on offshore islands along the southern New England coast have also rapidly disappeared. However, small populations still exist southward into Virginia and North Carolina and westward across the United States in prairie grasslands to Colorado and Montana. Western populations are more stable than those east of the Mississippi River. Although it has been reported from several counties in West Virginia, most of these records have resulted from temporary populations now extinct. The most recently known population occurred in northern Monongalia County, and it, too, has been threatened by habitat loss. A small population may still exist in Monroe County near Gap Mills. Other isolated populations are possible in local areas where suitable habitat is found, but recent surveys indicate that this species has probably disappeared from West Virginia.

Habitat: The Regal Fritillary is primarily a butterfly of the tall prairie grasslands, but it is found in other large grassland areas elsewhere. Grasslands adjacent to boggy or marshy areas or containing damp meadows are preferred in West Virginia. The grasslands that appear to support *S. idalia* populations are those at higher elevations, including the tops of hills where wind currents are strongest.

Life History and Habits: The Regal Fritillary is a patrolling species that flies in a fast, steady flight over large fields close to the grass. This butterfly, when not feeding, will land in the grass for long periods. Females usually mate shortly after emerging from the chrysalis. Females spend much of the late afternoon nectaring at various plants. They are more active and wander extensively in late summer in search of ovipositing areas. Similar to other fritillaries, females land in the grass dropping to the ground and walk around depositing eggs. Eggs are generally laid on or near violet leaves, many of which may be dried. Egg laying generally occurs in the afternoon. Like other *Speyeria,* this species is univoltine. Males emerge from late June into mid-July. Females begin to emerge about a week after the males and continue to fly into September, long after the males have disappeared. Females begin to oviposit in late July and continue the process until death. One female in captivity laid in excess of 1440 eggs in a period of 3 weeks. Once the larvae hatch they seek shelter in the leaf litter until spring when they become active and begin to feed. Caterpillars are gray black with a wide, dull yellow to reddish orange dorsal stripe. There are several fine yellow transverse stripes at each segment junction. The larva has 6 rows of fleshy setose spines. The 4 dorsolateral rows of spines are silver white and tipped with black, and the lateral rows have yellow or orange bases. The head is orange brown with black around the mouth parts. The chrysalis is brown with a yellowish abdomen and pinkish wing case. The entire chrysalis is covered with black blotches.

Nectar Sources: The various milkweeds, including common milkweed *(Asclepias syriaca)*, swamp milkweed *(A. incarnata)*, and butterfly weed *(A. tuberosa)*, are among the preferred nectar plants in July. In August and September ironweed *(Veronica)*, Joe-pye weed *(Eupatorium)*, thistle *(Cirsium)*, aster *(Aster)*, and on occasion boneset *(Eupatorium perfoliatum)* are visited. Red clover *(Trifolium)* is also reportedly used when available.

Larval Host Plant: As with other *Speyeria*, violets *(Viola* spp.) are the only accepted host for the Regal Fritillary.

Silver-bordered Fritillary

Boloria selene myrina (Cramer), 1777

Adult: Plate 14, Row 1
Larva: Plate 36, Row 3
Pupa: Plate 46, Row 4

Description: Wingspan is 1⅜ to 2 inches (35–51 mm). This is a small tawny-orange butterfly with black spots, dashes, and black margins containing small orange spots on the upper wing surfaces. It is the only small fritillary in West Virginia with silver spots on the underside of the hindwing against a background color of light to dark rust brown. A yellow patch occurs toward the outer margin of the hindwing.

Distribution: This is a northern species ranging from Alaska across Canada and northern United States to Labrador. It ranges southward from New

England and the Great Lakes states through the Appalachian Mountains into West Virginia and Virginia. In West Virginia the species is confined mostly to the mountains along the eastern border of the state in local populations. Some of these occur in the Spruce Knob Lake area of Randolph County and nearby Blister Swamp and at Pig's Ear in Pocahontas County.

Habitat: This fritillary is found in close association with wet meadows and marshes, often with willows and alders and various shrubs such as spiraea. The Silver-bordered Fritillary prefers those sites with taller vegetation.

Life History and Habits: Males of this species patrol their wetland habitat in a fairly rapid flight a few feet above the ground in search of females, resting periodically or stopping to nectar. Adults feed during much of the daylight hours. Oviposition by females takes place between nectar periods. This species is multibrooded in West Virginia, with the first flight occurring in May and June. A second flight begins in early July and extends into August. A partial third brood occurs in many years that flies from September into October. The caterpillar is brownish with black spots, and black patches occur around the spines. The numerous spines, in rows, are yellowish. Two long black spines project forward over the head. The chrysalis is brown, mottled with black. The species overwinters as a partially grown larva.

Nectar Sources: Various plants and shrubs associated with wetlands or nearby uplands are visited for nectar. They include dogbane *(Apocynum)*, milkweed *(Asclepias)*, ironweed *(Vernonia)*, yarrow *(Achillea millefolium)*, ox-eye daisies *(Chrysanthemum leucanthemum)*, red clover *(Trifolium pratense)*, mints *(Mentha)*, and goldenrods *(Solidago)*, as well as other composites.

Larval Host Plant: Violets are the hosts for this species, especially violets associated with wetland areas. Some of these may include marsh blue violet *(Viola cucullata)*, northern white violet *(V. pallens)*, striped violet *(V. striata)*, primrose-leaf violet *(V. primulifolia)*, and common blue violet *(V. papilionacea)* in adjacent uplands.

Meadow Fritillary

Boloria bellona bellona (Fabricius), 1775

Adult: Plate 14, Rows 2, 3
Larva: Plate 36, Row 4
Pupa: Plate 46, Row 4

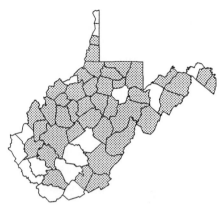

Description: Wingspan is 1¼ to 1⅞ inches (32–48 mm). The Meadow Fritillary is a small to medium orange butterfly with black spots, dashes, and crescents on the upper wing surface. The forewing tips are squared off (truncate). The basal portion of the forewings is darker than the outer portion. The underside of the wings is patterned with shades of brown. A yellowish patch occurs near the outer margin of the hindwing, and a grayish white area occurs near the base of the hindwing along the costal edge. Fresh specimens have a lavender cast to the outer third of the hindwings. The underside of the forewings is orange with black dashes and crescents. No silver spots occur on this species.

Distribution: The Meadow Fritillary ranges from Canada west to British Columbia and south to central Oregon and Colorado. In the East it ranges through the Appalachian Mountains to North Carolina and Tennessee. In West Virginia the species occurs statewide, with records from almost all counties except those along the southern border.

Habitat: This is a field species found in almost any weedy field, meadow, or pasture in the state. It prefers moist areas, although it can be readily found in the uplands as well.

Life History and Habits: Males patrol fields, flying just above the grass in search of females. Both sexes are frequently observed flying from one nectar plant to the next. Mating takes place soon after emergence of the female, and she carries the male. Mated pairs are often observed perched on tall vegetation. The species is multibrooded in West Virginia, with the spring flight from mid-April through May and into June. The second flight appears in late June and extends through August. There is a partial third brood in much of the state that flies in September into October and possibly November. The caterpillar is mottled black to brown with a velvety cast. The longitudinal row of short spines is yellow brown to brown, with black and cream around the base. The late instar larva overwinters.

Nectar Sources: Several field flowers are visited for nectar, especially composites. Some of the preferred plants include yarrow *(Achillea millefolium)*, Queen Anne's lace *(Daucus carota)*, ox-eye daisy *(Chrysanthemum leucanthemum)*, dandelions *(Taraxacum officinale)*, dogbane *(Apocynum)*, clovers *(Trifolium)*, wing-stem *(Verbesina alternifolia)*, thistles *(Cirsium)*, ironweed *(Vernonia)*, goldenrods *(Solidago)*, and asters *(Asters)*.

Larval Host Plant: Various species of violets are used as hosts by the Meadow Fritillary. The downy wood violet *(Viola soraria)* has been reported as one of the hosts for this species (Opler and Krizek 1984). It has been reared on common blue violet *(V. papilionacea)* in captivity.

Subfamily Nymphalinae—Brushfoots

The Nymphalinae is a diverse group consisting of many tribes, with approximately 110 species across North America. In West Virginia the group is represented by 22 species of regular inhabitants plus 4 species that are either rare or of historical occurrence.

Characteristics of this group are varied. Many species are brightly colored, although as a rule most are a combination of brown, orange, or black. They range from small to large. Adults are strong fliers, and males generally patrol or perch, or both, in search of receptive females. In mated pairs the female generally carries the male.

Adult Nymphalinae have varied feeding habits. The crescents and checkerspots, for instance, are mainly flower feeders, depending upon nectar for nourishment; the anglewings and tortoiseshells feed predominately on tree sap, fermenting fruit, dung, or carrion.

Mimicry and camouflage are common within this group. A few species resemble other distasteful species that contain toxins obtained from their host plants. Others are quite cryptic, resembling dead leaves or tree bark. And still others use eyespots in their wings for protection.

Larvae of the Nymphalinae feed on dicotyledons, and all have branched spines or spiny tubercles, referred to as "scoli." Eggs are deposited singly, in small stacks or in clusters, either on the host plant or nearby. Larvae may feed singly or communally, and some species feed from a web or leaf shelter. Most feed at night. The chrysalis is always suspended from a silk pad by a cremaster.

Winter is passed as hibernating larvae or nonreproductive adults. A few species migrate or immigrate from other zones. Nymphalinae that aestivate, hibernate, or migrate are long-lived butterflies with life spans of up to 10 months.

Gorgone Checkerspot

Chlosyne gorgone (Hiibner), 1810

Adult: Plate 14, Row 3

Description: Wingspan is 1⅛ to 1⅜ inches (28–35 mm). The Gorgone Checkerspot is tawny orange with black bands and blotches on the upper wing surface and resembles the Silvery Checkerspot *(Chlosyne nycteis).* A submarginal row of solid, black spots occurs on the hindwing. The underside of the hindwings is distinctive, however, being brown and having a strong zigzag pattern of alternating white and dark stripes crossing the wing. This pattern consists of sharply pointed chevrons or arrowheads in each cell. There is a row of pale marginal crescents on the outer hindwing and a submarginal row of black dots.

Distribution: The Gorgone Checkerspot is a midwestern species, ranging from Michigan and Minnesota west to Manitoba and southward to New Mexico, Texas, and Louisiana. In the East a few isolated populations are scattered throughout the Appalachian Mountains from New York to South Carolina and Kentucky, with a larger, pale form ("ismeria") occurring in Georgia and spilling over into adjacent states. In West Virginia Edwards recorded a specimen from Kanawha County on May 4, 1878. Although the specimen was probably that of a stray, there is a chance that it may show up elsewhere. Gorgone is a species whose populations fluctuate greatly, and in years of abundance it pioneers new areas establishing colonies.

Habitat: The Gorgone Checkerspot prefers open areas, such as fields, especially near streams. In the Appalachians it may be found in dry, grassy, burn-scared areas with blueberry and ground pine, as in New York, or open wooded areas, as in Georgia.

Life History and Habits: Males patrol slopes and fields in search of females. Scott (1975) reports perching behavior of males on ridge tops. The Gorgone Checkerspot is univoltine in the north but has 2 to 3 broods southward, although in South Carolina it is single-brooded. In West Virginia the species would probably be single- or double-brooded, with a flight occurring in May and June and a possible second flight in July, extending into August. Eggs are laid in clusters on host plant leaves, and young larvae are gregarious, feeding together. The caterpillar is yellow to orange, with black dorsal and lateral stripes and a black head. There are several rows of black, branched spines along the body. The chrysalis is gray to cream and is mottled.

Nectar Sources: Yellow composites are preferred nectar plants of the Gorgone Checkerspot and include goldenrods *(Solidago)* and tickseeds *(Coreopsis)*. They also visit white sweet clover *(Melilotus alba)*, milkweed *(Asclepias)*, and fleabane *(Erigeron)* for nectar.

Larval Host Plant: Composites in the genera *Helianthus* (sunflowers) and ragweeds *(Ambrosia)*, as well as loosestrife *(Lysimachia)*, are the most likely hosts for the species in West Virginia.

Silvery Checkerspot

Chlosyne nycteis nycteis (Doubleday and Hewitson), 1847

Adult: Plate 14, Row 4
Larva: Plate 36, Row 4
Pupa: Plate 47, Row 1

Description: Wingspan is 1⅜ to 1⅞ inches (35–48 mm). This species closely resembles Harris' Checkerspot *(Chlosyne harrisii)* on its upper surface. The butterfly is tawny orange with a large amount of black blotching toward the base of the wings. The wing borders are black. A submarginal row of black spots occurs on the upper and lower surface of the hindwing, some of which have orange centers. The remaining orange in the wings appears as a large irregular band and smaller, broken bands. The underside of the hindwing is yellow with brown veins, lines, and ovals. The outer portion of the hindwing is brown with a white crescent along the margin and a row of black spots, at least 1 of which has a white center.

Distribution: The Silvery Checkerspot ranges across Canada from the Maritime Provinces to Saskatchewan and south (inland from the coast) to the Gulf states and eastern Texas. In West Virginia, populations are spotty, but the species probably occurs in all counties. It is especially common in Fork Creek Wildlife Management Area, Boone County, as well as in other similar areas.

Habitat: The Silvery Checkerspot prefers moist habitat near streams or rivers where its host plant abounds. Populations seem to do as well in either semi-open habitats or shaded woods along streams. A moist woodland opening with an abundance of wing-stem *(Verbesina alternifolia)* or a moist stream bank through an open field of tall vegetation and shrubs will often have a colony of Silvery Checkerspots.

Life History and Habits: Males patrol along stream banks or dirt roads in a slow, gliding flight and often perch on vegetation. They also gather with other species at wet spots or dung to imbibe moisture and minerals. There are at least 2 and a partial third brood in West Virginia, with the first flight appearing in May and extending into June. At higher elevations the first flight may start somewhat later. The second flight usually occurs in late June and extends through July. A third flight occurs in late August and September. The female deposits a cluster of white eggs on the underside of a host leaf. The larvae are gregarious and feed together, breaking up in the late instars. Larvae from the last brood diapause in the third instar until the following spring. The caterpillar is variable but is usually black with a varying degree of yellow to orange along its sides in a band. There are several rows of shiny black, branched spines on the dorsal surface. The row of spines arising from the yellow lateral area is light brown. The chrysalis is white, or nearly so, with little to a large amount of black spotting. Some black and brown occurs on the short spines arising from the dorsal portion of the abdomen.

Nectar Sources: Several flowers are visited by the species for nectar, as well as dung for nutrients. Flowers include dogbane *(Apocynum)*, milkweeds *(Asclepias)*, fleabane *(Erigeron)*, winter cress *(Barbarea vulgaris)*, and clovers *(Trifolium)*. Other plants reported include dandelions *(Taraxacum officinale)*, Canada thistle *(Cirsium arvense)*, and wild parsnip *(Pastinaca sativa)* (Iftner et al. 1992).

Larval Host Plant: This species uses a wide variety of composites as hosts, although in West Virginia it prefers wing-stem *(Verbesina alternifolia)*. Sunflowers of the genus *Helianthus,* such as thinleaved sunflower *(H. decapetalus)*, Jerusalem artichoke *(H. tuberosus)*, pale-leaved sunflower *(H. strumosus)*, and possibly others are also used. Purple-stemmed aster *(Aster puniceus)* is also reported as a host plant in this region (Opler and Krizek 1984).

Harris' Checkerspot

Chlosyne harrisii liggetti (Avinoff), 1930

Adult: Plate 14, Row 5
Larva: Plate 37, Row 1

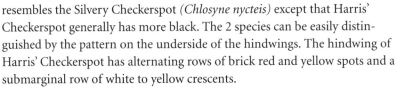

Description: Wingspan is 1¼ to 1¾ inches (32–44 mm). The Harris' Checkerspot is a black butterfly with bands of tawny-orange spots across the upperside of its wings. On the upper surface the species closely resembles the Silvery Checkerspot *(Chlosyne nycteis)* except that Harris' Checkerspot generally has more black. The 2 species can be easily distinguished by the pattern on the underside of the hindwings. The hindwing of Harris' Checkerspot has alternating rows of brick red and yellow spots and a submarginal row of white to yellow crescents.

Distribution: The Harris' Checkerspot is a northern species occurring across southern Canada from Manitoba to the Maritime Provinces and southward through New England to northern Pennsylvania and the Great Lakes states. Isolated populations occur in the higher mountains of West Virginia and are mainly distributed through the higher elevations of 4 counties: Pendleton, Pocahontas, Randolph, and Tucker. The butterfly is found commonly at Blackwater Falls and Canaan Valley State Parks in Tucker County and around Spruce Knob Lake in Randolph County.

Habitat: This species is restricted to wetland areas, marshes, and bogs that support good stands of its host plant. The butterfly strays into open or brushy upland fields for nectar and is often found along road banks.

Life History and Habits: Males patrol fields and wetlands a few feet above the ground in search of females, perching periodically on low vegetation with outstretched wings. They also gather at wet spots to sip moisture and minerals from the soil. The species is univoltine, with a single flight each year that begins in June and extends into July. The eggs are laid in a cluster on the underside of the host leaf. They are yellow when laid but turn red after a short period. The larvae, once hatched, feed together at or near the top of the plant in a silken web. Feeding ceases with the third instar, and the larvae diapause at the base of the plant. The following spring the larvae emerge and feed singly on young host leaves. The caterpillar is orange with transverse black stripes on each segment. There are several rows of branched, black spines. Laterally, the body is heavily mottled with black. The anterior and posterior ends of the body do not contain as much black as the Baltimore *(Euphydryas phaeton)* larva, which it resembles. The chrysalis is white with black, orange, and brown spots. The short spines along the dorsal surface are black tipped.

Nectar Sources: The Harris' Checkerspot visits a variety of field plants for nectar. These include daisy fleabane *(Erigeron),* hawkweeds *(Hieracium),* ox-eye daisy *(Chrysanthemum leucanthemum),* and dandelion *(Taraxacum officinale).*

Larval Host Plant: The flat-topped white aster *(Aster umbellatus)* is the only known host of Harris' Checkerspot. The aster is common in wetlands and bogs of the mountainous counties in West Virginia.

Pearl Crescent

Phyciodes tharos (Drury), 1773
Adult: Plate 15, Rows 1, 2
Larva: Plate 37, Row 1
Pupa: Plate 47, Row 1

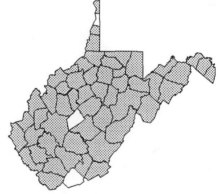

Description: Wingspan is 1 to 1½ inches (25–38 mm). The spring form ("Marcia," Edwards 1868) differs from the summer form ("Morpheus," Fabricius 1775). Spring males are tawny orange with broad, black borders and have a series of dark ovals, blotches, and spots on the upper surface of the wings. The upperside of the female's wings is similar to that of the male but contains more yellow. The underside of the spring male hindwing is brownish with white and dark blotches. The veins are brown. There is a white crescent in the outer hindwing margin. The female is similar but with more brown in the hindwing. The summer-form male is similar to the spring form on the upper surface but with fewer crescents visible. The female is similar to the spring form but with darker wing margins. On the underside the male is golden yellow with many fine striations in the hindwing. A brown patch containing a gray to whitish crescent occurs near the outer hindwing margin. The female hindwing has more obvious brown striations than the male. There is a brown patch at the outer hindwing margin containing a yellow marginal crescent followed by a white submarginal crescent. The antenna clubs are usually black or nearly so.

Distribution: This species ranges from New England across southern Canada west to Minnesota and southward into Mexico. The species occurs in the East to southern Florida. The Pearl Crescent occurs statewide in West Virginia and is one of the most common field butterflies.

Habitat: The Pearl Crescent occurs in almost any open area, such as fields, pastures, abandoned farms, woodland openings, roadsides, and yards, wherever asters *(Aster)* grow.

Life History and Habits: Males patrol open areas in an erratic, rapid flight in search of females. They also gather with other species at wet spots near streams or on gravel roads to sip moisture and will readily visit dung for nutrients. Mating usually takes place from noon to midafternoon (Opler and Krizek 1984). This species is multibrooded, and in West Virginia there are at least 3 flights. Although the species appears to fly all season long there are distinct flights that may overlap as a few worn and fresh individuals. The first brood appears in late April and continues through May into early June. A second brood appears in late June and extends through July and into early August. The third brood appears in mid-August, flying through September and into early October. Eggs are laid in small clusters on aster leaves, and larvae are gregarious. Larvae from the last generation overwinter in the third instar by diapausing in dried leaves. The caterpillar is light brown and speckled with small white spots and has several rows of branched, brown spines tipped with creamy white. There is a creamy white lateral stripe and broken, white dorsal stripes ending on the dark, almost black, head, which contains a scrolled, white line.

Nectar Sources: The Pearl Crescent visits almost any flower to obtain nectar. They generally prefer flowers that have a flattened inflorescence, such as dandelion *(Taraxacum officinale),* hawkweed *(Hieracium),* daisy *(Chrysanthemum),* black-eyed Susan *(Rudbeckia hirta),* milkweed *(Asclepias),* dogbane *(Apocynum),* aster *(Aster),* yarrow *(Achillea millefolium),* goldenrod *(Solidago),* and a host of other species.

Larval Host Plant: The Pearl Crescent selects a variety of asters (Compositae) as hosts. These include panicled aster *(Aster simplex),* white heath aster *(A. pilosus),* and smooth aster *(A. laevis).* Other asters are undoubtedly used as well. The species was reared in captivity on New England aster *(A. novae-angliae).*

Northern Crescent

Phyciodes selenis selenis (Kirby), 1837

Adult: Plate 15, Row 3

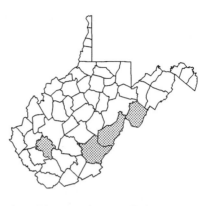

Description: Wingspan is 1¼ to 1¾ inches (35–45 mm). The Northern Crescent is similar to the Pearl Crescent *(Phyciodes tharos)* in appearance, but it is larger. Several differences distinguish the species, and males are the easiest to distinguish. The antenna clubs of the Northern Crescent are usually orange on the tips and ventral surface, whereas in the Pearl Crescent they are normally black. There are thin, orange, linear markings on the underside of the hindwings in the Northern Crescent. These markings are black in the Pearl Crescent. The marginal patch on the hindwing that contains the crescent spot is paler in the Northern Crescent. The patches of yellow scaling on the upperside of the forewings are heavier in the Northern Crescent than in *P. tharos*. Other distinguishing characteristics between the 2 species are habitat and flight. The Northern Crescent has a slow, gliding flight, whereas the Pearl Crescent has a rapid flight.

Distribution: The Northern Crescent ranges from Newfoundland west across Canada to British Columbia, and south through the northern states to New England. It ranges southward in spotty populations through the Appalachian Mountains to Pennsylvania, West Virginia, Virginia, and western North Carolina. Populations also occur in the western mountains of Utah, Arizona, and New Mexico. In West Virginia the species occurs in small populations recorded from 4 counties: Boone, Greenbrier, Pendleton, and Pocahontas. There are probably other colonies elsewhere in the state. A consistent site for the species is the Reddish Knob area near Sugar Grove in Pendleton County.

Habitat: The species prefers semi-open, moist woodlands along streams. It is associated with shale habitats in the eastern part of the state, but these open or semi-open areas are located in wooded habitats that are not as open as those preferred by *P. tharos*. In the southwestern portion of the state the species is found in semi-open, moist woodlands, usually close to streams. The species is most always found in close association with woods.

Life History and Habits: Males patrol in a slow, more or less gliding flight a few feet above the ground in search of females. They are often encountered in wooded areas usually close to streams. This species has a single flight that overlaps that of the Pearl Crescent. The flight begins in June and extends into late July in West Virginia. The development stages of the larvae are similar to those of the Pearl Crescent. The caterpillar is similar to the Pearl Crescent, but with pinkish gray tubercles (Oliver 1980). The species overwinters as a partially grown larva.

Nectar Sources: The Northern Crescent nectars at a variety of plants, including dogbane *(Apocynum),* fleabane *(Erigeron),* white clover *(Trifolium repens),* and ox-eye daisy *(Chrysanthemum leucanthemum).*

Larval Host Plant: Natural host plants are asters (Compositae). Larvae readily feed on panicled aster *(Aster simplex)* in captivity.

Tawny Crescent

Phyciodes batesii (Reakirt), 1865

Adult: Plate 15, Row 4
Larva: Plate 37, Row 1
Pupa: Plate 47, Row 1

Description: Wingspan is 1¼ to 1½ inches (32–38 mm). The Tawny Crescent is an orange-and-black butterfly and has more black on the upper surface of the wings in both sexes than the Pearl Crescent *(Phyciodes tharos).* The female has more yellow scaling in the orange than the male. The underside of the male's hindwing is tawny orange with pale markings. There is a submarginal row of black dots. The Tawny Crescent lacks the dark brown marginal patch on the hindwing found in the Pearl Crescent, and instead the patch is tawny orange in this species. The crescent is pale orange to white. The underside of the hindwing is darker on the female than the male, almost a rust color, with fine brown lines and yellow blotches. The pattern is less striking in the Tawny Crescent than in the Pearl Crescent.

Distribution: The Tawny Crescent ranges from Quebec west to Wisconsin and Nebraska. In the East it ranges south into New England, New York, and

Pennsylvania in small populations. There are records of the species sporadically through the Appalachian Mountains to northern Georgia. In West Virginia the species was recorded by Edwards in May 1875 and again in 1886, both in Kanawha County. No other recent populations have been found in the state, but it is possible that a small population exists. The species does occur in the mountains of North Carolina.

Habitat: Northern populations are found in moist or dry meadows (Shapiro 1966, 1974). The Appalachian colonies seem to prefer dry, rocky sites, such as pastures and hillsides on tops of mountains. In North Carolina the species prefers small openings along woodland roads in the mountains.

Life History and Habits: The Tawny Crescent, like the Northern Crescent *(P. selenis),* is univoltine. In this region, the flight should begin in early June and continue into early July. The female deposits eggs in clusters on the underside of host leaves. Once the eggs hatch the young larvae feed communally in webs on the host plant. Larvae diapause in the third instar for the winter and complete development the following spring. The caterpillar is brown with a pinkish cast and has pale, broken lateral stripes and a dark dorsal line. There are several rows of brown, branched spines. The head is black with a white, scrolled line similar to that of *P. tharos* (the Pearl Crescent). The chrysalis is mottled brown, more pointed than the Pearl Crescent, and has short dorsal projections.

Nectar Sources: Although nectar sources are not listed for the species, they probably feed on a variety of field flowers found in their habitat during June.

Larval Host Plant: Wavy-leaved aster *(Aster undulatus),* found throughout the state, is reported as the host plant for the Tawny Crescent. Other asters are probably also used. In Pennsylvania, released individuals selected panicled aster *(Aster simplex)* on which to oviposit (Oliver 1979). Panicled aster is also common in West Virginia but is found more in wet meadows and thickets, whereas *A. undulatus* is common in dry, semi-open woodland sites. The species has been reared on *A. undulatus* in captivity.

Baltimore

Euphydryas phaeton phaeton (Drury), 1773

Adult: Plate 15, Rows 4, 5
Larva: Plate 37, Row 2

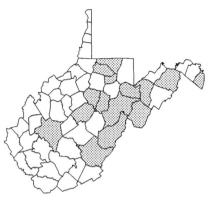

Description: Wingspan is 1⅝ to 2½ inches (41–64 mm). The Baltimore is a medium to large black butterfly with rust spots along the outer wing margins and 2 to 4 rows of pale yellow, submarginal spots and crescents on the upper surface. The underside of the wings has a marginal row of rust, triangular spots and a group of rust blotches at the base. A row of pale yellow, submarginal crescents followed by several rows of pale yellow spots occur across the wings.

Distribution: The Baltimore is found in local populations from Nova Scotia west across southern Canada to Manitoba and south to Georgia, Mississippi, and Oklahoma. In West Virginia the species should be found sporadically statewide in local colonies.

Habitat: The Baltimore is a wetland species occurring in bogs, marshes, and wet meadows.

Life History and Habits: Male Baltimores perch on vegetation 2 to 3 feet above the ground and await the passing of another Baltimore. They fly after it in search of a female and then glide to another perch. Females deposit a cluster of eggs, 100 to 700, on the underside of a host leaf, which in the summer is turtlehead *(Chelone glabra)*. The eggs are yellow at first but turn red in a day or 2. The Baltimore has only 1 flight per year. In West Virginia the flight may begin in late May but usually not until early June and continues into July. Once the eggs hatch, in about 3 weeks, the larvae feed gregariously on young leaves at the top of the host plant. They construct a web around the leaves and feed inside the web. By mid-August the larvae stop feeding and construct a thickened web around the eaten leaves and stems of the host plant. At times these webs are large, 1 to 2 feet in length, and encompass other plants as well. Hibernation occurs in the web, although a few larvae may leave, especially if disturbed. The following spring, larvae emerge from hibernation and feed singly on a variety of plants. At the time of their spring feeding, few turtlehead plants have begun to grow, especially at high elevations. When turtlehead is available in the spring, the larvae will use it. The caterpillar is tawny orange with several transverse rows of black lines and black, branched spines. The anterior and posterior segments of the body are black, differentiating it from the Harris' Checkerspot *(Chlosyne harrisii)*. The chrysalis is white with several black blotches on the wing cases and rows of black-and-orange tubercles on the abdomen.

Nectar Sources: The Baltimore visits flowers for nectar, usually in the adjacent uplands. These include milkweeds *(Asclepias)*, dogbane *(Apocynum)*, ox-eye daisy *(Chrysanthemum leucanthemum)*, clovers *(Trifolium)*, black-eyed Susan *(Rudbeckia hirta)*, and viburnum *(Viburnum)*. They will also sip moisture and nutrients from damp soil or dung.

Larval Host Plant: The primary host for the Baltimore is turtlehead *(Chelone glabra)*, and this is the plant on which the eggs are deposited and on which the larvae feed during the summer. When larvae emerge from hibernation, they feed on plants, such as English plantain *(Plantago lanceolata)*, arrowwood *(Viburnum recognitum)*, common lousewort *(Pedicularis canadensis)*, Japanese honeysuckle *(Lonicera japonica)*, and the primary host, turtlehead. Smooth yellow foxglove *(Aureolaria flava)* has also been reported as a host for the Baltimore (Shapiro 1974; Schweitzer, personal communication) and may be used as well in West Virginia. The use of other *Aureolaria* species have been reported by Opler and Krizek (1984) and Pyle (1981).

Question Mark

Polygonia interrogationis (Fabricius), 1798

Adult: Plate 16, Rows 1, 2, 3
Larva: Plate 37, Row 2
Pupa: Plate 47, Row 2

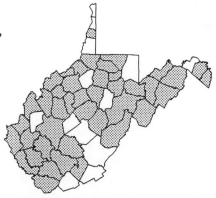

Description: Wingspan is 2⅜ to 2⅝ inches (60–67 mm). The Question Mark is the largest *Polygonia* found in West Virginia and has 2 distinct seasonal forms. It is a tawny-orange butterfly with ragged wing margins, strongly hooked at the tips, and has pronounced tails on the hindwings. The upper surface of the summer form is tawny orange on the forewing with a dark border and a group of dark spots in the center. The hindwing is almost entirely black, with some orange basally. The winter form has more orange on the upper surface and has black and orange spots on the hindwing. The wing margins are edged in violet more so on the winter form than on the summer form. The under surface is variable. It may be rust brown to brown, and either uniform in color with fine striations or strongly striated with dark bands and blotches. Summer forms often have a strong violet cast. There is a silver crescent, or comma, near the center of the hindwing, with a silver dot below, forming a question mark.

Distribution: The Question Mark ranges from Nova Scotia across southern Canada to the Rocky Mountains and south to the Gulf Coast. In the East it extends south to northern Florida. In West Virginia the species is found statewide, with records from most areas except the southeastern counties, although it should be common there as well.

Habitat: The Question Mark uses a variety of habitats, usually consisting of some open area. Woodland openings, gravel roads through wooded areas, forest edges, orchards, and stream banks seem to be the favorite habitats for the species.

Life History and Habits: Question Marks are rapid fliers, as are the other angle wings. Males prefer to perch on tree trunks or on the ground. They fly after almost any intruder passing through their territory. After a brief encounter they return to the same perch or another nearby. As with other angle wings, they are difficult to capture. Males and females readily visit dung, tree sap, or rotting fruit for nutrients. Females lay their eggs on or near host plants by depositing single or stacked eggs (2–6) on the underside of a leaf or stem. The Question Mark is double-brooded in West Virginia, with the first flight appearing in April and continuing into May. These individuals hibernated as adults through the winter or migrated north from warmer zones. Occasionally, Question Marks can be seen on warm days in late winter or early spring flying about with snow present on the ground. The resulting summer brood usually emerges during June and continues flying throughout the summer months into September. Individuals aestivate through many of the warmer summer days. The winter brood appears in late August and flies through September into October. Adults from this brood either hibernate or migrate south. In West Virginia, most probably hibernate. The caterpillar is variable in color and may be black, gray, or yellow, with pale cream to yellow longitudinal stripes and fine dots. There are several rows of branched spines along the body. The spines near the light to dark red head are usually black. Those to the rear may be red, orange, or yellow. The chrysalis is variable but is usually brown with a prominent thoracic keel and 8 silver spots along the dorsal surface to the rear of the keel.

Nectar Sources: Question Marks take nutrients from rotting fruit, tree sap, dung, carrion, and damp soil. On rare occasions they will visit flowers for nectar. This is usually done only when other foods are scarce. Flowers visited include milkweed *(Asclepias),* aster *(Aster),* dogwood *(Cornus),* and red clover *(Trifolium pratense).*

Larval Host Plant: A number of plants are utilized as hosts by the Question Mark. In West Virginia, elm *(Ulmus* spp.) and hackberry *(Celtis* spp.) are probably the most commonly used hosts. The Question Mark will also feed on nettles *(Urtica* spp.) and false nettle *(Boehmeria cylindrica).*

Eastern Comma

Polygonia comma (Harris), 1842

Adult: Plate 17, Rows 1, 2
Larva: Plate 37, Row 3
Pupa: Plate 47, Row 2

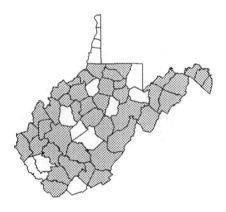

Description: Wingspan is 1¾ to 2 inches (44–51 mm). The Eastern Comma closely resembles the Question Mark *(Polygonia interrogationis)* except that it is smaller and has shorter tails. The butterfly is tawny orange with black blotches and spots, a black border, and a row of light orange or yellow, triangular spots near the outer margin on the upper wing surface. The summer brood has more black in the hindwing. The species has ragged wing edges, often edged with violet or gray. The underside is variable in pattern and color. It may be golden brown to red brown with fine lines or striations, or heavily marked with dark and light blotches, bands, and striations, resembling a dead leaf. There is a hooked, silver comma in the center of the hindwing.

Distribution: The Eastern Comma ranges from Nova Scotia across southern Canada to the Central Plains and south in the East to Florida, the Gulf states, and eastern Texas. In West Virginia the species is found statewide. The Eastern Comma may be common in some areas, especially in the southern counties.

Habitat: This species is usually found in close association with woodland habitats and is especially fond of riparian or moist woodlands where its host plant abounds. The Eastern Comma is most often encountered along semi-open woodland roads where it likes to perch on the sandy or rocky ground.

Life History and Habits: This species, like the Question Mark, has a rapid, erratic flight and perches on tree trunks or the ground, chasing intruders as they pass through the territory. The Eastern Comma is at least bivoltine in West Virginia, with the first flight emerging from hibernation in early spring. Individuals may be seen in late March and fly into May. The summer brood emerges in early June and flies through July. The overwintering brood emerges in August and flies through September, spending hot summer weather diapausing in hollow logs or trees. Most of these individuals hibernate for the winter. There may also be a partial third brood in late summer in some areas. Some may migrate south, although this is not confirmed for West Virginia. The pale green eggs are either deposited singly or in short stacks on host leaves. Later instar larvae seek shelter on the underside of leaves by pulling the edges together with silk and feeding on the leaves at night. The caterpillar is variable, from black to pale greenish brown, with several rows of branched, white spines and a white lateral band. Tubercles may be yellow in darker larvae. The head is black with white hairs. The chrysalis may be brown to gray with 2 rows of golden or silver projections on the dorsal surface of the abdomen.

Nectar Sources: Eastern Commas gather at moist soil, tree sap, rotting fruit, dung, or carrion for nutrients. On occasion they will visit such plants as boneset *(Eupatorium)*, blackberry *(Rubus)*, and other flowers to obtain nectar, but this practice is only done when fermenting fruit or sap is scarce or unavailable.

Larval Host Plant: In West Virginia the Eastern Comma utilizes nettle *(Urtica* spp.), false nettle *(Boehmeria cylindrica)*, wood nettle *(Laportea canadensis)*, elm *(Ulmus* spp.), and hops *(Humulus* spp.) as hosts. They will also use hackberry *(Celtis* spp.) on occasion.

Green Comma

Polygonia faunus smythi (Clark), 1937

Adult: Plate 17, Row 3

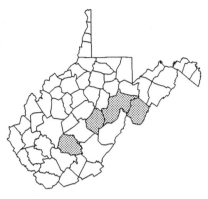

Description: Wingspan is 1⅞ to 2 inches (48–51 mm). The Green Comma is similar to the other anglewings except that the wing margins are more ragged and irregular. They are tawny orange with dark spots and dark wing borders. There is a row of pale orange to yellow, submarginal spots on the upper wing surface. The underside of the wings is mottled with light and dark brown and heavily striated. There are two rows of green chevrons along the outer margin of the wings, and a small silver comma toward the center of the hindwing.

Distribution: The Green Comma ranges from Newfoundland across Canada to the Pacific Coast. It ranges south into New England, New York, and Pennsylvania and west through the northern Great Lakes states. There is an isolated population in the Appalachian Mountains in West Virginia and Virginia south to northern Georgia. In West Virginia there are reports from 4 counties: Fayette, Pendleton, Randolph, and Webster.

Habitat: The Green Comma prefers northern hardwood forest habitats with an association of spruce and is usually found along roadways, trails, or streams. The amount of spruce present may vary. At higher elevations in the eastern mountains, beech-maple-birch with a spruce component is a typical forest type preferred by this species.

Life History and Habits: Males perch on the ground, on rocks, or even on the leaves of shrubs in lowland areas. The flight of the Green Comma is somewhat slower than the other anglewings. The Green Comma is univoltine in the Appalachians. Overwintering adults appear in early spring, often while snow is still present, and fly through May. The single brood emerges from late June to August and may aestivate during hot summer days. They become active again during fall, feeding and storing fat. These individuals hibernate during the winter months. Eggs are laid singly on host leaves, and the larvae feed beneath the leaf. The caterpillar is tan to brown or rust, with black and yellow transverse bands and spots and white blotches along the abdomen. A broken, orange lateral band occurs along the body. The branched spines are white and orange, and a pale marking in the shape of a "W" occurs on the head (Opler and Krizek 1984). The chrysalis is tan to brown, with greenish streaks and short metallic gold spurs on the dorsal surface.

Nectar Sources: The Green Comma is reported to feed on damp soil, tree sap, rotten fruit, dung, and carrion, as well as flower nectar (Scott 1986).

Larval Host Plant: The Green Comma selects willows *(Salix* spp.), birch *(Betula* spp.), and alders *(Alnus)* over much of its range; however, the Appalachian population may feed on gooseberry *(Ribes* spp.) as well (Opler and Krizek 1984).

Gray Comma

Polygonia progne (Cramer), 1776

Adult: Plate 17, Row 4
Larva: Plate 37, Row 3

Description: Wingspan is 1⅝ to 1⅞ inches (41–48 mm). The Gray Comma has 2 seasonal forms. The spring butterfly is tawny orange on the upper surface with a submarginal row of yellow spots along dark wing margins. There are small dark spots scattered through the wings. The summer form exhibits more black in the hindwing. The underside of the wings is heavily striated with brown-and-gray lines, and the hindwing is either darker basally or fairly uniform in color. The tips of the forewings are gray. A small, L-shaped, silver comma occurs in the hindwing. Wing margins are ragged, being squared off and pointed toward the tip of the forewing; and a tail-like protrusion occurs on the hindwing.

Distribution: The Gray Comma is found from the Maritime Provinces west across southern Canada to British Columbia and across the northern United States to the Great Plains. It ranges south in the East through the Appalachian Mountains to North Carolina. There is another southward extension of the range along the Mississippi River to Arkansas. In West Virginia the butterfly is found in scattered populations but is most common in the mountains of the eastern portion of the state. It has been reported most frequently from the Spruce Knob area in Randolph County.

Habitat: This species prefers deciduous woodlands and is often encountered along gravel roads, trails, and clearings.

Life History and Habits: The Gray Comma is most often found perched on gravel roads or trails. Males also perch on the trunks or leaves of trees and shrubs near open areas awaiting females. The Gray Comma is double-brooded throughout its range, with the first flight of overwintering adults appearing in April and May. The first brood of summer-form adults appears in mid-June and flies into late July. The fall, or overwintering, adults appear anywhere from late July through September. Eggs are deposited singly on the host leaves, and the larvae remain on the underside of the leaf. The caterpillar is variable. The body may be yellow to brown, with greenish blotches and lines. The several rows of branched spines are either yellow or black. The head is rust with long spines projecting from it. The chrysalis may be tan to brown, with dark streaks.

Nectar Sources: Adults prefer to visit sap flows, rotting fruit, or dung for nutrients, and visit flowers only occasionally. Those visited include teasel *(Dipsacus)* and burdock *(Arctium minus).*

Larval Host Plant: Gooseberry *(Ribes rotundifolia)* is the preferred host of the Gray Comma (Opler and Krizek 1984). They will also use elm *(Ulmus* spp.) on occasion. Shapiro (1966) reported the Gray Comma to feed on wild azalea *(Rhododendron nudiflorum)* as well. All 3 plants are common in West Virginia, especially in the mountains.

Compton Tortoiseshell

Nymphalis vau-album j-album
(Boisduval and LeConte), 1833

Adult: Plate 18, Row 1
Larva: Plate 37, Row 4

Description: Wingspan is 2½ to 2⅞ inches (64–73 mm). The Compton Tortoiseshell is a large rust-brown butterfly with black and yellow-gold blotches on the upper wing surface. A single, white spot occurs on the forewing and hindwing. The wings have a ragged margin and short hindwing tails. The underside is striated with browns, gray, and white, and is darker in the basal half. A series of gray crescents occurs along the outer wing margin, and a small silver "V" occurs on the hindwing. The butterfly is cryptic, and when the wings are folded, it resembles tree bark or dead leaves.

Distribution: This is a northern species occurring from eastern Canada west to British Columbia and Alaska. It ranges south into New England and the northern Great Lakes states. It is a frequent inhabitant of northern Pennsylvania but only migrates to West Virginia on occasion. In West Virginia the species might be found anywhere from the higher mountains to the lowlands. It has been recorded from 6 counties thus far: Grant, Hampshire, Hardy, Pendleton, Randolph, and Wood.

Habitat: This species prefers upland forest habitat primarily in a northern forest timber type with or without a conifer component. The butterfly perches on the ground along gravel or dirt roads or on bare spots in clearings.

Life History and Habits: The Compton Tortoiseshell immigrates into more southerly habitats when populations are high in the North. Hibernating adults become active in the spring from March through May when they mate and lay eggs. They are univoltine, with the single brood emerging from June to July. They may be active into November. Individuals in West Virginia are usually found during the summer and fall, but fresh individuals may be found as early as mid-June. Eggs are laid in clusters on host twigs. Larvae are gregarious and feed on the young foliage within a web. The caterpillar is pale green with yellow-green stippling and rows of black, bristly spines. The chrysalis varies from brown to green, is finely lined, has golden dorsal tubercles, and 2 hornlike projections from the head.

Nectar Sources: Compton Tortoiseshells prefer rotting fruit and sap to other foods. They also gather at moist soil to sip minerals, and on rare occasion they will sip flower nectar.

Larval Host Plant: Compton Tortoiseshells select aspens *(Populus* spp.), willows *(Salix* spp.), or birch *(Betula* spp.) as their primary host plants.

Mourning Cloak

Nymphalis antiopa antiopa (Linnaeus),
1758

Adult: Plate 18, Row 2
Larva: Plate 37, Row 4
Pupa: Plate 47, Row 2

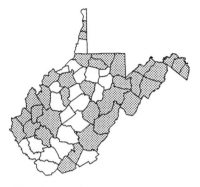

Description: Wingspan is 2 to 2⅜ inches
(73–86 mm). This is a large dark
maroon butterfly with pale tan to yellow
wing margins. A submarginal row of bright blue spots occurs across the upper
surface of both wings. On the underside the butterfly is dark brown, almost
black, and finely striated. It has a heavily flecked, yellow to tan border. The
wing edges are irregular, with a protrusion near the tip of the forewing and a
short tail on the hindwing.

Distribution: The Mourning Cloak is found throughout North America,
ranging south into Mexico. In the East it is rare in the Gulf states and almost
nonexistent in Florida. In West Virginia it is found throughout the state, but
records are still lacking for many counties.

Habitat: The Mourning Cloak is most frequently found along roads in
woodland habitats, although it may also be found in open areas, parks,
orchards, and yards. It also prefers riparian habitat since its host plant, willow
(Salix), usually abounds there.

Life History and Habits: The Mourning Cloak makes its first appearance from
hibernation during the first warm days of spring. It is often seen while snow is
still present. Males perch on the ground or low tree branches and await
females. They often fly back and forth along trails or through open areas
gliding much of the time in circles. Mating of overwintering adults takes place
in the spring. The Mourning Cloak is long-lived (up to 10 months) and
spends much of its time in aestivation during the summer (Young 1980).
They become active again during the fall. In cold weather, adults warm
themselves by basking on the ground with wings outspread. In warm weather
they often perch on tree trunks or branches with wings closed. The species is
single-brooded in West Virginia, although its behavior makes it appear as
though there are more broods. Eggs are laid in clusters on host leaves. Young
larvae are gregarious and feed together in silken webs. As they grow, the webs
are eliminated. The resulting brood appears in late June and July. These
individuals aestivate during hot weather and become active again in the fall to

feed and store fat. They then hibernate locally or migrate south for the winter. In West Virginia most adults probably hibernate rather than migrate. The caterpillar is black with white flecking in rows across the body. There is a dorsal row of brick red spots along the body, and the body is covered with several rows of black, branched spines. The prolegs are orange to red. The chrysalis is violet gray to light brown, with 2 rows of short dorsal projections. As with other Nymphalids, the chrysalis hangs inverted from its substrate.

Nectar Sources: Mourning Cloaks favor tree sap and rotting fruit for nutrients. They also take minerals from moist soil or dung. On occasion, Mourning Cloaks will visit flowers for nectar. These include milkweed *(Asclepias),* dogbane *(Apocynum),* and New Jersey tea *(Ceanothus),* as well as other species.

Larval Host Plant: Willows are the favorite host for the Mourning Cloak and include black willow *(Salix nigra)* and weeping willow *(S. babylonica)* as preferred species. Other hosts used include American elm *(Ulmus americana),* quaking aspen *(Populus tremuloides),* big-toothed aspen *(P. grandidentata),* and hackberry *(Celtis* spp.). Last instar larvae have a tendency to wander and may feed on unusual hosts, such as scrub oak *(Quercus ilicifolia)* (Schweitzer, personal communication).

Milbert's Tortoiseshell

Nymphalis milberti milberti (Godart), 1819
Adult: Plate 18, Row 3
Larva: Plate 38, Row 1
Pupa: Plate 47, Row 3

Description: Wingspan is 1¾ to 2 inches (44–51 mm). Milbert's Tortoiseshell is dark brown on the basal half of the upper wing surface, with yellow-and-orange bands on the outer third. Wing borders are dark and spotted with blue, and 1 black and 2 orange spots occur along the costal margin of the forewing. The underside is dark brown on the basal half and tan on the outer third, and heavily striated with fine lines. The wing borders are dark, and the wing edges are ragged.

Distribution: Milbert's Tortoiseshell is a northern species ranging across Canada from Newfoundland to British Columbia. In the United States it ranges from New England through the Great Lakes states to the Rocky Mountains. In the Appalachian Mountains the species occasionally strays south into West Virginia. Specimens have been taken as far south as North Carolina and Georgia. In West Virginia there are 2 county records from Monongalia County. Specimens taken in Monongalia County were collected in October 1973 and September 1980. There are occasional colonies nearby in Pennsylvania, and it is possible that the species will appear again in West Virginia.

Habitat: Milbert's Tortoiseshell prefers moist meadows and pastures, usually near streams and woodlands. The species is prone to wander.

Life History and Habits: Males prefer to perch on the ground or on fallen logs awaiting females. The species is multibrooded and probably has 2 broods in this region. Since the species hibernates as adults, the first adults appear in late March and April. The resulting brood appears in late May and June. A second brood appears in August and flies into October before hibernating. Milbert's Tortoiseshells may aestivate during periods of hot summer weather. The pale green eggs are deposited in clusters on the host plants; the larvae are gregarious and feed together in a web. As the larvae grow they feed singly from folded leaves. The caterpillar is black with 2 narrow, yellow or orange lateral bands. The ventral surface is grayish green. The body is speckled with white dots and has rows of short, black, branched spines. The chrysalis varies from gray to greenish and is flecked with dark brown.

Nectar Sources: Milbert's Tortoiseshells visit a variety of flowers for nectar. These include thistles *(Cirsium)*, milkweed *(Asclepias)*, ironweed *(Vernonia)*, clovers *(Trifolium)*, wing-stem *(Verbesina alternifolia)*, and asters *(Aster)*. Other plants are also visited, as well as fermenting fruit, damp soil, and probably sap flows.

Larval Host Plant: Nettles are the hosts for the species, and they include stinging nettle *(Urtica dioica)* and wild nettle *(U. gracilis)*.

American Lady

Vanessa virginiensis (Drury), 1773

Adult: Plate 18, Row 4; Plate 19, Row 1
Larva: Plate 38, Row 1
Pupa: Plate 47, Row 3

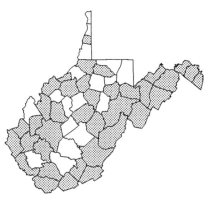

Description: Wingspan is 1¾ to 2⅛ inches (44–54 mm). The American Lady is a medium golden orange to pinkish butterfly with black markings in the upper surface of the forewing. Several white spots occur near the blackened forewing tip. A row of black spots ringed in blue occurs on the hindwing. The hindwing underside pattern distinguishes the American Lady from its close relative, the Painted Lady *(Vanessa cardui).* The hindwing of the American Lady has a complex pattern of olive brown, black, and white toward the base, with 2 large blue eyespots near the outer margin. The Painted Lady has 4 to 5 eyespots.

Distribution: The American Lady is a resident of the southern United States, reaching north along the East Coast to Virginia and then south through the Gulf states into Mexico, Central America, and northern South America. The species makes annual migrations into northern states and Canada. In West Virginia the species immigrates statewide and should be found in all counties, although records are still lacking for many counties.

Habitat: The American Lady prefers open areas, including fields, road banks, railroad grades, gas- and power-line right-of-ways, and stream banks. They are usually found in areas with low vegetation.

Life History and Habits: American Ladies are one of the first butterflies seen in early spring. Females are usually the first encountered; they fly close to the ground in a zigzag pattern searching for host plants on which to oviposit. Males are often encountered perching on bare spots in fields, on hill tops, or along gravel and sandy roads where they imbibe moisture with other butterflies. Perching may be done with wings folded or outstretched, and often males and females bask with wings outstretched. The American Lady is multibrooded, and probably 3 flights occur in West Virginia. The first flight, which results from immigrating adults, begins in early April and continues into May. The resulting brood emerges in late May or early June and flies into July, and a second brood flies in July and August. There is at least a partial third brood that flies in late August and September and continues into early October. The eggs are laid singly in the tomentose pubescence of the host leaves. The larva lives within a nest made by tying a leaf or leaves together with silk. As the larva grows, the web size increases. Pupation occurs on nearby plants. The caterpillar is black with a group of fine, transverse, yellowish lines between segments. There are 2 white spots in each of 7 body segments, and 4 rows of black to white, branched spines, each arising from a red base. The chrysalis is grayish white and finely marked with black dots, and has olive to bronze mottling in bands along the abdomen.

Nectar Sources: The American Lady utilizes a variety of plants for nectar. These include milkweed *(Asclepias)*, dogbane *(Apocynum)*, red and white clovers *(Trifolium)*, thistles *(Cirsium)*, dandelion *(Taraxacum officinale)*, ox-eye daisy *(Chrysanthemum leucanthemum)*, goldenrods *(Solidago)*, and asters *(Aster)*.

Larval Host Plant: The pussytoes *(Antennaria)* are widely selected hosts in West Virginia. They include field pussytoes *(A. neglecta)*, shale-barren pussytoes *(A. virginica)*, single-headed pussytoes *(A. solitaria)*, and plantainleaf everlasting *(A. plantaginifolia)*. The American Lady also uses pearly everlasting *(Anaphalis margaritacea)* where available and the cudweeds *(Gnaphalium* spp.) (Pyle 1981; Scott 1986).

Painted Lady

Vanessa cardui (Linnaeus), 1758
Adult: Plate 19, Rows 1, 2
Larva: Plate 38, Row 1
Pupa: Plate 47, Row 3

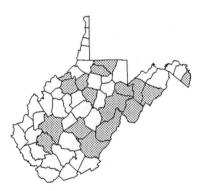

Description: Wingspan is 2 to 2¼ inches (51–57 mm). The Painted Lady is similar in color and pattern to the American Lady *(Vanessa virginiensis)*, except that on the underside of the hindwing there is a submarginal row of 4 to 5 small black eye spots rimmed with blue. The America Lady has only 2 large eye spots.

Distribution: The Painted Lady is a resident of the Mexican plateau. The species migrates and colonizes throughout North America into Canada as far north as Labrador and west to the Yukon. It is also found on all continents except Antarctica and Australia. In West Virginia, colonies probably occur statewide, although the butterfly is seldom abundant in any year.

Habitat: The species prefers open habitats, such as fields, pastures, railroad grades, gas- and power-line right-of-ways, vacant lots, and gardens.

Life History and Habits: The Painted Lady is a migratory species and is more abundant in the West than in the East. Northward migrations from Mexico occur during the spring, and at times they may be so numerous as to be a nuisance to motorists. Such migrations do not occur much in the East; however, all of the colonies established in West Virginia result from immigrations. Males perch on the ground on bare soil awaiting females. They are rapid fliers and when disturbed may fly a considerable distance before landing again. The number of broods in West Virginia depends on the season that immigration occurs, but usually there are 2 broods. In most years adults are not usually seen until the summer months; therefore, the first brood may not fly until July and August, and a second brood, if available, flies in September. This species cannot survive cold winters and may not be seen every year. Eggs are laid on young host leaves, and the larvae feed singly under a web on the leaf. The caterpillar is variable from pale greenish to black, with black mottling and a black head. There is a series of yellowish dashes along the sides and a yellow middorsal stripe. The several rows of branched spines are pale in color. The chrysalis is gray to brownish, with brown patches, and has a series of short metallic gold projections.

Nectar Sources: Painted Ladies visit many types of field or garden flowers for nectar and are especially attracted to composites. Some of these include thistles *(Cirsium)*, ironweed *(Vernonia)*, Joe-pye weed *(Eupatorium)*, milkweeds *(Asclepias)*, red clover *(Trifolium pratense)*, asters *(Aster)*, zinnias *(Zinnia)*, and marigolds *(Tagetes)*.

Larval Host Plant: The Painted Lady uses a variety of plants as hosts. The most commonly selected plant in this area is probably thistles *(Cirsium* spp.). Plants in the family Asteraceae are also used. Other host plants include the mallows *(Malvaceae)*, especially hollyhock *(Althaea* spp.) and common mallow *(Malva neglecta)*, and plants in the families Boraginaceae (Borage) and Fabaceae (legumes). The larvae will also feed on cultivated *Artemisia* species.

Red Admiral

Vanessa atalanta rubria (Fruhstorfer), 1909

Adult: Plate 19, Row 3
Larva: Plate 38, Row 2
Pupa: Plate 48, Row 1

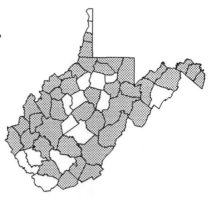

Description: Wingspan is 1¾ to 2¼ inches (44–57 mm). The Red Admiral is a distinctively marked, medium butterfly. The upper surface is dark brownish black with an orange-red band crossing the forewing and along the outer margin of the hindwing. There is a series of white spots near the tip of the forewing, and a row of black to blue spots occurs along the hindwing border. The underside of the hindwing is marbled with dark brown to black. The forewing underside is black with white spots near the tip, a blue swirl beneath, and a pinkish bar crossing the midwing.

Distribution: The Red Admiral colonizes northward throughout North America into northern Canada from the southern coastal and Gulf states and Mexico. It also occurs in Europe, Asia, North Africa, Hawaii, and New Zealand. In West Virginia the species is found statewide. Since the Red Admiral cannot survive winter weather, it recolonizes northern regions through annual migrations.

Habitat: The Red Admiral prefers woodland edges and roads and woodland clearings, as well as stream banks and bottomlands. However, they may be found in a number of places, such as fields, around abandoned farms, barnyards, railroad grades, and orchards, especially where they are attracted by scents of dung or fermenting fruit.

Life History and Habits: The Red Admiral is a rapid, erratic flier. Males perch in roads and are active at dusk. They are often seen perched along dirt or gravel roads after other butterflies have gone to roost in the evening. Egg laying by females usually begins around noon and continues late into the afternoon. One female was observed depositing eggs as late as 1830 hours (6:30 P.M.). There are at least 2 broods in West Virginia. Migrants may be seen from early April into May. The first brood emerges in June and flies into July, and the second flight occurs in August and early September. Immigrating adults colonize the state in the spring. In some years the species is locally common, and in other years it is difficult to find. Larvae live in leaf shelters constructed by folding a leaf or group of leaves together with silk. The caterpillar is variable. It may be black with cream to white lateral chevrons or dashes, and the several rows of branched spines may be white or black; or the caterpillar may appear grayish due to heavy specking of white on the body, with whitish spines that are brown or reddish at the base. The chrysalis varies from grayish brown to brown marked with black, and has gold flecking along the short dorsal tubercles. Where the species is able to overwinter, individuals do so as pupae.

Nectar Sources: In West Virginia, Red Admirals prefer to feed at sap flows, fermenting fruit, dung, or carrion more so than at flowers. Flowers are fed upon occasionally, and some of those selected include thistles *(Cirsium)*, milkweeds *(Asclepias)*, dogbane *(Apocynum)*, red clover *(Trifolium pratense)*, ox-eye daisy *(Chrysanthemum leucanthemum)*, Queen Anne's lace *(Daucus carota)*, and lilac *(Syringa)*.

Larval Host Plant: The Red Admiral prefers nettles as its host. These include stinging nettle *(Urtica dioica)* and wild nettle *(U. gracilis)*. It also uses false nettle *(Boehmeria cylindrica)*, Pennsylvania pellitory *(Parietaria pensylvanica)*, and wood nettle *(Laportea canadensis)*.

Common Buckeye

Junonia coenia (Hübner), 1822
Adult: Plate 19, Row 4
Larva: Plate 38, Row 2
Pupa: Plate 48, Row 1

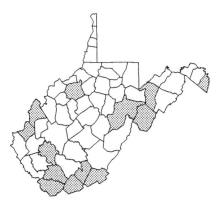

Description: Wingspan is 1¾ to 2¼ inches (45–58 mm). The Common Buckeye is a brown butterfly with a large and a small eyespot in the forewing and 2 large eyespots in the hindwing on the upperside. There are 2 short orange bars and a whitish bar in the forewing. The underside is light brown to rust, with small eyespots in the hindwing. The forewing underside contains a large eyespot and a light-colored band.

Distribution: The Common Buckeye is a resident of the southern Gulf states to Mexico and the Caribbean and along the East Coast to North Carolina. The butterfly colonizes the northern states each year, often as far north as New England and west through the Great Lakes states and Canada. It also colonizes west of the Rocky Mountains to Oregon. In West Virginia the species may be found in any county, although it is generally reported from warmer areas.

Habitat: The Common Buckeye is an inhabitant of open areas, such as fields, pastures, gas- and power-line right-of-ways, railroad grades, and roadside parks. The species likes bare ground for perching, in addition to short vegetation.

Life History and Habits: Males perch along sandy roads or on bare soil in fields or pastures, flying and gliding close to the ground from one spot to another. They are rapid fliers and are difficult to approach. Males perch with their wings outstretched or actively open and close their wings. Buckeyes immigrate into West Virginia in late spring but may not be seen until summer in many years. There are usually 1 to 2 broods over much of the state. A first brood from spring immigrants appears in June and early July, and a second flight appears in late August and continues into September. In most years cold weather prevents the completion of a third brood. The small green eggs are deposited singly on the host leaf. The caterpillar is black with pale yellow lateral and dorsal stripes. There are 4 rows of metallic blue and black spines, with the lateral row originating from an orange projection, called a chalazae. The head is orange and black.

Nectar Sources: The Common Buckeye visits a variety of flowers for nectar, which include Queen Anne's lace *(Daucus carota)*, sunflowers *(Helianthus)*, asters *(Aster)*, milkweeds *(Asclepias)*, ironweed *(Vernonia)*, and clovers *(Trifolium)*, as well as other field species.

Larval Host Plant: Common Buckeyes utilize members of the figwort (Scrophulariaceae), plantain (Plantaginaceae), and acanthus (Acanthaceae) families. The most commonly selected hosts in West Virginia are English plantain *(Plantago lanceolata)*, common plantain *(P. rugelii)*, and toadflax *(Linaria vulgaris)*. Other hosts include foxgloves *(Aureolaria* and *Agalinis* spp.) and ruellia *(Ruellia* spp.) (Opler and Krizek 1984).

Subfamily Limenitidinae—Admirals

The admirals are frequently combined with the Nymphalinae but are separated here because of the characteristics of the larvae and pupae.
    This subfamily is one of the most colorful groups, with many colorful

species found nationwide. It is represented by 2 species in West Virginia. Hybrids with a northern subspecies may also occur on rare occasions in West Virginia.

Larvae of this group lack the numerous branched spines that characterize the Nymphalinae. Instead, most of the spines are only represented by bristled tubercles. The pair of spines on the thorax and posterior section are the most developed and have a hornlike appearance. Many of the Limenitidinae have secondary spines arising as a rosette from the top of the primary spines. The larvae are cryptic, resembling bird droppings in their pattern and form. The pupa is slender and has a large hump, or keel, on the middorsal surface.

Red-spotted Purple

Limenitis arthemus astyanax (Fabricius), 1775

Adult: Plate 20, Rows 2, 3
Larva: Plate 38, Row 3

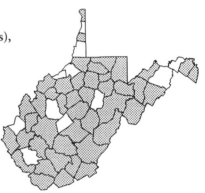

Description: Wingspan is 2⅝ to 3¾ inches (67–96 mm). The Red-spotted Purple is a large black butterfly with whitish dashes along the forewing margin on the upperside and a blue to blue-green iridescence on the outer portion of the hindwing. The female, which is larger than the male, usually has brick red spots near the tip of the forewing. The underside is charcoal black with 2 rows of blue marginal crescents followed by a submarginal row of brick red spots on the hindwing. There is also a cluster of blue and brick red spots in the basal portions of the wings. The forewing has a row of blue crescents, white dashes, and brick red spots near the outer margin. The Red-spotted Purple mimics the distasteful Pipevine Swallowtail *(Battus philenor)*. The Red-spotted Purple also interbreeds with the more northern White Admiral *(Limenitis arthemis arthemis)* where the 2 populations meet. On occasion hybrid *L. a. astyanax* x *L. a. arthemis* individuals can be found in the state. They are distinguished by varying amounts of white banding across the wings.

Distribution: The Red-spotted Purple ranges from New England south to Florida and west to the Dakotas, Colorado, and into Mexico. In West Virginia the species is found statewide, with records from most counties. Red-spotted

Purples and White Admiral hybrids have been reported from Marion and Mineral Counties. In West Virginia there are no pure *L. a. arthemis* individuals.

Habitat: The Red-spotted Purple is a forest butterfly preferring woodland roads, trails, clearings, and forest edges. Females are frequently found flying around small trees and shrubs in young deciduous forests, both perching and egg laying.

Life History and Habits: Males are most often encountered perched on gravel or dirt roads, although they also perch on leaves of trees several feet above the ground. When disturbed, males that were perched on the road usually fly to a perch 15 to 30 feet above the ground on a tree leaf. When the summer flight is at its peak, males may be seen perched along roads every few feet. They may also cluster in groups of a dozen or more. Females stay in second growth or young growth woodlands and shrubby areas gliding from perch to perch. They fly around the host tree and deposit a single large pale green egg on the tip of a leaf. The Red-spotted Purple is at least double-brooded in West Virginia, with a partial third brood in some areas. The first flight, resulting from overwintering larvae, begins in May and continues into June. The second brood emerges in late June and July and flies into August. A partial third brood may occur at times in late August and September. Larvae from the second and all of the third brood diapause partially grown in a tube hibernaculum constructed by rolling the basal portion (½–¾ in.) of an eaten leaf with silk and tying it along the stem to the branch. It will remain there throughout the winter. The caterpillar is similar to that of the Viceroy *(L. archippus)*. It is mottled brown to olive, with a white saddle across the back and along a portion of the ventral surface. It has 2 horny spines or projections behind the head and 2 large orange to brown, fleshy bumps on the back. The larva resembles a bird dropping. The chrysalis is brown and white, with a large keel-like projection on the middorsal surface.

Nectar Sources: The Red-spotted Purple prefers feeding at sap flows, fermenting fruit, damp soil, dung, or carrion. Flowers are used on occasion, and they include black cherry *(Prunus serotina)*, Viburnum *(Viburnum)*, and dogwood *(Cornus)*, as well as a few other tree species.

Larval Host Plant: Hosts used by the Red-spotted Purple in West Virginia include black cherry *(Prunus serotina)*, choke cherry *(P. virginiana)*, serviceberry *(Amelanchier* spp.), big-toothed aspen *(Populus grandidentata)*, quaking aspen *(P. tremuloides)*, silverleaf poplar *(P. alba)*, cottonwood *(P. deltoides)*, apple *(Pyrus malus)*, black oak *(Quercus velutina)*, scrub oak *(Q. ilicifolia)*, and willow *(Salix* spp.).

Viceroy

Limenitis archippus archippus
(Cramer), 1776

Adult: Plate 21, Rows 1, 2
Larva: Plate 38, Row 3
Pupa: Plate 48, Row 1

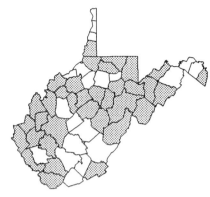

Description: Wingspan is 2½ to 3 inches (64–76 mm). Although somewhat smaller, the Viceroy mimics the Monarch *(Danaus plexippus)* in color and wing pattern. The upper surface of the wing is a rich russet orange, with black wing veins and black margins containing a row of white spots. The underside is pale orange brown with black veins and black margins that contain 1 to 3 rows of bluish white crescents. There is a black line across the center of the hindwing that is not present in the Monarch. On occasion the Viceroy hybridizes with the Red-spotted Purple *(L. Arthemis astyanax)* producing intermediate individuals, but this occurrence is rare.

Distribution: The Viceroy ranges from Canada south into Florida and west through much of the United States to the Sierra Nevada and Cascade Mountains. In West Virginia the species occurs statewide in suitable habitat.

Habitat: The Viceroy prefers semi-open to open shrub areas along streams, wet meadows, or ponds. Areas with alders *(Alnus),* willows *(Salix),* and aspens *(Populus)* are common sites for the Viceroy.

Life History and Habits: Males perch on low vegetation usually within a few feet of the ground. They patrol a small area in a gliding flight, returning to the same or a nearby perch after a short run. Mating takes place during the afternoon, with the female carrying the male. The pale green eggs are deposited singly at the tips of host leaves. The Viceroy is at least bivoltine in West Virginia, with the first brood emerging in mid-May and flying through June. A second brood emerges in July and flies into August, and a partial third brood may be found on occasion in September. At least some of the partially grown larvae from the second brood diapause in leaf shelters constructed by rolling the basal ½ to ¾ inch of an eaten leaf with silk and attaching it to the branch with silk. The larva remains in this tube shelter until spring. Where a partial third brood occurs, all partially grown larvae hibernate. The Viceroy caterpillar resembles a bird dropping, as do some of the swallowtail and other

Limenitis larvae, and, therefore, is left unharmed by many predators. Night feeding behavior aids in its protection. The caterpillar is brown and olive green, with a white dorsal saddle and white ventrally along the abdomen. There are 2 long horny spines in back of the head and 2 rows of fleshy knobs on the anterior and posterior dorsum. The chrysalis is brown with a cream to white abdomen and has a raised thorax with a rounded, keel-like projection arising from the dorsum at midbody.

Nectar Sources: Viceroys utilize a variety of food sources to obtain nutrients. They are fond of dung, carrion, fermenting fruit, moist sand, and soil. They also visit plants for nectar, including milkweeds *(Asclepias)*, thistles *(Cirsium)*, Joe-pye weed, boneset *(Eupatorium)*, teasel *(Dipsacus)*, and asters *(Aster)*.

Larval Host Plant: Willows *(Salix* spp.) and aspens *(Populus tremuloides* and *P. grandidentata)* are the main hosts used by the Viceroy in West Virginia. Other poplars that are not as common, but may be used where they occur, include silverleaf poplar *(P. alba)*, cottonwood *(P. deltoides)*, and black poplar *(P. nigra)*.

Subfamily Apaturinae—Hackberry Butterflies

The Apaturinae is an Old World subfamily with approximately 50 species worldwide. Only 12 species are recognized in North America, 2 of which are found in West Virginia. Most are tropical, and those that live in temperate regions do not extend further north than southern Canada. The subfamily is a closely related group made up of medium butterflies with stout bodies. Many are brightly colored. The hackberry butterflies are rapid, erratic fliers, although they also glide. Adults prefer tree sap, fermenting fruit, or dung as a food source rather than flowers.

The larvae are unique in this group and closely resemble those of Satyrinae more than the other nymphalids. Larvae are cylindrical, tapered at both ends, and lack body spines that characterize many nymphalids. Instead, there is a pair of branched horns that arise from the top of the head and a pair of projections forming a fork on the last abdominal segment. Larvae feed on hackberries *(Celtis)* in North America. The pupa is also different from that of other nymphalids; it is flattened laterally and arched dorsally from head to tail. Although it is attached to a silk pad from its cremaster, it lies against the underside of a leaf rather than hanging free. Larvae hibernate.

Hackberry Emperor

Asterocampa celtis celtis (Boisduval and Leconte), 1834

Adult: Plate 21, Rows 2, 3
Larva: Plate 38, Row 4
Pupa: Plate 48, Row 2

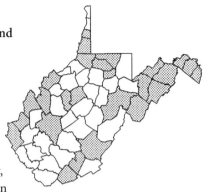

Description: Wingspan is 2 to 2½ inches (51–64 mm). Males are smaller than females and have narrow, more pointed wings. Both sexes are tan to brown, with white and dark spots on the upper surface. The character that most easily separates the Hackberry Emperor from its close relative, the Tawny Emperor *(Asterocampa clyton),* is the presence of a black eyespot ringed with white or pale orange on the outer forewing. On the hindwing there is a submarginal row of 5 to 6 black eyespots also ringed with white. The underside is completely marked in both sexes with a row of dark eyespots on the hindwing, white to dark spots, and purple-brown bars and chevrons. There are several pale spots on the forewing in rows. The single, black eyespot on the forewing is also present on the underside.

Distribution: The Hackberry Emperor is found throughout the eastern United States from southern New England west to Minnesota and south through Florida, the Gulf states, Texas, and northern Mexico. In West Virginia the butterfly can be found in scattered colonies throughout the state where its host plant occurs.

Habitat: The species inhabits woodland edges, trails, and roads, as well as old fields where hackberry trees *(Celtis* spp.) are found. The butterfly is closely associated with its host plant, hackberry, which is found in river bottoms, riparian habitat, and dry, shaley ridges of scrub oak and oak-pine forests; and the butterfly is usually found in these areas.

Life History and Habits: The Hackberry Emperor is an extremely fast flier, darting around an area and landing on the ground, a leaf of a tree, the trunk of a tree, or frequently on a person or other object. When landing on the side of a tree, the species prefers to face toward the ground. Males are active until late in the afternoon. Females stay close to the host tree landing on leaves within 6 to 12 feet of the ground or on the ground. Females lay their eggs in clusters on the underside of a host leaf, and they often perch on the underside of leaves. The Hackberry Emperor is bivoltine, with 2 broods occurring statewide. The first flight, resulting from overwintering third instar larvae, flies in May and June. The second brood flies from late July into September. Larvae from the second flight develop to the third instar and diapause in rolled leaves for the winter. The caterpillar is yellow green to green and tapered at both ends, with a forked projection at the rear. There is a yellow dorsal stripe and 3 lateral stripes, either white or yellow. The lower 2 are thin and irregular. The head is either black or green or a combination of both. There are 2 spiny, forked horns arising from the head, either green or black. Larvae are easily found in the spring on host leaves of smaller hackberries.

Nectar Sources: Hackberry Emperors obtain nutrients from tree sap, rotting fruit, dung, carrion, and soil moisture, but rarely do they visit flowers. They will also land on humans and imbibe salts from perspiration.

Larval Host Plant: The host plants for this species are the hackberries. Dwarf hackberry *(Celtis tenuifolia)* is common on the east slopes of the Alleghenies, whereas the larger hackberry or nettle-tree *(C. occidentalis)* is more widely distributed throughout the state in rich or dry soils often associated with limestone outcrops.

Tawny Emperor

Asterocampa clyton clyton (Boisduval and Leconte), 1833

Adult: Plate 21, Row 4
Larva: Plate 38, Row 4

Description: Wingspan is 2 to 2⅝ inches (51–67 mm). The upper surface is dark tawny orange with dark bars and patches, especially along the outer wing margin and wing tip. There are 2 irregular, submarginal rows of pale yellow and orange spots in the forewings. The hindwing contains a row of dark brown to black eye spots, often ringed with pale orange. The underside is brown with a strong purplish cast. There is a row of blue-centered eye spots in the hindwing. The forewing of both sexes lacks the eyespots found in the Hackberry Emperor *(A. celtis)*. Females are larger than males and lack the strongly concaved outer forewing found in the males. Females also tend to be lighter in color.

Distribution: The Tawny Emperor ranges across the southeastern United States to Mexico. Populations are rare to the north. In West Virginia the species is found in conjunction with the Hackberry Emperor since both feed on hackberry *(Celtis).* County records are scattered about the state, but the butterfly should be found wherever hackberry occurs.

Habitat: The habitat selected by this species is similar to that of the Hackberry Emperor. The species is frequently found along woodland roads or paved roads in areas where hackberry is prevalent. It also uses old wooded pastures and riparian areas where the hackberry is abundant.

Life History and Habits: The Tawny Emperor exhibits flight behavior similar to the Hackberry Emperor; however, it generally begins flying several days later in the spring. First emergents, which are males, appear in June and fly through July. Females appear later in June and fly into August. This species appears to be somewhat more secretive than the Hackberry Emperor. Females oviposit on the underside of host leaves. Eggs are laid in a stacked cluster of 200 to 500. Eggs turn gray shortly after they are deposited and hatch a few days later. A partial second brood may appear in late July and August. Some of the larvae from the first brood and all of the second brood feed into the third instar and then diapause. They are gregarious and feed together, following each other as they move from one leaf to another. Once feeding ceases, the green larvae roll a leaf or group of leaves with silk and remain inside until spring. Once they become dormant they turn a pale pink to brown. In spring, larvae ascend the host tree and begin feeding individually on new leaves. Frequently, small trees are chosen as hosts, and larvae are easily found on the leaves in the spring. Pupation occurs on the underside of a host leaf. The caterpillar closely resembles that of the Hackberry Emperor except that on the Tawny Emperor the horns on the head are more branched. Larvae are variable, but often they are pale green with a dark green dorsal stripe. There is a white lateral stripe followed by a band of darker green and 2 thin yellow stripes on pale green. The head is green. The chrysalis is pale green with fine yellow or white stripes, especially along the wing veins.

Nectar Sources: The Tawny Emperor prefers to feed from soil, dung, rotting fruit, and tree sap, similar to the Hackberry Emperor. On occasion they may visit milkweed *(Asclepias)* or other plants for nectar.

Larval Host Plant: Hackberry trees are the only host selected by the species. In West Virginia, nettle tree *(Celtis occidentalis)* and dwarf hackberry *(C. tenuifolia)* are the 2 species used.

Subfamily Satyrinae—Satyrs and Wood Nymphs

The Satyrinae are represented by 2000 species worldwide and 44 species in North America. Six species are regularly found in West Virginia, plus 1 occurrence of a subspecies. This group is composed of small to medium butterflies, either brown or blackish, with eyespots in the wings. The veins in the forewings are swollen at the base (fig. 14b). Males often have specialized scales on the forewings or hindwings.

The satyrs are slow, weak fliers and are quite sedentary. Satyrs generally stay in a small area, and none migrate. Adults have a short proboscis and prefer sap or fermenting fruit to flowers, with the exception of *Cercyonis*, which does frequently visit flowers. For the most part, satyrs are woodland or wetland species. They generally rest with wings closed and bask with wings outstretched.

The larvae lack the spines of many nymphalids, but they may have short hairs. Larvae of this group have a forked tail and often a pair of head horns. Larvae feed on monocotyledons, usually grasses or sedges. They are generally green or brown, striped longitudinally, and usually remain at the base of the host plant, feeding only at night. Larvae overwinter. Pupae have a humped thorax and 2 short anterior horns, and, lacking hooks on the cremaster, they are usually suspended close to the ground or in leaf litter.

Northern Pearly Eye

Enodia anthedon (A. H. Cook), 1936

Adult: Plate 22, Row 1
Larva: Plate 39, Row 1
Pupa: Plate 48, Row 2

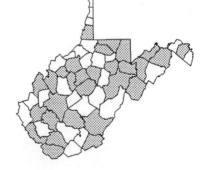

Description: Wingspan is 1⅝ to 2⅛ inches (41–54 mm). The Northern Pearly Eye is a medium soft brown butterfly with a submarginal row of dark eyespots on the upper wing surface (1 large and 2–3 small eyespots in the forewing and 5 medium to large ones in the hindwing). Females are similar to males but have larger eyespots. The wing margins in both sexes are scalloped, especially the hindwings. The underside is soft brown with a violet cast and contains dark, irregular lines traversing the wings. There is a submarginal row of gold-ringed, deep brown eyespots with a white dot in the center.

Distribution: The Northern Pearly Eye ranges from Quebec west to Manitoba and south to northern Georgia and west to Arkansas. The species is absent along the southern Atlantic and Gulf Coasts. In West Virginia the Northern Pearly Eye can probably be found in all counties in suitable habitat.

Habitat: This species prefers damp, deciduous woodlands and is often found in bottomland hardwoods and along streams. The butterfly may be encountered in heavily shaded woods or in semi-open grassy or brushy areas along woodland roads or trails.

Life History and Habits: The Northern Pearly Eye perches in wooded areas upside down on tree trunks more so than the other satyrs found in West Virginia. Males also perch on low vegetation or on the ground. They fly in an erratic, bouncing motion close to the ground and usually through vegetation and shrubs, making them somewhat difficult to capture on the wing. The species is bivoltine in West Virginia, with the first flight, resulting from overwintering larvae, appearing in mid- to late May and flying through June into early July. A second flight appears in July and flies through August into early September. The species has been observed as late as October in West Virginia, which suggests there may be a partial third brood in some localities. The large whitish eggs are deposited either singly or in small groups on blades of grass. Third instar larvae from the last brood overwinter in a rolled grass blade tied together with silk. The caterpillar is yellow green with a dark green middorsal line and 3 rows of greenish yellow lateral stripes. It has 2 pink to red-tipped tails and 2 red horns on the yellow-green head containing white lateral spurs. The chrysalis is pale green to blue green and is creamy white on the dorsal edge of the wing cases and on the head.

Nectar Sources: The Northern Pearly Eye obtains nutrients from tree saps (especially willows), fermenting fruit, dung, carrion, fungi, and damp soil. They do not visit flowers.

Larval Host Plant: Grasses are the primary host for this species. In West Virginia the species is known to use white grass *(Leersia virginica)* and panic grasses *(Panicum* spp.). Other grasses reported in the literature include bottle-brush grass *(Hystrix patula),* broad-leaved uniola *(Uniola latifolia),* plumegrass *(Erianthus alopecuroides),* and *Brachyelytrum erectum* (Opler and Krizek 1984; Iftner et al. 1992). All these grasses occur in West Virginia, with the most common being white grass. Other grasses may also be used.

Eyed Brown

Satyrodes eurydice eurydice (Johansson), 1763

Adult: Plate 22, Row 2
Larva: Plate 39, Row 1

Description: Wingspan is 1⅝ to 2 inches (41–51 mm). The Eyed Brown is a tan butterfly usually lighter tan to pale yellow near the tip of the forewing on the upper surface. A submarginal row of dark eyespots occurs in the forewing and hindwing. The underside is tan, lighter in the outer third, and contains a submarginal row of black eyespots that are ringed with yellow and have a white dot in the center. There are usually 4 eyespots in the forewing and 6 to 7 in the hindwing. There is also a sharply irregular, dark line separating the lighter and darker portions of the wings. The similar Appalachian Brown *(Satyrodes appalachia)* has a fairly regular or smooth line separating the 2 color zones.

Distribution: The Eyed Brown is a northern species that ranges across Canada to the Northwest Territories and south to Delaware, Pennsylvania, and northern Ohio and then west to North Dakota and Colorado. The species has not been recorded from West Virginia, but records in Pennsylvania are close to Preston County and the northern panhandle counties.

Habitat: The Eyed Brown prefers open sedge meadow habitats and cattail marshes.

Life History and Habits: This is a weak flying species that remains close to the ground, moving through vegetation and shrubs. Eyed Browns perch frequently and bask in the sun on vegetation with wings outstretched. There is a single brood, which flies from mid-June through early August in this region. The caterpillar is yellow green with red lateral stripes; it has 2 red-tipped horns arising from the top of the head and 2 tails. Partially grown larvae turn straw color in the fall and diapause for the winter to complete feeding the following spring. The chrysalis is green with buff stripes and a buff head, and is slender.

Nectar Sources: Like other satyrs, the Eyed Brown prefers sap, fermenting fruit, and fungi for nourishment, but on occasion it will use flowers. Flowers reportedly used include swamp milkweed *(Asclepias incarnata)*, Joe-pye weed *(Eupatorium)*, and wild bergamot *(Monarda fistulosa)* (Iftner et al. 1992; Opler and Krizek 1984).

Larval Host Plant: Sedges are reported as the normal host of the Eyed Brown. They include *Carex lacustris, C. lupulina, C. stricta, C. bromoides,* and *C. trichocarpa* (Opler and Krizek 1984; Iftner et al. 1992), all of which are found to some extent in West Virginia. Grasses may also be used since its close relative, the Appalachian Brown, feeds on grasses as well. Eyed brown larvae fed on grass in captivity.

Appalachian Brown

Satyrodes appalachia appalachia
(R. L. Chermock), 1947
Adult: Plate 22, Row 3
Larva: Plate 39, Row 1
Pupa: Plate 48, Row 2

Description: Wingspan is 1⅝ to 2⅛ inches (41–54 mm). The Appalachian Brown closely resembles its northern counterpart, the Eyed Brown *(Satyrodes eurydice).* This butterfly is a little darker brown on the upper surface, with 4 dark eyespots near the forewing border and 6 eyespots in the hindwing. The female is lighter than the male and usually has a light tan patch toward the forewing tip. The underside is soft brown, with a submarginal row of dark eyespots, doubly ringed with gold and tan. Each eyespot contains a white dot in the center. There are usually 4 eyespots in the forewing and 6 to 7 in the hindwing. The dark line separating the brown interior from the paler outer portion of the wings is fairly smooth and not jagged in this species.

Distribution: The Appalachian Brown occurs from southern New England west to Minnesota and south through the Appalachian Mountains. It ranges east along the coastal plains to central Florida, northern Alabama, and Mississippi. In West Virginia the species is widespread, found in most suitable habitats, and undoubtedly occurs in many other counties.

Habitat: The Appalachian Brown prefers grassy, wet glades in sparsely wooded areas. These lowland habitats, generally with streams running through them, are typified by dense grasses and sedges with a sparse overstory component of trees and shrubs. These sites may be at low elevations or on mountain tops.

Life History and Habits: The Appalachian Brown patrols wetland habitats in an erratic, bouncing flight through grasses, sedges, and shrubs. They fly short distances and stop frequently to perch on leafy vegetation. In the evening, adults will fly into trees to roost on leaves. Females fly through the grasses in a deliberate pattern seeking out plants on which to oviposit. Egg laying takes place anywhere from late morning (1200 hours, noon) throughout the afternoon until about 1600 hours (4:00 P.M.). Eggs may be deposited on nonhost plants—1 female was observed ovipositing on arrowleaf tearthumb (*Polygonum sagittatum*). This species is univoltine in West Virginia, with its only flight beginning in late June and flying through July into early August. The peak of the flight varies slightly from year to year but generally occurs between the second and third week of July. The caterpillar is green, striped with yellow, and has 2 red-tipped horns on the head and 2 hornlike tails. The chrysalis is green and slender. Larvae overwinter partially grown in rolled blades tied together with silk.

Nectar Sources: Sap flows, fermenting fruit, rotting fungi, and dung are the preferred food sources for the Appalachian Brown.

Larval Host Plant: Sedges are reported as the host plants for this species. In New York, *Carex lacustris* is reported as the host (Opler and Krizek 1984), and *Carex stricta* is frequently used as a host in Connecticut, New Jersey, and Pennsylvania (Schweitzer, personal observation). In West Virginia the Appalachian Brown also uses grasses as hosts. Fowl mannagrass (*Glyceria striata*) is a known host for the species.

Gemmed Satyr

Cyllopsis gemma gemma (Hübner), 1818
Adult: Plate 22, Row 4
Larva: Plate 39, Row 2
Pupa: Plate 48, Row 3

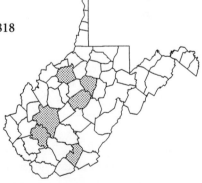

Description: Wingspan is 1¼ to 1⅝ inches (32–40 mm). The Gemmed Satyr is a small soft brown butterfly with only a small dark patch in the margin of the hindwing on the upperside. The underside is pale brown with 2 to 3 dark, irregular lines across the wings. Along the hindwing margin are a black patch ringed in gold and several silver spots.

Distribution: This is a southern species that ranges from Virginia south to Florida and west to Oklahoma, Texas, and into Mexico. In West Virginia the species has been found in a few southern and west-central counties. The Gemmed Satyr undoubtedly inhabits many other southern and western counties. The species has been found in Boone, Braxton, Kanawha, Lewis, Ritchie, and Summers Counties. The species is fairly common on the ridges above Stonecoal Lake Wildlife Management Area in Lewis County and Fork Creek Wildlife Management Area in Boone County.

Habitat: The Gemmed Satyr is a woodland species that prefers moist to wet, semi-open areas along streams and trails. The butterfly can be found in bottomland hardwoods or on ridge tops in West Virginia.

Life History and Habits: Gemmed Satyr males patrol in an erratic, bouncing flight close to the ground through woodland vegetation, perching periodically on vegetation or on dead leaves on the forest floor. They are somewhat difficult to pursue through vegetation, as are most of the wood nymphs. At least 2 to 3 broods occur in West Virginia. First flight individuals appear in mid-April and fly into May but may appear as early as March in some years. A second brood appears in late June and flies through July. A partial third flight occurs in some areas in late August and early September. The caterpillar varies in color among the spring, summer, and fall broods. In the summer the larva is pale green; in the fall it is light brown. Both forms are striped with pale lines and have 2 brown to red horns arising from the head and 2 anal tails. The head is striped with brown and cream. The chrysalis is brown or green with 2 pointed projections from the head. Eggs are pale green, small, and deposited on grass blades.

Nectar Sources: The Gemmed Satyr feeds mostly on damp soil, dung, fungi, tree sap, and fermenting fruit.

Larval Host Plant: The Gemmed Satyr selects grasses as its hosts. Bermuda grass *(Cynodon dactylon)* has been reported as a host plant (Opler and Krizek 1984). Since this grass occurs only rarely in a few counties in West Virginia, other grasses are undoubtedly used.

Carolina Satyr

Hermeuptychia sosybius (Fabricius), 1793

Adult: Plate 22, Row 4
Larva: Plate 39, Row 2
Pupa: Plate 48, Row 3

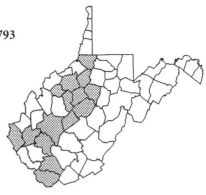

Description: Wingspan is 1⅛ to 1½ inches (28–38 mm). The Carolina Satyr is a small butterfly with plain, brown, unmarked wings on the upper surface. The underside is light brown, with 2 narrow, wavy lines across the midwings and a submarginal row of small yellow-ringed eyespots (4–5 in the forewing and 6 in the hindwing). Only 2 eyespots are large and distinct in the hindwing.

Distribution: This butterfly occurs across the southern United States from New Jersey west to south Texas and Mexico. In West Virginia it is found in the southern and western counties. There are no reports of the species inhabiting the mountainous region of the central and eastern portions of the state. The Carolina Satyr is generally more common than the Gemmed Satyr *(Cyllopsis gemma)* and is frequently found in the same areas. It is known to occur in Lewis Wetzel Wildlife Management Area in Wetzel County, Stonecoal Lake Wildlife Management Area in Lewis County, Elk River Wildlife Management Area in Braxton County, and Fork Creek Wildlife Management Area in Boone County, as well as other areas throughout the region.

Habitat: The Carolina Satyr is a woodland inhabitant often found along trails and roads near streams in low-lying areas. It is also found in woodland openings where there is an abundance of grass. The species may be quite common in many of the areas it inhabits.

Life History and Habits: Males patrol for females along roads, trails, or woodland openings in a slow, bouncing flight close to the ground. They perch frequently on the forest floor or on low vegetation. Mating and egg laying take place from late morning until at least midafternoon. In West Virginia the Carolina Satyr is multibrooded. The first flight usually begins in April and extends through May and into June. A flight of fresh individuals, which may be a second brood, occurs in late June and early July. Another flight appears in late July and continues into mid-August, and a fourth flight appears from late August into September. Whether there are 4 separate broods or 2 broods with extended flight periods has not been determined, but the species is present throughout most of the season from April to September. Eggs are pale green, small, and deposited on grass blades. The caterpillar is pale green with dark green, longitudinal stripes and is covered with short yellow hairs. The chrysalis is green, yellow green on the abdomen, and has 2 dorsal ridges with black dots on each side and along the outer margin of the wing cases.

Nectar Sources: This species is attracted to sap flows, fermenting fruit, and dung for nutrients as are the other satyrs. They also imbibe moisture and minerals from the soil or sand.

Larval Host Plant: The Carolina Satyr uses grasses as its hosts. In captivity it will feed on Kentucky bluegrass *(Poa pratensis)* as well as Bermuda grass *(Cynodon dactylon).* Various grasses in the genus *Poa,* as well as other species, probably serve as hosts in West Virginia.

Little Wood Satyr

Megisto cymela (Cramer), 1777
Adult: Plate 22, Row 5
Larva: Plate 39, Row 3
Pupa: Plate 48, Row 3

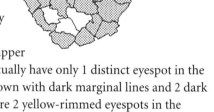

Description: Wingspan is 1⅜ to 1⅞ inches (35–48 mm). The Little Wood Satyr is a soft brown butterfly characterized by 2 pronounced eyespots rimmed in yellow on the upper surface of each wing; males may actually have only 1 distinct eyespot in the hindwing. The underside is pale brown with dark marginal lines and 2 dark lines crossing the midwing. There are 2 yellow-rimmed eyespots in the forewing and 2 to 3 in the hindwing.

Distribution: This butterfly ranges from New England south into the Florida peninsula and west to the central Plains and Colorado. In West Virginia the species is found statewide, with records from most counties.

Habitat: The Little Wood Satyr is found in tall, grassy fields, brushy, open areas, woodland edges, clearings, and along roads and trails. The species prefers uncut grassy habitats in close proximity to woodlands.

Life History and Habits: Males and females are frequently encountered flying methodically in a slow, bouncing flight through tall grasses and in and out of forest edges in brushy habitat. Males patrol for females in this manner. The butterflies perch on low vegetation, leaves of trees and shrubs, or even on the ground. Females can be observed from late morning into late afternoon (1600 hours, 4:00 P.M.) fluttering through field grasses, stopping periodically, and walking down into the base of grass clumps to oviposit. A single, pale green egg is laid each time on a live or dead grass blade or other nearby object. Larvae feed at night. The Little Wood Satyr is single-brooded in West Virginia; however, 2 peaks in its flight occur, which gives the appearance of 2 flights. Adults begin to emerge in early May and continue to fly into mid-July. The flight peaks in late May and early June and then again from late June to mid-July. Extreme dates for the flight are from April 23 to August 13. Larvae feed to the third or fourth instar and then diapause for the winter. The caterpillar is pale brown with brown lateral blotches and a dark stripe. The body is covered with small whitish tubercles. The head and anal forks are brown to grayish white. The chrysalis is yellow brown with lateral brown stripes and dots along the abdomen.

Nectar Sources: The Little Wood Satyr feeds on tree sap, fermenting fruit, fungi, aphid honeydew secretions, dung, and wet soil. On occasion adults will visit flowers and have been observed at milkweed *(Asclepias),* ox-eye daisy *(Chrysanthemum leucanthemum),* white sweet clover *(Melilotus alba),* dewberry *(Rubus* spp.), viburnum *(Viburnum* spp.), and staghorn sumac *(Rhus typhina)* (Iftner et al. 1992; Opler and Krizek 1984).

Larval Host Plant: Various grasses are used as hosts by the Little Wood Satyr. Females have been observed ovipositing on *Poa* spp. in West Virginia. In New York, larvae use orchard grass *(Dactylis glomerata)* (Opler and Krizek 1984), which is also common in West Virginia.

Common Wood Nymph

Cercyonis pegala pegala (Fabricius), 1775

Adult: Plate 23, Row 1
Larva: Plate 39, Row 3
Pupa: Plate 49, Row 1

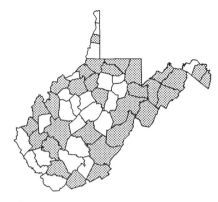

Description: Wingspan is 1⅞ to 2⅞ inches (48–73 mm). The Common Wood Nymph is a medium light to dark brown butterfly with 2 large eyespots in the outer forewing and usually a small eyespot in the hindwing on the upperside. There is a large yellow to orange patch surrounding the eyespots in the forewing. The hindwing margin is scalloped. The underside is medium to dark brown, finely striated with the same pattern in the forewing as the upperside, and several submarginal eyespots (usually 6) occur in the hindwing.

Distribution: The Common Wood Nymph occurs throughout eastern North America from southern Canada to central Florida and west to Kansas and central Texas. The species occurs throughout West Virginia and should be readily found in every county.

Habitat: The Common Wood Nymph prefers tall grass or shrubby, open areas usually in wet meadows or along streams. However, it is also readily encountered in dry, upland fields. This species prefers larger openings than the Little Wood Satyr *(Megisto cymela)* but can also be found in wooded areas and along woodland roads, trails, and forest edges.

Life History and Habits: Males patrol through grasses and along woodland edges in a low, bouncing flight. They fly through and around shrubs that are in their path. When disturbed they will fly up into trees or rapidly fly a short distance and land in the grass. They perch frequently in the grass or on low vegetation. Females perch more and fly less than males. Females are also longer-lived and remain active into late summer when the males have disappeared. The Common Wood Nymph is univoltine throughout its range, with a single flight each year. In West Virginia adults begin appearing in mid-June and continue their flight into late September. The peak of the flight occurs in July and early August. Eggs are deposited singly on the host plant, and newly hatched larvae diapause at the base of the plant for the winter. Feeding takes place in the spring. The caterpillar is green to yellow green, with a dark green dorsal stripe and 2 white to yellow lateral stripes. It has a green head and 2 red-tipped tails and is covered with fine white hairs. The chrysalis is yellow green to green, with white edging on the upper portion of the wing cases and the dorsal surface.

Nectar Sources: The Common Wood Nymph prefers sap flows, fermenting fruit, and dung as its food sources, but it does visit flowers more readily than the other satyrs. Favored flowers include milkweed *(Asclepias),* ox-eyed daisy *(Chrysanthemum leucanthemum),* black-eyed Susan *(Rudbeckia hirta),* Queen Anne's lace *(Daucus carota),* clovers *(Trifolium),* teasel *(Dipsacus),* ironweed *(Vernonia),* Joe-pye weed *(Eupatorium),* and wild bergamot *(Monarda fistulosa).*

Larval Host Plant: Various grasses are used as hosts for this species in West Virginia. These include poverty oatgrass *(Danthonia spicata),* purpletop *(Triodia flava),* bluestem grass *(Andropogon* spp.), and bluegrass *(Poa* spp.), as well as other grasses.

Dull-eyed Grayling

Cercyonis pegala nephele (W. Kirby), 1837

Adult: Plate 23, Row 2

Description: Wingspan is 1⅞ to 2½ inches (48–64 mm). The Dull-eyed Grayling is similar to the Common Wood Nymph *(Cercyonis p. pegala)* in size and appearance except that it lacks the yellow to orange forewing patch. In this subspecies, the patch is brown, often with faint yellow to orange rings around the eyespots.

Distribution: The Dull-eyed Grayling inhabits the more northern portion of the range of the Common Wood Nymph. It is rarely found in West Virginia, but on occasion a colony may establish itself for 2 to 3 years. The only record thus far is of a small colony in Marion County.

Habitat: This butterfly is found in habitats similar to those of the Common Wood Nymph and usually prefers wet, brushy, bottomland areas.

Life History and Habits: Refer to the Common Wood Nymph for details since both subspecies behave similarly.

Nectar Sources: Tree sap and fermenting fruit, as well as soil moisture, are favored foods for the species. Flowers are visited more frequently than they are by many of the satyrs. Ox-eye daisy *(Chrysanthemum leucanthemum)* is preferred, although milkweeds *(Asclepias)* and others are also used.

Larval Host Plant: Various grasses are selected as hosts by the Dull-eyed Grayling.

Subfamily Danainae—Milkweed Butterflies

The Danainae is a small tropical group of large butterflies represented by 200 species worldwide and only 4 species in North America, 3 of which are found in the South. The Monarch *(Danaus plexippus),* the only Danainae found in West Virginia, is the world's strongest migratory species, migrating to central Mexico in the fall to avoid cold weather. The species cannot withstand subfreezing temperatures but does migrate northward to southern Canada during the warmer seasons. Butterflies within this subfamily are strong fliers, although their flight is generally slow. Gliding is a regular part of their flight behavior. This group lacks the antennal scales found in other nymphalids. Males have either pencil-like tufts of long specialized scales near the tip of the abdomen or a scent gland along the vein in the hindwing; these produce pheromones used in mating. In mated pairs the male carries the female.

Larvae of this group feed on plants in the milkweed family (Asclepiadaceae) or the dogbane family (Apocynaceae), which produce cardiac glycosides (heart poisons that are toxic to vertebrates). These toxins are stored in the body of the larvae and passed on to the adults. As a result, the Danainae are mimicked by other species. In this region the Viceroy *(Limenitis archippus),* a willow *(Salix)* or aspen *(Populus)* feeder, mimics the Monarch. Some swallowtail *(Papilio* spp.) larvae also mimic Danainae larvae.

The larvae are brightly colored, usually a warning of toxicity to predators, and have long fleshy tubercles from both ends of the body. The pupa is stout. Adults diapause during periods of adversity.

Monarch

Danaus plexippus (Linnaeus), 1758

Adult: Plate 23, Rows 3, 4
Larva: Plate 39, Row 4
Pupa: Plate 49, Row 1

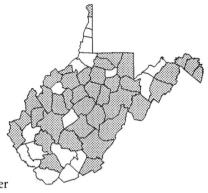

Description: Wingspan is 3½ to 4
inches (89–102 mm). The Monarch
is a large tawny-orange butterfly with
black veins and black wing borders
on the upper surface. Males are brighter
orange than females. There is a series of pale orange to white spots in
the forewing and along the wing borders. On the underside the hindwings are
pale burnt orange with heavy, black veins and 2 rows of cream to white spots
in the black borders. The forewing is orange to pinkish, with cream to white
spots near the tip and in the black border. Males have a noticeable scent patch
that appears as an enlarged, black spot along the vein in the lower hindwing.

Distribution: The Monarch is a summer resident from southern Canada across
the United States and into Mexico and Central and South America. Resident
populations also occur in a few Pacific Islands, including Hawaii and
Australia. Most North American populations winter in central Mexico,
although a few winter along the southern California coast and perhaps the
Gulf Coast as well as the Caribbean Islands.

Habitat: The Monarch prefers open habitats and may be found in fields,
pastures, wet meadows, abandoned farms, roadsides, and yards. Monarchs are
likely to be found wherever open areas occur with milkweed *(Asclepias).* In
West Virginia the Monarch occurs statewide.

Life History and Habits: The Monarch is a true migratory species. The fall
brood is programmed to migrate southward to areas where temperatures are
moderated. Migratory monarchs generally follow river courses and mountain
valleys, flying southwestward at considerable heights (from 20–150 ft. or
more). They nectar frequently during the flight and roost in trees at night.
Most Monarchs fly across the Gulf of Mexico to the Sierra Madre Mountains
in central Mexico where they roost by the millions, hanging from fir tree
limbs. A small group of eastern Monarchs migrate south through Florida to
the Caribbean Islands, and another group of western butterflies winters in
southern California. A few probably winter along the Gulf Coast in Florida
and Texas as well (Howe 1975; Scott 1986). By late February or early March,

much of the Monarch's fat reserves have been depleted, and the hibernating Monarchs begin seeking out nectar sources as they begin the return trip. Their reproductive organs develop, and mating occurs as they start northward. Probably no Monarchs return to the northern parts of their range from Mexico. Most produce a generation once they return to the southern United States and the resulting brood reinvades the northern states. Monarchs return to West Virginia, usually in May, at which time eggs are deposited singly on leaves of the host plants. The resulting brood flies during June and early July. A second brood appears in August, and a third brood, which is migratory, appears in September. Migrating Monarchs may be seen into November in small numbers, but the peak of the migration through West Virginia occurs in September and early October. Monarch larvae feed and rest on the leaves of milkweed plants. Because milkweeds contain toxins that are distasteful to birds and will actually make them ill, the larvae are seldom eaten. Their bright color pattern also serves as a warning to predators. The caterpillar is striped traversely with yellow, black, and white on each segment and has a white-and-black striped head. There are 2 long, fleshy, black tubercles projecting from the dorsal surface behind the head and at the posterior end. The chrysalis is pale green, stout, and has a gold dorsal band around the abdomen.

Nectar Sources: The Monarch visits many plants for nectar, including milkweed *(Asclepias)*, red clover *(Trifolium pratense)*, dogbane *(Apocynum)*, goldenrod *(Solidago)*, asters *(Aster)*, Joe-pye weed *(Eupatorium)*, ironweed *(Vernonia)*, thistle *(Cirsium)*, teasel *(Dipsacus)*, and many others. Around home gardens they readily feed on lilac *(Syringa)*, butterfly bush *(Buddleja)*, marigolds *(Tagetes)*, and chrysanthemums *(Chrysanthemum)*.

Larval Host Plant: Milkweeds are the host for the Monarch butterfly. The most commonly used milkweeds are common milkweed *(Asclepias syriaca)* and swamp milkweed *(A. incarnata)*, although butterfly weed *(A. tuberosa)*, four-leaved milkweed *(A. quadrifolia)*, and poke milkweed *(A. exaltata)* are also used on occasion, as well as other, less common milkweeds.

12

Superfamily Hesperioidae

Family Hesperiidae—Skippers

Skippers number approximately 3600 species worldwide, with 2300 found in the Americas. They are basically a tropical group, with most of the species occurring in the American tropics. Of the 292 species occurring in North America (Miller and Brown 1981), 45 species have been found in West Virginia.

Skippers are strikingly different from other butterflies; they are more robust, with broad heads and stout bodies. The antennae are widely separated, with the club tip curved or hooked. Skippers are generally small to medium insects with 6 well-developed legs. The Silver-spotted Skipper *(Epargyreus clarus)* is the only species in West Virginia that might be considered moderately large (wingspan is 2 in. plus). In general, skippers are not brightly colored and are either black, brown, orange, or yellow, with varying amounts of white.

Because of their well-developed and heavy flight muscles, skippers are powerful and rapid fliers, and they fly in a darting or skipping fashion—hence the name "skippers." When basking, skippers either hold their wings separated with the forewings just off the vertical plane and the hindwings in a horizontal plane, or all wings are fully extended.

Larvae are generally tapered at both ends and have a constricted neck and first thoracic segment for ease of manipulation when constructing leaf shelters or rolled grass stem shelters. Larvae lack spines and horns but are usually covered with fine hairs. The head is often quite pubescent. Larvae live in leaf shelters constructed by tying a leaf together with silk, or in rolled grass blades, or in silk shelters in grass clumps. Most skippers overwinter in the larval stage in closed shelters. The pupa is generally streamline and often covered with a waxy or powdery bloom. Pupation usually occurs in shelters.

The skippers found in West Virginia are divided into 2 subfamilies: the

Pyrginae (open-winged skippers) and the Hesperiinae (branded skippers). A discussion of each subfamily is presented at the respective introduction.

Many collectors refuse to collect or pay much attention to skippers for several reasons. Being rapid and strong flyers they are hard to capture. They are also very difficult to handle in a net without damaging the wings. When capturing skippers, one must be patient and stalk them carefully and methodically. Since they do not fly far, it is sometimes easier to capture them at nectar plants. Some skippers can be collected directly in a killing jar from the flower, others captured by net are best handled by quickly putting them in a fast-acting killing jar, which minimizes the damage to their wings. Skippers can also be difficult to identify because many species closely resemble each other. If one were identifying many hundreds of species of skippers, a microscope or at least a hand lens would be a necessity. However, the 45 species represented in West Virginia are distinct enough that almost all of them can be distinguished by visible characteristics. Only a couple of species are so similar that gross examination alone is insufficient to separate them, especially the females. Fortunately, these similar appearing species occupy different habitats, so the collector or enthusiast can sort them by noting their habitat.

Skippers are a challenge and should be considered by the serious observer as an integral part of West Virginia's butterfly fauna. Because they comprise a third of the total number of species within the state, they should not be overlooked.

For those who would like to pursue other literature on skippers, the following references are provided in the bibliography: MacNeill (1975), Lindsey et al. (1931), Burns (1964), and Evans (1951–55).

Subfamily Pyrginae—Open-winged Skippers

In West Virginia the subfamily Pyrginae is represented by 19 species of skippers, 16 of which are regular inhabitants of the state. Three species have approached West Virginia's borders but have not been reported from the state as yet. This group includes skippers that vary in size from small to the largest West Virginia skipper. Most are brown to black, with various markings. A few have large patches of white, silver, or gold, and still others are checkered black and white. Antennal clubs of this group are sickle- or boomerang-shaped.

FIG. 15.

(a) Pyrginae forewing;

(b) Hesperiinae forewing.

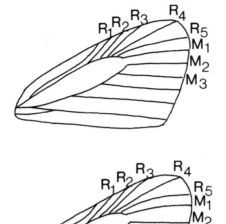

Vein M_2 of the forewing is only slightly curved at the base and arises midway between M_1 and M_3 (fig. 15a). The tibiae of the front legs lack spines; however, males of several species in this group contain specialized tufts of hair on the hind tibia. Another characteristic of males in some species is the presence of a costal fold in the forewing that contains scent scales. This group lacks the male stigma, or sex brand, found in the Hesperiinae. In mated pairs, the female usually carries the male when startled into flight.

Most Pyrginae males are perchers, but some also patrol, especially the *Pyrgus* genus. Pyrginae often rest with their wings wide open, basking on the ground. They visit flowers readily, although some frequent wet, muddy spots or dung. The pyrgines utilize a variety of dicotyledonous plants as larval hosts. Most deposit their eggs singly on the host plant, except for the Golden-banded Skipper *(Autochton cellus)*, which deposits its eggs in groups, and the Silver-spotted Skipper *(Epargyreus clarus)*, which often lays its eggs on nearby nonhost plants. The eggs of this group are drum-shaped or ovoid, with strong vertical ribs. Larvae are robust, with either rounded or heart-shaped heads. Some have 2 colored spots on the face. Larvae live in leaf shelters and pupate in loose cocoons constructed by pulling several leaves together.

Silver-spotted Skipper

Epargyreus clarus (Cramer), 1775

Adult: Plate 24, Row 1
Larva: Plate 39, Row 4
Pupa: Plate 49, Row 1

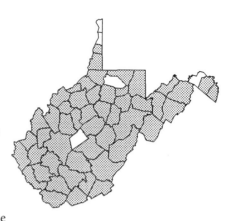

Description: Wingspan is 1¾ to 2⅜ inches (44–60 mm). The Silver-spotted Skipper is West Virginia's largest skipper. It is brown, with pointed forewings that contain a large translucent gold patch. On the underside of the hindwing is a large conspicuous white patch near the center, which makes the butterfly easily identifiable. The wing margins are frosted with lavender.

Distribution: The Silver-spotted Skipper is widely distributed throughout North America, ranging from southern Quebec west to British Columbia and south from Florida west to Baja California. In West Virginia it can be expected to occur in every county.

Habitat: This butterfly is found in most disturbed second growth forests or open areas of the state. It is especially common in areas where black locust *(Robinia pseudo acacia),* its preferred host food plant, abounds.

Life History and Habits: Males perch on leaves or twigs from a few to several feet above the ground and will pursue any large insect that passes nearby. They have a rapid, darting flight and are sometimes difficult to follow. The female usually deposits a single, green egg on a leaf of the host plant. The Silver-spotted Skipper is bivoltine, with at least 2 generations occurring in West Virginia. There may be a partial third brood in some areas. Adults first appear in late May and fly through June and then appear again in July in large numbers. The flight periods are long and overlap to the point where the skipper appears to be present throughout the entire summer. A partial third brood may appear in late August. Newly hatched caterpillars make leaf shelters by cutting a section of the leaf and then folding it over on the upper surface. The caterpillar lives under the folded leaf. As the larva grows, it moves and constructs a new shelter. Larger instars pull several leaves together to form shelters. The caterpillar is yellow with transverse dark stripes. The head is red brown with 2 red-orange spots low on the front. The chrysalis is brown with some lighter and darker markings. The last brood overwinters in the pupal stage.

Nectar Sources: The Silver-spotted Skipper nectars at a wide variety of flowers. Generally, pink, red, or purple flowers are selected, although white or cream flowers are also visited. Many of the summer flowers, such as ironweed *(Vernonia),* Joe-pye weed *(Eupatorium),* clovers *(Trifolium),* and dogbane *(Apocynum),* are widely used. This skipper is commonly seen in flower gardens around homes.

Larval Host Plant: Young shoots of black locust *(Robinia pseudo-acacia)* are the preferred host in West Virginia, although honeylocust *(Gleditsia triacanthos)* and other legumes, such as sticktights *(Desmodium* spp.), groundnut *(Apios americana),* lespedeza *(Lespedeza* spp.), and kudzu *(Pueraria lobata),* are also used.

Long-tailed Skipper

Urbanus proteus proteus (Linnaeus), 1758

Adult: Plate 30, Row 6
Larva: Plate 40, Row 1

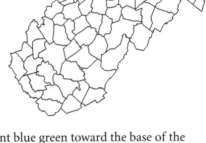

Description: Wingspan is 1½ to 2 inches (38–51 mm). The Long-tailed Skipper is a large brown skipper characterized by long tails. It is brown above with several glassy white windows in the forewings and iridescent blue green toward the base of the wings. The underside is brown, with white spots in the forewing and dark brown blotches and dark bands in the hindwing.

Distribution: This species is found in the southern portions of the Gulf states from Florida to Mexico and then south to Argentina. The Long-tailed Skipper immigrates into northern areas during summer and has been reported as far north as Long Island, New York. In the last few years it has approached West Virginia's border, being found in Maryland and in Pennsylvania at Pittsburgh. It has not been reported from West Virginia but is a likely species to watch for in the future.

Habitat: The Long-tailed Skipper prefers open, disturbed areas, especially brushy fields and woodland edges.

Life History and Habits: Males perch on low vegetation or leaves of shrubs and trees along forest edges awaiting females. They are rapid fliers. They readily visit flowers and are most often found nectaring in fields. The species has 2 to 3 broods in its southern habitat beginning in the spring and continuing into the fall. In this region, individuals are not likely to be seen until summer, and frequently not until July or August, when they could produce a single brood. Females lay their pale yellow eggs singly or in small groups of 2 to 6 on the underside of host leaves. Young larvae live in folded leaves on the host plant. As they grow, 2 or 3 leaves are tied together with silk. The caterpillar is yellow green, with yellow to brownish longitudinal stripes and black speckling. The head is reddish brown and black, with 2 orange or brownish spots on the lower portion of the face. An orange dash occurs at the posterior end of the lateral line, and the prolegs are orange. The chrysalis is brown with a white, powdery bloom.

Nectar Sources: Long-tailed Skippers feed at a variety of field flowers that include several composites as well as other species.

Larval Host Plant: Reported hosts include a variety of climbing legumes, such as beggar's ticks *(Desmodium* spp.), hog peanut *(Amphicarpa bracteata),* beans *(Phaseolus* spp.), butterfly pea *(Clitoria mariana),* and wisteria *(Wisteria* spp.).

Golden-banded Skipper

Autochton cellus (Boisduval and LeConte), 1837
Adult: Plate 24, Row 2

Description: Wingspan is 1⅝ to 2 inches (41–54 mm). The Golden-banded Skipper is a large brown butterfly with rounded wings; it has a large translucent gold band crossing the forewing and extending almost to its outer margin. Unlike the Silver-spotted Skipper *(Epargyreus clarus),* no white patch occurs on the hindwings. The underside of the hindwings is brown with 2 dark, irregular bands crossing each wing. Grayish white scales along the outer margin of the ventral hindwing give it a frosted appearance. The male has a small white ring on each antenna just below the club.

Distribution: Although the Golden-banded Skipper is widely distributed geographically, it is usually rare and local throughout its range. It is found in a broad band from Pennsylvania southwest to Texas, southern Arizona, and south into Mexico. In the East, it extends to the Gulf states and northern Florida. In West Virginia, local populations have been reported from a tri-county area of Boone, Kanawha, and Lincoln—in particular, Fork Creek Wildlife Management Area, Boone County, and Big Ugly Wildlife Management Area, Lincoln County. However, other small colonies are certain to occur elsewhere in West Virginia in suitable habitat. This is a rare species that should be collected sparingly.

Habitat: The Golden-banded Skipper is usually found in moist, wooded areas either along streams or wetlands. In southern West Virginia it is found along trails or roads in steep, shaded hollows.

Life History and Habits: The flight of the Golden-banded Skipper is rapid and darting. Males usually perch on the leaves of low vegetation or shrubs and sip moisture from wet areas along sandy roads. In West Virginia the skipper is probably univoltine, with a single flight occurring in May and extending through June. Farther south a partial second brood has been reported. Unlike most skippers, the yellow eggs are deposited in strings of 2 to 7 on the host plant. Larvae feed at night, and during the day they stay in nests made by tying leaves together with silk. The caterpillar is bright yellow green with small yellow dots and a broad, yellow lateral line. The head is red brown with 2 round, yellow spots on the front (Opler and Krizek 1984). The chrysalis turns from green to brown within a few hours (Clark 1936). The skipper hibernates in the pupal stage.

Nectar Sources: Most woodland flowering plants that are in bloom in midsummer are visited. A few include blackberry *(Rubus)*, hydrangea *(Hydrangea arborescens)*, and dogbane *(Apocynum)*.

Larval Host Plant: The only recorded host plant in West Virginia for the Golden-banded Skipper is hogpeanut *(Amphicarpa bracteata)*.

Hoary Edge

Achalarus lyciades (Geyer), 1832

Adult: Plate 24, Row 3
Larva: Plate 40, Row 1

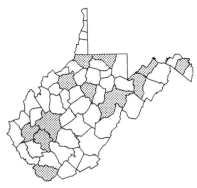

Description: Wingspan is 1½ to 1¾ inches (38–44 mm). Although the Hoary Edge is similar to the Silver-spotted Skipper *(Epargyreus clarus)*, its wings are less angular. The wings are dark brown above; the forewing contains 4 or 5 translucent, almost square, golden spots. The underside of the hindwing is mottled and contains a large patch of white frosting along the outer margin. The hindwing fringes are heavily checkered.

Distribution: The Hoary Edge ranges from southern New England west to southern Minnesota and south to northern Florida and through the Gulf states to eastern Texas. In West Virginia, scattered records have been reported from several counties. This skipper probably occurs in most West Virginia counties, but it occurs in restricted populations and is not often encountered.

Habitat: The Hoary Edge can be found in wooded areas along roads but is most often encountered in open woodlands and adjacent brushy areas. It nectars readily in open fields where red or white clover *(Trifolium)* is found.

Life History and Habits: In West Virginia the Hoary Edge is generally univoltine at higher elevations, with a flight occurring in late May and extending through June. In warmer areas of the state it produces a partial second brood, with some individuals being found in July and August. Males perch in forest openings or along woodland roads. They may perch either on a twig or leaf up to several feet above the ground, or on the ground in bare spots. They are rapid fliers and readily chase other butterflies or insects. Females deposit a single, whitish egg on the leaf of the host plant. Hosts are usually selected in shaded areas. The caterpillar is dark green with a bluish dorsal stripe, a narrow, orange lateral stripe, and a profuse scattering of yellowish speckling. The head is black. The chrysalis is light brown with both dark and yellowish patches.

Nectar Sources: The Hoary Edge visits a wide variety of nectar plants; red clover *(Trifolium pratense),* white clover *(T. ripens),* dogbane *(Apocynum),* and common milkweed *(Asclepias)* are the most commonly used plants, but Japanese honeysuckle *(Lonicera japonica)* and others are also used.

Larval Host Plant: Large-leaved legumes are preferred hosts, and in West Virginia sticktights *(Desmodium* spp.) are the usual host. Wild indigo *(Baptisia tinctoria)* and bush clover *(Lespedeza* spp.) have been reported as possible hosts elsewhere, but there is no evidence that they are used in West Virginia.

Northern Cloudywing

Thorybes pylades (Scudder), 1870
Adult: Plate 24, Row 4
Larva: Plate 40, Row 2

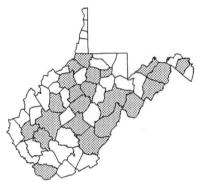

Description: Wingspan is 1¼ to 1¾ inches (32–44 mm). Northern Cloudywings are medium brown skippers. The wings of the male Northern Cloudywing are distinctive—they possess a fold in the costal margin of the forewing that the other 2 species *(Thorybe bathyllus* and *T. confusis)* lack. The hyaline spots in the forewing tend to be smaller than in *T. bathyllus,* and they are nonaligned. The outer fringe of the forewing is checkered. On the underside of the hindwing there are 2 dark brown bands crossing the wing. The bands are finely outlined with irregular, dark brown lines. The outer margin of the wing is slightly frosted with gray.

Distribution: The Northern Cloudywing ranges from Nova Scotia west to British Columbia and south to Florida, the Gulf states, Texas, and Mexico. It is the most common and widely distributed of the cloudywing skippers. Although records in West Virginia are scattered throughout several eastern and central counties, this skipper can be expected to be found throughout the state in most counties.

Habitat: The Northern Cloudywing is most often found in open or scrubby woodland habitats, especially along woodland edges, fields, brushy roadsides, meadows, and clearings.

Life History and Habits: The Northern Cloudywing is a rapid flier. Males perch on brushy vegetation, close to the ground, along trails or in clearings awaiting females, and occasionally use hilltops. Freshly emerged males often sip minerals at wet spots along woodland roads or streams. *T. pylades* is univoltine in West Virginia, with adults appearing in mid-May and flying through June and possibly into early July. The egg is pale greenish white. The caterpillar is dark green to maroon green, with a dark maroon middorsal stripe and 2 pale reddish or salmon lateral stripes. The body is covered with small yellow-orange tubercles bearing short hairs. The head is dark maroon to black and covered with fine pale hairs. Larvae live in leaf shelters constructed by tying leaves together with silk. Larvae overwinter in a leaf shelter. The chrysalis is dark brown, tan, and olive mottled with black.

Nectar Sources: The Northern Cloudywing is frequently found nectaring with the Southern Cloudywing. A wide variety of field plants are visited to obtain nectar during June. Red clover *(Trifolium pratense)* is visited regularly along roadsides and open fields. Dogbane *(Apocynum)*, milkweed *(Asclepias)*, vetch *(Vicia)*, Japanese honeysuckle *(Lonicera japonica)*, thistle *(Cirsium)*, and others are also visited.

Larval Host Plant: A variety of legumes are used as larval hosts. Sticktights *(Desmodium* spp.) and bush clover *(Lespedeza* spp.) are commonly selected hosts in West Virginia; however, various clovers *(Trifolium* spp.), alfalfa *(Medicago* spp.), and vetch *(Vicia* spp.) may also be used.

Southern Cloudywing

Thorybes bathyllus (J. E. Smith), 1797

Adult: Plate 24, Row 5
Larva: Plate 40, Row 2

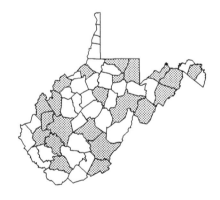

Description: Wingspan is 1¼ to 1⅝ inches (32–41 mm). The Southern Cloudywing is a medium brown skipper with several hyaline spots in the forewing, aligned in more of a straight row than in the Northern Cloudywing *(T. pylades)*. The cell spot in this species is large and hourglass-shaped. The hindwing forms a rudimentary tail. The wing fringes are light buff and checkered. The underside of the hindwings contains 2 darker brown cross bands and is slightly frosted along the outer margin. Males lack a costal fold.

Distribution: The Southern Cloudywing ranges from southern New England west to southern Ontario and Minnesota and then south to Colorado and, rarely, northern New Mexico. In the East it ranges south to Florida, the Gulf states, and Texas. This species is widespread in West Virginia and has been reported from almost half the counties. The skipper should be found in all counties of the state.

Habitat: The Southern Cloudywing is a skipper of open habitats using dry meadows, hayfields, power- and gas-line right-of-ways, and roadsides.

Life History and Habits: The Southern Cloudywing is a rapid, erratic flier. Males perch near the ground on hill tops or in open fields on the tips of tall grass or twigs of shrubs. They use the same perch repeatedly for several days. Females lay a single, pale green egg on a leaf of the host plant. Females have been observed egg laying during the afternoon hours (1530 hours, 3:30 p.m.). This species is bivoltine in West Virginia, with its first flight in May and June and a second flight in late July and August. The caterpillar is greenish brown, with light dorsal and lateral lines and a black head covered with short golden hairs. Caterpillars live in a leaf shelter made by tying leaves together with silk. The chrysalis is brown. The skipper hibernates as a fully grown larva.

Nectar Sources: Southern Cloudywings visit a wide variety of nectar plants found in open areas. These include dogbane *(Apocynum),* common milkweed *(Asclepias syriaca),* red clover *(Trifolium pratense),* crown vetch *(Coronilla varia),* viper's bugloss *(Echium vulgare),* Joe-pye weed *(Eupatorium),* and ironweed *(Vernonia).*

Larval Host Plant: In West Virginia various legumes are selected as hosts, such as sticktights *(Desmodium* spp.) and bush clover *(Lespedeza).* Wild bean *(Strophostyles helvola),* wild kidney bean *(Phaseolus polystachios),* ground nut *(Apios americana),* butterfly pea *(Clitoria mariana),* hogpeanut *(Amphicarpa bracteata),* and milk vetch *(Astragalus canadensis)* are also reported as hosts and are all found in West Virginia.

Confused Cloudywing

Thorybes confusis (Bell), 1922

Adult: Plate 25, Row 1

Description: Wingspan is 1⅛ to 1⅝ inches (30–41 mm). The Confused Cloudywing is similar to the Northern Cloudywing *(T. pylades)* except that it is slightly smaller, and males lack the costal fold in the forewing. The hyaline spots in the forewing are usually smaller and less distinct than those in the Northern Cloudywing, and some spots may even be lacking. This species is difficult to separate from the Northern Cloudywing unless males are captured and examined for the presence of the fold. The Confused Cloudywing can be confused with the Southern Cloudywing *(T. bathyllus)* if the hyaline spots are developed. However, the wings are more pointed in the Confused Cloudywing. Some specimens are difficult to separate without examining the genitalia.

Distribution: The Confused Cloudywing is a southern species but strays northward into southeastern Pennsylvania and Virginia, west to Illinois and Kansas. In the South it ranges into the Florida peninsula and along the Gulf Coast to Texas. To date there are no confirmed records of the Confused Cloudywing in West Virginia. Although the species is not as common as the other 2 members of the genus, the Confused Cloudywing is found to the south and east of the state and could migrate into southern and possibly eastern West Virginia on occasion, as do many southern species.

Habitat: This species prefers open areas near woods. It is often found in and around fields, meadows, abandoned pastures, and woodland clearings along with *T. pylades* and *T. bathyllus*. However, *T. confusis* is generally less common.

Life History and Habits: Because of the obscurity of this species, little is known about its life history. If the species immigrates into West Virginia, it may be double-brooded, with adults appearing in mid-May and flying into early July. A partial second flight may occur in August. The species is multibrooded to the south. Although there are behavioral differences among the various *Thorybes* species, it is expected that the life cycle of the Confused Cloudywing closely parallels that of *T. pylades*.

Nectar Sources: The Confused Cloudywing can be found nectaring along with *T. pylades* and *T. bathyllus* on plants occurring in open areas. Dogbane *(Apocynum)*, red clover *(Trifolium pratense)*, milkweed *(Asclepias)*, vetch *(Vicia)*, honeysuckle *(Lonicera)*, and thistle *(Cirsium)* are among the favorite species chosen.

Larval Host Plant: A variety of legumes are reported as the possible hosts. Bush Clover *(Lespedeza* spp.) and sticktights *(Desmodium* spp.) would be the most likely hosts in West Virginia, although they are not confirmed.

Dreamy Duskywing

Erynnis icelus (Scudder and Burgess), 1870

Adult: Plate 25, Row 2
Larva: Plate 40, Row 3

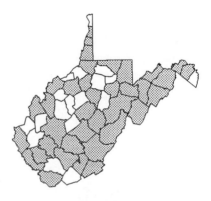

Description: Wingspan is 1 to 1⅜ inches (25–35 mm). The Dreamy Duskywing is a small dark brown to black skipper, with blue-gray and black crescents forming a chain across the upperside of the forewing. This skipper resembles the Sleepy Duskywing *(E. b. brizo)* but is smaller. A patch of gray scaling occurs near the outer costal margin of the forewing. The glassy white spots that are present in several *Erynnis* are lacking in the Dreamy Duskywing. The species also has long pointed antennal clubs and long labial palpi. The underside is dark brown, with 2 irregular rows of pale spots in the outer hindwing.

Distribution: The Dreamy Duskywing is a northern species occurring from Nova Scotia west to British Columbia and southward in the East to northern Georgia, Alabama, and Arkansas. It is absent from the Deep South. In West Virginia the Dreamy Duskywing should be found in every county.

Habitat: This skipper is found along roadsides, trails, and clearings in open woods and forest edges. It likes the borders of damp woods in hilly or mountainous terrain.

Life History and Habits: Males patrol close to the ground perching either on low twigs or bare soil and gather at moist, sandy areas along streams or wet depressions along roads and trails. Females can be found flitting about low vegetation along woodland edges and brushy areas. Eggs are deposited singly on new leaves or stems of host trees. Eggs of the Dreamy Duskywing are green when laid but turn red within a short period. The caterpillar is light green and has a white lateral and a dark dorsal stripe and is covered with white, setiferous tubercles. The head is black with yellow, orange, or red spots and is strongly angled and depressed on top. The larva overwinters in a leaf shelter and pupates in the spring. The Dreamy Duskywing is univoltine, with adults emerging in late April. The flight continues into June and in some years into July in West Virginia, especially in the central mountain counties.

Nectar Sources: A wide variety of plants and trees are visited by the skipper for nectar. Some of these include redbud *(Cercis canadensis),* blueberry *(Vaccinium),* strawberry *(Fragaria),* spring beauty *(Claytonia),* vetch *(Vicia),* bird's-foot violet *(Viola pedata),* blackberry *(Rubus),* mustard *(Brassica),* dogbane *(Apocynum),* Queen Anne's lace *(Daucus carota),* and black-eyed Susan *(Rudbeckia hirta).*

Larval Host Plant: Larval host trees in West Virginia include willows *(Salix* spp.), poplars *(Populus* spp.), and possibly locust *(Robinia* spp.).

Sleepy Duskywing

Erynnis brizo brizo (Boisduval and Leconte), 1834

Adult: Plate 25, Row 3
Larva: Plate 40, Row 3

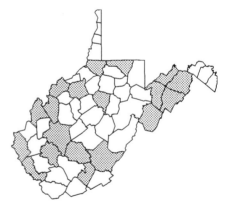

Description: Wingspan is 1⅛ to 1⅝ inches (28–41 mm). The Sleepy Duskywing is a medium skipper that is dark brown. This skipper, as well as the smaller Dreamy Duskywing *(E. icelus),* lacks the hyaline spots in the forewing that characterize the other duskywings. There is a gray band surrounded by black in the form of opposite crescents that runs across the outer portion of the forewing and gives the appearance of a gray chain. Usually, a similar, less visible gray band occurs basally to the outer band in both sexes. There is also a series of buff spots on the hindwing upper surface and 2 rows of white to buff spots along the outer margin of the hindwing beneath. The outer fringe on the wings is brown. Females are paler brown than the males but are similarly marked.

Distribution: The Sleepy Duskywing ranges from Prince Edward Island across to southern Ontario, Manitoba, and south from Wisconsin to Texas. In the West the population extends from the central Rocky Mountain states to northern California. In the East it ranges south to northern Florida and the Gulf states. In West Virginia the skipper should be found in all counties despite the lack of records in the central portion of the state.

Habitat: The Sleepy Duskywing prefers oak, pine-oak, and scrub oak sites on sandy or shale soils. For that reason the species is quite common in the eastern counties. It is generally found in woodland areas along trails, roads, or edges of open areas.

Life History and Habits: The Sleepy Duskywing is a rapid flier. It stays close to the ground in a bouncing flight, landing either on the ground or on twigs close to it. Males gather at wet, sandy places along streams or in dirt roads. When at rest, its wings are held open in a horizontal position. Males are territorial and will return after a few minutes if chased away. The Sleepy Duskywing is univoltine, with a single flight peaking during May. Individuals may be found in April and fly well into June. Females are found later than males. The egg is green and deposited singly on the leaves of host plants. The caterpillar is pale green with a yellow lateral stripe and is covered with small white tubercles and short hairs. The head is brownish, with bright orange dots along the margin, and is strongly angled with a depression on top. Larvae live in leaf shelters constructed with silk. The fully grown larva overwinters in the shelter, pupating in spring and emerging shortly thereafter as an adult. The chrysalis is brown or dark green.

Nectar Sources: Males and females of the species frequently sip minerals from damp soil. Various heath flowers, such as blueberries *(Vaccinium)* and azalea *(Rhododendron),* are visited for nectar, as well as trees, including redbud *(Cercis canadensis).* Blackberry *(Rubus)* and dandelions *(Taraxacum)* are also visited.

Larval Host Plant: The chief host in West Virginia is scrub oak *(Quercus ilicifolia);* however, other oaks are also utilized where scrub oak is lacking. American chestnut *(Castanea dentata)* has also been reported as a host of the Sleepy Duskywing.

Juvenal's Duskywing

Erynnis juvenalis (Fabricius), 1793

Adult: Plate 25, Row 4
Larva: Plate 40, Row 3
Pupa: Plate 49, Row 2

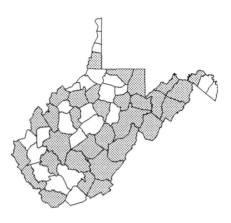

Description: Wingspan is 1¼ to 1¾ inches (32–44 mm). Juvenal's Duskywing is a medium skipper. Males are dark brown to blackish, with black spots and chevrons on the upperside of the forewing. Several clear hyaline spots occur in the forewing with a close group of 4 to 5 small spots occurring near the outer costal margin. The hindwing is quite plain above, lighter brown than the forewing, with 2 inconspicuous rows of buff spots near the outer margin. Long hairs obscure the spots. Females are much paler brown than males, and the markings are much more conspicuous. The hyaline spots are larger in the females. Wing fringes are buff. The underside of the wings in both sexes is plain brown to blackish, with pale spots. However, there are usually 2 conspicuous white to buff spots near the outer edge of the hindwing. The spots are nearly always conspicuous in females, but in males one or both spots may only be present as black dots. The other duskywings in West Virginia lack these spots.

Distribution: Juvenal's Duskywing ranges from Nova Scotia west to Manitoba and northeastern Wyoming, and south to Florida, the Gulf states, and Texas. A population occurs from west Texas to Arizona, New Mexico, and Mexico. The species is not found in the Rocky Mountains. Juvenal's Duskywing is the most common dark skipper in West Virginia during early spring. It can be easily found in all counties.

Habitat: This skipper is associated with oak woodlands and abounds along edges of fields and along roads near or within wooded areas. This butterfly is often found in woodlands with a partially opened canopy.

Life History and Habits: Males perch on twigs or on bare ground along roads or forest edges. They patrol around these perches in a rapid, bounding flight pursuing other skippers or insects that pass by. Males also gather at moist areas along streams with other butterflies. When perching or basking, these butterflies hold their wings in an outstretched position. When roosting they generally clasp a twig, with their wings rooflike as a moth, and fold the antennae back. Juvenal's Duskywing is univoltine, with the first adults appearing in April. Their flight continues into June in the higher elevations. Pale green eggs are laid singly on host leaves, turning a pinkish red before hatching. Larvae develop slowly, not completing their growth until September, at which time they hibernate for the winter. Pupation occurs in early spring. The caterpillar is light green with a thin white lateral stripe and is covered with fine short hairs. The head is orange brown with a row of yellow to orange spots along the outer edge. The chrysalis is dark green or brown.

Nectar Sources: Many spring flowers are visited for nectar. Vetch *(Vicia)*, bird's-foot violet *(Viola pedata)*, cinquefoil *(Potentilla)*, spring beauty *(Claytonia)*, wild plum *(Prunus)*, redbud *(Cercis)*, autumn olive *(Elaeagnus umbellata)*, hawthorn *(Crataegus)*, blackberry *(Rubus)*, and blueberry *(Vaccinium)* are among some of the favorite nectar plants.

Larval Host Plant: In West Virginia a variety of red and white oaks *(Quercus* spp.) are selected as hosts for the larvae. The use of white oak *(Q. alba)* has been more commonly observed than the other species.

Horace's Duskywing

Erynnis horatius (Schuuder and Burgess), 1870

Adult: Plate 25, Row 5
Larva: Plate 40, Row 4

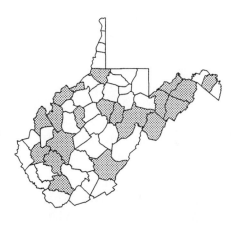

Description: Wingspan is 1¼ to 1¾ inches (32–44 mm). Horace's Duskywing is a medium brown skipper with strongly patterned forewings. The pattern consists of black patches scattered about the forewing, stronger in both sexes than the pattern of Juvenal's Duskywing *(E. juvenalis)*. Juvenal's Duskywing males are darker than Horace's Duskywing, being almost black. Otherwise these 2 skippers are quite similar in appearance. The forewings of both sexes contain clear hyaline spots similar to Juvenal's Duskywing. The hyaline spots are larger in the female *E. horatius*. The hindwing is plain brown above, with faint buff and dark spots along the outer margin. The wing fringes are buff. The underside of the hindwings contains light and dark spots on brown and lacks the 2 whitish spots near the outer edge that characterize *E. juvenalis*. Male Horace's Duskywings can also be confused with the Wild Indigo Duskywing *(E. baptisiae),* although *E. baptisiae* is generally smaller and usually found in close association with its host, a legume (Fabaceae).

Distribution: In the East, Horace's Duskywing occurs from southern New Hampshire southward to Florida, and west to Minnesota and South Dakota in the North and eastern Texas in the South. The population also extends into southeastern Utah and northern Arizona. In West Virginia, Horace's Duskywing has been found in several counties around the state and probably occurs in all counties in small populations. Even in years of abundance, Horace's Duskywing is never as common as Juvenal's Duskywing.

Habitat: Horace's Duskywing prefers warm, sunny openings in oak woodlands or forest edges. It can be found in oak scrub and adjacent open spaces or roadsides. The skipper often wanders a considerable distance into open fields and gardens in search of nectar.

Life History and Habits: Males perch in sunny spots on hilltops or slopes generally within 2 feet of the ground. Males may also be found at wet areas along sandy road edges taking moisture from the soil. When at rest or basking, they hold their wings outspread. Females oviposit on young host leaves of sapling trees. In West Virginia, the species is bivoltine, with the first flight occurring in late April and May and flying into early June. A second flight occurs in late July and August. Depending on the year, the skipper may be quite abundant during the July flight. The eggs are green at first, changing to pink or reddish after a short period. The caterpillar is light green and covered with short hairs. It is speckled with white and has a red-, orange-, or yellow-spotted head. Larvae from the second brood overwinter in leaf litter before forming a dark green to brown chrysalis.

Nectar Sources: Horace's Duskywing nectars at a variety of plants and trees, including several field plants. White and yellow flowers are favored, including dogbane *(Apocynum),* peppermint *(Mentha),* buttonbush *(Cephalanthus occidentalis),* and goldenrod *(Solidago).*

Larval Host Plant: The red oak group is favored, with northern red oak *(Quercus rubra)* and scrub oak *(Q. ilicifolia)* the preferred hosts. In the white oak group, post oak *(Q. stellata)* is frequently selected. Other white oaks may also be utilized.

Mottled Duskywing

Erynnis martialis

Adult: Plate 25, Row 6

Description: Wingspan is 1 to 1⅜ inches (25–35 mm). The Mottled Duskywing is a small to medium skipper, light brown above and a lavender cast below. The upper wing surfaces are strongly patterned with dark blotches, giving it a mottled or almost banded appearance. Several small hyaline spots occur in the outer portion of the forewings. The fringes are brown. Spring adults have more white scaling and are smaller than the summer brood.

Distribution: The Mottled Duskywing occurs from southern New England west through southern Ontario to Minnesota, Wyoming, and Colorado. It ranges southward in the East to Georgia and the Gulf states to Texas. In West Virginia this skipper colonizes where its host plant, New Jersey tea *(Ceanothus americanus),* is found. Although this skipper has been reported from only 7 counties in West Virginia—Boone, Greenbrier, Hampshire, Lincoln, Mercer, Pendleton, and Wyoming—it can be expected to be found sporadically throughout the eastern and southern counties and may be found in other counties as well since New Jersey tea is widespread. A population has been reported from Springfield Wildlife Management Area in Hampshire County and Big Ugly Wildlife Management Area in Lincoln County.

Habitat: The Mottled Duskywing prefers wooded uplands or open woods and woodland edges, often on acid soil where the terrain is hilly.

Life History and Habits: Males perch with outstretched wings on twigs close to the ground or on bare soil. This skipper visits wet spots along sandy roads to sip moisture and minerals. The Mottled Duskywing is bivoltine everywhere but is never abundant. The spring brood appears in late April or early May and flies into June. The second flight appears in mid-July and extends into August. The eggs are pale green, turning pink shortly after being deposited. The caterpillar is light green and covered with short hairs and white specks. The head is spotted with red, orange, or yellow. Larvae from the first brood develop directly, whereas fully grown second brood larvae overwinter. The chrysalis is dark green or brown.

Nectar Sources: Mottled Duskywings nectar at a variety of plants available at the time of their flight. Since it occurs along roads, it utilizes plants found along forest edges. It has been observed nectaring at houstonia *(Houstonia)*, gromwell, *(Lithospermum)*, dogbane *(Apocynum)*, and New Jersey tea *(Ceanothus americanus)*, as well as sipping minerals from damp soil and dung. It has also been observed feeding on the carcass of a snake. Several butterfly species will feed at carrion.

Larval Host Plant: The Mottled Duskywing selects the *Ceanothus* plants in the buckthorn family (Rhamnaceae) as its host. New Jersey tea *(Ceanothus americanus)* is the species used in West Virginia.

Columbine Duskywing

Erynnis lucilius (Scudder and Burgess), 1870

Adult: Plate 26, Row 1
Larva: Plate 40, Row 4

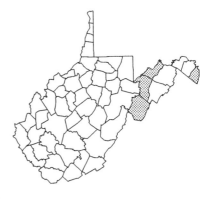

Description: Wingspan is ⅞ to 1¼ inches (22–32 mm). The Columbine Duskywing is a small dark brown skipper, smaller than but otherwise similar to the Wild Indigo Duskywing *(E. baptisiae).* The Columbine Duskywing has short rounded wings; the forewing is patterned with bands of darker brown. Males are grayer between bands, especially next to the hyaline spots, than females, which are a lighter brown. There are 4 glassy white hyaline dots near the tip of the forewing along the costal margin and 1 to 2 dots below those. The hindwing is dark brown with 2 rows of buff spots near the margin on the dorsal and ventral surfaces. The males lack most of the hairlike scaling on the dorsal forewing found in other *Erynnis* species. Males have a hind tibia tuft. They are also closely associated with their host plant and can be separated from the Wild Indigo Duskywing on that basis when confusion occurs.

Distribution: The Columbine Duskywing ranges from southern Quebec west to Minnesota and south to New Jersey, Pennsylvania, and through the Appalachian Mountains to Virginia and Kentucky. In West Virginia it is found in close proximity to its host plant, wild columbine *(Aquilegia canadensis)*. Although wild columbine occurs throughout West Virginia in woods and on rocky banks, the skipper is difficult to find. It has been reported only from Grant, Jefferson, Mineral, and Pendleton counties. It may also occur in the other eastern counties as far south as Monroe County.

Habitat: The skipper's favorite habitat is rocky, wooded ravines, gorges, and semi-exposed rocky mountain tops associated with limestone outcrops where columbine is abundant; it should also be found along woodland edges or glades, and especially along shale slopes below limestone cliffs.

Life History and Habits: The Columbine Duskywing has a low, bouncing flight typical of the *Erynnis* group, although its flight may be rapid when disturbed. Males tend to perch on the ground or rocks but visit flowers regularly for nectar. The Columbine Duskywing is trivoltine in West Virginia. The first flight occurs from mid- to late April and extends through mid-May, and the second flight occurs from early to late July. A partial third flight may be present in late August and September. The egg is green, turning pink before hatching. Eggs are deposited singly on either the upper or lower surface of the host leaf. Caterpillars are pale green with a single white lateral line on each side of a dorsal, dark green stripe. The head is purple brown, flattened anteriorly, and deeply cleft. Larvae live in leaf shelters with each instar folding a larger portion of the leaf. Some larvae from the second brood and all from the third overwinter in a leaf shelter constructed by tying several leaves together with silk. Pupation occurs in the shelter in spring. The chrysalis is pale green and has 2 small black projections between the eyes.

Nectar Sources: The Columbine Duskywing nectars at a variety of wild flowers in bloom at the time of its flight. These include phlox *(Phlox)*, violets *(Viola)*, rock sandwort *(Arenaria)*, rock twist *(Draba)*, downy woodmint *(Blephilia)*, hawkweeds *(Hieracium)*, and others. Favorite flower colors include pink, white, and yellow.

Larval Host Plant: The only native host in West Virginia is wild columbine *(Aquilegia canadensis)*, although the larvae will feed on garden columbine *(Aquilegia vulgaris)* if it is provided.

Wild Indigo Duskywing

Erynnis baptisiae (Forbes), 1936

Adult: Plate 26, Row 2
Larva: Plate 41, Row 1

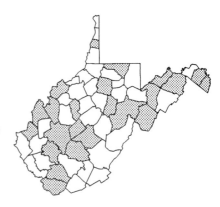

Description: Wingspan is 1⅛ to 1⅝ inches (21–41 mm). The Wild Indigo Duskywing is a medium dark brown to black skipper with a discernible pattern on the upper surface of the forewing. The basal half of the forewing is almost black, and several small, clear hyaline spots occur near the tip, with a light brown patch basal to the hyaline spots. Pale brown and dark spots occur in bands across the outer margin of the forewings. The wing fringes are brown. The hindwings are brown with light spots along the outer margin. The hindwing underside is similar to the upperside but with lighter markings.

Distribution: This species ranges from southern New England west to Iowa and south to Florida, the Gulf states, and central Texas. The Wild Indigo Duskywing has become more common in West Virginia in recent years since one of its host plants, crown vetch *(Coronilla varia)*, is a widely used ground cover along roads. Records of *Erynnis baptisiae* are scattered throughout the state. This skipper should be found in all counties near its host plant.

Habitat: This species is found frequently in open fields and along roads and railroad banks where stands of crown vetch are planted. It also prefers dry, open woods and barrens of sandy or acid soils.

Life History and Habits: Males perch on low shrubs or twigs in open areas. They may also gather at moist areas along dirt roads or streams. Frequently, they can be found visiting various flowers in open fields for nectar. Females are often seen in a low, bouncing flight in and about their host plants where they may land periodically to rest or oviposit. The Wild Indigo Duskywing is trivoltine, having 2 full flights and a partial third each year. The first emergents appear in late April and early May and fly into June. The second flight does not appear until mid-July and extends into August. A partial third flight occurs in some areas during late August and extends into September. Eggs are deposited singly on the leaves of the host plant and are green, turning pink before hatching. The caterpillar is light green with numerous, small white tubercles, and is covered with short hairs. The head is patterned with red, orange, or yellow. The chrysalis is green to brown. Fully grown larvae from a portion of the second brood and all of the third brood overwinter. Pupation occurs in the spring.

Nectar Sources: The Wild Indigo Duskywing visits a wide variety of field flowers to obtain nectar, including dogbane *(Apocynum)*, blackberry *(Rubus)*, and red and white clovers *(Trifolium)*.

Larval Host Plant: The Wild Indigo Duskywing selects members of the legume family as hosts. The preferred hosts are wild indigo *(Baptisia tinctoria)* and crown vetch *(Coronilla varia)*. However, wild blue indigo *(B. australis)* and lupine *(Lupinus* spp.) are also used as hosts, but stands of lupine are uncommon in West Virginia.

Persius Duskywing

Erynnis persius persius (Scudder)

Adult: Plate 26, Row 3

Description: Wingspan is 1 to 1⅜ inches (25–35 mm). The Persius Duskywing is a small to medium dark brown skipper. Darker markings in the basal portion of the forewings of males are obscured by elevated, curved, whitish, hairlike scales that give it a soft appearance. Females are more heavily patterned than males. Both sexes contain a short row of 2 to 3 glassy white spots near the outer margin of the forewings. The underside is brown with pale spotting along the outer margin.

Distribution: In the East, the Persius Duskywing is found sporadically from Ontario south through New England and the Appalachian Mountains. A western population occurs from Alaska south to California, southern Arizona, and southwestern Mexico. As yet the Persius Duskywing has not been reported from West Virginia but should be searched for in the eastern counties.

Habitat: In the Great Lakes region this skipper prefers oak-savannah habitats and has typically been found along power-line right-of-ways; and in the East it is found in pine barrens. The Persius Duskywing may be found in association with the Frosted Elfin *(Incisalia irus)*, which utilizes the same host plants and flight season. The Persius Duskywing is also found in open sites within the northern forest. Such areas may consist of willow seeps and sandy sites where small aspens abound or marshy areas near woods. The skipper is rare throughout its range in the East. In West Virginia the Persius Duskywing should be searched for in sandy or open areas where lupine *(Lupinus)* or wild indigo *(Baptisia tinctoria)* occurs in large patches.

Life History and Habits: Males actively patrol and perch on the ground or close to the ground on twigs in open areas. Females are generally found flitting about close to their host plants or visiting flowers for nectar. The Persius Duskywing is univoltine, with a single flight each year. It generally flies a little later than the Sleepy Duskywing *(E. brizo)* and Juvenal's Duskywing *(E. juvenalis)* and should be searched for from mid-May to early June in West Virginia. Eggs are deposited singly on host plant leaves. Larvae live in leaf shelters constructed by tying 1 or more leaves together with silk. The caterpillar is pale green and covered with small white tubercles, each bearing a whitish hair. There is a thin dark green dorsal line and a light lateral line. The head, which is cleft on top, is brown to black, with reddish and yellowish spots. Larvae overwinter in leaf shelters and pupate in the spring.

Nectar Sources: Various low-growing plants found in early spring serve as nectar sources for the skippers.

Larval Host Plant: Although willows and aspen are reported as host plants in the East (Opler and Krizek 1984), lupine *(Lupinus* spp.) and wild indigo *(Baptisia tinctoria)* are probably utilized more often in this region. However, other possible hosts should not be ruled out.

Grizzled Skipper

Pyrgus centaureae wyandot (Edwards), 1863

Adult: Plate 26, Row 4
Larva: Plate 41, Row 1
Pupa: Plate 49, Row 2

Description: Wingspan is ⅞ to 1¼ inches (22–32 mm). The Grizzled Skipper is small, dark brown black above, with 2 irregular bands of white spots across the forewing. The hindwing has 2 rows of partly diffused, white patches. The body and inner third of the upper wing surface are covered with long, fine, bluish hairs. The underside is olive with 2, and a partial third, irregular white bands of zigzag blotches crossing the hindwing. The fringes are boldly checkered. The Grizzled Skipper could be confused with the Common Checkered-Skipper *(Pyrgus communis),* which is lighter in color.

Distribution: The Grizzled Skipper is a northern species that occurs in scattered populations in the boreal regions of North America and Eurasia. In North America, populations occurs from Labrador to British Columbia and Alaska and south in the Rocky Mountains to New Mexico. The subspecies *wyandot* is found in portions of Michigan and New York and southward through the Appalachian Mountains to North Carolina and Kentucky. In West Virginia it is found in the eastern counties of Hampshire, Hardy, Mineral, and Pendleton. There is a historic record from Kanawha County. The butterfly may be found in the other surrounding counties where its preferred habitat exists. This skipper has been disappearing from its eastern range in recent years in conjunction with increased spraying programs to control gypsy moths *(Lymantria dispar).* As a result the Grizzled Skipper is now listed as a Federal species of concern.

Habitat: The Grizzled Skipper is generally found on open or semi-open shale slopes in close proximity to woodlands. It can be found along trails through oak woods or shale barrens, semi-open clearings, or power- and gas-line right-of-ways where its host plant, cinquefoil *(Potentilla canadensis),* is found.

Life History and Habits: Males patrol along trails and open areas close to the ground in a bouncing flight. They visit plants readily for nectar as they travel. Males either perch on low plants, shrubs, or on the ground in bare spots. When at rest, the wings are held open. Females also travel along these open areas flitting around cinquefoil patches in search of suitable plants on which to oviposit. The tiny, pale green eggs are laid singly on the underside of the host leaf. The female then moves on a few feet in search of another suitable plant. Egg laying occurs from midday until approximately 1600 hours (4:00 P.M.). The skipper is univoltine, with adults appearing in mid-April and flying into mid-May. The larvae live in leaf shelters created by rolling the leaf with silk. Larvae are slow growing and do not reach full size until August. The caterpillar is pale green with a brownish black, round head and a small brown collar on the dorsum of the prothorax. The head and body are covered with stiff (bristly), translucent hairs. The larvae of the Michigan population of the Grizzled Skipper are tan to pinkish instead of green. The pale brown head and body are covered with short, translucent hairs. Larvae pupate in late summer and spend the winter in leaf shelters created by tying several leaves together either on the host plant or close to it. The chrysalis is dark brown and speckled with white on the dorsal surface. The abdomen is brownish, and the wing cases are covered with a white, powdery bloom.

Nectar Sources: Adults nectar on low growing flowers found along the open or woodland habitat used. These include Canada cinquefoil *(Potentilla canadensis)*, strawberry *(Fragaria* spp.), spring beauty *(Claytonia)*, bird's-foot violet *(Viola pedata)*, and phlox *(Phlox subulata)*.

Larval Host Plant: In West Virginia Canada cinquefoil *(Potentilla canadensis)* is the primary host for the Grizzled Skipper. However, the larvae will readily accept strawberry *(Fragaria* spp.) (the host for *P. centaureae* populations in Michigan), as well as other cinquefoils. Cinquefoil is by far the most common host in the areas where the Grizzled Skipper flies in this region.

Common Checkered-Skipper

Pyrgus communis communis (Grote), 1872

Adult: Plate 26, Row 5
Larva: Plate 41, Row 2
Pupa: Plate 49, Row 3

Description: Wingspan is ¾ to 1¼ inches (19–32 mm). The Common Checkered-Skipper is easily distinguished from other skippers by its black-and-white checkered pattern on the upper surface of the wings. It is lighter in color than its close relative, the Grizzled Skipper *(P. centaureae wyandot)*. On the hindwing underside there are 2 to 4 bands of dark gray to olive connected spots crossing the wing on a background of eggshell white. The skipper appears to be bluish white when seen darting through the grass due to the bluish, hairy scaling toward the base of the wings on the upper surface. Female Common Checkered-Skippers may be darker with little white checkering, whereas the males are quite pale with broad bands of white checkers. The wing fringes are checkered gray and white.

Distribution: The Common Checkered-Skipper is resident from Virginia and West Virginia westward through the central United States and south to Mexico and tropical America. The species strays north into New England and

New York and west across central Canada to the Pacific coast. In West Virginia the skipper has been reported from the dryer regions of the state in the eastern counties along the Virginia border. It has also been reported from McDowell and Monongalia Counties. However, it should also be found in the counties along the Ohio River and occasionally in the central and southern mountain counties. Its presence in the mountain counties at higher elevations is sporadic because it cannot survive cold winters.

Habitat: The Common Checkered-Skipper is found in open fields, usually sunny areas with low vegetation and some bare ground. Quite often the species can be found along streams and on sandy, rocky islands where it frequently lands on the ground. It also uses wet or dry meadows, rocky hillsides, pastures, farmyards, landfills, and highway edges.

Life History and Habits: The Common Checkered-Skipper is a patrolling species. Males patrol a well-defined territory most of the day in an erratic flight close to the ground. They occasionally perch on low vegetation or on bare soil. When at rest the wings are held fully extended. There are 2 to 3 broods in West Virginia, with the first flight appearing in late April and continuing through May. The second flight appears in July and extends through August into September. The second brood is generally larger than the first. The skipper has been found as late as mid-October, so a partial third brood is apparent. The egg is a pale green and deposited singly on host leaves. Larvae live in leaf shelters made by folding the leaf over with silk. As the larva grows, several leaves may be tied together. The caterpillar is pale yellow green to brownish, with a gray or greenish brown dorsal stripe and 2 white stripes on each side. The body is covered with small white tubercles. The head is black and densely covered with short light hairs. The chrysalis is light brown toward the head and light green behind, with black dots and dashes in bands on the dorsal surface. The wing cases are greenish. The species hibernates as a fully grown larva.

Nectar Sources: Common Checkered-Skippers nectar at a variety of small white flowers, such as fleabane *(Erigeron)* and asters *(Aster)*. They also use red clover *(Trifolium pratense),* sticktights *(Desmodium),* and knapweed *(Centaurea).*

Larval Host Plant: Plants in the mallow family are used as the primary host. In West Virginia, these include mallow *(Malva* spp.), velvet leaf *(Abutilon theophrasti),* hollyhock *(Althaea* spp.), and sida *(Sida* spp.).

Common Sootywing

Pholisora catullus (Fabricius), 1793

Adult: Plate 26, Row 6
Larva: Plate 41, Row 2

Description: Wingspan is ⅞ to 1¼ inches (22–32 mm). The Common Sootywing is a small black skipper with somewhat rounded wings. There are 2 curved rows of tiny white spots on the outer portion of the forewing and, less often, a row of tiny spots on the upper surface of the hindwing. The amount of spotting varies considerably. On the underside, the wings are brownish black, and the fringes of the hindwings may be brown. The Hayhurst's Scallopwing *(Staphylus hayhurstii),* which can be easily confused with the Common Sootywing, has gold flecking on the upper wing surfaces. There is no gold flecking on the Common Sootywing.

Distribution: The Common Sootywing ranges through the central United States south to northern Florida and the Gulf states to Mexico. It strays north to southern Canada. It is rare in northern habitats and is absent from the Florida peninsula. It has been found sporadically in West Virginia. While this skipper may occur throughout the state, it appears most commonly in the eastern counties. It can also be found in many of the western counties bordering the Ohio River.

Habitat: The Common Sootywing is found in close association with its favored host plant, lamb's quarters *(Chenopodium),* which grows in disturbed soils, such as landfills, roadsides, vacant lots, gardens, and farmyards. Following heavy flooding in 1985, *Chenopodium* was abundant along river courses, which resulted in an increase in skipper populations.

Life History and Habits: Males patrol in a bouncing, erratic flight close to the ground during much of the daylight hours, resting either on plants or in bare spots on the ground. At rest, the wings are held open. Newly emerged males may be found sipping moisture from soil along streams or puddles. Mating occurs from midmorning to early afternoon (930–1430 hours, 9:30 A.M.–2:30 P.M.), with the female carrying the male on short nuptial flights (Opler and Krizek 1984). Females lay their eggs during the warmest part of the day, usually from 1100 hours (11:00 A.M.) throughout the afternoon. A single, pink to reddish egg is rapidly deposited on the upper surface of the host leaf, and then the female quickly flits off in search of another plant. This sequence is repeated in such rapid fashion that it is difficult to keep watch of a female ovipositing. The Common Sootywing is bivoltine throughout West Virginia. The first flight occurs from May to mid-June, and the second flight occurs from late July through August. Larvae live in leaf shelters created by cutting the leaf inward from the edge in 2 places and pulling the flap over with a strand or 2 of silk. The flap is then tacked in place along its margin. The larva feeds on the margin of the leaf away from its shelter at night. As the larva grows, larger shelters are constructed. The caterpillar is pale green with straw-colored dots and 2 greenish lateral stripes. It has a brownish black head and a black collar patch on the prothorax. The larva is covered with a fine down. The chrysalis is purple brown and covered with a whitish bloom. Full-grown larvae overwinter in silk-lined leaf shelters and pupate in the spring.

Nectar Sources: The Common Sootywing nectars at clovers *(Trifolium)*, dogbane *(Apocynum)*, wood sorrel *(Oxalis)*, mints *(Mentha)*, milkweed *(Asclepias)*, and cucumber and squash flowers *(Cucurbita)*.

Larval Host Plant: Hosts include members of the goosefoot and amaranth families. Lamb's quarters *(Chenopodium album)* is the most widely used host in West Virginia, although amaranths *(Amaranthus* spp.) and cockscomb *(Celosia* spp.) may be used on occasion.

Hayhurst's Scallopwing
Staphylus hayhurstii (Edwards), 1870
Adult: Plate 26, Row 7
Larva: Plate 41, Row 2

Description: Wingspan is 1 to 1¼ inches (25–32 mm). The Hayhurst's Scallopwing is a small dark skipper. It is distinguished from the Common Sootywing *(Pholisora catullus)* by the scalloped margin of its hindwings. The hindwings also contain dark bands on a deep brown background, and both sets of wings are covered with gold flecking on their upper surface. The female is browner than the male and has more gold flecking. There are 2 to 3 small white dots near the anterior margin of the forewing and 1 white dot near the center of the forewing. On females this center dot is larger than on males—on males it may be minute or absent.

Distribution: The Hayhurst's Scallopwing is confined mainly to the southern states, ranging from southern Pennsylvania and New Jersey west to Nebraska and southward to Florida, the Gulf states, and central Texas. In West Virginia it has been reported from the confluence of the Potomac and Shenandoah Rivers at Harpers Ferry, Jefferson County, and along the Ohio River in Mason and Cabell Counties. It may also be found in adjoining counties, such as Wayne and Jackson or in the southeastern counties of Mercer and Monroe, although no records have been reported from these counties to date.

Habitat: The Hayhurst's Scallopwing prefers moist and rather shady areas where its host plant occurs. Frequently, it will be found along creeks flowing through wooded areas. It can also be found along weedy edges of railroad tracks and in weedy, vacant lots where lamb's quarters *(Chenopodium)* grows.

Life History and Habits: Males tend to perch in sunny spots on low vegetation along woodland edges. They move quickly from flower to flower in open areas in search of nectar. The butterfly holds its wings fully extended when at rest or perched. Egg laying occurs from midday to late afternoon. The pale pink eggs are deposited singly on the underside of host leaves. The Hayhurst's Scallopwing is bivoltine in West Virginia, with the first flight appearing in the spring from May into June. The second flight does not appear until mid- to late July and continues into September. Larvae live in silk-lined, folded leaf shelters and feed on the leaves at night. The caterpillar is deep green, with a rosy cast toward the rear, and a dark green dorsal stripe. The body is covered with fine, short white hairs. The prothoracic shield is pale brown, and the rounded head is deep purple to almost black, with a vertical groove in the center. The shelter constructed in the final instar consists of the entire leaf lined in silk. The chrysalis is pale olive brown becoming orange brown on the abdomen. The abdomen and head are covered with fine orange hairs (Heitzman 1963). The chrysalis is covered with a white, powdery bloom. Full-grown larvae from the second brood overwinter in leaf shelters and pupate in the spring. Those that pupate in late summer emerge as adults a couple of weeks later and may produce a partial third brood.

Nectar Sources: Hayhurst's Scallopwings nectar at a variety of flowers in bloom at the time of their flight, including clovers *(Trifolium)*, dogbane *(Apocynum)*, spearmint *(Mentha)*, knotweed *(Polygonum)*, and marigolds *(Tagetes)*.

Larval Host Plant: Lamb's quarters *(Chenopodium album)* is the only known larval host in West Virginia.

Subfamily Hesperiinae—Branded Skippers

The subfamily Hesperiinae is represented by 26 species in West Virginia. Skippers of this group are small to medium and predominately orange or black, with pointed wings. Males have a black stigma (androconial scales), or sex brand, on the dorsal surface of the forewings. The Hesperiinae lack the costal fold and hind tibia hair tufts found in the Pyrginae. The antennal club is oval and ends in a small angled point, called an apiculus. The M_2 vein in this group is closer to the M_3 vein than to the M_1 (fig. 15b). The Hesperiinae rest with their wings folded over their back and bask with the hindwings fully extended and the forewings extended to about a 45 degree angle. Males are generally perchers, although 2 species, the Least Skipper *(Ancyloxypha numitor)* and the European Skipper *(Thymelicus lineola),* patrol in a slow flight in search of females.

The eggs of Hesperiinae are usually hemispherical without prominent ribbing, although they have pitlike reticulations. Eggs are deposited singly on the host leaf. The larvae of this group feed on monocotyledons (grasses and sedges in West Virginia), as well as palms elsewhere. Many species are not highly selective and will feed on more than 1 species of grass if grass feeders; however, sedge feeders tend to be more specialized. The larvae live in silken leaf shelters usually at the base of the host plant. They are green, tan, or brown, with a green or dark head and black collar. The larvae usually hibernate, and pupation occurs within the leaf shelter. Females carry the male when mated pairs are startled.

Swarthy Skipper

Nastra lherminier (Latreille), 1824

Adult: Plate 27, Row 1
Larva: Plate 41, Row 3
Pupa: Plate 49, Row 3

Description: Wingspan is ⅞ to 1 inch (22–25 mm). The Swarthy Skipper is a small, dull gray-brown skipper with triangular forewings. There are 2 pale, often vague, spots in the forewing toward the tip. The underside is plain olive brown with no distinct markings; however, the veins in the hindwings may be a yellowish. This skipper is the only West Virginia species with no distinct markings.

Distribution: The Swarthy Skipper ranges from southern New England to Kansas, south to Florida, and west to Texas. In the northern portion of its range it cannot survive the winter and must colonize from the south. The skipper may overwinter in the warmer parts of West Virginia, but since it cannot survive cold weather its populations fluctuate from year to year. It has been found in scattered counties around the state, including Jefferson, Lewis, Mineral, Monongalia, Nicholas, Randolph, Summers, Tyler, and Wirt. Because of its wide distribution in West Virginia it probably colonizes all counties from time to time, but it is undoubtedly less common in areas where woodlands predominate.

Habitat: The Swarthy Skipper is found in open fields, either dry or moist, or on grassy hillsides where its host plant, little bluestem *(Andropogon scoparius)*, occurs. In years of abundance it may be found in yards, vacant lots, landfills, and roadsides. Because of the lack of large stands of little bluestem grass in West Virginia, populations are seldom high enough to be noticeable.

Life History and Habits: The Swarthy Skipper, as with most skippers, is a rapid flier. Males tend to dart back and forth, perching on the tips of grass stems. Females can be found flitting about through the grass. In West Virginia this skipper is bivoltine, with the first flight occurring in May and extending into early June. The second flight appears in July and extends into August and perhaps even September. The egg is pearly white. The caterpillar is pale green with a dark dorsal stripe. The head is reddish brown with pale or cream, longitudinal stripes on the face. Caterpillars live in a partly rolled leaf blade tied with silk strands. The chrysalis is pale green with a pointed projection on the point of the head.

Nectar Sources: This skipper visits a variety of low-growing field plants, with white, pink, or blue flowers preferred. Some of these include peppermint *(Mentha)*, vetch *(Vicia)*, red and white clovers *(Trifolium)*, tick-trefoil *(Desmodium)*, and New Jersey tea *(Ceanothus americanus)*.

Larval Host Plant: Little bluestem *(Andropogon scoparius)* is used in West Virginia along with bluegrass *(Poa)*. Other grasses are also used.

Clouded Skipper

Lerema accius
Adult: Plate 27, Rows 1, 2
Larva: Plate 41, Row 3
Pupa: Plate 49, Row 4

Description: Wingspan is 1 to 1⅜ inches (25–35 mm). This skipper is medium-sized, has pointed forewings, and is blackish brown above with a row of 4 to 5 small hyaline spots near the tip of the forewing. Males have a black stigma in the forewing. Against the dark wing the stigma is difficult to see. There is a purple sheen to the wing in fresh males. The hindwing is unmarked and is brownish black. The underside of the forewing is dark basally becoming dusted with violet on the outer half. The hindwing is dusted to varying degrees with bands of purple.

Distribution: The Clouded Skipper is a resident of the Deep South, ranging from southern Georgia and Florida west along the Gulf states to Texas, and south through Mexico and Central America. It wanders into West Virginia during years of abundance and may be found in almost any county, although it is more likely to be found along the eastern border. It has been reported thus far from Greenbrier, Jefferson, and Randolph Counties. Only 1 to 2 individuals have been reported at any time, and the species rarely breeds in West Virginia. However, a fresh male was taken in Jefferson County along the Shenandoah River and 2 fresh males were found along the Greenbrier River in Greenbrier County. These may have resulted from broods in those areas. The fact that a specimen was taken in Randolph County indicates that it can be found in the mountains away from river systems.

Habitat: The Clouded Skipper is usually found around wet areas near rivers or streams. It may also be found in fields along woodland edges or clearings and around home gardens.

Life History and Habits: Males perch close to the ground on grass or other objects in sunlit openings. They may also be found nectaring at plants in semi-shaded areas. The caterpillar is greenish white, with a dark dorsal stripe and a white lateral stripe. The head is white with a black margin and has 3 vertical, black stripes on the front. The chrysalis is greenish white, smooth, and slender. There are no breeding records in West Virginia. This species is likely to be found during late summer and early fall, often into October.

Nectar Sources: Several white, pink, or purple flowers are visited for nectar, including buttonbush *(Cephalanthus occidentalis)*, selfheal *(Prunella vulgaris)*, vervain *(Verbena)*, and clovers *(Trifolium)*. They also visit such plants as marigolds *(Tagetes)*, butterfly bush *(Buddleja* spp.), and blazing star *(Liatris* spp.) if planted in yards.

Larval Host Plant: The Clouded Skipper selects various grasses, including plumegrass *(Erianthus alopecuroides)* (Opler and Krizek 1984) and perhaps millets *(Echinochloa* spp.), as hosts. In West Virginia, plumgrass occurs sporadically in the southwestern counties; however, millets are common throughout the state.

Least Skipper

Ancyloxypha numitor (Fabricius), 1793

Adult: Plate 27, Row 2
Larva: Plate 41, Row 4
Pupa: Plate 49, Row 4

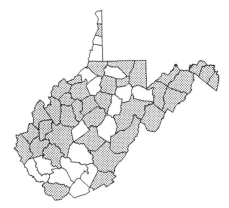

Description: Wingspan is ¾ to 1 inch (19–25 mm). The Least Skipper is a small orange-and-black skipper. The forewing of the male is variable but often blackish with some orange along the costal margin and interior area. The hindwing above is gold with a broad, black border. The forewing of the female may be entirely black or almost so. The forewing is black beneath along the base, blending to an orange gold, whereas the hindwing is orange gold. This skipper is easily distinguished from other skippers by its small size, orange-and-black color pattern, and its moderately slow flight close to the ground, usually among grasses.

Distribution: The Least Skipper ranges throughout the eastern United States from Nova Scotia west to Saskatchewan and south to Florida, the Gulf states, and Texas. It has been reported from almost all counties in West Virginia and is undoubtedly found throughout the state.

Habitat: The Least Skipper is typically found in wet or moist areas with tall grasses, especially in pastures and meadows along streams, ditches, and marshes. Frequently the skipper will become abundant, especially in summer, and will spread to fields and hillsides where grasses are present.

Life History and Habits: Males fly through tall grasses in a fairly feeble flight in search of females. The skipper has at least 2 broods in West Virginia and possibly a third. The first flight is seen in May and extends through June, and the second flight appears in mid-July and extends through August. On occasion there may be a partial third flight in September that extends into October. The eggs are laid on host leaves and are glossy yellow, acquiring an orange-red band around the middle before hatching. The caterpillar is light green with a pale brown head that contains a white line around the front surface. Four white patches occur on the ventral surface of the abdomen. The chrysalis is cream with brown lines and a black blotch on the dorsal surface of the head extending to the pronotum.

Nectar Sources: The Least Skipper visits low-growing plants with small flowers for nectar. These may include wood sorrel *(Oxalis),* chicory *(Cichorium),* and white clover *(Trifolium).* They are also reported to visit dogbane *(Apocynum)* and buttonbush *(Cephalanthus).*

Larval Host Plant: The larvae feed on various grasses in West Virginia, including rice cutgrass *(Leersia oryzoides)* and bluegrass *(Poa).*

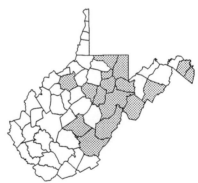

European Skipper

Thymelicus lineola
(Ochsenheimer), 1808
Adult: Plate 27, Row 3
Larva: Plate 41, Row 4
Pupa: Plate 50, Row 1

Description: Wingspan is ¾ to 1 inch (19–25 mm). The European Skipper is a relatively small brassy orange skipper with a narrow, dark brown wing border. The fringe is pale orange. The male has a small, narrow, black forewing stigma. The wing veins are slightly darkened above, especially in the female. The forewing undersides are orange, whereas the hindwings have a greenish tinge or are copper.

Distribution: This is an introduced species first being found in London, Ontario, in 1910. Since then it has expanded its range southward in the East from New England west to Iowa and south to Virginia and Kentucky. The species probably occurs throughout West Virginia, although most of the records are in the eastern half of the state. This skipper can be abundant at times in fields where it occurs.

Habitat: The European Skipper prefers open, grassy fields, including pastures, abandoned farms, and grassy road edges where tall grasses abound.

Life History and Habits: Males patrol in search of females in a slow, somewhat feeble flight amongst the grass stems, resting periodically on blades of grass or on flowers to sip nectar. When at rest the skipper holds its wings partially opened. The European Skipper is univoltine over most of its range, with adults flying from the first week of June through mid- to late July. The round, white egg is laid on the stem of grasses. Although the larva develops quickly, the eggs do not hatch until the following spring. The caterpillar is green with a dark dorsal stripe and pale lateral stripes and has a greenish tan head with 2 white or yellow longitudinal stripes on the front. The chrysalis is pale green to yellow green, with a dark dorsal stripe and has a hornlike projection in front.

Nectar Sources: European Skippers select several field plants for nectar during their flight period. A favorite, however, is red clover *(Trifolium pratense)*, although fleabane *(Erigeron)*, ox-eye daisy *(Chrysanthemum leucanthemum)*, hawkweed *(Hieracium)*, milkweeds *(Asclepias)*, thistles *(Cirsium)*, dogbane *(Apocynum)*, and white clover *(Trifolium repens)* are readily visited.

Larval Host Plant: Orchard grass *(Dactylis glomerata)*, velvet grass *(Holcus lanatus)*, and timothy *(Phleum pratense)* are the hosts most often selected in West Virginia. Other field grasses may also be used.

Fiery Skipper

Hylephila phyleus
Adult: Plate 27, Row 4
Larva: Plate 42, Row 1
Pupa: Plate 50, Row 1

Description: Wingspan is 1 to 1¼ inches (25–32 mm). The Fiery Skipper is a medium yellow-orange skipper with pointed wings. Males have a wide black stigma toward the base of the forewing and a black patch just above the stigma. There is a zigzag black outer border in both wings above, and below the hindwings have numerous small brown checks on a yellow-orange background. Females are larger than males, with long wings containing large tawny spots. The female has orange along the costal margin of the forewing, and the hindwing upperside has a band of tawny-orange spots on a brown background. The underside of the female's hindwing is a little more orange than male's, with numerous dark flecks. The Fiery Skipper has short antennae. The brown dots on the underside of the hindwing are the distinguishing characteristic of this species. No hyaline spots occur on the wings of either sex.

Distribution: The Fiery Skipper is a resident of the southern United States from southern Georgia through Florida, and along the Gulf Coast to Mexico and tropical America. It strays north to Connecticut, the Great Lakes states, and west to northern California. This southern skipper readily colonizes areas of West Virginia in favorable years and may be found in any county. At present it has been recorded only from a few central and southeastern counties, but it may be found elsewhere during the summer, especially on marigolds *(Tagetes)* and other composites planted around homes.

Habitat: This is a skipper of sunny, open grassy areas, including lawns, roadsides, dry fields, pastures, and clearings.

Life History and Habits: The Fiery Skipper is a rapid flier. Males generally perch close to the ground on twigs or vegetation and spend much time visiting flowers for nectar. In West Virginia the Fiery Skipper may be found as early as May and may be common until late September. There are probably 2 successful broods during that period. The small, pale green eggs are laid on various grasses, and larvae live in shelters at the base of the plants close to the ground. The caterpillar varies from pale greenish brown to brown, with a dark dorsal stripe and 2 lateral stripes. The head is brown with a short black stripe on the face bordered by 2 tan to white lines. The chrysalis is light tan to yellow brown, with a dark dorsal stripe and 2 dark, dorsolateral dashes behind the head. Two oval, brown spots occur on each side of the head in front of the dashes.

Nectar Sources: Many flowers that bloom during summer are visited for nectar, including thistles *(Cirsium)*, milkweed *(Asclepias)*, ironweed *(Vernonia)*, Joe-pye weed *(Eupatorium)*, knapweed *(Centaurea)*, asters *(Aster)*, and marigolds *(Tagetes)*.

Larval Host Plant: Weedy grasses are selected, especially crab grass *(Digitaria)* and bent grass *(Agrostis)*. Although other grasses, such as Bermuda grass *(Cynodon dactylon)*, are also used.

Leonard's Skipper

Hesperia leonardus leonardus
(Harris), 1862

Adult: Plate 27, Row 5

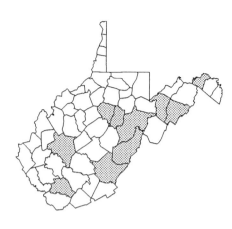

Description: Wingspan is ⅞ to 1⅜
inches (22–35 mm). Leonard's
Skipper is a medium brown-and-
orange skipper. Males are dark
brown above with a broad, dark
border. The forewings are tawny orange toward the base and contain a long,
narrow stigma. Several small orange dots occur in the outer forewing. The
hindwing has a short central band of 4 to 6 orange spots. The hairs along the
base of the hindwing are orange. Females are dark brown with tawny-orange
spots in bands on each wing; the forewing is orange toward the base, and, as
in the male, the long hairs on the hindwing are orange. In both sexes, the
background color on the underside is red brown to rust with a row of yellow
spots in the central area of the hindwing. One to 2 additional yellow spots
occur toward the base in the hindwing.

Distribution: Leonard's Skipper ranges throughout the northeastern United
States from Nova Scotia to Minnesota, south to northern Georgia, and west to
Missouri. This skipper is probably more widespread in West Virginia than
records indicate; however, it seems to be more abundant in the eastern
counties. The species is not very abundant in most parts of its range, although
several individuals can be found during its flight period.

Habitat: Leonard's Skipper is generally found in open areas with tall grass and
weeds. Low-lying wet meadows with ironweed in flower are good places to
look for the species. They also inhabit grassy slopes, pine-oak barrens, and
grassy or wetland areas along roads or woodland edges.

Life History and Habits: Like the other *Hesperia,* Leonard's Skipper is a rapid
flier. Males perch on vegetation or patrol back and forth in search of females,
and they can be readily found visiting flowers for nectar. There is a single, late
summer flight in this species that does not begin until mid- to late August and
continues well into September. The caterpillar is maroon with green
highlights. The young larva overwinters and develops the following spring
and early summer.

Nectar Sources: Blazing star, or gay feathers *(Liatris* spp.), is a favorite nectar source for Leonard's Skipper (Schweitzer, personal communication). In areas lacking *Liatris,* other purple or pink flowers are selected for nectaring, especially ironweed *(Vernonia),* Joe-pye weed *(Eupatorium),* asters *(Aster),* teasel *(Dipsacus),* and thistles *(Cirsium).*

Larval Host Plant: Grasses are reported as the primary host, especially panic grasses *(Panicum* spp.), poverty oat grass *(Danthonia spicata),* and bent grasses *(Agrostis* spp.) (McGuire 1982). Leonard's Skipper is also associated with bluestem grass *(Andropogon* spp.) and bluegrass *(Poa* spp.).

Cobweb Skipper

Hesperia metea metea
Adult: Plate 27, Row 6
Larva: Plate 42, Row 1

Description: Wingspan is 1 to 1⅜ inches (25–35 mm). The Cobweb Skipper is a small to medium brown skipper. Males are medium brown on the upper surface with tawny orange patches above and below the narrow stigma. A few orange patches occur near the tip of the forewing. On the hindwing there is a V-shaped, orange patch pointing toward the outer margin. The female is similarly marked above but not as conspicuously, and the patches may be more creamy colored than orange. The underside of both sexes possesses a white, V-shaped band pointed toward the outer margin of the hindwing. There is a small white patch in the basal area of the hindwing as well. White may extend along the veins of the wing causing them to be quite noticeable and giving the wing a webbed appearance. The markings on the female are less noticeable.

Distribution: The Cobweb Skipper ranges from southern Maine south to the Gulf states and eastern Texas in sporadic populations. Its range in West Virginia is restricted to those sites that have a considerable amount of beard grass *(Andropogon)* on them. Thus far the species has only been reported from 5 counties: Grant, Hampshire, Lewis, Monroe, and Pendleton; however, it is certain to be found elsewhere in the state, especially in the eastern region where suitable habitat occurs.

Habitat: The Cobweb Skipper is found on dry hillsides, usually rocky sites, where its host plant is found. These areas may include shale barrens, pine-oak barrens, and cedar-oak glades. They are often fairly open sites that have been burned or cleared and have a considerable amount of beard grass.

Life History and Habits: Males perch on or near the ground and readily visit low flowers. The skipper is univoltine, with a single brood that flies in April and early May. The flight is short, and by late May adults are gone. The eggs are white. The caterpillar is light brown with a greenish dorsal stripe and a black head. There is a narrow, black prothoracic collar. The chrysalis is a drab green and is probably the overwintering stage.

Nectar Sources: Early spring flowers are visited for nectar by the species. Bird's-foot violet *(Viola pedata)*, spring beauty *(Claytonia)*, wild strawberry *(Fragaria)*, and clovers *(Trifolium)* are among the common plants visited.

Larval Host Plant: The beard grasses *(Andropogon)* are the host plants for this species, especially little bluestem *(A. scoparius)*, although big bluestem *(A. gerardii)* and other *Andropogon* grasses are also used.

Indian Skipper

Hesperia sassacus sassacus (Harris), 1862
Adult: Plate 27, Row 7
Larva: Plate 42, Row 2
Pupa: Plate 50, Row 2

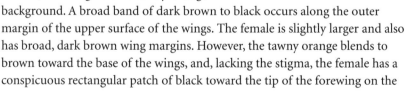

Description: Wingspan is 1 to 1⅜ inches (25–35 mm). The Indian Skipper is a small to medium butterfly with triangular wings. The male has a slender, black stigma on a tawny-orange background. A broad band of dark brown to black occurs along the outer margin of the upper surface of the wings. The female is slightly larger and also has broad, dark brown wing margins. However, the tawny orange blends to brown toward the base of the wings, and, lacking the stigma, the female has a conspicuous rectangular patch of black toward the tip of the forewing on the upper surface. The underside of both sexes is greenish orange with a faint row of light yellow, rectangular patches in the hindwing. A few yellow patches occur near the tip of the forewing underside.

Distribution: The Indian Skipper ranges from Maine west across southern Ontario to Minnesota, and then southward through the mountains into West Virginia, Virginia, and western North Carolina. In West Virginia the Indian Skipper has been reported from the counties along the eastern portion of the state. Because it is a northern species, its range in West Virginia is restricted to the counties within the higher mountain region. It is fairly easy to find in open fields at high elevations during spring.

Habitat: This skipper occurs in old brushy fields, woodland clearings, grazed or ungrazed pastures, and rocky hillsides.

Life History and Habits: Males and females spend much of the day flitting among various spring field flowers obtaining nectar. Males frequently perch on grass or broad-leafed plants close to the ground. This skipper is a rapid flier and, except for its short flights between plants, is difficult to follow or capture. The Indian Skipper is univoltine in West Virginia and flies during May and June into early July. Females oviposit as late as 1630 hours (4:30 P.M.). The pale green, hemispherical eggs are deposited singly on host leaves or stems. The caterpillar is brown to reddish brown, often mottled with green highlights or light speckling, and has a black head. Larvae live in silk-structured shelters at the base of grass clumps. The slender chrysalis is light brown.

Nectar Sources: Various spring plants are visited for nectar, such as henbit *(Lamium),* orange and yellow hawkweed *(Hieracium),* gromwell *(Lithospermum),* phlox *(Phlox),* viper's bugloss *(Echium vulgare),* and blackberry *(Rubus).*

Larval Host Plant: Panic grasses *(Panicum* spp.) are readily chosen along with little bluestem *(Andropogon scoparius)* and red fescue *(Festuca rubra).* Bluegrass *(Poa* spp.) and poverty oatgrass *(Danthonia spicata)* are also known hosts in West Virginia. Other grasses are probably utilized as well.

Peck's Skipper

Polites peckius (Kirby), 1837

Adult: Plate 28, Row 1
Larva: Plate 42, Row 2
Pupa: Plate 50, Row 2

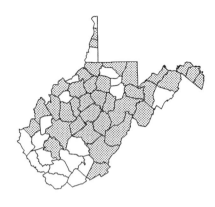

Description: Wingspan is ¾ to 1 inch (19–25 mm). Peck's Skipper is a small butterfly easily recognized by the bright yellow patch against a rust background on the underside of the hindwing. Males are dark brown above with a tawny-orange patch along the costal margin of the forewing extending to its base. The black stigma is prominent and narrow. There is a large gray-brown patch next to the outside edge of the stigma. The distal end of the forewing has a broad, dark brown band. The upperside of the hindwing has square yellow spots on a dark brown background. Females are dark brown with several tawny-yellow spots on the upper surface of both wings. Both sexes have an expanding row of bright yellow, rectangular spots on the underside of the hindwing. The veins between the spots are dark.

Distribution: Peck's Skipper ranges from Newfoundland west across southern Canada to British Columbia , south to northern Georgia, and west to Colorado, Idaho, and northern California. It is rare in the South. This skipper is common in open areas of West Virginia and should be found in all counties.

Habitat: Peck's Skipper is an inhabitant of a variety of open areas, including fields, pastures, meadows (wet and dry), power- and gas-line right-of-ways, lawns, landfills, roadsides, and marshes.

Life History and Habits: This is a rapid-flying skipper. Males and females can be found most often at various nectar plants. Males have a tendency to perch on low vegetation in sunny areas. Peck's Skipper is bivoltine in West Virginia, although the second flight may only be a partial one at times. The first flight begins in late May and extends through June, and the second flight occurs in late July and extends through August. Individuals may be found in September. The egg is white to pale green, small, and almost spherical. The caterpillar is maroon to dark brown, covered with short amber hairs, and has a black head. The species overwinters in the larval stage.

Nectar Sources: Red clover is a favorite nectar plant during the first flight, but many plants serve as nectar sources during summer, including dogbane

(*Apocynum*), milkweed *(Asclepias)*, thistle *(Cirsium)*, Joe-pye weed *(Eupatorium)*, ironweed *(Vernonia)*, vetch *(Vicia)*, New Jersey tea *(Ceanothus americanus)*, selfheal *(Prunella vulgaris)*, viper's bugloss *(Echium vulgare)*, and blue vervain *(Verbena hastata)*.

Larval Host Plant: Grasses are the host for the species. Shapiro (1974) reported rice cutgrass *(Leersia oryzoides)* as a host plant for Peck's Skipper. Other grasses belonging to the genus *Poa* are also selected in West Virginia, as well as rice cutgrass.

Tawny-edged Skipper

Polites themistocles (Latreille), 1824

Adult: Plate 28, Row 2
Larva: Plate 42, Row 3

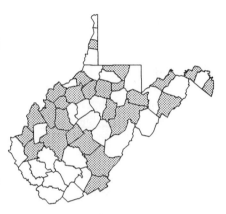

Description: Wingspan is 1 to 1¼ inches (25–32 mm). The Tawny-edged Skipper is a small butterfly with somewhat pointed, triangular wings. Males are olive brown on the upperside with a bright tawny-orange patch along the costal margin of the forewing above an S-shaped, black stigma. The upperside of the female is dark brown with some orange along the costal margin and a band of yellow spots in the outer portion of the forewing. The hindwing is plain brown. The underside of both sexes is greenish to mustard, and either plain or with a curved row of faint spots on the hindwing. The forewing has some orange along the costal margin with black at the base.

Distribution: The Tawny-edged Skipper is found throughout the eastern United States and Canada, and west to British Columbia and northern California. The species occurs southward in the West to Arizona and New Mexico. In West Virginia the Tawny-edged Skipper should be found in all counties, although records thus far have been scattered throughout the state.

Habitat: This skipper prefers wetter sites than does its close relative, the Crossline Skipper *(P. origines)*. It can be found in fields and wet meadows, along stream banks, and basking or sipping moisture from damp or muddy soil at stream edges. This is a skipper of open areas.

Life History and Habits: Males perch on low vegetation, often on the tops of grass stems, awaiting females. They also perch frequently on bare ground, usually in a wet area along a stream. They are rapid fliers and generally fly back and forth, landing close to the same spot from which they were disturbed. Pairs mate from midday to midafternoon (1200–1500 hours, 12:00–3:00 P.M.). Females oviposit from midday to late afternoon. The skipper is bivoltine in West Virginia, flying from late May through June and into July and then again in August to late September, and occasionally into October. The caterpillar is yellowish brown to maroon, covered with short black hairs, and has a black head that may contain pale, vertical stripes when fully grown.

Nectar Sources: This skipper utilizes a variety of field flowers for nectar, including dogbane *(Apocynum),* clovers *(Trifolium),* thistles *(Cirsium),* milkweed *(Asclepias),* viper's bugloss *(Echium vulgare),* and chicory *(Cichorium intybus).*

Larval Host Plant: Panic grasses *(Panicum* spp.) are reported as the main host for the larva, and usually the smaller species are selected. *Panicum microcarpon* is a known host for the skipper in West Virginia. Other grasses are also used, including bluegrass *(Poa)* and mannagrass *(Glyceria).* The species will also feed on sedge and has accepted *Carex scabrata* in rearing studies.

Crossline Skipper

Polites origenes (Fabricius), 1793

Adult: Plate 28, Row 3
Larva: Plate 42, Row 3
Pupa: Plate 50, Row 3

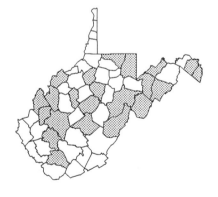

Description: Wingspan is 1 to 1¼ inches (25–32 mm). The Crossline Skipper male is a small, pointed-winged, brown skipper with a tawny-orange patch along the costal margin of the forewing above the stigma. The stigma is black, not as bright or sinuous as that of the Tawny-edged Skipper *(P. themistocles),* and lacks the hooked ends that form a reversed "S" that is prominent in *P. themistocles.* A pale spot occurs at the tip of the stigma in males. The female is also dark brown, with or without orange scaling near the base of the forewing above, and has several pale spots in the distal end of the forewing; the spot at the end of the forewing cell is often square. The underside of both sexes is plain brownish with an olive-green cast in fresh specimens. A faint, curved band of pale spots may occur across the center of the hindwing in many individuals.

Distribution: This skipper is found throughout the eastern United States from Maine across southern Canada to North Dakota and south to northern Florida, the Gulf states, and Texas. In West Virginia the skipper is probably found in all counties, with records scattered around the state.

Habitat: The Crossline Skipper can be distinguished from its close relative, the Tawny-edged Skipper, by its habitat. The Crossline Skipper is most often found in dry, grassy areas away from water, whereas the Tawny-edged Skipper prefers wet areas near water. Typical areas to look for the Crossline Skipper would be in old fields, pastures, meadows, dry grassy or brushy openings in woodlands, and power- or gas-line right-of-ways.

Life History and Habits: The Crossline Skipper is a rapid flier. Males perch on low vegetation or on short grass. On occasion they are found at wet puddles in pastures where they sip moisture. Courtship and mating take place during midday, and egg laying by females usually occurs in the afternoon. In West Virginia the Crossline Skipper is bivoltine, with the first flight occurring during late May and June and into July. A second flight of generally larger individuals occurs from August through September. The egg is a pale green hemisphere and is deposited singly on the host plant. The caterpillar is dark brown with dirty white marbling and has a black head. Larvae live in shelters constructed by tying grass blades together with silk. They pull leaves and other cut grass blades into the shelter.

Nectar Sources: This skipper visits many flowering plants found in fields during its flight periods. Some of the favored plants include dogbane *(Apocynum)*, common vetch *(Vicia)*, clovers *(Trifolium)*, ironweed *(Vernonia)*, milkweeds *(Asclepias)*, and viper's bugloss *(Echium vulgare)*.

Larval Host Plant: Several grasses are used as hosts by this skipper, including mannagrass *(Glyceria melicaria)*, bluegrass *(Poa)*, and little bluestem *(Audrapogon scoparius)*. Purpletop *(Triodia flava)* has also been reported as a host. The Crossline Skipper feeds on sedges as well, and used *Carex scabrata* in rearing studies in West Virginia.

Whirlabout

Polites vibex vibex (Geyer), 1832

Adult: Plate 28, Row 4
Larva: Plate 42, Row 3
Pupa: Plate 50, Row 3

Description: Wingspan is 1 to 1¼ inches (25–32 mm). The male Whirlabout is a tawny-yellow skipper with a broad, black stigma connected to a grayish dash at the forewing tip. The wing borders are black. The underside of the male is yellow with 2 rows of unconnected black spots on the hindwing. The female is dark brown above with a bronze cast near the base. There is a series of 2 to 5 pale yellow spots near the outer forewing. On the underside, the female is bronze to greenish with 2 rows of unconnected, dark brown to black spots on the hindwing.

Distribution: The Whirlabout is a southern species that occurs from coastal North Carolina through Florida to Texas and south to tropical America. It is only an occasional stray into West Virginia and may be found in the warmer regions along water courses. The only record in the state for this species is from Charleston in Kanawha County.

Habitat: The Whirlabout is found in open, dry or damp, grassy areas, fields, rolling hills, and urban habitats. In West Virginia it may be found in open areas along rivers that are probably followed in the skippers' northward movement. Likely areas to look for this skipper are along the Kanawha and Ohio Rivers.

Life History and Habits: Males are quite active and fly rapidly, perching on low vegetation. Both sexes can be found visiting a variety of flowers from midmorning to late afternoon. There are 2 broods in Georgia, and in Florida the skipper is found year round. Following mild winters the skipper may migrate into southern West Virginia and could reproduce here if it finds a suitable host. However, because of the lack of records, this species is probably a rare breeder in West Virginia and more likely is an occasional visitor. The egg is smooth, white, and hemispherical. The caterpillar is pale green with a dark dorsal stripe and has a black head containing 2 yellow-white patches and 2 pale stripes on the front. The body is speckled with fine black dots, and there are 2 white, ventral patches between the last 2 abdominal segments. The chrysalis is light green with a pale abdomen.

Nectar Sources: Various field flowers are visited for nectar. Summer flowers, such as fleabane *(Erigeron)*, dogbane *(Apocynum)*, viper's bugloss *(Echium vulgare)*, and many others, are favored.

Larval Host Plant: Bermuda grass *(Paspalum setaceum)* is the favored host of the species (Opler and Krizek 1984), and though it has been found only in Pendleton County, other species of *Paspalum* are found more commonly in the state and may also serve as hosts. Panic grasses or weedy lawn grasses of the family Poaceae may also be utilized as hosts.

Long Dash

Polites mystic mystic (Edwards), 1863
Adult: Plate 28, Row 5

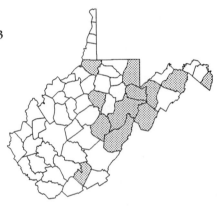

Description: Wingspan is 1 to 1¼ inches (25–32 mm). The Long Dash is a medium tawny-orange skipper with a broad, dark brown border and a broad, black stigma. A black dash occurs at the forewing tip, giving the stigma an elongated appearance in the males. Black veins are visible in the orange patch of the hindwing. Females are more tawny orange than males, darker at the base, and have 2 connecting, black patches from the base to the tip of the forewing. The wing borders are black. The underside is golden to brown or rust, with a curved, submarginal row of pale, elongated spots and a pale, basal spot in the hindwing.

Distribution: The Long Dash is found throughout the northern United States and southern Canada west to British Columbia. It extends southward through the mountains into West Virginia and western Virginia. In West Virginia it is found mainly in the eastern half of the state, with records from several counties. It can probably be found in many of the remaining eastern and northern counties as well.

Habitat: The Long Dash is usually associated with wetlands and is found in moist, open areas, such as wet meadows, seeps, stream banks, marshes, and woodland edges. At times this skipper can also be found in large numbers on Spruce Knob along the grassy hillsides above the lake some distance from the water.

Life History and Habits: The Long Dash is a rapid flier, and males perch on low vegetation in open areas. Courtship and mating take place during the afternoon. Females have been observed egg laying from late morning to late afternoon. In West Virginia, especially at high elevations, the species is univoltine, with adults flying from late May through June and into July. The egg is pale green, hemispherical, and finely reticulated. The caterpillar is dark brown, mottled with dull white, and has short black hairs arising from black tubercles. It has a dark dorsal stripe and a black head. The larva feeds on grasses and constructs a protective cylinder in grass clumps by tying the leaf blades together with silk. Other grass-feeding *Polites* construct similar shelters. The Long Dash overwinters as a half-grown larva in a cylindrical shelter.

Nectar Sources: The Long Dash visits flowers for nectar, such as milkweed *(Asclepias)*, tick-trefoil *(Desmodium)*, mountain laurel *(Kalmia latifolia)*, hawkweeds *(Hieracium)*, dogbane *(Apocynum)*, and red clover *(Trifolium pratense)*.

Larval Host Plant: Grasses are the host for the larvae of the Long Dash. Bluegrass *(Poa)* has been reported as the larval host in Pennsylvania (Shapiro 1966), but other grasses in the Poaceae family are used as well.

Northern Broken-Dash

Wallengrenia egeremet (Scudder), 1864
Adult: Plate 28, Row 6

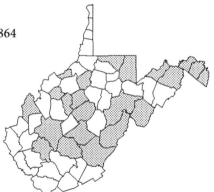

Description: Wingspan is 1 to 1¼ inches (25–32 mm). The Northern Broken-Dash is a medium, uniformly brown skipper. Males possess a divided stigma. There is a narrow, apricot dash extending from the outer portion of the stigma near the tip of the forewing on the upperside. The hindwing is plain brown. In the female there are several apricot spots in the outer portion of the forewing and a faint, curved row of spots on the hindwing. The underside of both sexes is purplish to reddish brown, with a faint, curved row of pale spots on the hindwing.

Distribution: The Northern Broken-Dash ranges throughout the eastern United States from Canada south into Florida, and west beyond the Mississippi River. In West Virginia the skipper should be found in all counties. Present records are scattered throughout the state.

Habitat: This species prefers open areas, such as weedy or brushy fields, usually in close proximity to woods. It may also be found in fields near wet areas. Abandoned farm land would be excellent habitat for this skipper in West Virginia.

Life History and Habits: Males are active during the morning hours searching for mates. They tend to perch on low shrubs, twigs, or vegetation a few feet above the ground. In West Virginia the Northern Broken-Dash is univoltine, with a single flight occurring in late June and extending into August. Eggs are deposited singly on grass blades; they are large, hemispherical, and lime green. Shortly after being deposited, a red ring appears around the egg. Newly hatched larvae are yellow with a black head, and they diapause in that stage. The caterpillar is apple green with darker green mottling and has faint dorsal and lateral stripes. The head is brown and also contains a dark central stripe and pale lateral stripes on the face. The chrysalis is green with a yellow abdomen and brown head.

Nectar Sources: This skipper visits many summer flowers found in second-growth fields. Purple, pink, or white are the preferred colors and include such plants as red and white clovers *(Trifolium)*, knapweed *(Centaurea)*, and New Jersey tea *(Ceanothus americanus)*.

Larval Host Plant: Preferred host plants are the panic grasses *(Panicum* spp.), with deertongue *(Panicum clandestinum)* and switch grass *(P. virgatum)* reported as commonly selected hosts.

Little Glassywing

Pompeius verna verna (Edwards), 1862

Adult: Plate 28, Row 7

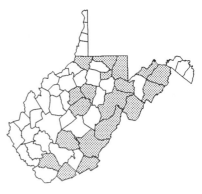

Description: Wingspan is 1 to 1⅜ inches (26–34 mm). The Little Glassywing male is a dark brown skipper with a short row of pale glassy spots in the outer forewing and along the black stigma on the upperside. The female is similar to the male, with large glassy spots in the forewing, but lacks the stigma. On the underside of the forewing the glassy spots are visible. The hindwing underside is purplish brown with a few pale submarginal spots.

Distribution: The Little Glassywing is found throughout the eastern United States and southern Canada from New England south to Florida, and west to Texas and eastern Nebraska. In West Virginia it should be found in all counties, but records to date are scattered throughout the state.

Habitat: The Little Glassywing is an inhabitant of openings, including cleared areas, open fields, and openings in forest habitat. It can be frequently found nectaring at flowers in fields. It prefers moist habitat and is most often found in clearings near streams, marshes, and bogs.

Life History and Habits: Males utilize open fields where they perch on low vegetation awaiting females. Mating occurs around midday. Over much of the southern part of its range, the Little Glassywing is reported to be double-brooded. In West Virginia it is single-brooded, especially in the mountains. Adults are found from early June into August, with the peak of the flight occurring in early July. The hemispherical egg is whitish when deposited and turns greenish before hatching. The caterpillar is yellowish green to yellowish brown and covered with numerous brown tubercles, each projecting a short light hair. There is a single, dark dorsal stripe and 2 to 3 lateral stripes on the body. The head is dark reddish brown with a black posterior margin. The species probably overwinters in an early larval instar.

Nectar Sources: Several field plants are utilized by the species during its flight period. White, pink, and purple flowers are preferred. These include milkweeds *(Asclepias),* dogbane *(Apocynum),* mints *(Mentha),* ironweed *(Vernonia),* and viper's bugloss *(Echium vulgare).*

Larval Host Plant: The only reported host for the species is purpletop grass *(Triodia flava),* which is common throughout the state in open areas, road banks, and waste places (Opler and Krizek 1984).

Sachem

Atalopedes campestris huron (Edwards),
1863

Adult: Plate 29, Row 1
Larva: Plate 42, Row 4
Pupa: Plate 50, Row 3

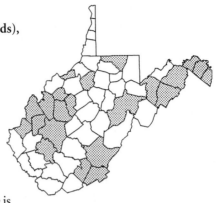

Description: Wingspan is 1 to 1½
inches (25–37 mm). Male Sachems
are tawny orange with brown wing
borders. The stigma forms a large
black oval in the forewing. The female is
dark brown with tawny orange in the wing centers and large, glassy
white windows in the outer forewing, one being a large rectangular window in
the distal end of the discal cell. There is a black patch at the base of the large
window spot. The underside of the hindwing is dusky yellow to olive, with a
band of paler spots along the outer margin. The female has a darker hindwing
than the male.

Distribution: The Sachem is a resident of the southern United States from
coastal Virginia through Florida, the Gulf states to California, and then south
through Central America. It is a regular migrant northward over much of the
United States, and in the East to northern Pennsylvania. The Sachem migrates
into West Virginia almost annually, and though it reproduces in the state, it
cannot winter this far north. It has been found in several counties and can be
expected to occur in all counties when flights are strong.

Habitat: The Sachem prefers open, sunny areas, such as fields, pastures, lawns,
roadsides, landfills, and gas- and power-line right-of-ways. Any disturbed,
weedy site is a good place to look for the Sachem.

Life History and Habits: Male Sachems perch in sunlit openings either on the
ground or on low vegetation within 1 to 2 feet of the ground. Courtship and
mating take place from midmorning into midafternoon. Egg laying occurs
during the afternoon, with females laying a single egg on a grass blade. Adult
Sachems have been observed in West Virginia from late March through
September, and flights probably extend into October. Most Sachems are
observed during August and September. If the skipper arrives early in the
season, there may be as many as 3 broods in West Virginia, with 1 occurring
during May, another in July, and a third in September. The egg is a small white
hemisphere. The caterpillar is dark green and covered with dark tubercles,
each bearing a short dark hair. The head is black. Larvae live in silk shelters

constructed at the base of the grass clump. The chrysalis is brown with white patches on the thorax and is covered with a white, powdery bloom.

Nectar Sources: Sachems visit a wide variety of flowers, including milkweed *(Asclepias),* dogbane *(Apocynum),* clovers *(Trifolium),* mints *(Mentha),* thistles *(Cirsium),* ironweed *(Vernonia),* Joe-pye weed *(Eupatorium),* asters *(Asters),* and marigolds *(Tagetes).* In late summer and fall they are readily found at patches of marigolds.

Larval Host Plant: Grasses are the host for the Sachem, with crabgrass *(Digitaria* spp.) and goose grass *(Eleusine indica)* the species most often selected in West Virginia. Bermuda grass *(Cynodon dactylon)* is also reported as a preferred host but is quite scarce in the state, although it does occur sporadically at elevations under 1800 feet.

Delaware Skipper

Atrytone logan logan (Edwards), 1863
Adult: Plate 29, Row 2

Description: Wingspan is 1 to 1⅜ inches (25–35 mm). The Delaware Skipper is bright tawny orange with a thin brown border and brown veins. The stigma is narrow and extends almost to the base of the forewing. A dark dash occurs along the distal edge of the discal cell. The female is similar to the male but has wider marginal bands and is darker toward the base of the wings. The underside is bright golden yellow with black at the base and along the lower margin of the forewings.

Distribution: The Delaware Skipper occurs from southern Maine west across southern Ontario to Montana, and south to Florida, Texas, and Mexico. In West Virginia the skipper might be found in all counties if suitable wetlands exist. At present the skipper has only been reported from 10 counties but probably occurs in several other counties as well.

Habitat: The Delaware Skipper prefers damp meadows, fields, and marshes. The species is occasionally found in dry fields but most often is found in wet areas, which may be suburban lots and roadsides.

Life History and Habits: Males perch on grasses in lowland fields or depressions and are rapid flyers. At times they perch on the ground, especially near water or along paths. Mating occurs during the afternoon. Although the Delaware Skipper is reported to be double-brooded over much of its range, it is reported to be single-brooded in Indiana (Shull 1987). In West Virginia it is probably single-brooded. Most adults are found during July, resulting from a flight that begins in June and extends into August. The eggs are small and white. The caterpillar is bluish white and covered with minute, dark tubercles and a black crescent band near the anal plate. The head is white with a black margin and contains 3 dark stripes on the face. The chrysalis is slender and greenish white with a black head, and the last abdominal segment is black.

Nectar Sources: This skipper favors a variety of white or pink flowers, including milkweeds *(Asclepias),* buttonbush *(Cephalanthus occidentalis),* mints *(Mentha),* and thistles *(Cirsium),* for nectar.

Larval Host Plant: The reported larval hosts are bluestem grasses *(Andropogon* spp.) and switch grass *(Panicum virgatum),* with switch grass being the more common throughout the state. Other grasses associated with wetlands are probably also used as hosts but have not been confirmed.

Hobomok Skipper

Poanes hobomok (Harris), 1862
Adult: Plate 29, Rows 3, 4
Larva: Plate 42, Row 4

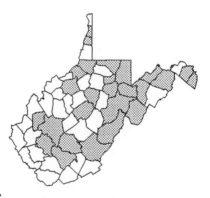

Description: Wingspan is 1⅛ to 1½ inches (29–39 mm). The Hobomok Skipper is a medium skipper. The male is yellow orange on the upperside, with broad, dark brown wing borders. A dark dash occurs in the outer end of the discal cell. The female is also yellow orange with wide, dark brown wing borders and wing bases restricting the amount of orange present to the center areas of the wings. The underside is yellow to yellow orange with brown wing margins and bases. The outer margins of the wings are dusted with gray and violet. The female Hobomok occurs in 2 color forms. In the dark form "Pocahontas" the wings are dark brown above with a series of pale spots near the tip of the forewing. The hindwing is brown above with a faint patch of tawny color. Individuals can be quite variable. The underside of "Pocahontas" is dark brown. The hindwing contains a pale band of brown, and the forewing contains a yellow patch with a few pale spots near the tip.

Distribution: The Hobomok Skipper occurs in the northern United States from Nova Scotia to Saskatchewan south through the mountains to northern Georgia and west to Kansas and Oklahoma. An isolated population occurs in Colorado and New Mexico. In West Virginia, the skipper is widely distributed and can probably be found in all counties.

Habitat: The Hobomok Skipper prefers sunlit openings in woods, woodland edges, trails, and along woodland roads. It is also found in damp areas along bog edges or woodland streams.

Life History and Habits: Like many skippers, the Hobomok is a rapid flyer. Males perch on tree leaves in sunlit openings generally 5 to 6 feet above the ground and fly after other butterflies passing close by. Males are aggressive toward other males, and chase flights are common. The Hobomok Skipper is univoltine throughout its range. In West Virginia the skipper flies from May through June and into early July. The peak of its flight is in June. The egg of the Hobomok is white and is deposited singly on grass blades. Larvae are pale brownish green and covered with small tubercles and short white hairs, which give them a velvety appearance. They have round, brown heads. Caterpillars live in rolled leaf shelters and feed mainly at night. Larvae overwinter in tubular shelters made by rolling the edges of a grass blade together, and they complete development the following spring.

Nectar Sources: Adults visit several species of flowers and shrubs for nectar, including blackberry *(Rubus)*, privet *(Ligustrum)*, milkweed *(Asclepias)*, viper's bugloss *(Echium vulgare)*, and henbit *(Lamium)*.

Larval Host Plant: Several grasses are utilized as hosts. Panic grasses *(Panicum)* are most frequently selected, with *P. microcarpon* the preferred host in West Virginia. Deertongue *(P. clandestinum)* is also used on occasion. However, other grasses, such as blue grass *(Poa* spp.), little bluestem *(Andropogan scoparium)*, poverty oatgrass *(Danthonia spicata)* and rice cutgrass *(Leersia oryzoides)*, are also readily fed upon.

Zabulon Skipper

Poanes zabulon (Boisduval and LeConte), 1834

Adult: Plate 29, Rows 4, 5
Larva: Plate 43, Row 1
Pupa: Plate 50, Row 4

Description: Wingspan is 1 to 1⅜ inches (25–35 mm). The male Zabulon is a medium yellow orange skipper with dark brown borders. A thin black dash occurs near the tip of the forewing. The underside of the male is yellow orange with several small brown spots along the outer margin of the hindwing, and a larger spot near the base. The female is dark blackish brown with conspicuous, pale yellow, angular spots in the forewing forming a zigzag pattern. The underside of the female is dark brown with rust spots in the hindwing and a violet flush along the outer wing margins.

Distribution: The Zabulon Skipper ranges from southern New England, south to northern Florida, and west to Texas and Kansas. In West Virginia the skipper has been found in many counties and probably occurs in all counties. At times it is more abundant than the Hobomok Skipper and is generally encountered more frequently.

Habitat: This skipper prefers sunlit openings around woodland edges, stream banks, and openings along woodland roads. These areas are often brushy, and in a transitional stage of growth.

Life History and Habits: Males are rapid flyers and perch on tree or shrub leaves 4 to 6 feet above the ground. Sunny spots are selected for perching. Like the Hobomok Skipper, Zabulon males interact with other males flying through their territory. Males often use the same perching site repeatedly as long as it remains sunlit. Females are not as conspicuous as males and are frequently seen in shaded, brushy areas perched within a foot of the ground or visiting flowers for nectar. The Zabulon Skipper is bivoltine in West Virginia, with the first adults flying from early May through June and into July, and those of the resulting brood flying in late July and August and extending into late September. The eggs are small, pale green, and laid singly on grass blades. The caterpillar is pale brown to greenish with a dark dorsal stripe and a white lateral stripe and is covered with fine short hairs, giving it a velvety appearance. The head is reddish brown. Two white patches occur between the last 2 abdominal segments on the ventral surface. The pupa is almost white, pink toward the thorax, and is covered with a white, powdery bloom.

Nectar Sources: The Zabulon Skipper visits many flowers and shrubs, both native and exotic, for nectar. Some of these include Japanese honeysuckle *(Lonicera japonica),* privet *(Ligustrum),* blackberry *(Rubus),* buttonbush *(Cephalanthus occidentalis),* common vetch *(Vicia),* clovers *(Vernonia),* violets *(Viola),* milkweeds *(Asclepias),* ironweed *(Vernonia),* and Joe-pye weed *(Eupatorium).*

Larval Host Plant: Females are reported to select grasses, such as purpletop *(Triodia flava)* and lovegrass *(Eragrostis* spp.), as their primary hosts. In West Virginia a readily selected host is small-fruited panic grass *(Panicum microcarpon).* The larvae will also feed on white grass *(Leersia virginica)* and bluegrass in the genus *Poa.*

Black Dash

Euphyes conspicuus conspicuus (Edwards), 1863

Adult: Plate 29, Row 6
Larva: Plate 43, Row 1

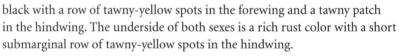

Description: Wingspan is 1 to 1⅜ inches (25–35 mm). Males are tawny orange with broad, brown borders and wing bases and a conspicuous black stigma. The female is dark brownish black with a row of tawny-yellow spots in the forewing and a tawny patch in the hindwing. The underside of both sexes is a rich rust color with a short submarginal row of tawny-yellow spots in the hindwing.

Distribution: In the East the Black Dash occurs from Massachusetts southward into Virginia and then south of the Great Lakes from northern Ohio to Minnesota and Nebraska. In West Virginia the Black Dash occurs in 1 known population along the Maryland border at Cranesville in Preston County. It may also occur in other wetland sites in Grant, Jefferson, Mineral, Preston, Randolph, and Tucker Counties where its preferred host is found. The skipper may also occur in other northern counties.

Habitat: The Black Dash is an inhabitant of wet, marshy areas and wet meadows where stands of sedges are abundant.

Life History and Habits: Males of the Black Dash are rapid flyers and perch on tall grasses in dense marsh vegetation. Females can also be found perched on marsh vegetation or visiting flowers of various wetland plants for nectar. The Black Dash is single-brooded, with its flight occurring in late June and extending through July. Worn adults can be found into August. Larvae hibernate in shelters constructed by tying several sedge blades together in the second or third instar and complete development the following spring. The caterpillar is dark green with wavy, longitudinal, fine white lines. The head is brown with cream-colored bands and a black oval ringed in white or cream in the center of the forehead.

Nectar Sources: Several large flowering plants found in wetlands are visited for nectar during the flight period. They include swamp milkweed *(Asclepias incarnata)*, thistles *(Cirsium)*, ironweed *(Vernonia)*, and Joe-pye weed *(Eupatorium)*.

Larval Host Plant: Sedges *(Carex* spp.) are the hosts for the species. In West Virginia *Carex stricta* is the commonly selected host.

Two-spotted Skipper

Euphyes bimacula (Grote and Robinson), 1867

Adult: Plate 29, Row 7
Larva: Plate 43, Row 2

Description: Wingspan is 1⅛ to 1¼ inches (29–32 mm). Males are dark brown with a tawny-orange patch around a black stigma on the upper surface. The underside is tawny brown with 2 pale spots in the forewing. There is a dark brown patch along the lower margin of both wings beneath, with pale veins in the hindwing. The female is also dark brown on the upperside with 3 to 5 small, pale yellow, rectangular spots in a row across the outer forewing. On the underside, the female is tawny brown with light veins and white scaling along the wing fringes, inner wing margins, and body.

Distribution: The Two-spotted Skipper is a northern species occurring from Maine across southern Canada and south into West Virginia through the mountains. A separate population occurs in Colorado and Nebraska. It also ranges south to Georgia along the coastal plain. In West Virginia the skipper has been found in wetlands in Hampshire, Pendleton, Pocahontas, and Webster Counties, with a small known population on Deer Creek at Greenbank. It may also occur in other surrounding counties.

Habitat: The Two-spotted Skipper is found only in wet, sedge meadows, marshes, and bogs, most often in close proximity to woods.

Life History and Habits: Males and females perch on grass blades within the marsh 2 to 3 feet above the ground. They perch with their wings partly open, as do many of the branded skippers. They interact readily with other skippers or males of the same species. The species is univoltine, with a single flight in West Virginia occurring in June and July. The pale green eggs are deposited singly on blades of the host sedge. Within 2 days, an orange ring appears around the egg. Larvae feed on the sedge from shelters constructed by tying several blades together. They hibernate for the winter in shelters in the third or fourth instar. The caterpillar is pale green with a dark dorsal stripe. The head is chestnut brown, ridged toward the rear, and has a dark chestnut band around its edge. A black oval ringed with white occurs in the center of the forehead.

Nectar Sources: Various wetland plants and shrubs are visited for nectar. These include swamp milkweed *(Asclepias incarnata),* ironweed *(Vernonia),* spiraea *(Spiraea),* and maleberry *(Lyonia ligustrina).*

Larval Host Plant: Sedges are the hosts for this skipper, with *Carex stricta* a known host in West Virginia.

Dun Skipper

Euphyes vestris metacomet (Harris), 1862

Adult: Plate 30, Row 1
Larva: Plate 43, Row 3

Description: Wingspan is 1 to 1¼ inches (25–32 mm). The male Dun Skipper is a medium brownish black skipper with a thin black stigma on the forewing. The female is also brownish black with 4 to 5 pale spots in the outer forewing. The underside is brownish black with a black area at the base of the forewing and a faint row of lighter spots on the hindwing. There is a greenish sheen to the hindwings.

Distribution: The Dun Skipper's range extends from Nova Scotia across Canada to Manitoba and south to Florida and eastern Texas. In West Virginia the skipper probably occurs statewide, with scattered records from several counties.

Habitat: The Dun Skipper is associated with wet areas in and near deciduous woodlands, such as wet meadows, marshes, and boggy areas. They may also use wet seeps along roads or power- and gas-line right-of-ways.

Life History and Habits: Males perch on grasses or other vegetation 2 to 3 feet above the ground in the wet areas they inhabit. They can also be found on bare ground along stream edges where they sip moisture and minerals. Mating generally occurs in the afternoon. Egg laying occurs during late morning and into midafternoon when females are actively flying through the sedges. In West Virginia the species is bivoltine, with the first flight in May and extending through June. The second flight occurs from mid-July through August and into late September. The eggs are hemispherical and lime green, turning red before hatching. The caterpillar is translucent green with numerous wavy, white dashes, giving it a whitish cast. The head is brown and black with 2 creamy bands and an oval, black spot high on the center of the face outlined with cream. The chrysalis is whitish green with a pale yellow-green abdomen and a pale brown head and is covered with a whitish bloom. Pupation occurs in a silk-lined tube at the base of the host plant.

Nectar Sources: Adults seem to prefer white, pink, or purple flowers for nectar, and they visit milkweed *(Asclepias)*, dogbane *(Apocynum)*, New Jersey tea *(Ceanothus americanus)*, selfheal *(Prunella vulgaris)*, mints *(Mentha)*, and viper's bugloss *(Echium vulgare)* most frequently.

Larval Host Plant: Various sedges are selected as hosts by the species. In West Virginia *Carex stricta* is a known host for the Dun Skipper. Sedges in the genus *Cyperus,* of which there are several species in West Virginia, have also been reported as hosts by Heitzman (1964).

Dusted Skipper

Atryonopsis hianna hianna (Scudder), 1868

Adult: Plate 30, Row 2

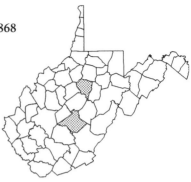

Description: Wingspan is 1¼ to 1½ inches (32–39 mm). This medium skipper has pointed wings. It is dark brown on the upper surface with several tiny white dots in the outer forewing. The female is also dark brown with larger spots in the forewing than the male. The underside is brown with a band of violet to pale gray frosting along the outer wing margins. A small white dot occurs near the base of the hindwing.

Distribution: The Dusted Skipper occurs from southern New England west to eastern Wyoming and Colorado. It ranges south to peninsula Florida and west through northern Texas to Oklahoma. In West Virginia it is found in scattered colonies where it has pioneered disturbed areas. To date, the Dusted Skipper has only been recorded from 2 counties, Lewis and Nicholas, but probably occurs in small colonies in several other counties within the state. The most consistent population occurs near the Summersville Dam in Nicholas County.

Habitat: The Dusted Skipper prefers open, dry areas that have been subjected to fire or some type of disturbance. It can be found in old fields of acid soil, woodland openings, acid pine-oak barrens, and power- or gas-line right-of-ways.

Life History and Habits: Males perch on low vegetation close to the ground during sunlit hours. The species is univoltine in West Virginia, with 1 flight beginning in mid-May and extending into June. Females fly close to the ground through grasses depositing eggs on the host grass stems from midday to midafternoon. The egg is a lemon yellow hemisphere. Caterpillars are pale pinkish lavender on the back turning to gray along the sides and behind the head. The anal segment is brown with a dark shield, and the head is dark reddish purple. The body is covered with long cream hairs. Larvae live in shelters constructed by tying several blades together. The fully grown larva winters in a sealed case constructed at the base of the grass clump 1 to 3 inches above the ground (Heitzman 1974). Pupation occurs in the sealed case.

Nectar Sources: The Dusted Skipper visits a variety of plants for nectar, including white and red clover *(Trifolium)*, strawberry *(Fragaria)*, blackberry *(Rubus)*, and phlox *(Phlox).*

Larval Host Plant: In West Virginia, little bluestem *(Andropogon scoparius)* is the host most often selected by the Dusted Skipper. Big bluestem *(A. gerardii)* may also be used on occasion.

Pepper and Salt Skipper

Amblyscirtes hegon (Scudder), 1864

Adult: Plate 30, Row 3
Larva: Plate 43, Row 3

Description: Wingspan is ⅞ to 1 inch (22–25 mm). This small skipper is dark brown with a greenish cast. There are several small, pale yellow spots in an angled row on the outer third of the forewing upper surface. The fringe is checkered. The female is similar to the male. The underside is brownish gray with a curved row of pale spots in both wings. A few pale spots occur near the base of the hindwing.

Distribution: The Pepper and Salt Skipper is found from Nova Scotia and Maine west to Minnesota and southward through the mountains to Georgia and west to Texas. The species is absent from the coastal plains, although a small population occurs in northwest Florida. In West Virginia it has been found in scattered colonies across the state. It can be expected to occur in several other counties as well, especially in the mountains. It has been regularly found along the East Fork of Glady Creek in the Monongahela National Forest in Randolph County, as well as Blackwater Falls State Park in Tucker County.

Habitat: This skipper prefers wet areas and is found along streams, bogs, low-lying wet meadows, and glades at the edges of mixed or coniferous forests.

Life History and Habits: Male Pepper and Salt Skippers perch on grass stems from the ground up to 2 feet within the marshes they inhabit. They often leave the wetland to nectar on nearby plants along trails or roads. They will also sip minerals from wet areas on sandy soil. This skipper is univoltine throughout its range. Its flight in West Virginia occurs from late April into late June. The flight is generally brief, with the early flights occurring in the warmer climates and the later flights occurring at higher elevations. The egg is a large, pale green hemisphere. Larvae overwinter in tightly sealed leaf shelters. The caterpillar is pale green with 3 dark green dorsal stripes and a pale lateral stripe. The head is brown and contains vertical stripes on the front and sides. The chrysalis is straw colored, with greenish wing pads.

Nectar Sources: The Pepper and Salt Skipper visits viburnums *(Viburnum)*, blackberry *(Rubus)*, and fleabane *(Erigeron)*, as well as other plants for nectar. It will also sip minerals from moist soil or dung.

Larval Host Plant: Grasses are the hosts for this skipper, and in West Virginia the skipper is known to feed on fowl mannagrass *(Glyceria striata)*. Other grasses selected include Kentucky bluegrass *(Poa pratensis)*, Indian grass *(Sorghastrum nutans)*, and broad-leaved uniola *(Uniola latifolia)* (Opler and Krizek 1984).

Common Roadside-Skipper

Amblyscirtes vialis (Edwards), 1862

Adult: Plate 30, Row 4

Description: Wingspan is ⅞ to 1 inch (22–25 mm). The Common Roadside-Skipper is a small, dark brownish black skipper with tiny pale spots on the outer third of the forewing. The fringe is checkered in both sexes. The female is also dark brown with a cluster of tiny pale spots near the tip of the forewing. The underside is dark brownish black with violet-gray frosting near the tip of the forewing and along the outer margin of the hindwing.

Distribution: This skipper is found from Nova Scotia and Maine to British Columbia, south to northern Florida, and west to Texas. It also occurs in northern New Mexico and central California. In West Virginia the skipper has been found in several counties scattered throughout the state. It probably occurs in all counties.

Habitat: The Common Roadside-Skipper is frequently found in open, often grassy areas near or within woodlands. It may frequent areas along streams, dry grassy hillsides, shale barrens, or power- and gas-line right-of-ways.

Life History and Habits: Males and females perch on the ground, low rocks, or low vegetation. They fly short distances when disturbed and land again on the ground. The Common Roadside-Skipper is bivoltine in West Virginia, with the first flight occurring from mid-April into June and the second flight in July through August. The egg is a pale green hemisphere. The caterpillar is pale green and covered with small green tubercles, each bearing a hair. The head is frosty white with vertical, rust stripes. Larvae live in leaf shelters. The chrysalis is green with reddish spots at both ends. The chrysalis overwinters.

Nectar Sources: The skipper visits many low spring and summer flowers for nectar. These include bird's-foot violet *(Viola pedata)*, phlox *(Phlox)*, cinquefoil *(Potentilla)*, blue vervain *(Verbena hastata)*, selfheal *(Prunella vulgaris)*, rock twist *(Draba)*, and downy woodmint *(Blephilia)*.

Larval Host Plant: Various grasses are reportedly used as host plants, including bluegrass *(Poa* spp.), broad-leaved Uniola *(Uniola latifolia)*, bent grass *(Agrostis* spp.), and Bermuda grass *(Cynodon dactylon)* if present.

Ocola Skipper

Panoquina ocola (Edwards), 1863

Adult: Plate 30, Row 5
Larva: Plate 43, Row 4
Pupa: Plate 50, Row 4

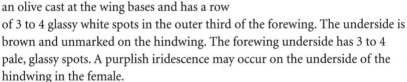

Description: Wingspan is 1¼ to 1⅜ inches (32–35 mm). The Ocola Skipper is a medium skipper with long, slender, pointed forewings. It is dark brown with an olive cast at the wing bases and has a row of 3 to 4 glassy white spots in the outer third of the forewing. The underside is brown and unmarked on the hindwing. The forewing underside has 3 to 4 pale, glassy spots. A purplish iridescence may occur on the underside of the hindwing in the female.

Distribution: The Ocola Skipper is a resident of the Deep South, including Florida, Georgia, and the Gulf Coast, and then south through the West Indies to Argentina. It strays northward as far as New Jersey and Ohio. The skipper probably follows river courses northward and has been found in West Virginia in a few scattered counties. At times, when its population is high, it might be expected to wander into West Virginia in other counties, especially along the Ohio River, or eastern counties along the New and Potomac Rivers.

Habitat: This skipper prefers damp clearings, fields, and openings along woods, especially wet areas that abound with nectar plants. These areas may include small streams and seeps.

Life History and Habits: Ocola Skipper males perch on low vegetation in weedy areas. The species is most often found visiting nectar plants. This skipper rarely breeds in West Virginia. It has only been found in the state on a few occasions and not until midsummer at which time a partial brood may occur. Larvae from eggs deposited in July and August are usually not successful in completing development before frost since they are slow growing. The egg is a smoky white hemisphere. The caterpillar is pale green to gray green with a dark dorsal stripe and pale lateral stripes. The head is lime green. The chrysalis is green with 4 yellow stripes along the abdomen and has a long, pointed projection in front.

Nectar Sources: The skipper nectars at many species of flowers, especially those of buttonbush *(Cephalanthus occidentalis),* milkweed *(Asclepias),* ironweed *(Vernonia),* and Joe-pye weed *(Eupatorium).*

Larval Host Plant: In its southern range this skipper prefers sugar cane *(Saccharum* spp.), but grasses (Poaceae) are also used. In West Virginia the species is known to use rice cutgrass *(Leersia oryzoides).*

PLATES

Collection information for all plates can be found in Appendix C.

The color plates show the adult butterflies in actual size with the exception of Papilionidae, plates 1 to 3, and Nymphalidae, plates 11 to 13, which are shown two-thirds actual size.

PLATE 1

SWALLOWTAILS
(Papilionidae)
*Subfamily Papilioninae:
Swallowtails*

Row 1
Pipevine Swallowtail. *Battus philenor.* Male. *Upperside:* Iridescent bluish green. Light blue-green submarginal spots on hindwing. p. 41
Battus philenor. Female. *Upperside:* Slight iridescence on hindwing. Lavender submarginal spots on hindwing. Pale submarginal spots on forewing.

Row 2
Battus philenor. Male. *Underside:* Curved row of 7 circular orange spots on background of iridescent blue green.
Zebra Swallowtail. *Eurytides marcellus.* Male (spring form). *Upperside:* Smaller and lighter than summer form. Tails half as long as summer individuals. p. 42

Row 3
Eurytides marcellus. Male (summer form). *Upperside:* Transverse whitish stripes on black. Large red spot on inner margin of hindwing.
Eurytides marcellus. Female (summer form). *Upperside:* Transverse whitish stripes on black. Similar to male.
Eurytides marcellus. Male. *Underside:* Transverse whitish stripes on black. Single curved transverse red stripe in hindwing.

PLATE 1 • 249

PLATE 2

SWALLOWTAILS
(Papilionidae)

Row 1
Black Swallowtail. *Papilio polyxenes asterius.* Male. *Upperside:* Narrow, postmedian yellow band on both wings. Black spot in center of orange anal patch on hindwing does not touch edge. p. 44
Papilio polyxenes asterius. Female. *Upperside:* Series of 1 or 2 rows of small, yellow spots on both wings. Large, blue band on hindwing.
Papilio polyxenes asterius. Male. *Underside:* Two rows of yellow, and orange on yellow spots on both wings.

Row 2
Giant Swallowtail. *Papilio cresphontes.* Male. *Upperside:* Prominent band of yellow spots from forewing tip to inner margin, continuing across hindwing as solid band. Yellow spot in tail and red anal crescent in hindwing. p. 45
Papilio cresphontes. Male. *Underside:* Large amount of yellow on black on both wings. Thin median band of blue and orange in hindwing.

Row 3
Spicebush Swallowtail. *Papilio troilus troilus.* Male. *Upperside:* Hindwing has row of pale, submarginal spots below dusting of greenish scales. Large orange spot along upper margin of hindwing. p. 47
Papilio t. troilus. Female. *Upperside:* Similar to male except dusting of pale green is replaced by blue.
Papilio t. troilus. Male. *Underside:* Two submarginal rows of discrete orange spots separated by area of blue scaling.

PLATE 2 · 251

PLATE 3

SWALLOWTAILS
(Papilionidae)

Row 1
Eastern Tiger Swallowtail.
Papilio glaucus. Male.
Upperside: First submarginal spot in hindwing orange in both sexes. p. 48
Papilio glaucus. Male.
Underside: Submarginal row of spots in the hindwing contain orange. Orange also extends on basal side of submarginal band (hindwing).

Row 2
Papilio glaucus. Female.
Upperside: Large patch of blue on hindwing.
Papilio glaucus. Female (black). *Upperside:* Similar to Spicebush Swallowtail but forewing submarginal spots smaller.

Row 3
Papilio glaucus. Female (intermediate). *Upperside:* Peppering of black scaling on yellow.
Papilio glaucus. Female (black). *Underside:* Darker transverse stripes visible on both wings. Submarginal row of large yellow spots with orange centers in band of blue scaling.

PLATE 3 · 253

PLATE 4

WHITES AND SULPHURS
(Pieridae)
Subfamily Pierinae: Whites

Row 1
Checkered White. *Pontia protodice.* Male. *Upperside:* White with brownish black blotches. p. 54
Pontia prodotice. Female. *Upperside:* White with heavier charcoal pattern than male.

Row 2
Pontia protodice. Female (fall brood). *Upperside:* Not as dark as spring or summer brood.
Pontia prodotice. Male. *Underside:* Nearly immaculate white hind wing below.
Pontia prodotice. Female (fall brood). *Underside:* Veins lined with brown to olive green.
Pontia prodotice. Female (spring brood). *Underside:* Veins much darker in spring brood.

Row 3
West Virginia White. *Pieris virginiensis.* Male. *Upperside:* White with slight smoky-gray fusing along wing margin and wing base. p. 55
Pieris virginiensis. Female. *Upperside:* More smoky gray in wings above.
Pieris virginiensis. Male. *Underside:* Veins streaked with varying amounts of brownish gray on hindwing.

Row 4
Cabbage White. *Pieris rapae.* Male. *Upperside:* Charcoal wing tips. Single black spot in FW and top of hindwing. p. 57
Pieris rapae. Female *Upperside:* Two black spots in FW.

Row 5
Pieris rapae. Male (spring brood). *Upperside:* Black markings in wings often diminished or completely lacking.
Pieris rapae. Male. *Underside:* Pale yellow hindwing. Forewing spots present.
Pieris rapae. Female (spring brood). *Underside:* hindwing may be dusted with smoky gray on pale yellow background. Forewing spots present.

PLATE 4 · 255

PLATE 5

WHITES AND SULPHURS
(Pieridae)
Subfamily Pierinae: Whites

Subfamily Coliadinae: Sulphurs

Row 1

Olympia Marble. *Euchloe olympia.* Male. *Upperside:* White with light to dark gray markings in FW. p. 58
Euchloe olympia. Female. *Upperside:* Similar to male.
Euchloe olympia. Male. *Underside:* Yellow-green marbling in discrete pattern on hindwing.

Row 2

Falcate Orangetip.
Anthocharis midea annickae. Male. *Upperside:* White with bright orange patch at FW tip. p. 59
Anthocharis m. annickae. Female. *Upperside:* White. Wing tips pointed and slightly hooked.
Anthocharis m. annickae. Male. *Underside:* Finely marbled pattern of chartreuse or greenish brown on hindwing. Female similar.

Row 3

Clouded Sulphur. *Colias p. philodice.* Male. *Upperside:* Yellow with sharp black border. Black FW spot. p. 61
Colias p. philodice. Female. *Upperside:* Yellow with broad black border spotted with yellow. Black FW spot.
Colias p. philodice. Female (Albino form). *Upperside:* White with white-spotted black border. Black FW spot.

Row 4

Colias p. philodice. Male. *Underside:* Yellow to greenish hindwing. Central hindwing silver spot double rimmed in red. Brown row of submarginal spots in hindwing. Fringe pink.
Orange Sulphur. *Colias eurytheme.* Male. *Upperside:* Bright orange yellow with black wing margin. p. 63

Row 5

Colias eurytheme. Female. *Upperside:* Orange yellow with black wing margin spotted with yellow. Orange spot in hindwing.
Colias eurytheme. Male. *Underside:* Orange, yellow, or greenish with single or double red-rimmed silvery spot in hindwing. Submarginal row of brown spots in hindwing.
Colias eurytheme x Colias philodice hybrid. Male. *Upperside:* Intergrades of orange to yellow. Occurs where populations are high.

PLATE 5 · 257

PLATE 6

WHITES AND SULPHURS
(Pieridae)
Subfamily Coliadinae: Sulphurs

Row 1
Pink-edged Sulphur. *Colias interior.* Male. *Upperside:* Black spot in FW light with yellow center. Pink wing fringes. p. 64
Colias interior. Female. *Upperside:* Black wing margin in FW barely reaching hindwing. Black FW spot pale with yellow center. Pink fringes.

Row 2
Colias interior. Male. *Underside:* Yellow to greenish. Silver spot in hindwing rimmed with pink. Pink wing fringes.
Cloudless Sulphur. *Phoebus sennae eubule.* Male. *Upperside:* Pale, unmarked greenish yellow. Pointed wings. p. 66

Row 3
Phoebus sennae eubule. Male. *Underside:* Yellow, often mottled with reddish brown.
Phoebus sennae eubule. Female. *Upperside:* Lemon yellow to golden. Dark markings along wing margin and FW spot variable.
Phoebus sennae eubule. Female. *Underside:* Pale yellow mottled with reddish brown. Double silver spot in hindwing. Forewing spot variable, rimmed in red-brown.

Row 4
Little Yellow. *Eurema lisa.* Male. *Upperside:* Bright yellow with black FW tips and margin. p. 67
Eureme lisa. Female. *Upperside:* Bright to pale yellow with reduced black in FW and margin. Hindwing margin with series of black connected spots.
Eurema lisa. Male. *Underside:* Dark smudges across hindwing. Rust spot in upper margin of hindwing.
Eurema lisa. Female. *Underside:* Similar to male. Pale yellow to white.

PLATE 6 · 259

PLATE 7

WHITES AND SULPHURS
(Pieridae)
Subfamily Coliadinae: Sulphurs

Row 1
Sleepy Orange. *Eurema nicippe.* Male. *Upperside:* Bright to dark orange with wide irregular black margins. p. 69
Eurema nicippe. Female. *Upperside:* Bright to pale orange. Black border breaks down halfway across hindwing.

Row 2
Eurema nicippe. Male. *Underside:* Yellow with small brown blotches on hindwing.
Eurema nicippe. Female. *Underside:* Yellow with brown and whitish blotches on hindwing.
Eurema nicippe. Female. *Underside:* Yellow FW. Pale brown hindwing with darker brown blotches.

GOSSAMER WINGS
(Lycaenidae)
Subfamily Miletinae: Harvesters

Row 3
Harvester. *Feniseca tarquinius.* Male. *Upperside:* Yellow orange with blackish borders and blotches. p. 73
Feniseca tarquinius. Female. *Upperside:* Similar to male. May have more black along margins.
Feniseca tarquinius. Male. *Underside:* FW brownish along outer margin with dark brown blotches on yellow interior. Hindwing brown with white-rimmed blotches.

Subfamily Lycaeninae: Coppers

Row 4
American Copper. *Lycaena phlaeas americana.* Male. *Upperside:* Bright golden-orange FW with black spots and gray margin. Hindwing gray with orange band along margin. p. 75
Lycaena phlaeas americana. Female. *Upperside:* Similar to male. Black spots in FW slightly larger.
Lycaena phlaeas americana. Male. *Underside:* Silver-gray hindwing with small black spots and red-orange irregular line in hindwing outer margin.

Row 5
Bronze Copper. *Lycaena hyllus.* Male. *Upperside:* Copper FW and darker hindwing with purple sheen. Orange margin in hindwing spotted with black. p. 76
Lycaena hyllus. Female. *Upperside:* Pale orange FW spotted with black. Charcoal outer margin. Hindwing charcoal with black spotted orange margin.
Lycaena hyllus. Male. *Underside:* Silver hindwing with black spots and orange margin spotted with black. Forewing black spotted on orange. Silver tips.

PLATE 7 · 261

PLATE 8

GOSSAMER WINGS
(Lycaenidae)
Subfamily Lycaeninae: Copper

Row 1
Bog Copper. *Lycaena epixanthe epixanthe.* Male. *Upperside:* Purplish with dark border. Dark spots in both wings. Orange in hindwing margin. p. 78
Lycaena e. epixanthe. Female. *Upperside:* Brown with dark spots in both wings. Orange in hindwing margin to tip.
Lycaena e. epixanthe. Male. *Underside:* Silver with black spots in forewing, smaller in hindwing. Irregular red line near hindwing margin.

Subfamily Theclinae: Hairstreaks

Row 2
Great Purple Hairstreak. *Atlides halesus.* Male. *Upperside:* Black with large patches of bright iridescent blue. p. 80
Atlides halesus. Female. *Upperside:* Black with pale iridescent blue in basal half of wings.
Atlides halesus. Male. *Underside:* Black with iridescent blue markings at tip of hindwing. Red-orange abdomen and red at base of forewing on costal margin.

Row 3
Coral Hairstreak. *Satyrium titus mopsus.* Male. *Upperside:* Brown; stigma gray. p. 81
Satyrium titus mopsus. Female. *Upperside:* Brown with 2 to 3 orange spots in outer hindwing margin.
Satyrium titus mopsus. Male. *Underside:* Gray with faint rows of black spots and submarginal row of red spots in hindwing.
Edwards' Hairstreak. *Satyrium edwardsii.* Male. *Upperside:* Brown with pale orange spot in hindwing margin. Stigmas slightly darker. p. 82

Row 4
Satyrium edwardsii. Female. *Upperside:* Brown with pale orange spot in hindwing margin.
Satyrium edwardsii. Male. *Underside:* Gray. Inner band of dark spots not connected; spots ringed with white.
Banded Hairstreak. *Satyrium calanus falacer.* Male. *Upperside:* Dark brown black. Stigma gray. p. 84

Row 5
Satyrium calanus falacer. Male. *Underside:* Dark brown inner band in forewing narrow, connected, and usually has white line on outside edge.
Hickory Hairstreak. *Satyrium caryaevorum.* Male. *Upperside:* Dark brown; stigmas present. p. 85
Satyrium caryaevorum. Male. *Underside:* Gray. Inner band in forewing offset. Band in hindwing broadens at upper margin. Band edges white.

Row 6
Striped Hairstreak. *Satyrium liparops strigosum.* Male. *Upperside:* Dark blackish brown. Stigmas large and gray. p. 87
Satyrium liparops strigosum. Female. *Upperside:* Brown. Lacks spots.
Satyium liparops strigosum. Male. *Underside:* Gray and brown. Darker band in wings wider than other species; broken with white edges.
Satyrium liparops strigosum. Female. *Underside:* Same as male but with wider bands.

PLATE 8 • 263

PLATE 9

GOSSAMER WINGS
(Lycaenidae)
Subfamily Theclinae: Hairstreaks

Row 1
Red-banded Hairstreak.
Calycopis cecrops. Male.
Upperside: Charcoal gray with
blue iridescence in hindwing
and base of forewing. p. 88
Calycopis cecrops. Female.
Upperside: Charcoal gray.
Calycopis cecrops. Female.
Underside: Gray with medium
red band in both wings.

Row 2
(Olive) Juniper Hairstreak.
Mitoura grynea grynea. Male.
Upperside: Pale brown with
dark brown borders. Pale
stigma in forewing. p. 89
Mitoura g. grynea. Female.
Upperside: Medium brown
with dark borders. Wing veins
dark.
Mitoura g. grynea. Female
(summer form). *Upperside:*
Dark brownish black.
Mitoura g. grynea. Male.
Underside: Green with
irregular bands of white edged
in brown on basal side.

Row 3
Brown Elfin. *Incisalia*
augustinus croesoides. Male.
Upperside: Brown with dark
stigmas; hindwing pointed at
lower edge. p. 91
Incisalia a. croesoides. Female.
Upperside: Brown to brownish
black.
Incisalia a. croesoides. Female.
Underside: Reddish brown
hindwing. Darker toward base.
No gray.
Hoary Elfin. *Incisalia polia.*
Male. *Upperside:* Brown with
pale stigma. p. 92

Row 4
Incisalia polia. Female.
Upperside: Brown without
markings.
Incisalia polia. Male.
Underside: Brownish gray.
Darker at base. Broad gray
band along margin of
hindwing.
Frosted Elfin. *Incisalia irus*
irus. Male (*Baptisia* feeding
population). *Upperside:* Brown
with darker stigma. p. 93
Incisalia i. irus. Female.
Upperside: Brown.

Row 5
Incisalia i. irus. Male.
Underside: Brown with gray
band along hindwing.
Henry's Elfin. *Incisalia henrici*
henrici. Male. *Upperside:*
Brown with reddish brown
along hindwing margin. p. 94
Incisalia h. henrici. Female.
Upperside: Brown, but not as
red brown as male.
Incisalia h. henrici. Female.
Underside: Banded. Deep
brown black at base of
hindwing to paler brown to
gray at margin. Forewing
greenish at tip.

Row 6
Eastern Pine Elfin. *Incisalia*
niphon niphon. Male.
Upperside: Dark gray brown.
Pale stigmas present. p. 95
Incisalia n. niphon. Female.
Upperside: Orange brown with
dark borders. Hindwing dark
at base.
Incisalia n. niphon. Male.
Underside: Gray brown
marbled with deep brown
irregular bands.

Row 7
White M Hairstreak.
Parrhasius m-album. Male.
Upperside: Bright iridescent
blue with broad black borders.
Stigmas present. p. 97
Parrhasius m-album. Female.
Upperside: Similar to male, but
lacks stigma.
Parrhasius m-album. Male.
Underside: Gray brown with
thin white band in both wings,
forming inverted "M" in
hindwing. Red spot also
present in hindwing.

PLATE 9 · 265

PLATE 10

GOSSAMER WINGS
(Lycaenidae)
Subfamily Theclinae: Hairstreaks

Row 1
(Northern) Southern Hairstreak. *Fixsenia favonius ontario.* Male. *Upperside:* Brownish black with pale orange spot in both wings. Stigmas present. p. 98
Fixsenia favonius ontario. Male. *Underside:* Grayish brown, with a thin white band in both wings. Band in hindwing forms a "W" at distal end.
Gray Hairstreak. *Strymon melinus humuli.* Male. *Upperside:* Charcoal gray with orange-and-black spot in margin of hindwing. p. 99
Strymon m. humuli. Female. *Upperside:* Charcoal gray with orange-and-black spot in margin of hindwing.

Row 2
Strymon m. humuli. Male. *Underside:* Silver gray with thin red-and-white band in hindwing. Hindwing contains two bright orange-and-black spots in margin.
Early Hairstreak. *Erora laeta.* Male. *Upperside:* Charcoal gray with pale blue in hindwing margin. p. 100
Erora laeta. Female. *Upperside:* Iridescent blue purple with dark charcoal to black borders.
Erora laeta. Male. *Underside:* Gray with greenish cast. Thin irregular rust band in hindwing.

Subfamily Polyommatinae: Blues

Row 3
Eastern Tailed-Blue. *Everes comyntas comyntas.* Male. *Upperside:* Deep blue with small orange-and-black spot in hindwing. p. 103
Everes c. comyntas. Female. *Upperside:* Charcoal gray with

dusting of blue near base of forewing. Two orange-and-black spots in hindwing margin.
Everes c. comyntas. Female (summer brood). *Upperside:* Charcoal gray with 2 orange-and-black spots in hindwing margin.
Everes c. comyntas. Female. *Underside:* Pale silver with black spotting and 2 orange spots in hindwing margins.

Row 4
Spring Azure. *Celastrina ladon ladon.* Male (race "violacea" Type I). *Upperside:* Pale blue with fine black margins. p. 104
Celastrina l. ladon . Female (race "violacea" Type I). *Upperside:* Pale violet blue with broad black margins on forewing.
Celastrina l. ladon. Male *(lucia Auct.,* form "violacea"). *Underside:* Dull gray with black spotting on both wings.
Celastrina l. ladon. Male (race "violacea" Type II, form "marginata"). *Underside:* Dull gray with black spotting and dark gray marginal band on hindwing.

Row 5
Celastrina l. ladon. Male (race "neglecta"). *Upperside:* Violet blue with white in hindwing.
Celastrina ladon. Female (race "neglecta"). *Upperside:* Violet blue with white in both wings and broad black marginal band in forewing.
Celastrina l. ladon. Male (race "neglecta"). *Underside:* Pale silvery gray with small black spots and crescents.
Celastrina l. ladon. Male *(lucia Auct.,* form "lucia"). *Underside:* Dull gray with darker gray pattern in center of hindwing and dark gray marginal band.

Row 6
Appalachian Azure. *Celastrina neglectamajor.* Male. *Upperside:* Violet blue with

some white possible in hindwing. p. 107
Celastrina neglectamajor. Female. *Upperside:* Violet blue with white in both wings and broad black marginal band in forewing.
Celastrina neglectamajor. Male. *Underside:* Pale silvery gray with fine pale spotting.

Row 7
Dusky Azure. *Celastrina nigra.* Male. *Upperside:* Charcoal gray. p. 108
Celastrina nigra. Female. *Upperside:* Pale whitish blue with broad black borders on both wings.
Celastrina nigra. Male. *Underside:* Dull gray with small black spots and crescents.
Silvery Blue. *Glaucopsyche lygdamus lygdamus.* Male. *Upperside:* Silvery blue with narrow black border on both wings. p. 110

Row 8
Glaucopsyche l. lygdamus. Female. *Upperside:* Silver blue with broad black margins.
Glaucopsyche l. lygdamus. Male. *Underside:* Uniform gray with round black spots ringed with white in rows across wings.

METALMARKS
(Riodinidae)
Subfamily Riodininae: Metalmarks
Northern Metalmark. *Calephelis borealis.* Male. *Upperside:* Rust brown with thin metallic gray submarginal band on both wings. p. 113
Calephelis borealis. Female. *Upperside:* Rust brown with darker markings and metallic gray submarginal band.
Calephelis borealis. Female. *Underside:* Pale orange with brown to black spotting and metallic gray submarginal band.

PLATE 10 • 267

PLATE 11

BRUSH-FOOTED BUTTERFLIES
(Nymphalidae)
Subfamily Heliconiinae: Longwings

Row 1
Variegated Fritillary.
Euptoieta claudia. Male.
Upperside: Tawny brown with
zigzag black bands, black dots,
circles, crescents, and 2
marginal bands. p. 119
Euptoieta claudia. Female.
Upperside: Similar to male.
Euptoieta claudia. Male.
Underside: Hindwing mottled
with cream to brown.
Hindwing margin lighter with
a few dark submarginal spots.

Row 2
Diana. *Speyeria diana.* Male.
Upperside: Deep brown inner
two-thirds, orange outer third
of forewing with small dark
spots. p. 121
Speyeria diana. Male.
Underside: Pale orange
hindwing with 2 rows of fine
silver dashes. Basal half
forewing heavily marked with
black.

Row 3
Speyeria diana. Female.
Upperside: Black with blue to
blue-green ovals in a band
across outer third of hindwing.
White spots outer third of
forewing.
Speyeria diana. Female.
Underside: Chocolate brown
hindwing with green
iridescence. Two bands of fine
silver dashes in hindwing.

Row 4
Great Spangled Fritillary.
Speyeria cybele cybele. Male.
Upperside: Orange with series
of black dashes, crescents, and
spots. p. 123
Speyeria c. cybele. Male.
Underside: Hindwing with
broad pale yellow-brown
submarginal band. Several
silver spots and crescents in
hindwing.

PLATE 11 • 269

PLATE 12

BRUSH-FOOTED BUTTERFLIES
(Nymphalidae)
Subfamily Heliconiinae: Longwings

Row 1
Great Spangled Fritillary.
Speyeria cybele cybele. Female.
Upperside: Similar to male, but
darker brown basal half of
wings. p. 123
Speyeria c. cybele. Female.
Underside: Wide pale yellow-
brown submarginal band in
hindwing. Many silver spots
and crescents in hindwing.

Row 2
Aphrodite Fritillary. *Speyeria
aphrodite aphrodite.* Male.
Upperside: Orange with several
black dashes and spots. Basal
third of wings darker. p. 124
Speyeria a. aphrodite. Male.
Underside: Cinnamon-brown
hindwing. Narrow, pale
yellow-brown submarginal
band in hindwing. Many silver
spots in hindwing.

Row 3
Speyeria a. aphrodite. Female.
Upperside: Golden orange with
black dashes, spots and
crescents.
Speyeria a. aphrodite. Female.
Underside: Deep red-brown
hindwing with narrow,
irregular, pale, yellow-brown
submarginal band. Silver spots
in hindwing.

Row 4
Atlantis Fritillary. *Speyeria
atlantis atlantis.* Male.
Upperside: Orange with black
dashes and spots. Solid black
band on outer margin of
forewing. p. 126
Speyeria a. atlantis. Male.
Underside: Greenish brown
hindwing with narrow pale
yellow-brown submarginal
band. Many silver spots in
hindwing.

PLATE 12 • 271

PLATE 13

BRUSH-FOOTED BUTTERFLIES
(Nymphalidae)
Subfamily Heliconiinae: Longwings

Row 1
Atlantis Fritillary. *Speyeria a.
atlantis.* Female. *Upperside:*
Similar to male. Greenish cast
in basal third of wings. p. 126
Speyeria a. atlantis. Female.
Underside: Hindwing dark
brown mixed with pale yellow.
Pale yellow-brown submar-
ginal band in hindwing. Silver
spots in hindwing.

Row 2
Regal Fritillary. *Speyeria
idalia.* Male. *Upperside:*
Hindwing dark blue black
with submarginal row of
orange spots and inner row of
cream spots. p. 127
Speyeria idalia. Male.
Underside: Rich golden brown
with several triangular silvery
white spots, many rimmed in
black.

Row 3
Speyeria idalia. Female.
Upperside: Hindwing blue
black with 2 submarginal rows
of cream spots.
Speyeria idalia. Female.
Underside: Golden brown
hindwing with several
triangular silvery white spots.

PLATE 13 • 273

PLATE 14

BRUSH-FOOTED BUTTERFLIES
(Nymphalidae)
Subfamily Heliconiinae: Longwings

Row 1
Silver-bordered Fritillary.
Boloria selene myrina. Male.
Upperside: Tawny-orange
wings with black dashes and
spots. p. 129
Boloria selene myrina. Female.
Upperside: Similar to male.
Boloria selene myrina. Male.
Underside: Reddish brown
hindwing with yellow and
silver spots. Black spot rimmed
with silver near base of
hindwing.

Row 2
Meadow Fritillary. *Boloria
bellona bellona.* Male.
Upperside: Orange with black
blotches and spots. Forewing
squared at tip from bulge in
margin. p. 131
Boloria b. bellona. Female.
Upperside: Same as male.
Darker basal third of wings.
Boloria b. bellona. Male
(summer brood). *Underside:*
Basal half of hindwing mottled
reddish and yellow. Outer
third of hindwing soft brown,
beige, gray, or violet.

Row 3
Boloria b. bellona. Female
(spring brood). *Underside:*
Whitish keel along upper
margin of hindwing. Soft
brown, gray to violet outer
third of hindwing.

*Subfamily Nymphalinae:
Brushfoots*
Gorgone Checkerspot.
Chlosyne gorgone. Male.
Upperside: Tawny orange with
black bands. Row of black
spots in hindwing. p. 133
Chlosyne gorgone. Male.
Underside: Hindwing, band of
white arrowheads or chevrons
across midwing, zigzag near
margin. Black submarginal

spots.

Row 4
Silvery Checkerspot. *Chlosyne
nycteis nycteis.* Male.
Upperside: Orange with black
margins and bands. Row of
black spots on hindwing.
Center spot hollow. p. 134
Chlosyne n. nycteis. Female.
Upperside: Similar to male.
One or 2 spots hollow in
hindwing.
Chlosyne n. nycteis. Male.
Underside: Short row of silver-
white crescents in hindwing
margin. Row of hollow dark
spots on brown in hindwing.

Row 5
Harris' Checkerspot. *Chlosyne
harrisii liggetti.* Male.
Upperside: Blackish brown
with orange bands. Row of
black spots in hindwing. p. 136
Chlosyne harrisii liggetti.
Female. *Upperside:* Similar to
male. Amount of black
variable.
Chlosyne harrisii liggetti.
Male. *Underside:* Alternating
bands of brick red and pale
yellow spots. Row of
submarginal white to yellow
crescents in hindwing.

PLATE 14 • 275

PLATE 15

PLATE 15

BRUSH-FOOTED BUTTERFLIES
(Nymphalidae)
Subfamily Nymphalinae: Brushfoots

Row 1
Pearl Crescent. *Phyciodes tharos.* Male (spring form). *Upperside:* Orange with black margins and series of dark circles, blotches, and spots. Row of light crescents near margin of hindwing. p. 137
Phyciodes tharos. Male (spring form). *Underside:* Hindwing brownish with white and dark blotches. White crescent in outer hindwing margin.
Phyciodes tharos. Female (spring form). *Upperside:* Similar to male only lighter with more yellow in forewing.
Phyciodes tharos. Female (spring form). *Underside:* Similar to male only browner on hindwing.

Row 2
Phyciodes tharos. Male (summer form). *Upperside:* Very similar to spring form only with darker margins and fewer crescents visible.
Phyciodes tharos. Male (summer form). *Underside:* Golden yellow with numerous fine striations in hindwing. Brown patch in hindwing margin with gray to whitish crescent present.
Phyciodes tharos. Female (summer form). *Upperside:* Similar to spring form but with darker wing margins.
Phyciodes tharos. Female (summer form). *Underside:* Golden yellow hindwing with many striations. Brown margin in hindwing with white-and-yellow crescent.

Row 3
Northern Crescent. *Phyciodes selenis selenis.* Male. *Upperside:* Larger than pearl crescent but very similar in appearance. Antenna clubs are orange tipped. p. 139
Phyciodes s. selenis. Male. *Underside:* Similar to pearl crescent except wing veins are orange, not dark brown to black.
Phyciodes s. selenis. Female. *Upperside:* Large, but similar markings as in Pearl Crescent.
Phyciodes s. selenis. Female. *Underside:* Similar to Pearl Crescent except larger. Orange-tipped antennae usually present. Refer to text for behavior and habitat differences.

Row 4
Tawny Crescent. *Phyciodes batesii.* Male. *Upperside:* Similar to Pearl Crescent except blotches and markings more defined. Orange patches smaller. p. 140
Phyciodes batesii. Female. *Upperside:* Dark blotches and margins covering much of wings. Orange patch in hindwing more fused than in Pearl Crescent female.
Phyciodes batesii. Male. *Underside:* Pale yellow-orange hindwing with faint striations. Brown hindwing margin missing. White to pale orange crescent present in hindwing margin. Row of black dots in hindwing.
Baltimore. *Euphydryas phaeton phaeton.* Male. *Underside:* Black with rust wing margins and basal blotches. Series of pale yellow spots and crescent in rows across wings. p. 142

Row 5
Euphydryas p. phaeton. Male. *Upperside:* Black with rust spots in wing margins and 2 to 4 rows of pale yellow spots and crescent across outer wings.
Euphydryas p. phaeton. Female. *Upperside:* Black, larger than male with larger pale yellow spots across outer portion of wings.

PLATE 15 • 277

PLATE 16

PLATE 16

BRUSH-FOOTED BUTTERFLIES
(Nymphalidae)
Subfamily Nymphalinae: Brushfoots

Row 1
Question Mark. *Polygonia interrogationis.* Male. *Upperside:* Wing margins ragged. Hindwing distinctly tailed. Wing margins lined with violet. p. 143
Polygonia interrogationis. Male (fall brood). *Underside:* Red brown with violet cast. Silver comma in hindwing with offset dot forming a question mark.

Row 2
Polygonia interrogationis. Male (fall brood). *Underside:* Variable. Silver comma with offset dot in hindwing.
Polygonia interrogationis. Male (summer brood). *Upperside:* Hindwing mostly black with some orange at base.
Polygonia interrogationis. Male (summer brood). *Underside:* Heavily mottled wings. Silver comma with offset dot in hindwing.

Row 3
Polygonia interrogationis. Female (summer brood). *Upperside:* Similar to male except larger.
Polygonia interrogationis. Female (summer brood). Underside: Red brown with strong violet cast. Silver comma with offset dot in hindwing.

PLATE 16 • 279

PLATE 17

BRUSH-FOOTED BUTTERFLIES
(Nymphalidae)
Subfamily Nymphalinae: Brushfoots

Row 1
Eastern Comma. *Polygonia comma.* Male (fall brood). *Upperside:* Wing margins ragged. Short tails. Dark borders with submarginal row of yellow spots. p. 145
Polygonia comma. Male (fall brood). *Underside:* Heavily mottled brown; silver comma hooked at both ends in hindwing.

Row 2
Polygonia comma. Male (summer brood). *Underside:* Hindwing suffused with brownish black.
Polygonia comma. Male (fall brood). *Underside:* Patterned brown with silver comma hooked at both ends.
Polygonia comma. Female (summer brood). *Underside:* Patterned golden brown with silver comma hooked at both ends.

Row 3
Green Comma. *Polygonia faunus smythi.* Male. *Upperside:* Wing margins very irregular and ragged. Tails present. Russet with dark borders. Row of submarginal yellow spots. p. 147
Polygonia faunus smythi. Male. *Underside:* Strongly striated with dark browns to tan. Two rows of green chevrons along outer margin.

Silver comma in hindwing.

Row 4
Gray Comma. *Polygonia progne.* Male (fall brood). *Upperside:* Tawny orange with small dark spots and broad brown-black border. Submarginal row of yellow spots in hindwing. p. 148
Polygonia progne. Female (summer brood). *Underside:* Dark chocolate brown hindwing, tawny at base, row of yellow submarginal spots. Wings ragged; short tails present.
Polygonia progne. Male (summer brood). *Underside:* Gray brown with heavy striations. Gray at tip of forewing. Silver comma in L-shape on hindwing.

PLATE 17 • 281

PLATE 18

PLATE 18

BRUSH-FOOTED BUTTERFLIES
(Nymphalidae)
Subfamily Nymphalinae: Brushfoots

Row 1
Compton Tortoiseshell.
*Nymphalis vau-album j-
album.* Female. *Underside:*
Shades of gray, brown, and tan
in striated pattern. Gray
crescents along wing margin.
Small silver "V" in hindwing.
p. 149
*Nymphalis vau-album j-
album.* Male. *Upperside:*
Ragged wings. Rich rust-
brown base blending into
yellow gold with heavy black
spotting. Single white mark on
forewing and hindwing.

Row 2
Mourning Cloak. *Nymphalis
antiopa antiopa.* Male.
Upperside: Wing margins
ragged. Deep chocolate brown
or maroon with yellow or pale
margins. Bright blue
submarginal spots. p. 151
Nymphalis a. antiopa. Female.
Underside: Dark brown, finely
striated. Light border marked
with dark flecking.

Row 3
Milbert's Tortoiseshell.
Nymphalis milberti milberti.
Male. *Upperside:* Dark brown
inner half. Light yellow and
orange bands outer third. Dark
margins. Two orange spots in
forewing. p. 152
Nymphalis m. milberti. Male.
Underside: Basal half brown,
lighter tan outer half with dark
border. Finely striated.

Row 4
American Lady. *Vanessa
virginiensis.* Male. *Upperside:*
Golden orange to pinkish with
black markings in forewing.
Forewing tip has white spots.
Row of black submarginal
spots ringed with blue on
hindwing. p. 154
Vanessa virginiensis. Female.
Upperside: Similar to male;
may be more pink than
orange.

PLATE 18 • 283

PLATE 19

BRUSH-FOOTED BUTTERFLIES
(Nymphalidae)
Subfamily Nymphalinae: Brushfoots

Row 1
American Lady. *Vanessa virginiensis.* Female. *Underside:* Complex pattern of olive brown, black, and white in hindwing. Two large blue eyespots in hindwing near outer margin. p. 154
Painted Lady. *Vanessa cardui.* Male. *Upperside:* Salmon orange with black blotches. Black forewing tips with white spots. Row of small black submarginal spots rimmed with blue in hindwing. p. 155

Row 2
Vanessa cardui. Female. *Upperside:* Similar to male.
Vanessa cardui. Male. *Underside:* Complex pattern of white, olive, and black on hindwing. Four or 5 blue submarginal spots ringed with gold and black in hindwing.

Row 3
Red Admiral. *Vanessa atalanta rubria.* Female. *Upperside:* Dark brown black with orange-red bar across forewing and along hindwing border. White spots on forewing tip. Black-and-blue dots on hindwing border. p. 157
Vanessa atalanta rubria. Male. *Underside:* Mottled brown and black hindwing. Black forewing with white at tip. Blue swirl and pinkish bar across midwing of forewing.

Row 4
Common Buckeye. *Junonia coenia.* Male. *Upperside:* One large and 1 small eyespot in forewing and 2 large eyespots on gray-brown background on hindwing. Two orange bars and a whitish bar on forewing. p. 158
Junonia coenia. Female. *Upperside:* Similar to male with large eyespots.
Junonia coenia. Male. *Underside:* Light brown to rust hindwing with small eyespots. Forewing contains large eyespot.

PLATE 19 • 285

PLATE 20

SWALLOWTAILS
(Papilionide)
Subfamily Papilioninae: Swallowtails

Row 1
Canadian Tiger Swallowtail.
Papilio canadensis. Male.
Upperside: First submarginal
spot in hindwing orange. p. 50
Papilio canadensis x P. glaucus.
Male. *Underside:* First
submarginal spot in hindwing
orange.

BRUSH-FOOTED BUTTERFLIES
(Nymphalidae)
Subfamily Limenitidinae:
Admirals

Row 2
Red-spotted Purple. *Limenitis*
a. arthemis x Limenitis a.
astyanax. Male. *Upperside:*
Varying amounts of white
forming partial band on
forewing. p. 160
Limenitis a. arthemis x
Limenitis a. astyanax. Male.
Underside: Varying amounts of
white forming a band across
the forewing.
Limenitis arthemis astyanax.
Male. *Upperside:* Black with
blue to blue-green iridescence
especially on hindwing.

Row 3
Limenitis arthemis astyanax.
Female. *Upperside:* Similar to
male except larger. Brick red
spots near forewing tip usually
prominent.
Limenitis arthemis astyanax.
Male. *Underside:* Blue
crescents along wing margins.
Submarginal row of brick red
spots. Similar spots clustered
at wing bases.

PLATE 20 • 287

PLATE 21

BRUSH-FOOTED BUTTERFLIES
(Nymphalidae)
Subfamily Limenitidinae: Admirals

Row 1
Viceroy. *Limenitis archippus archippus.* Male. *Upperside:* Rich russet orange with black veins. Borders black with row of white spots. Black line across center of hindwing. p. 162
Limenitis a. archippus. Female. *Upperside:* Similar to male.

Row 2
Limenitis a. archippus. Male. *Underside:* Pale orange brown with black veins. One to 3 rows of bluish white crescents in black margins.

Subfamily Aparturinae: Hackberry Butterflies
Hackberry Emperor. *Asterocampa celtis celtis.* Male (light phase). *Upperside:* Mixed pattern of white, gray, and brown spots and blotches. Dark near wing tips. One pale- to white-ringed black eyespot in forewing and 5 similar spots in hindwing forming a band. p. 164
Asterocampa c. celtis. Female (light phase). *Upperside:* Similar to male with cream predominating.

Row 3
Asterocampa c. celtis. Male. *Upperside:* Same as light phase with tawny brown dominating.
Asterocampa c. celtis. Male. *Underside:* Lighter with 1 white-centered black eyespot near forewing tip. Series of bluish-centered black eyespots in hindwing.
Asterocampa c. celtis. Female. *Upperside:* Similar to male.

Row 4
Tawny Emperor. *Asterocampa clyton clyton.* Male. *Upperside:* Tawny marked with blackish brown forewing tips containing pale spots. Submarginal row of black spots in hindwing. p. 165
Asterocampa c. clyton. Female. *Upperside:* Larger than male; more tawny brown containing bands of pale yellow brown spots in forewing. Row of dark spots in hindwing.
Asterocampa c. clyton. Male. *Underside:* Brownish with lavender cast. Submarginal row of dark eyespots with blue centers in hindwing. Dark and light banding in forewing.

PLATE 21 • 289

PLATE 22

BRUSH-FOOTED BUTTERFLIES
(Nymphalidae)
Subfamily Satyrinae: Satyrs and Wood Nymphs

Row 1
Northern Pearly Eye. *Enodia anthedon.* Male. *Upperside:* Soft brown with row of submarginal dark eyespots— one large and 2 to 3 small in forewing, and 5 medium to large in hindwing. Hindwing margins scalloped. p. 167
Enodia anthedon. Female. *Upperside:* Similar to male but usually with larger eyespots.
Enodia anthedon. Male. *Underside:* Soft brown with violet cast. Dark striations traverse wings. Single row of gold-ringed, deep brown eyespots with white dot in center near outer wing margin.

Row 2
Eyed Brown. *Satyrodes eurydice eurydice.* Male. *Upperside:* Pale brown with submarginal row of dark eyespots—4 in forewing and 6 in hindwing. p. 169
Satyrodes e. eurydice. Female. *Upperside:* Similar to male except lighter brown to tan.
Satyrodes e. eurydice. Male. *Underside:* Tan with row of small eyespots in both wings— 4 in forewing and 6 to 7 in hindwing. Eyespots contain white dots in center.

Row 3
Appalachian Brown. *Satyrodes appalachia appalachia.* Male. *Upperside:* Soft brown with smooth wing margins. Generally small eyespots in forewing—6 in hindwing. p. 170
Satyrodes a. appalachia. Female. *Upperside:* Paler brown than male with 4 small eyespots in forewing and 6 in hindwing.
Satyrodes a. appalachia. Male. *Underside:* Soft brown with thin striations across wings. Submarginal row of eyespots with double ring of gold and tan. Eyespots contain white dot. Four spots in forewing and 6 to 7 in hindwing.

Row 4
Gemmed Satyr. *Cyllopsis gemma gemma.* Male. *Upperside:* Even brown, with small dark patch in hindwing margin. p. 171
Cyllopsis g. gemma. Female. *Underside:* Brown with 2 to 3 striations across wings. Black patch ringed in gold and silver in hindwing margin.
Carolina Satyr. *Hermeuptychia sosybius.* Male. *Upperside:* Dark brown. No markings. p. 173
Hermeuptychia sosybius. Female. *Underside:* Light brown with 2 narrow wavy lines across wings and row of small eyespots near wing margins—4 to 5 in forewing and 6 in hindwing.

Row 5
Little Wood Satyr. *Megisto cymela.* Male. *Upperside:* Medium brown with 2 eyespots in forewing and 1 to 2 in hindwing. p. 174
Megisto cymela. Female. *Upperside:* Medium brown with 2 eyespots in forewing and 2 in hindwing. Female larger than male.
Megisto cymela. Male. *Underside:* Light brown with 2 striations across wings. Two eyespots in forewing and 3 in hindwing. Several silver dots between eyespots.

PLATE 22 • 291

PLATE 23

BRUSH-FOOTED BUTTERFLIES
(Nymphalidae)
Subfamily Satyrinae: Satyrs and Wood Nymphs

Row 1
Common Wood Nymph.
Cercyonis pegala pegala. Male.
Upperside: Brown with yellow-orange patch containing 2 eyespots in forewing. p. 176
Cercyonis p. pegala. Female.
Upperside: Similar to male; a little larger with larger eyespots.
Cercyonis p. pegala. Male.
Underside: Brown with dark striations. Numerous eyespots in hindwing. Yellow patch with 2 eyespots in forewing.

Row 2
Dull-eyed Grayling. *Cercyonis pegala nephele.* Male.
Upperside: Brown with 2 small eyes in forewing and one in hindwing. p. 177
Cercyonis pegala nephele. Female. *Upperside:* Brown with 2 large eyespots in forewing and 1 small eyespot in lower hindwing.
Cercyonis pegala nephele. Male. *Underside:* Brown with dark striations in basal half of wings. Two eyespots present in forewing and 3 to 5 small eyespots in hindwing.

Subfamily Danainae:
Milkweed Butterflies

Row 3
Monarch. *Danaus plexippus.* Male. *Upperside:* Bright orange brown with black margins and wing veins. White to orange spots present in margins. Gland present in cubitus (CU2) vein of hindwing. p. 179
Danaus plexippus. Male. *Underside:* Tan hindwing, orange forewing with black margins containing 2 rows of numerous white spots.

Row 4
Danaus plexippus. Female. *Upperside:* Similar to male only more brown than orange.
Subfamily Libytheinae:
Snouts
American Snout. *Libytheana carinenta bachmanii.* Male. *Upperside:* Dark brown-black margins and wing base. Orange patches in both wings. White spots near forewing tip. Long labial palpi. p. 117
Libytheana carinenta bachmanii. Male. *Underside:* Brown with lighter and darker patches in hindwing. Two to 3 white spots in forewing. Often violet sheen to hindwing.

PLATE 23 • 293

PLATE 24

SKIPPERS
(Hesperiidae)
Subfamily Pyrginae: Open-winged Skippers

Row 1
Silver-spotted Skipper.
Epargyreus clarus. Male.
Upperside: Large pointed
wings. Irregular band of glassy
yellow-gold connected spots
across forewing with dark
veins. p. 184
Epargyreus clarus. Male.
Underside: Large silver-white
patch in middle of hindwing.
Frosted lavender wing
margins.

Row 2
Golden-banded Skipper.
Autochton cellus. Male.
Upperside: Smooth golden
yellow band across forewing.
Wing veins also gold in band.
p. 186
Autochton cellus. Male.
Underside: forewing band
visible on underside.
Hindwing brown with 2
irregular broken bands of
darker brown crossing wing.
Light grayish white frosting on
hindwing margin.

Row 3
Hoary Edge. *Achalarus*
lyciades. Male. *Upperside:*
Cluster of 4 to 5 golden yellow
spots in forewing. p. 188
Achalarus lyciades. Male.
Underside: Hindwing mottled
with light and dark brown
near base. Heavily frosted with
white on outer half of
hindwing.

Row 4
Northern Cloudywing.
Thorybes pylades. Male.
Upperside: Several small glassy
white spots in outer forewing;
not connected and not in a
distinct band. p. 189
Thorybes pylades. Male.
Underside: Two dark-edged
bands across hindwing. Lightly
frosted gray on outer wing
margins.

Row 5
Southern Cloudywing.
Thorybes bathyllus. Male.
Upperside: Series of rectangu-
lar glassy white spots more or
less in a row across forewing.
One spot offset toward wing
tip. p. 190
Thorybes bathyllus. Female.
Underside: Two dark bands
across hindwing. Slight gray
frosting along outer margin.

PLATE 24 • 295

PLATE 25

SKIPPERS
(Hesperiidae)
Subfamily Pyrginae: Open-winged Skippers

Row 1
Confused Cloudywing.
Thorybes confusis. Male.
Upperside: Series of thin linear glassy white spots in forewing. Center spot offset toward tip of wing. p. 192
Thorybes confusis. Male.
Underside: Brown, hindwing crossed by 2 darker bands. Slight gray frosting at wing tips and along margins.

Row 2
Dreamy Duskywing. *Erynnis icelus.* Male. *Upperside:* Gray patch on upper margin of forewing. Forewing lacks glassy white spots. p. 193
Erynnis icelus. Female.
Upperside: forewing more patterned than male. Chain of gray-centered dark spots on forewing near tip. Two rows of pale spots on hindwing.
Erynnis icelus. Male.
Underside: Pale brown with less conspicuous markings. Pale spots in rows along outer wing margins.

Row 3
Sleepy Duskywing. *Erynnis brizo brizo.* Male. *Upperside:* forewing patterned with row of gray-centered chain links rimmed in black across forewing. p. 194
Erynnis b. brizo. Female.
Upperside: Lighter than male. Forewing patterned with 2 rows of dark chainlike spots with gray centers. Hindwing with several pale spots in rows near margin.
Erynnis b. brizo. Male.
Underside: Gray brown to pale brown. Rows of pale spots along wing margins.

Row 4
Juvenal's Duskywing. *Erynnis juvenalis.* Male. *Upperside:* forewing patterned, dark brown with black spots and chevrons. Several glassy white spots on outer third of forewing. p. 196
Erynnis juvenalis. Female.
Upperside: Strongly patterned with tan, brown, black, and gray. Several glassy white spots on outer forewing. Rows of pale spots near hindwing margin.
Erynnis juvenalis. Male.
Underside: Pale brown with light spots along outer wing margins. Two pale spots near hindwing tip.

Row 5
Horace's Duskywing. *Erynnis horatius.* Male. *Upperside:* Patterned forewing with dark blotches on brown. Glassy white spots on forewing, usually in a row near outer margin. p. 197
Erynnis horatius. Female.
Upperside: More strongly patterned forewing than male with dark brown blotches. Large glassy white spots in a row on forewing.
Erynnis horatius. Male.
Underside: Weakly patterned brown with pale spotting near outer wing margins.

Row 6
Mottled Duskywing. *Erynnis martialis.* Male. *Upperside:* Strong contrasting dark blotches on forewing and hindwing. Glassy white spots near forewing tip. p. 199
Erynnis martialis. Female.
Upperside: More strongly patterned than male with lighter lavender cast to forewing. Glassy forewing spots present.
Erynnis martialis. Male.
Underside: Brown. Hindwing mottled with dark blotches adjoining lighter spots in outer half.

PLATE 25 • 297

PLATE 26

SKIPPERS
(Hesperiidae)
Subfamily Pyrginae: Open-winged Skippers

Row 1
Columbine Duskywing.
Erynnis lucilius. Male.
Upperside: Small, marked similar to the Dreamy Duskywing but with small glassy white spots on outer forewing. p. 200
Erynnis lucilius. Female.
Upperside: Similar to male but with more gray in forewing. Rows of pale submarginal spots in hindwing.
Erynnis lucilius. Female.
Underside: Dark brown with 2 rows of light spots along outer wing margins.

Row 2
Wild Indigo Duskywing.
Erynnis baptisiae. Male.
Upperside: forewing patterned with dark blotches in bands. Basal area of forewing very dark. Small glassy white spots on outer forewing. p. 202
Erynnis baptisiae. Female.
Upperside: Similar to male, may be more strongly patterned. Glassy white spots on outer forewing.
Erynnis baptisiae. Male.
Underside: Dark blackish brown with pale spots along outer wing margins.

Row 3
Persius Duskywing. *Erynnis persius persius.* Male.
Upperside: Very dark brown-black forewing with obscured pattern. Small glassy white spots on outer forewing. p. 203
Erynnis p. persius. Female.
Upperside: Forewing with more gray. Wings strongly patterned. Glassy white spots on outer forewing. Pale spots on hindwing in rows.
Erynnis p. persius. Male.
Underside: Brown with pale spotting along outer margin.

Row 4
Grizzled Skipper. *Pyrgus centaureae wyandot.* Male.
Upperside: Dark brown black with white spots on outer half of forewing. Hindwing faintly patterned with pale spots. Wing fringes checkered. p. 204
Pyrgus centaureae wyandot. Female. *Upperside:* Similar to male.
Pyrgus centaureae wyandot. Male. *Underside:* hindwing olive, with white blotches in rows across wing. Fringes strongly checkered.

Row 5
Common Checkered Skipper. *Pyrgus communis communis.* Male. *Upperside:* Variable. Almost black with numerous white patches across forewing and hindwing. Bluish scaling at wing bases and on body. p. 206
Pyrgus c. communis. Female. *Upperside:* Variable, but usually with less white than male.
Pyrgus c. communis. Male. *Underside:* Hindwing white with olive to gray irregular bands crossing wing.

Row 6
Common Sootywing.
Pholisora catullus. Male.
Upperside: Small. Black brown with small white spots in forewing. p. 208
Pholisora catullus. Female.
Upperside: Similar to male. White spots may be larger.
Pholisora catullus. Male.
Underside: Black brown with zigzag row of white spots in forewing. One to 3 small white spots near center of forewing.

Row 7
Hayhurst's Scallopwing.
Staphylus hayhurstii. Male.
Upperside: Black with gold flecking in wings. Hindwing margins scalloped. Two to 4 white dots in forewing. p. 209
Staphylus hayhurstii. Female.
Upperside: Dark brown with black bands crossing wings. Gold flecking on wings. Hindwing scalloped. Two to 4 white dots in forewing.
Staphylus hayhurstii. Female.
Underside: Brown black with few to no markings.

PLATE 26 • 299

PLATE 27

(Hesperiidae)
Subfamily Hesperiinae: Branded Skippers

Row 1
Swarthy Skipper. *Nastra lherminier.* Male. *Upperside:* Small. Dull gray brown, often 2 pale spots in center of forewing. Greenish sheen to wings. p. 211
Nastra lherminier. Female. *Upperside:* Darker brown than male. Lacks greenish sheen.
Nastra lherminier. Female. *Underside:* Dull olive brown with no spots. Veins in hindwing thin and yellow.
Clouded Skipper. *Lerema accius.* Male. *Upperside:* Pointed wings. Blackish brown with short row of white spots near forewing tip and 1 toward middle. Thin linear stigma in lower center of forewing. p. 213

Row 2
Lerema accius. Male. *Underside:* Dark blackish brown with light violet dusting along margin of forewing and over hindwing with dark patch in center.
Least Skipper. *Ancyloxypha numitor.* Male. *Upperside:* Small. Forewing orange to brown with black around borders and in center. Hindwing orange gold with black border. p. 214
Ancyloxypha numitor. Female. *Upperside:* Forewing blackish; may have some orange. Hindwing orange gold with black border.
Ancyloxypha numitor. Male. *Underside:* Forewing black with orange-gold upper margin and tip. Hindwing bright orange gold.

Row 3
European Skipper. *Thymelicus lineola.* Male. *Upperside:* Brassy orange with narrow dark border. Faint stigma present. Veins somewhat darkened especially near edge. p. 215
Thymelicus lineola. Female. *Upperside:* Brassy orange with narrow black border and black veins.
Thymelicus lineola. Female. *Underside:* Pale orange forewing. Greenish ochre hindwing with orange ray from outer margin to base in lower wing.

Row 4
Fiery Skipper. *Hylephila phyleus.* Male. *Upperside:* Yellow orange with zigzag black border on both wings. Large black stigma with black dash toward tip of forewing. p. 216
Hylephila phyleus. Female. *Upperside:* Long wings, blackish with tawny-orange spots.
Hylephila phyleus. Male. *Underside:* Yellow orange with small black spots scattered on hindwing.

Row 5
Leonard's Skipper. *Hesperia leonardus leonardus.* Male. *Upperside:* Tawny orange at base of forewing with broad blackish borders. Tawny spots in forewing and short row in hindwing. Stigma in forewing. p. 218
Hesperia l. leonardus. Female. *Upperside:* Dark brown with tawny-orange bands in forewing and across hindwing. Forewing dark orange brown at base.

Hesperia l. leonardus. Male. *Underside:* Rust brown with row of orange spots in hindwing and 1 offset toward base.

Row 6
Cobweb Skipper. *Hesperia metea metea.* Male. *Upperside:* Medium brown to olive with tawny spots in forewing above and below stigma. Faint tawny spots in angled band on hindwing. p. 219
Hesperia m. metea. Female. *Upperside:* Dark brown with pale yellow spots near tip of forewing. Faint tawny spots in angled band on hindwing.
Hesperia m. metea. Male. *Underside:* Hindwing olive brown with irregular bands of white dashes and white veins, giving cobweb appearance.

Row 7
Indian Skipper. *Hesperia sassacus sassacus.* Male. *Upperside:* Tawny orange with broad blackish brown borders. Long, narrow black stigma in forewing. p. 220
Hesperia s. sassacus. Female. *Upperside:* Yellow orange in wing centers. Broad, dark brown borders and black dash near forewing tip. Wing bases darker.
Hesperia s. sassacus. Male. *Underside:* forewing tawny orange with black at base.

PLATE 27 · 301

PLATE 28

SKIPPERS
(Hesperiidae)
Subfamily Hesperiinae: Banded Skippers

Row 1
Peck's Skipper. *Polites peckius.*
Male. *Upperside:* Dark brown
with tawny orange patch above
black stigma. Tawny patch
near forewing tip and in
hindwing. p. 222
Polites peckius. Female.
Upperside: Variable. Dark
brown with tawny yellow spots
in forewing and tawny patch
in hindwing.
Polites peckius. Male.
Underside: hindwing rust with
bright yellow patch of
rectangular spots in center of
wing.

Row 2
Tawny-edged Skipper. *Polites
themistocles.* Male. *Upperside:*
Olive brown with yellow-
orange patch along upper
margin above black stigma.
p. 223
Polites themistocles. Female.
Upperside: Dark brown with
band of yellow spots in outer
forewing. Plain dark brown
hindwing.
Polites themistocles. Male.
Underside: Tawny orange along
upper margin of forewing with
black at base. Hindwing olive
brown, usually plain.

Row 3
Crossline Skipper. *Polites
origines.* Male. *Upperside:* Dark
brown with faint tawny orange
along upper forewing margin
above stigma. Pale spot at tip
of stigma. Hindwing with pale
submarginal spots. p. 224
Polites origines. Female.
Upperside: Dark brown with
orange scaling near base. Pale
yellow-orange spots in broken
band on forewing.
Polites origines. Male.
Underside: Orange brown to
bronze with faint pale spots in
center of forewing and faint
submarginal row of spots on
hindwing.

Row 4
Whirlabout. *Polites vibex
vibex.* Male. *Upperside:* Tawny
yellow with broad black stigma
connected to grayish dash at
forewing tip. Wing borders
dark charcoal. p. 226
Polites v. vibex. Female.
Upperside: Dark brown with
bronze cast near base. Series of
2 to 5 pale yellow spots near
outer forewing.
Polites v. vibex. Male.
Underside: Yellow with 2 rows
of unconnected black spots on
hindwing.
Polites v. vibex. Female.
Underside: Bronze to greenish
with 2 rows of dark brown to
black unconnected spots on
hindwing.

Row 5
Long Dash. *Polites mystic
mystic.* Male. *Upperside:* Tawny
orange with dark brown
borders. Black veins in
hindwing. Broad black stigma
with black dash near forewing
tip. p. 227
Polites m. mystic. Female.
Upperside: More tawny orange
than male, darker at base with
2 connecting black patches
from base to tip of forewing.
Broad black borders.
Polites m. mystic. Male.
Underside: Wings golden to
brown or rust with a row of
submarginal pale or yellow
spots and a pale basal spot in
the hindwing.

Row 6
Northern Broken-Dash.
Wallengrenia egeremet. Male.
Upperside: Brown with pale
apricot spot at tip of divided
black stigma and near tip of
forewing. p. 228
Wallengrenia egeremet.
Female. *Upperside:* Brown with
row of pale orange spots in
outer forewing.
Wallengrenia egeremet. Male.
Underside: Purplish to reddish
brown with submarginal row
of very pale spots on
hindwing.

Row 7
Little Glassywing. *Pompeius
verna verna.* Male. *Upperside:*
Very dark brown with row of
pale glassy spots in outer
forewing and along black
stigma. Greenish hairs at base.
p. 230
Pompeius verna verna. Female.
Upperside: Similar to male
with large, square glassy spot
in forewing.
Pompeius verna verna. Male.
Underside: Dark brown. Pale
glassy spots in forewing.
Hindwing purplish brown
with a few pale submarginal
spots.

PLATE 28 · 303

PLATE 29

SKIPPERS
(Hesperiidae)
Subfamily Hesperiinae: Banded Skippers

Row 1
Sachem. *Atalopedes campestris huron.* Male. *Upperside:* Tawny orange with brown margins. Stigma forming large black oval in forewing. p. 231
Atalopedes campestris huron. Female. *Upperside:* Dark brown with tawny orange in wing centers. Large glassy white windows in outer forewing. Black patch at base of large window spot.
Atalopedes campestris huron. Male. *Underside:* hindwing dusky yellow with band of paler spots along outer margin. Female with darker hindwing than male.

Row 2
Delaware Skipper. *Atrytone logan logan.* Male. *Upperside:* Bright tawny orange with thin dark brown margin and brown veins. Stigma narrow. p. 232
Atrytone l. logan. Female. *Upperside:* Similar to male with wider brown margins and brown veins.
Atrytone l. logan. Male. *Underside:* Bright yellow gold with black at base of forewing and along lower margin of the forewing.

Row 3
Hobomok Skipper. *Poanes hobomok.* Male. *Upperside:* Yellow orange with broad dark borders. Dark dash in forewing near tip. p. 233
Poanes hobomok. Female. *Upperside:* Tawny orange restricted. Broad dark brown borders and wing bases.
Poanes hobomok. Male. *Underside:* Yellow to yellow orange with brown wing borders and base of hindwing. Hindwing may be edged in violet.

Row 4
Poanes hobomok. Female (form "Pocahontas"). *Upperside:* Dark brown with pale forewing spots near tip. Hindwing may be brown with a little tawny color.
Poanes hobomok. Female (form *Pocahontas*). *Underside:* Brown hindwing with paler brown band. Forewing brown with yellow patch and a few pale spots near tip.
Zabulon Skipper. *Poanes zabulon.* Male. *Underside:* Yellow orange with small brown dots along margin and in hindwing. Large spot at base of hindwing. p. 235

Row 5
Poanes zabulon. Male. *Upperside:* Yellow orange with dark brown borders. Black dash near tip of forewing. p. 235
Poanes zabulon. Female. *Upperside:* Dark blackish brown with conspicuous pale yellow angular spots in forewing forming a zigzag pattern.
Poanes zabulon. Female. *Underside:* Dark brown. Rust spots in hindwing and violet flush along margin.

Row 6
Black Dash. *Euphyes conspicuus conspicuus.* Male. *Upperside:* Tawny, with broad brown borders and wing bases. Conspicuous black stigma in forewing. p. 236
Euphyes c. conspicuus. Female. *Upperside:* Dark brown black with row of tawny yellow spots in forewing and tawny patch in hindwing.
Euphyes c. conspicuus. Male. *Underside:* hindwing rich rust color with short submarginal row of tawny yellow spots.

Row 7
Two-spotted Skipper. *Euphyes bimacula.* Male. *Upperside:* Dark brown with tawny-orange patch around a black stigma. p. 237
Euphyes bimacula. Female. *Upperside:* Dark brown with 3 to 5 small pale yellow rectangular spots in row across outer forewing.
Euphyes bimacula. Male. *Underside:* Tawny brown with 2 pale spots in forewing. Dark brown along lower margin of both wings. Veins in hindwing pale.

PLATE 29 • 305

PLATE 30

PLATE 30

SKIPPERS
(Hesperiidae)
Subfamily Pyrginae: Open-winged Skippers

Row 1
Dun Skipper. *Euphyes vestris metacomet.* Male. *Upperside:* Brownish black with thin black stigma in forewing. p. 238 *Euphyes vestris metacomet.* Female. *Upperside:* Brownish black with 4 to 5 pale spots in outer forewing. *Euphyes vestris metacomet.* Male. *Underside:* Brownish black with black forewing base and faint row of lighter spots in hindwing.

Row 2
Dusted Skipper. *Atrytonopsis hianna hianna.* Male. *Upperside:* Pointed wings. Dark brown with several tiny white dots in outer forewing. p. 240 *Atrytonopsis h. hianna.* Female. *Upperside:* Dark brown with larger pale glassy spots in forewing than in male. *Atrytonopsis h. hianna.* Male. *Underside:* Brown with violet to pale gray frosting along margins. Small white spot near base of hindwing.

Row 3
Pepper and Salt Skipper. *Amblyscirtes hegon.* Male. *Upperside:* Dark brown with greenish cast. Small pale yellow spots on outer third of forewing. Fringe checkered. p. 241 *Amblyscirtes hegon.* Female. *Upperside:* Dark brown with angled row of small pale spots on outer third of forewing. Fringe checkered. *Amblyscirtes hegon.* Male. *Underside:* Brownish gray with angled row of small pale spots in forewing and hindwing. A few pale spots near base of hindwing.

Row 4
Common Roadside-Skipper. *Amblyscirtes vialis.* Male. *Upperside:* Dark brown black. Tiny pale spots on outer third of forewing. Fringe checkered. p. 242 *Amblyscirtes vialis.* Female. *Upperside:* Dark brown black with small cluster of tiny pale spots near tip of forewing. Fringe checkered. *Amblyscirtes vialis.* Male. *Underside:* Dark brown black with violet frosting near tip of forewing and along outer margin of hindwing.

Row 5
Ocola Skipper. *Panoquina ocola.* Male. *Upperside:* forewing slender and pointed. Dark brown with olive cast near bases. Pale glassy spots on outer third of forewing. p. 243 *Panoquina ocola.* Male. *Underside:* Brown on hindwing, unmarked. Pale glassy spots on forewing.

Row 6
Long-tailed Skipper. *Urbanus proteus proteus.* Male. *Upperside:* Long tails, glassy windows in forewing and iridescent blue green toward wing base. p. 185 *Urbanus p. proteus.* Male. *Underside:* Brown with white spots in forewing and dark blotches and bands in hindwing.

PLATE 30 • 307

PLATE 31

PLATE 31 • 309

PLATE 32

PLATE 32

BUTTERFLY LARVAE

Row 1

Olympia Marble *(Euchloe olympia)* on smooth rockcress *(Arabis laevigata).* p. 58

Falcate Orangetip *(Anthocharis midea annickae)* on hairy bittercress *(Cardamine hirsuta).* p. 59

Clouded Sulphur *(Colias philodice philodice)* on white clover *(Trifolium ripens).* p. 61

Row 2

Orange Sulphur *(Colias eurytheme)* on white clover *(Trifolium ripens).* p. 63

Pink-edged Sulphur *(Colias interior)* on lowbush blueberry *(Vaccinium angustifolium).* p. 64

Row 3

Cloudless Sulphur *(Phoebus sennae eubule)* on wild senna *(Cassia hebecarpa).* p. 66

Little Yellow *(Eurema lisa)* on wild sensitive plant *(Cassia nictitans).* p. 67

Row 4

Sleepy Orange *(Eurema nicippe)* on wild senna *(Cassia hebecarpa).* p. 69

Harvester *(Feniseca tarquinius)* feeding on woolly aphids on alder *(Alnus* sp.). p. 73

PLATE 32 • 311

PLATE 33

PLATE 33 • 313

PLATE 34

Row 1
Red-banded Hairstreak
(*Calycopis cercrops*) on
staghorn sumac *(Rhus typhina)*. p. 88
(Olive) Juniper Hairstreak
(*Mitoura grynea grynea*) on
eastern red cedar *(Juniperus virginiana)*. p. 89

Row 2
Brown Elfin *(Incisalia*
***augustinus croesoides)* on**
blueberry *(Vaccinium* sp.).
p. 91
Frosted Elfin *(Incisalia irus*
***irus)* on** wild indigo *(Baptisia tinctoria)*. p. 93
Henry's Elfin *(Incisalia henrici*
***henrici)* on** redbud *(Cercis canadensis)*. p. 94

Row 3

Eastern Pine Elfin *(Incisalia*
***niphon niphon)* on** Virginia
pine *(Pinus virginiana)*. p. 95

White M Hairstreak
(*Parrhasius m-album)* on
white oak *(Quercus alba)*. p. 97

Row 4
Gray Hairstreak *(Strymon*
***melinus humuli)* on**
bushclover *(Lespedeza* sp.).
p. 99
Early Hairstreak *(Erora laeta)*
on American beech fruit
(Fagus grandifolia). p. 100

PLATE 34 • 315

PLATE 35

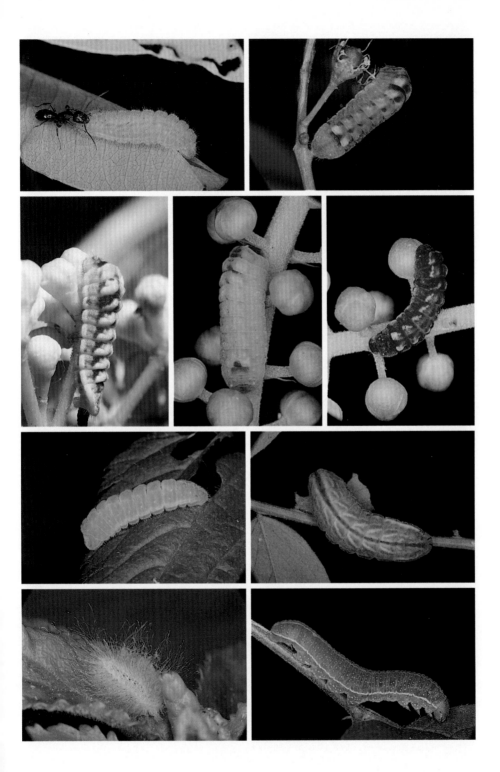

PLATE 35 • 317

PLATE 36

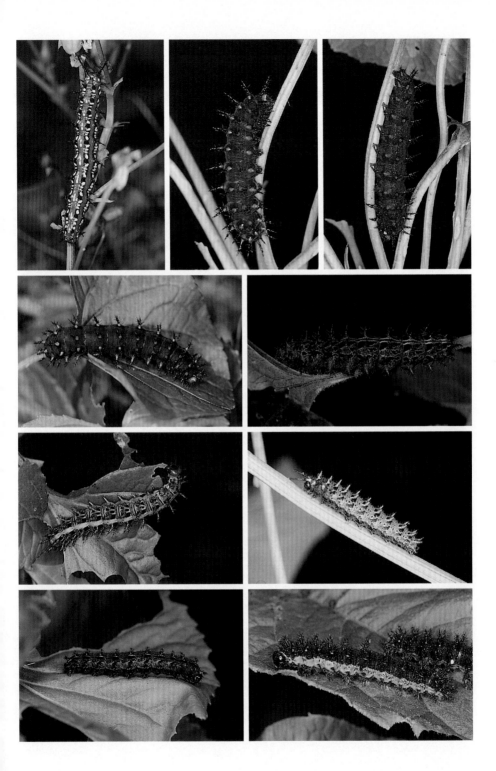

PLATE 36 • 319

PLATE 37

BUTTERFLY LARVAE

Row 1

Harris' Checkerspot *(Chlosyne harrisii liggetti)* on flat-topped white aster *(Aster umbellatus)*. p. 136

Pearl Crescent *(Phyciodes tharos)* on aster *(Aster* sp.*)*. p. 137

Tawny Crescent *(Phyciodes batesii)* on wavy-leaf aster *(Aster undulatus)*. p. 140

Row 2

Baltimore *(Euphydryas phaeton phaeton)* on turtlehead *(Chelone glabra)*. p. 142

Question Mark *(Polygonia interrogationis)* on dwarf hackberry *(Celtis tenuifolia)*. p. 143

Row 3

Eastern Comma *(Polygonia comma)* on nettle *(Urtica* sp.*)*. p. 145

Gray Comma *(Polygonia progne)* on gooseberry *(Ribes cyosloati)*. p. 148

Row 4

Compton Tortoiseshell *(Nymphalis vau-album j-album)*. p. 149

Mourning Cloak *(Nymphalis antiopa)* on weeping willow *(Salix babylonica)*. p. 151

PLATE 37 • 321

PLATE 38

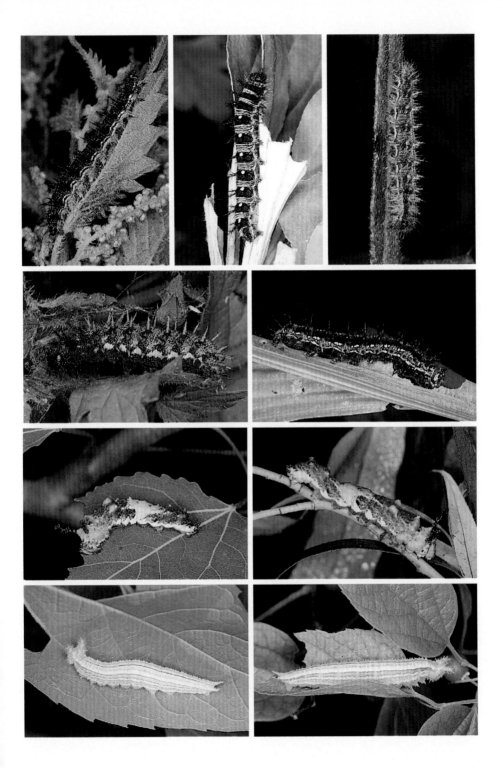

PLATE 38 · 323

PLATE 39

PLATE 39 • 325

PLATE 40

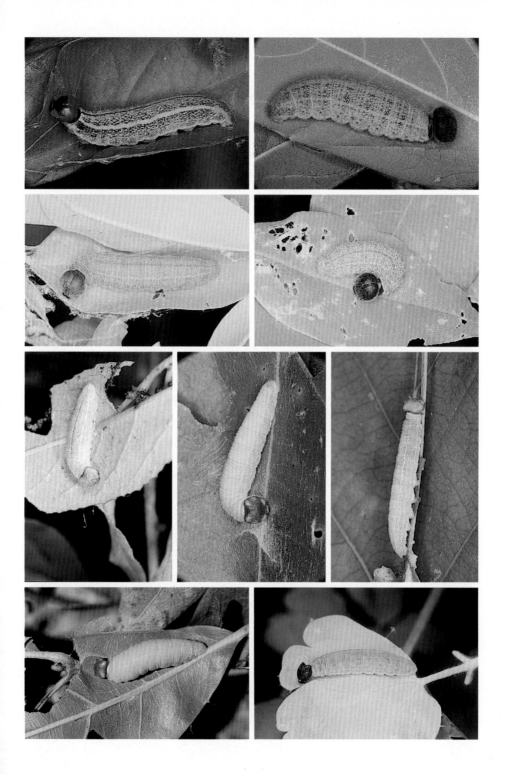

PLATE 40 · 327

PLATE 41

Row 1

Wild Indigo Duskywing
(Erynnis baptisiae) on crown
vetch *(Coronilla varia)*. p. 202
Grizzled Skipper *(Pyrgus
centaureae wyandot)* on
Canada cinquefoil *(Potentilla
canadensis)*. p. 204

Row 2

Common Checkered-Skipper
(Pyrgus communis communis)
on common mallow *(Malva
neglecta)*. p. 206
Common Sootywing
(Pholisora catullus) on lamb's
quarters *(Chenopodium
album)*. p. 208
Hayhurst's Scallopwing
(Staphylus hayhurstii) on
lamb's quarters *(Chenopodium
album)*. p. 209

Row 3

Swarthy Skipper *(Nastra
lherminier)* on little bluestem
grass *(Andropogan scoparius)*.
p. 211
Clouded Skipper *(Lerema
accius)* on grass (Poaceae).
p. 213

Row 4

Least Skipper *(Ancyloxypha
numitor)* on rice cutgrass
(Leesia oryzoides). p. 214
European Skipper
(Thymelicus lineola) on
orchard grass *(Dactylis
glomerata)*. p. 215

PLATE 41 • 329

PLATE 42

BUTTERFLY LARVAE

Row 1

Fiery Skipper *(Hylephila phyleus)* on crabgrass *(Digitaria somguinalis).* p. 216

Cobweb Skipper *(Hesperia metea metea)* at base of little bluestem grass *(Andropogon scoparius).* p. 219

Row 2

Indian Skipper *(Hesperia sassacus sassacus)* on poverty oatgrass *(Danthonia spicata).* p. 220

Peck's Skipper *(Polites peckius)* on rice cutgrass *(Leersia oryzoides).* p. 222

Row 3

Tawny-edged Skipper *(Polites themistocles)* on blue grass *(Poa* spp.*).* p. 223

Crossline Skipper *(Polites origines)* on little bluestem grass *(Andropogon scoparius).* p. 224

Whirlabout *(Polites vibex vibex)* on Bermuda grass *(Cynodon dactylon).* p. 226

Row 4

Sachem *(Atalopedes campestris huron)* on Bermuda grass *(Cynodon dactylon).* p. 231

Hobomok Skipper *(Poanes hobomok)* on panic grass *(Panicum microcarpon).* p. 233

PLATE 42 • 331

PLATE 43

PLATE 43 • 333

PLATE 44

BUTTERFLY PUPAE

Row 1
Zebra Swallowtail *(Eurytides marcellus)*. p. 42
Giant Swallowtail *(Papilio cresphontes)*. p. 45

Row 2
Spicebush Swallowtail *(Papilio troilus)*. p. 47
Eastern Tiger Swallowtail *(Papilio glaucus)*. p. 48

Row 3
Checkered White *(Papilio protodice)*. p. 54
West Virginia White *(Pieris virginiensis)*. p. 55
Olympia Marble *(Euchloe olympia)*. p. 58

Row 4
Falcate Orangetip *(Anthocharis midea annickae)*. p. 59
Orange Sulphur *(Colias eurytheme)*. p. 63

PLATE 44 • 335

PLATE 45

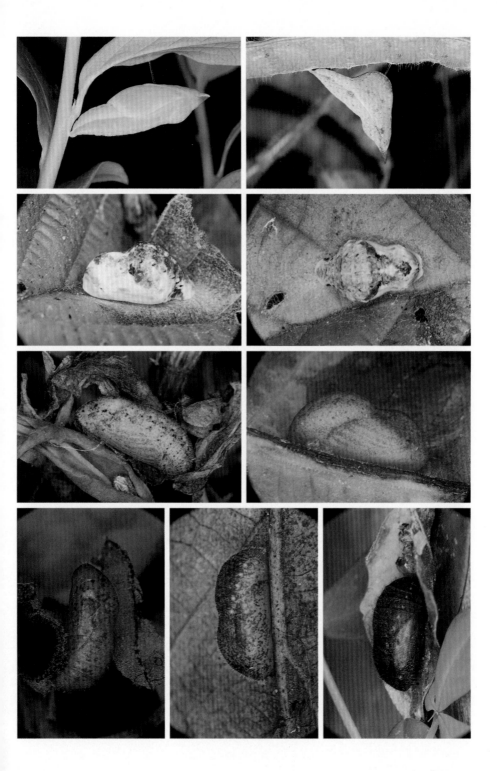

PLATE 45 • 337

PLATE 46

PLATE 46 • 339

PLATE 47

PLATE 47 · 341

PLATE 48

PLATE 48 · 343

PLATE 49

PLATE 49 • 345

PLATE 50

PLATE 50 • 347

Appendix A

List of Scientific and Common Names of Plants

Abutilon theophrasti	velvet leaf	*Arabis glabra*	rockcress
Acer saccharinum	silver maple	*Arabis laevigata*	smooth rockcress
Achillea millefolium	yarrow	*Arabis serotina*	shale barren
Achillea spp.	yarrow		rockcress
Actinomeris		*Arabis* spp.	rock cresses
alternifolia	wing-stem	*Aralia hispida*	bristly sarsaparilla
Agalinis spp.	gerardia	*Aralia spinosa*	Hercules' club
Agrostis spp.	bent grass	*Arctium minus*	burdock
Albizia julibrissin	mimosa	*Arctium* spp.	burdock
Alliaria officinalis	garlic mustard	*Arctostaphylos*	
Alnus spp.	alder	*uvaursi*	bearberry
Althaea spp.	hollyhock	*Arenaria* spp.	rock sandwort
Amaranthus spp.	amaranths	*Aristolochia*	
Ambrosia spp.	ragweeds	*macrophylla*	dutchman's pipe
Amelanchier spp.	serviceberry	*Aristolochia*	
Amphicarpa		*serpentaria*	Virginia snakeroot
bracteata	hog peanut	*Artemisia* spp.	artemisia
Anaphalis		*Aruncus dioicus*	goatsbeard
margaritacea	pearly everlasting	*Asclepias exaltata*	poke milkweed
Andropogon gerardii	big bluestem	*Asclepias incarnata*	swamp milkweed
Andropogon scoparius	little bluestem	*Asclepias quadrifolia*	four-leaved
Andropogon spp.	beard grasses		milkweed
Anethum graveolens	dill	*Asclepias syriaca*	common milkweed
Antennaria neglecta	field pussytoes	*Asclepias tuberosa*	butterfly weed
Antennaria	plantainleaf	*Asclepias* spp.	milkweed
plantaginifolia	everlasting	*Asimina triloba*	paw paw
Antennaria solitaria	single-headed	*Aster laevis*	smooth aster
	pussytoes	*Aster novae-angliae*	New England aster
Antennaria virginica	shale-barren	*Aster pilosus*	white heath aster
	pussytoes	*Aster puniceus*	purple stemmed
Antennaria spp.	pussytoes		aster
Apios americana	groundnut	*Aster simplex*	paniculed aster
Apocynum spp.	dogbane	*Aster umbellatus*	flat-topped white
Aquilegia canadensis	wild columbine		aster
Aquilegia vulgaris	garden columbine	*Aster undulatus*	wavy-leaved aster
Arabidopsis thaliana	mouse-eared cress	*Aster* spp.	aster

Astragalus canadensis	milk vetch	*Cirsium* spp.	thistle
Aureolaria spp.	foxgloves	*Citrus* spp.	citrus
Baptisia australis	blue false indigo	*Claytonia* spp.	spring beauty
Baptisia tinctoria	wild indigo	*Clethra acuminata*	sweet pepperbush
Barbarea vulgaris	winter cress	*Clitoria mariana*	butterfly pea
Betula allegh=eniensis	yellow birch	*Comandra umbellata*	bastard toadflax
Betula lenta	sweet birch	*Coreopsis* spp.	tickseeds
Betula spp.	birch	*Cornus florida*	flowering dogwood
Blephilia	downy woodmint	*Cornus* spp.	dogwood
Boehmeria cylindrica	false nettle	*Coronilla varia*	crown vetch
Brachyelytrum		*Corylus* spp.	hazelnut
erectum	grass	*Crataegus* spp.	hawthorn
Brassica spp.	mustard	*Cucurbita* spp.	cucumber, squash
Buddleja spp.	butterfly bush	*Cynodon dactylon*	Bermuda grass
Capsella		*Cyperus* spp.	sedge
bursa-pastoris	shepherd's purse	*Dactylis glomerata*	orchard grass
Cardamine hirsuta	hairy bittercress	*Danthonia spicata*	poverty oat grass
Cardamine spp.	bittercress	*Daucus carota*	
Carex bromoides	sedge	var. *sativa*	cultivated carrot
Carex lacustris	sedge	*Daucus carota*	Queen Anne's lace
Carex lupulina	sedge	*Dentaria diphylla*	two-leaved toothwort
Carex stricta	sedge	*Dentaria laciniata*	cutleaf toothwort
Carex trichocarpa	sedge	*Dentaria* spp.	toothwort
Carex spp.	sedges	*Desmodium* spp.	tick-trefoil, sticktights
Carpinus caroliniana	American hornbeam	*Digitaria sanguinalis*	crabgrass
Carya cordiformis	bitternut hickory	*Dipsacus* spp.	teasel
Carya glabra	pignut hickory	*Draba* spp.	rock twist
Carya ovata	shagbark hickory	*Echinochloa* spp.	millet
Carya spp.	hickories	*Echium vulgare*	viper's bugloss
Cassia fasciculata	partridge pea	*Elaeagnus umbellata*	autumn olive
Cassia hebecarpa	wild senna	*Eleusine indica*	goose grass
Cassia marilandica	wild senna	*Epigaea repens*	trailing arbutus
Cassia nictitans	wild sensitive plant	*Eragrostis* spp.	lovegrass
Cassia spp.	sennas	*Erianthus alopecuroides*	plume grass
Castanea dentata	American chestnut	*Erigeron* spp.	fleabane, daisy
Ceanothus americanus	New Jersey tea		fleabane
Celosia spp.	cockscomb	*Eupatorium*	
Celtis occidentalis	nettle tree	*perfoliatum*	boneset
Celtis tenuifolia	dwarf hackberry	*Eupatorium* spp.	Joe-pye weed, boneset
Celtis spp.	hackberry	*Fagus grandifolia*	American beech
Centaurea	knapweed	*Fagus* spp.	beech
Cephalanthus		*Festuca rubra*	red fescue
occidentalis	buttonbush	*Foeniculum vulgare*	fennel
Cercis canadensis	redbud	*Fragaria* spp.	strawberry
Chelone glabra	turtlehead	*Fraxinus americana*	white ash
Chenopodium album	lamb's quarters	*Fraxinus nigra*	black ash
Chrysanthemum		*Fraxinus* spp.	ash
leucanthemum	ox-eye daisy	*Gaylussacia brachycera*	box huckleberry
Cichorium intybus	chicory	*Gaylussacia* spp.	huckleberry
Cichorium spp.	chicory	*Geranium* spp.	wild geranium
Cimicifuga racemosa	black cohosh	*Gleditsia triacanthos*	honeylocust
Cirsium arvense	Canada thistle	*Glyceria striata*	fowl mannagrass
Cirsium vulgare	Common thistle	*Gnaphalium* spp.	cudweeds

Hamamelis virginiana	witch hazel	*Menispermum* spp.	moonseed
Helianthus decapetalus	thinleaved sunflower	*Mentha* spp.	peppermint, spearmint, mint
Helianthus strumosus	pale-leaved sunflower		
Helianthus tuberosus	Jerusalem artichoke	*Monarda clinopodia*	basal balm
Helianthus spp.	sunflowers	*Monarda fistulosa*	wild bergamot
Hibiscus syriacus	Rose-of-Sharon	*Oxalis* spp.	wood sorrel
Hieracium	hawkweeds	*Oxydendrum*	
Holcus lanatus	velvet grass	*arboreum*	sourwood
Houstonia	bluets	*Panicum clandestinum*	deertongue
Humulus spp.	hops	*Panicum virgatum*	switch grass
Hydrangea arborescens	hydrangea	*Panicum* spp.	panic grasses
Hystrix patula	bottle-brush grass	*Parietaria pensylvanica*	Pennsylvania pellitory
Ilex opaca	American holly	*Paspalum setaceum*	Bermuda grass
Impatiens spp.	touch-me-not	*Pastinaca sativa*	wild parsnip
Juglans cinerea	butternut	*Pedicularis canadensis*	common lousewort
Juglans nigra	black walnut	*Petroselinum crispum*	parsley
Juniperus virginiana	red cedar	*Phaseolus polystachios*	wild kidney bean
Kalmia latifolia	mountain laurel	*Phaseolus* spp.	beans
Lactuca sativa		*Philadelphus* spp.	mock orange
var. *crispa*	lettuce	*Phleum pratense*	timothy
Lamium spp.	henbit	*Phlox subulata*	phlox
Laportea canadensis	wood nettle	*Phlox* spp.	phlox
Leersia oryzoides	rice cutgrass	*Phoradendron*	
Leersia virginica	white grass	*flavescens*	mistletoe
Lepidium campestre	field cress	*Pinus echinata*	shortleaf pine
Lepidium densiflorum	dense-flowered peppergrass	*Pinus rigida*	pitch pine
		Pinus sylvestris	scotch pine
Lepidium virginicum	wild peppergrass	*Pinus virginiana*	scrub pine
Lepidium spp.	peppergrass	*Plantago rugelii*	common plantain
Lespedeza spp.	bush clover	*Plantago* spp.	plantain
Liatris spp.	blazing star	*Poa* spp.	grass
Ligustrum spp.	privet	*Podophyllum peltatum*	may-apple
Lilium spp.	lilies	*Polygonum sagittatum*	arrowleaf tearthumb
Linaria vulgaris	toadflax	*Polygonum* spp.	knotweed
Lindera benzoin	spicebush	*Populus alba*	silverleaf poplar
Liriodendron tulipifera	yellow poplar	*Populus deltoides*	cottonwood
Lithospermum spp.	gromwell	*Populus grandidentata*	big-toothed aspen
Lobelia cardinalis	cardinal flower	*Populus nigra*	black poplar
Lonicera japonica	Japanese honeysuckle	*Populus* spp.	aspens
Lonicera spp.	honeysuckle	*Populus tremuloides*	quaking aspen
Lotus corniculatus	bird's-foot-trefoil	*Portulaca* spp.	purslane
Lupinus perennis	lupine	*Potentilla canadensis*	Canada cinquefoil
Lupinus spp.	lupine	*Potentilla* spp.	cinquefoil
Lyonia ligustrina	maleberry	*Prunella vulgaris*	selfheal, heal-all
Lysimachia spp.	loosestrife	*Prunus serotina*	black cherry
Malus spp.	apple	*Prunus virginiana*	choke cherry
Malva neglecta	common mallow	*Prunus* spp.	wild plum
Malva spp.	mallow	*Ptelea trifoliata*	wafer ash
Marrubium vulgare	horehound	*Pueraria lobata*	kudzu
Medicago sativa	alfalfa	*Pycnanthemum*	narrowleaf
Medicago spp.	alfalfa	*flexuosum*	mountain-mint
Melilotus alba	white sweet clover	*Pyrus* spp.	chokeberry
Melilotus officinalis	yellow sweet clover	*Quercus alba*	white oak

Quercus ilicifolia	scrub oak	*Syringa* spp.	lilac
Quercus marilandica	blackjack oak	*Tagetes* spp.	marigolds
Quercus prinus	chestnut oak	*Taraxacum officinale*	dandelion
Quercus rubra	red oak	*Taraxacum* spp.	dandelions
Quercus stellata	post oak	*Tilia* spp.	basswood
Quercus velutina	black oak	*Trifolium arvense*	rabbitfoot clover
Ranunculus spp.	buttercups	*Trifolium pratense*	red clover
Rhododendron		*Trifolium repens*	white clover
calendulaceum	flame azalea	*Trifolium* spp.	clovers
Rhododendron		*Triodia flava*	purpletop
nudiflorum	wild azalea	*Ulmus americana*	American elm
Rhododendron spp.	azalea	*Ulmus* spp.	elm
Rhus copallina	dwarf sumac	*Uniola latifolia*	broad-leaved uniola
Rhus glabra	smooth sumac	*Urtica dioica*	stinging nettle
Rhus typhina	staghorn sumac	*Urtica gracilis*	wild nettle
Rhus spp.	sumac	*Urtica* spp.	nettles
Ribes rotundifolia	gooseberry	*Vaccinium*	
Ribes spp.	gooseberry	*angustifolium*	lowbush blueberry
Robinia pseudo acacia	black locust	*Vaccinium*	
Robinia spp.	locust	*macrocarpon*	large cranberry
Rubus spp.	dewberry, blackberry	*Vaccinium oxycoccos*	small cranberry
Rudbeckia hirta	black-eyed Susan	*Vaccinium* spp.	blueberries, heaths
Ruellia spp.	ruellia, wild petunia	*Verbena hastata*	blue vervain
Rumex acetosella	sheep sorrel	*Verbena* spp.	vervain
Rumex crispus	curly dock	*Verbesina alternifolia*	wing-stem
Rumex verticillatus	water dock	*Vernonia* spp.	ironweed
Ruta graveolens	common rue	*Viburnum recognitum*	arrowhead
Saccharum spp.	sugar cane	*Viburnum* spp.	viburnum
Salix babylonica	weeping willow	*Vicia caroliniana*	wild vetch
Salix nigra	black willow	*Vicia* spp.	vetches
Salix spp.	willow	*Viola blanda*	sweet white violet
Sambucus canadensis	elderberry	*Viola canadensis*	Canada violet
Sambucus spp.	elderberry	*Viola cucullata*	marsh blue violet
Saponaria officinalis	bouncing bet	*Viola pallens*	northern white violet
Sassafras albidum	white sassafras	*Viola papilionacea*	common blue violet
Satureja vulgaris	field basil	*Viola pedata*	bird's-foot violet
Sedum spp.	stonecrop	*Viola pennsylvanica*	smooth yellow violet
Senecio obovatus	squaw-weed	*Viola primulifolia*	primrose-leaf violet
Sida spp.	sida	*Viola soraria*	downy wood violet
Sisymbrium	hedge mustards	*Viola striata*	striped violet
Smilax spp.	greenbrier, carrion	*Viola tricolor*	Johnny-jump-ups
	flower	*Viola* spp.	violets, pansies
Solidago spp.	goldenrods	*Wisteria* spp.	wisteria
Sorghastrum nutans	Indian grass	*Zanthoxylum*	
Spiraea spp.	spiraea,	*americanum*	prickly ash
	meadowsweet	*Zanthoxylum*	
Stellaria spp.	chickweed	*clava-herculis*	Hercules' club
Strophostyles helvola	wild bean	*Zinnia* spp.	zinnia
Syringa vulgaris	lilac		

Appendix B

List of Scientific and Common Names of Butterflies

Swallowtails—Papilioninae

Battus philenor	Pipevine Swallowtail
Eurytides marcellus	Zebra Swallowtail
Papilio polyxenes asterius	Black Swallowtail
Papilio cresphontes	Giant Swallowtail
Papilio troilus troilus	Spicebush Swallowtail
Papilio glaucus	Eastern Tiger Swallowtail
Papilio canadensis	Canadian Tiger Swallowtail

Whites—Pierinae

Pontia protodice	Checkered White
Pieris virginiensis	West Virginia White
Pieris rapae	Cabbage White
Euchloe olympia	Olympia Marble
Anthocharis midea annickae	Falcate Orangetip

Sulphurs—Coliadinae

Colias philodice philodice	Clouded Sulphur
Colias eurytheme	Orange Sulphur
Colias interior	Pink-edged Sulphur
Phoebis sennae eubule	Cloudless Sulphur
Eurema lisa	Little Yellow
Eurema nicippe	Sleepy Orange

Harvesters—Miletinae

Feniseca tarquinius	Harvester

Coppers—Lycaeninae

Lycaena phlaeas americana	American Copper
Lycaena hyllus	Bronze Copper
Lycaena epixanthe epixanthe	Bog Copper

Hairstreaks—Theclinae

Atlides halesus	Great Purple Hairstreak
Satyrium titus mopsus	Coral Hairstreak
Satyrium edwardsii	Edwards' Hairstreak
Satyrium calanus falacer	Banded Hairstreak
Satyrium caryaevorum	Hickory Hairstreak
Satyrium liparops strigosum	Striped Hairstreak
Calycopis cecrops	Red-banded Hairstreak
Mitoura grynea grynea	(Olive) Juniper Hairstreak
Incisalia augustinus croesoides	Brown Elfin
Incisalia polia	Hoary Elfin
Incisalia irus irus	Frosted Elfin
Incisalia henrici henrici	Henry's Elfin
Incisalia niphon niphon	Eastern Pine Elfin
Parrhasius m-album	White M Hairstreak
Fixsenia flavonius ontario	(Northern) Southern Hairstreak
Strymon melinus humuli	Gray Hairstreak
Erora laeta	Early Hairstreak

Blues—Polyommatinae

Everes comyntas comyntas	Eastern Tailed-Blue
Celatrina ladon	Spring Azure
Celastrina neglectamajor	Appalachian Azure
Celastrina nigra	Dusky Azure
Glaucopsyche lygdamus lygdamus	Silvery Blue

Metalmarks—Riodininae

Calephelis borealis	Northern Metalmark

Snouts—Libytheinae

Libytheana carinenta bachmanii	American Snout

Longwings—Heliconiinae

Euptoieta claudia	Variegated Fritillary
Speyeria diana	Diana
Speyeria cybele cybele	Great Spangled Fritillary
Speyeria aphrodite aphrodite	Aphrodite Fritillary
Speyeria atlantis atlantis	Atlantis Fritillary
Speyeria idalia	Regal Fritillary
Boloria selene myrina	Silver-bordered Fritillary
Boloria bellona bellona	Meadow Fritillary

Brushfoots—Nymphalinae

Chlosyne gorgone	Gorgone Checkerspot
Chlosyne nycteis nycteis	Silvery Checkerspot
Chlosyne harrisii liggetti	Harris' Checkerspot
Phyciodes tharos	Pearl Crescent
Phyciodes selenis selenis	Northern Crescent
Phyciodes batesii	Tawny Crescent
Euphydryas phaeton phaeton	Baltimore
Polygonia interrogationis	Question Mark
Polygonia comma	Eastern Comma
Polygonia faunus smythi	Green Comma
Polygonia progne	Gray Comma
Nymphalis vau-album j-album	Compton Tortoiseshell

Nymphalis antiopa antiopa	Mourning Cloak
Nymphalis milberti milberti	Milbert's Tortoiseshell
Vanessa virginiensis	American Lady
Vanessa cardui	Painted Lady
Vanessa atalanta rubria	Red Admiral
Junonia coenia	Common Buckeye

Admirals—Limenitidinae

Limenitis arthemis astyanax	Red-spotted Purple
Limenitis archippus archippus	Viceroy

Hackberry Butterflies—Apaturinae

Asterocampa celtis celtis	Hackberry Emperor
Asterocampa clyton	Tawny Emperor

Satyrs and Wood Nymphs—Satyrinae

Enodia anthedon	Northern Pearly Eye
Satyrodes eurydice eurydice	Eyed Brown
Satyrodes appalachia appalachia	Appalachian Brown
Cyllopsis gemma gemma	Gemmed Satyr
Hermeuptychia sosybius	Carolina Satyr
Megisto cymela	Little Wood Satyr
Cercyonis pegala pegala	Common Wood Nymph
Cercyonis pegala nephele	Dull-eyed Grayling

Milkweed Butterfly—Danainae

Danaus plexippus	Monarch

Open-winged Skippers—Pyrginae

Epargyreus clarus	Silver-spotted Skipper
Urbanus proteus proteus	Long-tailed Skipper
Autochton cellus	Golden-banded Skipper
Achalarus lyciades	Hoary Edge
Thorybes pylades	Northern Cloudywing
Thorybes bathyllus	Southern Cloudywing
Thorybes confusis	Confused Cloudywing
Erynnis icelus	Dreamy Duskywing
Erynnis brizo brizo	Sleepy Duskywing
Erynnis juvenalis	Juvenal's Duskywing

Erynnis horatius	Horace's Duskywing	*Polites peckius*	Peck's Skipper
Erynnis martialis	Mottled Duskywing	*Polites themistocles*	Tawny-edged Skipper
Erynnis lucilius	Columbine Duskywing	*Polites origenes*	Crossline Skipper
Erynnis baptisiae	Wild Indigo Duskywing	*Polites vibex vibex*	Whirlabout
		Polites mystic mystic	Long Dash
Erynnis persius persius	Persius Duskywing	*Wallengrenia egeremet*	Northern Broken-Dash
Pyrgus centaureae wyandot	Grizzled Skipper	*Pompeius verna verna*	Little Glassywing
Pyrgus communis communis	Common Checkered-Skipper	*Atalopedes campestris huron*	Sachem
Pholisora catullus	Common Sootywing	*Atrytone logan logan*	Delaware Skipper
Staphylus hayhurstii	Hayhurst's Scallopwing	*Poanes hobomok*	Hobomok Skipper
		Poanes zabulon	Zabulon Skipper

Branded Skippers—Hesperiinae

		Euphyes conspicuus conspicuus	Black Dash
Nastra lherminier	Swarthy Skipper	*Euphyes bimacula*	Two-spotted Skipper
Lerema accius	Clouded Skipper	*Euphyes vestris metacomet*	Dun Skipper
Ancyloxypha numitor	Least Skipper	*Atryonopsis hianna hianna*	Dusted Skipper
Thymelicus lineola	European Skipper	*Amblyscirtes hegon*	Pepper & Salt Skipper
Hylephila phyleus	Fiery Skipper	*Amblyscirtes vialis*	Common Roadside-Skipper
Hesperia leonardus leonardus	Leonard's Skipper	*Panoquina ocola*	Ocola Skipper
Hesperia metea metea	Cobweb Skipper		
Hesperia sassacus sassacus	Indian Skipper		

Appendix C
Collection Information for Plates

PLATE 1

Row 1

Pipevine Swallowtail. *Battus philenor.* Elkins, Randolph Co., W.Va. September 5, 1986.

Battus philenor. Nellis, Boone Co., W.Va. July 4, 1986.

Row 2

Battus philenor. Elkins, Randolph Co., W.Va. September 5, 1986.

Zebra Swallowtail. *Eurytides marcellus.* Fork Creek Wildlife Management Area (WMA), Nellis, Boone Co., W.Va. April 18, 1980.

Row 3

Eurytides marcellus. McClintic Wildlife Station, near Point Pleasant, Mason Co., W.Va. July 30, 1979.

Eurytides marcellus. Danville, Boone Co., W.Va. July 5, 1986.

Eurytides marcellus. Harman, Randolph Co., W.Va. July 16, 1974.

PLATE 2

Row 1

Black Swallowtail. *Papilio polyxenes asterius.* Elkins, Randolph Co., W.Va. August 24, 1987.

Papilio polyxenes asterius. Roaring Plains, Randolph Co., W.Va. May 26, 1980.

Papilio polyxenes asterius. Elkins, Randolph Co., W.Va. August 7, 1983.

Row 2

Giant Swallowtail. *Papilio cresphontes.* Sleepy Creek Mtn., Berkeley Co., W.Va. July 11, 1988.

Papilio cresphontes. Sleepy Creek Mtn., Berkeley Co., W.Va. July 28, 1986.

Row 3

Spicebush Swallowtail. *Papilio troilus troilus.* Huttonsville, Randolph Co., W.Va. May 17, 1987.

Papilio t. troilus. Nellis, Boone Co., W.Va. July 4, 1986.

Papilio t. troilus. Fork Creek WMA, Nellis, Boone Co., W.Va. July 18, 1980.

PLATE 3

Row 1

Eastern Tiger Swallowtail. *Papilio glaucus.* Rt. 41, Prince, Fayette Co., W.Va. May 22, 1987.

Papilio glaucus. East Lynn Lake, Wayne Co., W.Va. April 16, 1984.

Row 2

Papilio glaucus. Fort Martin, Monongalia Co., W.Va. July 8, 1982.

Papilio glaucus. East Fork of Glady Creek, Randolph Co., W.Va. June 18, 1984.

Row 3

Papilio glaucus. East Fork of Glady Creek, Randolph Co., W.Va. June 18, 1984.

Papilio glaucus. Elkins, Randolph Co., W.Va. July 28, 1986.

PLATE 4

Row 1

Checkered White. *Pontia protodice.* Ohio River at Russellville, Ohio. September 1, 1988.

Pontia prodotice. South of Ashford, Boone Co., W.Va. July 6, 1987.

Row 2

Pontia protodice. Ohio River at Russellville, Ohio. September 1, 1988.

Pontia prodotice. Ohio River at Russellville, Ohio. September 1, 1988.

Pontia prodotice. Ohio River at Russellville, Ohio. September 1, 1988.

Pontia prodotice. Petersburg, Grant Co., W.Va. May 6, 1987.

Row 3

West Virginia White. *Pieris virginiensis.* Fork Creek WMA, Boone Co., W.Va. April 12, 1985.

Pieris virginiensis. Files Creek, near Beverly, Randolph Co., W.Va. April 14, 1986.

Pieris virginiensis. Files Creek, near Beverly, Randolph Co., W.Va. April 14, 1986.

Row 4

Cabbage White. *Pieris rapae.* Larenim Park, north of Burlington, Mineral Co., W.Va. September 20, 1984.

Pieris rapae. Larenim Park, north of Burlington, Mineral Co., W.Va. September 20, 1984.

Row 5

Pieris rapae. Blennerhassett Island, Wood Co., W.Va. April 16, 1989.

Pieris rapae. Larenim Park, north of Burlington, Mineral Co., W.Va. September 20, 1984.

Pieris rapae. Blennerhassett Island, Wood Co., W.Va. April 16, 1989.

PLATE 5

Row 1

Olympia Marble. *Euchloe olympia.* Larenim Park, north of Burlington, Mineral Co., W.Va. April 27, 1984.

Euchloe olympia. Larenim Park, north of Burlington, Mineral Co., W.Va. April 20, 1986.

Euchloe olympia. Larenim Park, north of Burlington, Mineral Co., W.Va. April 27, 1984.

Row 2

Falcate Orangetip. *Anthocharis midea annickae.* Larenim Park, north of Burlington, Mineral Co., W.Va. April 27, 1984.

Anthocharis midea annickae. Blennerhassett Island, Wood Co., W.Va. April 16, 1989.

Anthocharis midea annickae. Middle Mtn., Neola, Greenbrier Co., W.Va. May 15, 1974.

Row 3

Clouded Sulphur. *Colias p. philodice.* Elkins, Randolph Co., W.Va. August 7, 1983.

Colias p. philodice. Elkins, Randolph Co., W.Va. August 5, 1983.

Colias p. philodice. Elkins, Randolph Co., W.Va. August 7, 1983.

Row 4

Colias p. philodice. Elkins, Randolph Co., W.Va. August 5, 1983.

Orange Sulphur. *Colias eurytheme.* Elkins, Randolph Co., W.Va. October 14, 1984.

Row 5

Colias eurytheme. Elkins, Randolph Co., W.Va. August 7, 1983.

Colias eurytheme. Elkins, Randolph Co., W.Va. August 7, 1983.

Colias eurytheme x Colias philodice hybrid. Elkins, Randolph Co., W.Va. August 7, 1983.

PLATE 6

Row 1

Pink-edged Sulphur. *Colias interior.* Canaan Heights, Tucker Co., W.Va. July 18, 1983.

Colias interior. Canaan Heights, Tucker Co., W.Va. July 18, 1983.

Row 2

Colias interior. Canaan Heights, Tucker Co., W.Va. July 18, 1983.

Cloudless Sulphur. *Phoebus sennae eubule.* Rt. 55, west of Wardensville, Hardy Co., W.Va. August 6, 1987.

Row 3

Phoebus sennae eubule. Smokey Mtn.,
Gatlinburg, Tenn. September 6, 1986.

Phoebus sennae eubule. Huttonsville Prison,
Randolph Co., W.Va. August 25, 1987.

Phoebus sennae eubule. Ormond Beach, Volutia
Co., Fla. August 25, 1982.

Row 4

Little Yellow. *Eurema lisa.* Burnsville Lake,
Braxton Co., W.Va. August 23, 1983.

Eurema lisa. Clothier, Boone Co., W.Va.
September 26, 1972.

Eureme lisa. Stonewall Jackson Lake, Lewis Co.,
W.Va. September 6, 1983.

Eureme lisa. Muddy Creek, Greenbrier Co.,
W.Va. August 26, 1983.

PLATE 7

Row 1

Sleepy Orange. *Eurema nicippi.* Rt. 55, west of
Wardensville, Hardy Co., W.Va. August 14,
1987.

Eurema nicippi. Trout Run, south of
Wardensville, Hardy Co., W.Va. August 18,
1987.

Row 2

Eurema nicippi. Potts Creek, Jefferson National
Forest (NF), Monroe Co., W.Va. September
14, 1984.

Eurema nicippi. Trout Run, south of
Wardensville, Hardy Co., W.Va. August 30,
1987.

Eurema nicippi. Trout Run, south of
Wardensville, Hardy Co., W.Va. August 17,
1987.

Row 3

Harvester. *Feniseca tarquinius.* Bluestone
WMA, Indian Mills, Summers Co., W.Va.
April 25, 1984.

Feniseca tarquinius. Fork Creek WMA, Boone
Co., W.Va. April 12, 1985.

Feniseca tarquinius. Fork Creek WMA Boone
Co., W.Va. April 14, 1989.

Row 4

American Copper. *Lycaena phlaeas americana.*
Beverly, Randolph Co., W.Va. July 7, 1972.

Lycaena phlaeas americana. Ridge, Morgan
Co., W.Va. August 26, 1984.

Lycaena phlaeas americana. Beverly, Randolph
Co., W.Va. July 9, 1972.

Row 5

Bronze Copper. *Lycaena hyllus.* Greenbottom
WMA, Cabell Co., W.Va. September 6,
1989.

Lycaena hyllus. Huttonsville Prison, Randolph
Co., W.Va. June 14, 1985.

Lycaena hyllus. Spring Brook, Kalamazoo Co.,
Mich. June 24, 1974.

PLATE 8

Row 1

Bog Copper. *Lycaena epixanthe epixanthe.*
Cranesville Swamp, Preston Co., W.Va. July
16, 1983.

Lycaena e. epixanthe. Cranesville Swamp,
Preston Co., W.Va. July 16, 1983.

Lycaena e. epixanthe. Cranesville Swamp,
Preston Co., W.Va. July 8, 1983.

Row 2

Great Purple Hairstreak. *Atlides halesus.*
Dismal Swamp, N.C. August 7, 1976.

Atlides halesus. New Bridge, Dorchester Co.,
Md. July 21, 1985 (reared).

Atlides halesus. Dismal Swamp, N.C. August 7,
1976.

Row 3

Coral Hairstreak. *Satyrium titus mopsus.*
Reddish Knob, near Sugar Grove,
Pendleton Co., W.Va. July 12, 1983.

Satyrium titus mopsus. The Jug WMA, Tyler
Co., W.Va. June 25, 1987.

Satyrium titus mopsus. Reddish Knob, near
Sugar Grove, Pendleton Co., W.Va. July 12,
1983.

Edwards' Hairstreak. *Satyrium edwardsii.* Potts
Creek, Jefferson NF, Monroe Co., W.Va.
July 8, 1987.

Row 4

Satyrium edwardsii. Port Franks, Ontario,
Canada. July 15, 1983.

Satyrium edwardsii. Port Franks, Ontario,
Canada. July 7, 1986.

Banded Hairstreak. *Satyrium calanus falacer.*
Sleepy Creek WMA, Berkeley Co., W.Va.
June 26, 1986.

Plate 8, continued

Row 5

Satyrium calanus falacer. Sleepy Creek WMA, Berkeley Co., W.Va. June 25, 1986.

Hickory Hairstreak. *Satyrium caryaevorum.* London, Middlesex Co., Ontario, Canada. July 5, 1988.

Satyrium caryaevorum. London, Middlesex Co., Ontario, Canada. July 5, 1988.

Row 6

Striped Hairstreak. *Satyrium liparops strigosum.* Sleepy Creek WMA, Berkeley Co., W.Va. June 27, 1984.

Satyrium liparops strigosum. Cranesville, Preston Co., W.Va. 29 June 1987

Satyrium liparops strigosum. Sleepy Creek WMA, Berkeley Co., W.Va. June 27, 1984.

Satyrium liparops strigosum. Twin Falls State Park, Wyoming Co., W.Va. July 9, 1987.

PLATE 9

Row 1

Red-banded Hairstreak. *Calycopis cecrops.* Greenbottom WMA, Cabell Co., W.Va. September 6, 1989.

Calycopis cecrops. Big Ugly WMA, Lincoln Co., W.Va. July 7, 1987.

Calycopis cecrops. Fork Creek WMA, Boone Co., W.Va. May 12, 1990.

Row 2

(Olive) Juniper Hairstreak. *Mitoura grynea grynea.* Petersburg, Grant Co., W.Va. April 27, 1984.

Mitoura g. grynea. Petersburg, Grant Co., W.Va. May 11, 1983.

Mitoura g. grynea. Cabins, Grant Co., W.Va. August 2, 1989.

Mitoura g. grynea. Larenim Park, north of Burlington, Mineral Co., W.Va. April 28, 1984.

Row 3

Brown Elfin. *Incisalia augustinus croesoides.* Brady Gap, Ruddle, Pendleton Co., W.Va. April 28, 1994

Incisalia a. croesoides. George Washington NF, west of Wardensville, Hardy Co., W.Va. April 25, 1985.

Incisalia a. croesoides. George Washington NF, west of Wardensville, Hardy Co., W.Va. April 25, 1985.

Hoary Elfin. *Incisalia polia.* Ipperwash, Ontario, Canada. May 11, 1980.

Row 4

Incisalia polia. Ipperwash, Ontario, Canada. May 11, 1980.

Incisalia polia. Myles Standish State Forest, Plymouth, Mass. May 20, 1984.

Frosted Elfin. *Incisalia irus irus.* Mizpah, Atlantic Co., N.J. May 6, 1993.

Incisalia i. irus. Mizpah, Atlantic Co., N.J. May 6, 1993.

Row 5

Incisalia i. irus. Mizpah, Atlantic Co., N.J. May 6, 1993.

Henry's Elfin. *Incisalia henrici henrici.* Bluestone WMA, Summers Co., W.Va. April 25, 1984.

Incisalia h. henrici. East Lynn Lake, Wayne Co., W.Va. April 12, 1984.

Incisalia h. henrici. Bluestone WMA, Summers Co., W.Va. April 25, 1984.

Row 6

Eastern Pine Elfin. *Incisalia niphon niphon.* Sugar Grove, Pendleton Co., W.Va. May 10, 1984.

Incisalia n. niphon. Bluestone WMA, Summers Co., W.Va. April 25, 1984.

Incisalia n. niphon. Larenim Park, north of Burlington, Mineral Co., W.Va. April 27, 1984.

Row 7

White M Hairstreak. *Parrhasius m-album.* Near Elderton, Indian Co., Pa. May 18, 1988.

Parrhasius m-album. Near Elderton, Indian Co., Pa. June 21, 1988.

Parrhasius m-album. North Madison, Conn. July 15, 1967.

PLATE 10

Row 1

(Northern) Southern Hairstreak. *Fixsenia favonius ontario.* Meramec State Park, Franklin Co., Mo. May 28, 1988.

Fixsenia favonius ontario. Meramec State Park, Franklin Co., Mo. May 28, 1988.

Gray Hairstreak. *Strymon melinus humuli.* River Rd. east of Moorefield, Hardy Co., W.Va. April 19, 1985.

Strymon melinus humuli. Stonewall Jackson Lake, Lewis Co., W.Va. July 13, 1983.

Row 2

Strymon melinus humuli. Stonecoal Lake, Lewis Co., W.Va. July 5, 1983.

Early Hairstreak. *Erora laeta.* Indian Mills, Summers Co., W.Va. May 9, 1985.

Erora laeta. West of Cass, Pocahontas Co., W.Va. May 6, 1985.

Erora laeta. Fork Creek WMA, Boone Co., W.Va. April 14, 1989.

Row 3

Eastern Tailed-Blue. *Everes comyntas comyntas* Fork Creek WMA, Boone Co., W.Va. May 12, 1982.

Everes c. comyntas. Fork Creek WMA, Boone Co., W.Va. May 12, 1982.

Everes c. comyntas. Fork Creek WMA, Boone Co., W.Va. June 4, 1985.

Everes c. comyntas. Burnsville Lake, Braxton Co., W.Va. August 23, 1983.

Row 4

Spring Azure. *Celastrina ladon.* Fork Creek WMA, Boone Co., W.Va. April 14, 1989.

Celastrina ladon. Larenim Park, north of Burlington, Mineral Co., W.Va. April 27, 1984.

Celastrina ladon. River Rd., east of Moorefield, Hardy Co., W.Va. May 6, 1987.

Celastrina ladon. Spruce Knob, 4200 ft. elev., Randolph Co., W.Va. May 22, 1988.

Row 5

Celastrina ladon. Fork Creek WMA, Boone Co., W.Va. June 4, 1985.

Celastrina ladon. Grassy Knob Tower, Greenbrier Co., W.Va. June 17, 1985.

Celastrina ladon. Elkins, Randolph Co., W.Va. July 27, 1987.

Celastrina ladon. Sleepy Creek WMA, Berkeley Co., W.Va. April 4, 1986.

Row 6

Appalachian Azure. *Celastrina neglectamajor.* Spruce Laurel Fork, Clothier, Boone Co., W.Va. May 18, 1972.

Celastrina neglectamajor. Neola, Greenbrier Co., W.Va. May 22, 1974.

Celastrina neglectamajor. Neola, Greenbrier Co., W.Va.May 9, 1974.

Row 7

Dusky Azure. *Celastrina nigra.* Fork Creek WMA, Boone Co., W.Va. April 14, 1989.

Celastrina nigra. Fork Creek WMA, Boone Co., W.Va. April 12, 1985.

Celastrina nigra. Bluestone WMA, Indian Mills, Summers Co., W.Va. April 25, 1984.

Silvery Blue. *Glaucopsyche lygdamus lygdamus.* Fork Creek WMA, Boone Co., W.Va. April 14, 1989.

Row 8

Glaucopsyche l. lygdamus. Fork Creek WMA, Boone Co., W.Va. April 14, 1989.

Glaucopsyche l. lygdamus. Fork Creek WMA, Boone Co., W.Va. April 14, 1989.

Northern Metalmark. *Calephelis borealis.* Stonecoal Lake, Lewis Co., W.Va. July 5, 1983.

Calephelis borealis. Ridgeville, Mineral Co., W.Va. July 14, 1982.

Calephelis borealis. Big Draft Rd., Blue Bend, Greenbrier Co., W.Va. July 16, 1986.

PLATE 11

Row 1

Variegated Fritillary. *Euptoieta claudia.* Greenbrier Co., W.Va. August 26, 1983.

Euptoieta claudia. Petersburg, Grant Co., W.Va. October 16, 1984.

Euptoieta claudia. Petersburg, Grant Co., W.Va. August 26, 1984.

Row 2

Diana. *Speyeria diana.* Prince, Raleigh Co., W.Va. May 31, 1987 (reared).

Speyeria diana. Rt. 41 near Grandview State Park, Raleigh Co., W.Va. October 4, 1986 (reared).

Plate 11, continued

Row 3

Speyeria diana. Potts Creek, Jefferson NF, Monroe Co., W.Va. June 26, 1989 (reared).

Speyeria diana. Pinnacle Creek, Wyoming Co., W.Va. July 12, 1978.

Row 4

Great Spangled Fritillary. *Speyeria cybele cybele.* Pigs Ear, Pocahontas Co., W.Va. July 7, 1983.

Great Spangled Fritillary. *Speyeria cybele cybele.* Middle Mtn., Greenbrier Co., W.Va. July 3, 1975.

PLATE 12

Row 1

Great Spangled Fritillary. *Speyeria cybele cybele.* Reddish Knob, Sugar Grove, Pendleton Co., W.Va. July 12, 1983.

Speyeria c. cybele. Elkins, Randolph Co., W.Va. June 25, 1985.

Row 2

Aphrodite Fritillary. *Speyeria aphrodite aphrodite.* Elkins, Randolph Co., W.Va. June 25, 1985.

Speyeria a. aphrodite. Spruce Knob Lake, Randolph Co., W.Va. July 3, 1987.

Row 3

Speyeria a. aphrodite. Pigs Ear, Pocahontas Co., W.Va. July 7, 1983.

Speyeria a. aphrodite. Reddish Knob, Pendleton Co., W.Va. June 30, 1983

Row 4

Atlantis Fritillary. *Speyeria atlantis atlantis.* Spruce Knob Lake, Randolph Co., W.Va. June 28, 1987.

Speyeria a. atlantis. Spruce Knob Lake, Randolph Co., W.Va. June 28, 1987.

PLATE 13

Row 1

Atlantis Fritillary. *Speyeria a. atlantis.* Pigs Ear, Pocahontas Co., W.Va. July 7, 1983.

Speyeria a. atlantis. Pigs Ear, Pocahontas Co., W.Va. July 7, 1983.

Row 2

Regal Fritillary. *Speyeria idalia.* Fort Martin, Monongalia Co., W.Va. July 8, 1982.

Speyeria idalia. Gap Mills, Monroe Co., W.Va. August 26, 1987 (reared).

Row 3

Speyeria idalia. Fort Martin, Monongalia Co., W.Va. August 5, 1986.

Speyeria idalia. Fort Martin, Monongalia Co., W.Va. July 8, 1982.

PLATE 14

Row 1

Silver-bordered Fritillary. *Boloria selene myrina.* Pigs Ear, Pocahontas Co., W.Va. July 27, 1983.

Boloria selene myrina. Pigs Ear, Pocahontas Co., W.Va. July 27, 1983.

Boloria selene myrina. Blister Swamp, Pocahontas Co., W.Va. June 22, 1983.

Row 2

Meadow Fritillary. *Boloria bellona bellona.* Reddish Knob, Pendleton Co., W.Va. July 12, 1983.

Boloria b. bellona. Elkins, Randolph Co., W.Va. October 22, 1987 (reared).

Boloria b. bellona. Elkins, Randolph Co., W.Va. August 7, 1983.

Row 3

Boloria b. bellona. Elkins, Randolph Co., W.Va. May 13, 1984.

Gorgone Checkerspot. *Chlosyne gorgone.* Luther, Oklahoma Co., Okla. April 11, 1985.

Chlosyne gorgone. Luther, Oklahoma Co., Okla. April 11, 1985.

Row 4

Silvery Checkerspot. *Chlosyne nycteis nycteis.* Cass, Pocahontas Co., W.Va. June 22, 1984.

Chlosyne n. nycteis. Fork Creek WMA, Boone Co., W.Va. June 4, 1985.

Chlosyne n. nycteis. Rt. 41, Prince, Fayette Co., W.Va. August 1, 1984.

Plate 14, continued

Row 5

Harris' Checkerspot. *Chlosyne harrisii liggetti.* Gandy Creek, Randolph Co., W.Va. June 23, 1983.

Chlosyne harrisii liggetti. Blackwater Falls State Park, Tucker Co., W.Va. June 8, 1985.

Chlosyne harrisii liggetti. Gandy Creek, Randolph Co., W.Va. June 22, 1983.

PLATE 15

Row 1

Pearl Crescent. *Phyciodes tharos.* Larenim Park, north of Burlington, Mineral Co., W.Va. May 17, 1984.

Phyciodes tharos. Webster Co., W.Va. May 25, 1987.

Phyciodes tharos. Reddish Knob, near Sugar Grove, Pendleton Co., W.Va. May 30, 1985.

Phyciodes tharos. River Rd., north of Moorefield, Hardy Co., W.Va. April 19, 1985.

Row 2

Phyciodes tharos. Springfield WMA, Hampshire Co., W.Va. August 10, 1983.

Phyciodes tharos. Elkins, Randolph Co., W.Va. August 7, 1983.

Phyciodes tharos. Elkins, Randolph Co., W.Va. August 14, 1983.

Phyciodes tharos. Burnsville Lake, Braxton Co., W.Va. August 23, 1983.

Row 3

Northern Crescent. *Phyciodes selenis selenis.* Reddish Knob, near Sugar Grove, Pendleton Co., W.Va. July 12, 1983.

Phyciodes s. selenis. Reddish Knob, near Sugar Grove, Pendleton Co., W.Va. July 12, 1983.

Phyciodes s. selenis. Reddish Knob, near Sugar Grove, Pendleton Co., W.Va. July 12, 1983.

Phyciodes s. selenis. Reddish Knob, near Sugar Grove, Pendleton Co., W.Va. July 12, 1983.

Row 4

Tawny Crescent. *Phyciodes batesii.* Pinery Prov. Park, Lambton Co., Ontario. June 16, 1984.

Phyciodes batesii. Pinery Prov. Park, Lambton Co., Ontario. June 16, 1984.

Phyciodes batesii. Pinery Prov. Park, Lambton Co., Ontario. June 16, 1983.

Baltimore. *Euphydryas phaeton phaeton.* Blackwater Falls State Park, Davis, Tucker Co., W.Va. July 1, 1983.

Row 5

Euphydryas p. phaeton. Elkins, Randolph Co., W.Va. June 10, 1984.

Euphydryas p. phaeton. Elkins, Randolph Co., W.Va. June 20, 1989.

PLATE 16

Row 1

Question Mark. *Polygonia interrogationis.* Stonewall Jackson Lake, Lewis Co., W.Va. September 6, 1983.

Polygonia interrogationis. Stonewall Jackson Lake, Lewis Co., W.Va. September 6, 1983.

Row 2

Polygonia interrogationis. Lewis Co., W.Va. September 24, 1983.

Polygonia interrogationis. Rough Run, George Washington NF, Pendleton Co., W.Va. July 12, 1989.

Polygonia interrogationis. Rough Run, George Washington NF, Pendleton Co., W.Va. July 12, 1989.

Row 3

Polygonia interrogationis. Rough Run, George Washington NF, Pendleton Co., W.Va. July 12, 1989.

Polygonia interrogationis. Rough Run, George Washington NF, Pendleton Co., W.Va. July 12, 1989.

PLATE 17

Row 1

Eastern Comma. *Polygonia Comma.* Muddy Creek, Greenbrier Co., W.Va. August 26, 1983.

Polygonia comma. Clothier, Boone Co., W.Va. August 24, 1972.

Row 2

Polygonia comma. Fork Creek WMA, Boone Co., W.Va. June 4, 1985.

Polygonia comma. Stonewall Jackson Lake, Lewis Co., W.Va. September 6, 1983.

Polygonia comma. Cass, Pocahontas Co., W.Va. June 24, 1989.

Plate 17, continued

Row 3

Green Comma. *Polygonia faunus.* Passadumkeag, Maine. June 24, 1989.

Polygonia faunus. Fayette Co., W.Va. 1978.

Row 4

Gray Comma. *Polygonia progne.* Potts Creek, Jefferson NF, Monroe Co., W.Va. September 14, 1987.

Polygonia progne. Spruce Knob Lake, Monongahela NF, Randolph Co., W.Va. July 27, 1987.

Polygonia progne. Muddy Creek, Greenbrier Co., W.Va. June 14, 1984.

PLATE 18

Row 1

Compton Tortoiseshell. *Nymphalis vau-album j-album.* Big Meadow Rd., Latah Co., Idaho. September 1984.

Nymphalis vau-album j-album. Hickory Rd., north Attleboro, Mass. July 1, 1984.

Row 2

Mourning Cloak. *Nymphalis antiopa antiopa.* Elkins, Randolph Co., W.Va. July 15, 1980.

Nymphalis a. antiopa. Elkins, Randolph Co., W.Va. August 7, 1986.

Row 3

Milbert's Tortoiseshell. *Nymphalis milberti milberti.* Cambridge, Washington Co., N.Y. June 10, 1987.

Nymphalis m. milberti. Troy, Latah Co., Idaho. July 1989.

Row 4

American Lady. *Vanessa virginiensis.* Rt. 30, 1 mile south of I-79, Lewis Co., W.Va. May 31, 1985.

Vanessa virginiensis. Elkins, Randolph Co., W.Va. July 9, 1989.

PLATE 19

Row 1

American Lady. *Vanessa virginiensis.* Beverly, Randolph Co., W.Va. June 22, 1988.

Painted Lady. *Vanessa cardui.* Petersburg, Grant Co., W.Va. October 16, 1984.

Row 2

Vanessa cardui. Pigs Ear, Pocahontas Co., W.Va. July 27, 1983.

Vanessa cardui. Gap Mills, Monroe Co., W.Va. September 2, 1988.

Row 3

Red Admiral. *Vanessa atalanta rubria.* Burnsville Lake, Braxton Co., W.Va. August 23, 1983.

Vanessa atalanta rubria. Elkins, Randolph Co., W.Va. July 15, 1980.

Row 4

Common Buckeye. *Junonia coenia.* Greenbottom WMA, Cabell Co., W.Va. September 6, 1989.

Junonia coenia. Greenbottom WMA, Cabell Co., W.Va. September 6, 1989.

Junonia coenia. Greenbottom WMA, Cabell Co., W.Va. September 6, 1989.

PLATE 20

Row 1

Canadian Tiger Swallowtail. *Papilio canadensis.* Coe Hill, Ontario, Canada. June 6, 1986.

Papilio canadensis x P. glaucus. Lanesville, Tucker Co., W.Va. 18 June 1973.

Row 2

Red-spotted Purple. *Limenitis a. arthemis x Limenitis a. astyanax.* Dillon's Hollow Rd., Columbia Co., Pa. August 15, 1972.

Limenitis a. arthemis x Limenitis a. astyanax. Laporte, Sullivan Co., Pa. July 4, 1966.

Limenitis arthemis astyanax. Beverly, Randolph Co., W.Va. 19 June 1972.

Row 3

Limenitis arthemis astyanax. Rough Run, Pendleton Co., W.Va. July 12, 1989.

Limenitis arthemis astyanax. Cass, Pocahontas Co., W.Va. 29 June 1989.

PLATE 21

Row 1

Viceroy. *Limenitis archippus archippus.* Stonewall Jackson Lake, Lewis Co., W.Va. September 6, 1988.

Limenitis a. archippus. Elkins, Randolph Co., W.Va. July 25, 1987.

Row 2

Limenitis a. archippus. Elkins, Randolph Co., W.Va. July 23, 1983.

Hackberry Emperor. *Asterocampa celtis celtis.* Near Ravenswood, Wood Co., W.Va. May 28, 1982.

Asterocampa c. celtis. Inwood, Berkeley Co., W.Va. August 5, 1986 (reared).

Row 3

Asterocampa c. celtis. Martinsburg, Berkeley Co., W.Va. August 16, 1986.

Asterocampa c. celtis. Larenim Park, north of Burlington, Mineral Co., W.Va. August 10, 1984.

Asterocampa c. celtis. River Rd., east of Moorefield, Hardy Co., W.Va. August 27, 1989.

Row 4

Tawny Emperor. *Asterocampa clyton clyton.* River Rd., east of Moorefield, Hardy Co., W.Va. June 10, 1986.

Asterocampa c. clyton. Upper Tract, Pendleton Co., W.Va. June 25, 1990.

Asterocampa c. clyton. Leetown, Jefferson Co., W.Va. July 26, 1985.

PLATE 22

Row 1

Northern Pearly Eye. *Enodia anthedon.* Burnsville Lake, Braxton Co., W.Va. August 23, 1983.

Enodia anthedon. Elk River WMA, Braxton Co., W.Va. May 13, 1985.

Enodia anthedon. Fork Creek WMA, Boone Co., W.Va. June 3, 1980.

Row 2

Eyed Brown. *Satyrodes eurydice eurydice.* Coe Hill, Ontario, Canada. July 1, 1986.

Satyrodes e. eurydice. Port Franks, Lambton, Ontario, Canada. July 20, 1988.

Satyrodes e. eurydice. Flambem State Forest,

Sawyer Co., Wis. July 7, 1984.

Row 3

Appalachian Brown. *Satyrodes appalachia.* Dowthas Creek, Minnehaha Springs, Pocahontas Co., W.Va. July 18, 1985.

Satyrodes appalachia. Dowthas Creek, Minnehaha Springs, Pocahontas Co., W.Va. July 18, 1985.

Satryrodes appalachia. Dowthas Creek, Minnehaha Springs, Pocahontas Co., W.Va. July 18, 1985.

Row 4

Gemmed Satyr. *Cyllopsis gemma.* Burnsville Lake, Braxton Co., W.Va. August 23, 1983.

Cyllopsis gemma. Pinnacle Creek, Mullens, Wyoming Co., W.Va. July 6, 1987.

Carolina Satyr. *Hermeuptychia sosybius.* Ormond Beach, Volutia Co., Fla. August 24, 1982.

Hermeuptychia sosybius. Fork Creek WMA, Boone Co., W.Va. May 12, 1982.

Row 5

Little Wood Satyr. *Megisto cymela.* Elkins, Randolph Co., W.Va. June 10, 1984.

Megisto cymela. Elk River WMA, Braxton Co., W.Va. May 31, 1985.

Megisto cymela. Beverly, Randolph Co., W.Va. August 2, 1971.

PLATE 23

Row 1

Common Wood Nymph. *Cercyonis pegala pegala.* Beverly, Randolph Co., W.Va. July 15, 1984.

Cercyonis p. pegala. Sinks of Gandy, Randolph Co., W.Va. July 27, 1987.

Cercyonis p. pegala. Fort Martin, Monongalia Co., W.Va. July 4, 1983.

Row 2

Dull-eyed Grayling. *Cercyonis pegala nephele.* Drummond Island, Lake Huron, Mich. August 5, 1984.

Cercyonis pegala nephele. Perry Sound Dist., Ontario, Canada. August 6, 1988.

Cercyonis pegala nephele. Near Katy, Marion Co., W.Va. June 15, 1965.

Plate 23, continued

Row 3

Monarch. *Danaus plexippus.* Beverly, Randolph Co., W.Va. September 9, 1975.

Danaus plexippus. Beverly, Randolph Co., W.Va. August 31, 1975.

Row 4

Danaus plexippus. Greenbottom WMA, Cabell Co., W.Va. September 6, 1989.

American Snout. *Libytheana carinenta bachmanii.* Leetown Hatchery, Leetown, Jefferson Co., W.Va. September 24, 1985

Libytheana carinenta bachmanii. Hinton, Summers Co., W.Va. June 12, 1978.

PLATE 24

Row 1

Silver-spotted Skipper. *Epargyreus clarus.* Reddish Knob, Pendleton Co., W.Va. June 30, 1983.

Epargyreus clarus. Medina Rd., Wood Co., W.Va. June 6, 1986.

Row 2

Golden-banded Skipper. *Autochton cellus.* Fork Creek WMA, Nellis, Boone Co., W.Va. May 25, 1988.

Autochton cellus. Fork Creek WMA, Nellis, Boone Co., W.Va. May 25, 1988.

Row 3

Hoary Edge. *Achalarus lyciades.* Rt.30, 1 mile south of I-79, Lewis Co., W.Va. May 24, 1985.

Achalarus lyciades. Rt. 30, 1 mile south of I-79, Lewis Co., W.Va. May 24, 1985.

Row 4

Northern Cloudywing. *Thorybes pylades.* Beverly, Randolph Co., W.Va. June 17, 1984.

Thorybes pylades. Fork Creek WMA, Nellis, Boone Co., W.Va. June 13, 1984.

Row 5

Southern Cloudywing. *Thorybes bathyllus.* Rt. 30, 1 mile south of I-79, Lewis Co., W.Va. May 24, 1985.

Thorybes bathyllus. Fort Martin, Monongalia Co., W.Va. July 4, 1983.

PLATE 25

Row 1

Confused Cloudywing. *Thorybes confusis.* Mobile, Ala. July 16, 1988.

Thorybes confusis. Kingfisher Landing, S.C. August 6, 1976.

Row 2

Dreamy Duskywing. *Erynnis icelus.* Webster Co., W.Va. May 25, 1983.

Erynnis icelus. Cabins, Grant Co., W.Va. May 6, 1985.

Erynnis icelus. Webster Co., W.Va. May 25, 1983.

Row 3

Sleepy Duskywing. *Erynnis brizo brizo.* Indian Mills, Summers Co., W.Va. April 25, 1984.

Erynnis b. brizo. Larenim Park, north of Burlington, Mineral Co., W.Va. April 27, 1984.

Erynnis b. brizo. East Lynn Lake WMA, Wayne Co., W.Va. April 12, 1984.

Row 4

Juvenal's Duskywing. *Erynnis juvenalis.* East Lynn Lake WMA, Wayne Co., W.Va. April 12, 1984.

Erynnis juvenalis. Sugar Grove, Pendleton Co., W.Va. May 10, 1984.

Erynnis juvenalis. Larenim Park, north of Burlington, Mineral Co., W.Va. April 27, 1984.

Row 5

Horace's Duskywing. *Erynnis horatius.* Big Ugly WMA, Lincoln Co., W.Va. July 7, 1987.

Erynnis horatius. Danville, Boone Co., W.Va. July 5, 1986.

Erynnis horatius. Big Ugly WMA, Lincoln Co., W.Va. July 7, 1987.

Row 6

Mottled Duskywing. *Erynnis martialis.* Big Ugly WMA, Lincoln Co., W.Va. July 7, 1987.

Erynnis martialis. Springfield WMA, Hampshire Co., W.Va. August 15, 1984.

Erynnis martialis. Big Draft Rd., Blue Bend, Greenbrier Co., W.Va. July 16, 1986.

PLATE 26

Row 1

Columbine Duskywing. *Erynnis lucilius.* Cabins, Grant Co., W.Va. May 15, 1987.

Erynnis lucilius. Cabins, Grant Co., W.Va. September 2, 1986.

Erynnis lucilius. Cabins, Grant Co., W.Va. July 31, 1986.

Row 2

Wild Indigo Duskywing. *Erynnis baptisiae* Fort Martin, Monongalia Co., W.Va. August 28, 1985.

Erynnis baptisiae. Summersville Dam, Nicholas Co., W.Va. August 1, 1984.

Erynnis baptisiae. Summersville Dam, Nicholas Co., W.Va. August 1, 1984.

Row 3

Persius Duskywing. *Erynnis persius persius.* Necedah Wildlife Refuge, Juneau Co., Wis. May 15, 1987.

Erynnis p. persius. Milford, Pike Co., Pa. June 1, 1989.

Erynnis p. persius. Necedah Wildlife Refuge, Juneau Co., Wis. May 15, 1987.

Row 4

Grizzled Skipper. *Pyrgus centaureae wyandot.* Larenim Park, north of Burlington, Mineral Co., W.Va. December 29, 1986 (reared).

Pyrgus centaureae wyandot. Larenim Park, north of Burlington, Mineral Co., W.Va. January 5, 1987 (reared).

Pyrgus centaureae wyandot. Larenim Park, north of Burlington, Mineral Co., W.Va. December 31, 1986 (reared).

Row 5

Common Checkered Skipper. *Pyrgus communis communis.* River Rd. near Romney, Hampshire Co., W.Va. August 10, 1983.

Pyrgus c. communis. River Rd. south of Romney, Hampshire Co., W.Va. August 2, 1983.

Pyrgus c. communis. River Rd. south of Romney, Hampshire Co., W.Va. August 10, 1983.

Row 6

Common Sootywing. *Pholisora catullus.* Inwood, Berkeley Co., W.Va. July 27, 1986.

Pholisora catullus. Moorefield, Hardy Co., W.Va. August 4, 1987.

Pholisora catullus. Petersburg, Grant Co., W.Va. August 15, 1984.

Row 7

Hayhurst's Scallopwing. *Staphylus hayhurstii.* Harpers Ferry, Jefferson Co., W.Va. September 15, 1986 (reared).

Staphylus hayhurstii. Harpers Ferry, Jefferson Co., W.Va. September 5, 1986 (reared).

Staphylus hayhurstii. Harpers Ferry, Jefferson Co., W.Va. August 30, 1986 (reared).

PLATE 27

Row 1

Swarthy Skipper. *Nastra lherminier.* Fort Martin Power Station, Fort Martin, Monongalia Co., W.Va. August 9, 1985.

Nastra lherminier. Fort Martin Power Station, Fort Martin, Monongalia Co., W.Va. August 28, 1985.

Nastra lherminier. Fort Martin Power Station, Fort Martin, Monongalia Co., W.Va. August 28, 1985.

Clouded Skipper. *Lerema accius.* Ormond Beach, Volusia Co., Fla. October 26, 1984.

Row 2

Lerema accius. Shenandoah River, Charles Town, Jefferson Co., W.Va. August 24, 1984.

Least Skipper. *Ancyloxypha numitor.* Medina Rd., Wood Co., W.Va. August 21, 1986.

Ancyloxypha numitor. Elkins, Randolph Co., W.Va. August 7, 1983.

Ancyloxypha numitor. Elkins, Randolph Co., W.Va. August 7, 1983.

Row 3

European Skipper. *Thymelicus lineola.* Beverly, Randolph Co., W.Va. June 17, 1984.

Thymelicus lineola. Beverly, Randolph Co., W.Va. June 17, 1984.

Thymelicus lineola. Pleasants Creek WMA, Taylor Co., W.Va. June 21, 1984.

Plate 27, continued

Row 4

Fiery Skipper. *Hylephila phyleus.* Coonskin Park, north of Charleston, Kanawha Co., W.Va. September 10, 1985.

Hylephila phyleus. Coonskin Park, north of Charleston, Kanawha Co., W.Va. September 10, 1985.

Hylephila phyleus. Huttonsville Prison, Huttonsville, Randolph Co., W.Va. August 9, 1982.

Row 5

Leonard's Skipper. *Hesperia leonardus leonardus.* North Fork of Anthony Creek, Greenbrier Co., W.Va. August 27, 1987.

Hesperia l. leonardus. Dowthas Creek Rd., south of Minnehaha Springs, Pocahontas Co., W.Va. August 29, 1983.

Hesperia l. leonardus. Branch Mtn., Hardy Co., W.Va. August 15, 1983.

Row 6

Cobweb Skipper. *Hesperia metea metea.* 1 mile north of Smoke Hole, Pendleton Co., W.Va. April 30, 1987.

Hesperia m. metea. 1 mile north of Smoke Hole, Pendleton Co., W.Va. April 30, 1987.

Hesperia m. metea. 1 mile north of Smoke Hole, Pendlelton Co., W.Va. April 30, 1987.

Row 7

Indian Skipper. *Hesperia sassacus sassacus.* Grassy Knob Tower, Greenbrier Co., W.Va. June 15, 1984.

Hesperia s. sassacus. Spruce Knob, Randolph Co., W.Va. June 11, 1985.

Hesperia s. sassacus. Grassy Knob Tower, Greenbrier Co., W.Va. June 15, 1984.

PLATE 28

Row 1

Peck's Skipper. *Polites peckius.* Elkins, Randolph Co., W.Va. June 10, 1984.

Polites peckius. Elkins, Randolph Co., W.Va. June 10, 1984.

Polites peckius. Helvetia, Randolph Co., W.Va. August 24, 1989.

Row 2

Tawney-edged Skipper. *Polites themistocles.* U.S. Rt. 20 near Wallace, Harrison Co., W.Va. May 25, 1985.

Polites themistocles. Ormond Beach, Volutia Co., Fla. June 17, 1980.

Polites themistocles. Deer Creek, south of Greenbank, Pocahontas Co., W.Va. June 22, 1984.

Row 3

Crossline Skipper. *Polites origines.* Stonewall Jackson Lake WMA, Lewis Co., W.Va. September 6, 1983.

Polites origines. Fort Martin Power Station, Ft. Martin, Monongalia Co., W.Va. August 28, 1986.

Polites origines. Rt.30, 1 mile south of I-79, Lewis Co., W.Va. May 31, 1985.

Row 4

Whirlabout. *Polites vibex vibex.* Ormond Beach, Volutia Co., Fla. October 26, 1984.

Polites v. vibex. South Charleston, Kanawha Co., W.Va. June 27, 1976.

Polites v. vibex. Ormond Beach, Volutia Co., Fla. October 20, 1983.

Polites v. vibex. Ormond Beach, Volutia Co., Fla.October 26, 1984.

Row 5

Long Dash. *Polites mystic mystic.* Elkins, Randolph Co., W.Va. June 10, 1984.

Polites m. mystic. Spruce Knob Lake, Randolph Co., W.Va. July 7, 1983.

Polites m. mystic. Elkins, Randolph Co., W.Va. June 10, 1984.

Row 6

Northern Broken-Dash. *Wallengrenia egeremet.* Files Creek Rd., Beverly, Randolph Co., W.Va. July 15, 1984.

Wallengrenia egeremet. Reddish Knob, near Sugar Grove, Pendleton Co., W.Va. July 12, 1983.

Wallengrenia egeremet. Files Creek Rd., Beverly, Randolph Co., W.Va. July 15, 1984.

Plate 28, continued

Row 7

Little Glassywing. *Pompeius verna verna.* Stonecoal Lake WMA, Lewis Co., W.Va. July 5, 1983.

Pompeius v. verna. George Washington NF, Sugar Grove, Pendleton Co., W.Va. June 28, 1985.

Pompeius v. verna. Pleasants Creek WMA., Taylor Co., W.Va. June 21, 1984.

PLATE 29

Row 1

Sachem. *Atalopedes campestris huron.* Charleston, Kanawha Co., W.Va. September 19, 1984.

Atalopedes campestris huron. Charleston, Kanawha Co., W.Va. September 19, 1984.

Atalopedes campestris huron. Nellis, Boone Co., W.Va. September 19, 1984.

Row 2

Delaware Skipper. *Atrytone logan logan.* Beverly, Randolph Co., W.Va. July 24, 1972.

Atrytone l. logan. Deer Creek, south of Greenbank, Pocahontas Co., W.Va. July 12, 1984.

Atrytone l. logan. Larenim Park, north of Burlington, Mineral Co., W.Va. June 28, 1984.

Row 3

Hobomok Skipper. *Poanes hobomok.* Grassy Knob Tower, Greenbrier Co., W.Va. June 15, 1984.

Poanes hobomok. East Fork of Glady Creek, Glady, Randolph Co., W.Va. June 11, 1985.

Poanes hobomok. Sugar Grove, Pendleton Co., W.Va. June 7, 1984.

Row 4

Poanes hobomok. East Fork of Glady Creek, Glady, Randolph Co., W.Va. June 11, 1985.

Poanes hobomok. Sugar Grove, Pendleton Co., W.Va. June 7, 1984.

Zabulon Skipper. *Poanes zabulon.* Springfield WMA, Hampshire Co., W.Va. August 15, 1984.

Row 5

Poanes zabulon. Muddy Creek, Percey's Mill, Greenbrier Co., W.Va. May 24, 1984.

Poanes zabulon. Burnsville Lake, Braxton Co., W.Va. August 23, 1983

Poanes zabulon. Cacapon State Park, Morgan Co., W.Va. August 24, 1984.

Row 6

Black Dash. *Euphyes conspicuus conspicuus.* Cranesville Wetland, Preston Co., W.Va. July 19, 1987.

Euphyes c. conspicuus. Cranesville Wetland, Preston Co., W.Va. July 19, 1987.

Euphyes c. conspicuus. Cranesville Wetland, Preston Co., W.Va. July 19, 1987.

Row 7

Two-spotted Skipper. *Euphyes bimacula.* Deer Creek Wetland, south of Greenbank, Pocahontas Co., W.Va. June 22, 1984.

Euphyes bimacula. Deer Creek Wetland, south of Greenbank, Pocahontas Co., W.Va. June 22, 1984.

Euphyes bimacula. Deer Creek Wetland, south of Greenbank, Pocahontas Co., W.Va. June 22, 1984.

PLATE 30

Row 1

Dun Skipper. *Euphyes vestris metacomet.* Larenim Park, north of Burlington, Mineral Co., W.Va. June 27, 1984.

Euphyes vestris metacomet. Files Creek Rd., Beverly, Randolph Co., W.Va. July 15, 1984.

Euphyes vestris metacomet. Larenim Park, north of Burlington, Mineral Co., W.Va. June 27, 1984.

Row 2

Dusted Skipper. *Atrytonopsis hianna hianna.* Summersville Dam, Nicholas Co., W.Va. May 22, 1987.

Atrytonopsis h. hianna. Summersville Dam, Nicholas Co., W.Va. May 22, 1987.

Atrytonopsis h. hianna. Summersville Dam, Nicholas Co., W.Va. May 22, 1987.

Plate 30, continued

Row 3

Pepper and Salt Skipper. *Amblyscirtes hegon.*
  Blackwater Falls State Park, Davis, Tucker
  Co., W.Va. June 2, 1987.

Amblyscirtes hegon. East Fork of Glady Creek,
  Glady, Randolph Co., W.Va. May 29, 1987.

Amblyscirtes hegon. East Fork of Glady Creek,
  Glady, Randolph Co., W.Va. May 29, 1987.

Row 4

Common Roadside-Skipper. *Amblyscirtes
  vialis.* Powers Hollow, Cabins, Grant Co.,
  W.Va. May 3, 1985.

Amblyscirtes vialis. Powers Hollow, Cabins,
  Grant Co., W.Va. May 3, 1985.

Amblyscirtes vialis. Larenim Park, north of
  Burlington, Mineral Co., W.Va. May 17,
  1984.

Row 5

Ocola Skipper. *Panoquina ocola.* Ormond
  Beach, Volutia Co., Fla. October 26, 1984.

Panoquina ocola. Ormond Beach, Volutia Co.,
  Fla.October 26, 1984.

Row 6

Long-tailed Skipper. *Urbanus proteus proteus.*
  Ormond Beach, Volusia Co., Fla.
  December 27, 1983.

Urbanus p. proteus. Ormond Beach, Volusia
  Co., Fla. December 27, 1983.

Glossary

Aberration. An abnormal appearing individual resulting from environmental conditions or a genetic deviation.

Abdomen. The soft, slender, segmented portion of the body behind the thorax.

Aestivate. To spend periods of hot summer weather in an inactive state.

Anal plate. The plate or shield covering the dorsal portion of the last segment of the abdomen.

Androconial scales. Specialized scales, usually in patches along the wing veins, that produce pheromones used in mate attraction and mating behavior. Found in males of several groups.

Antenna(ae). Long, segmented sensory appendage arising from the top of a butterfly's head.

Anterior. Toward the front, or the head end.

Anticlines. Relating to a fold in which the sides dip away from a common line or crest. An arch of layered rock in the earth's surface.

Apex. The tip or outer angle of a butterfly's wing.

Apiculus. The curved tip of the antenna in skippers.

Basal. The inner portion of a butterfly's wing closest to the body (fig.4).

Bask. Exposing the wing surface to sun rays to obtain heat energy for flight.

Bifurcate. To divide or branch into 2 parts.

Bivoltine. Refers to species that have 2 generations, or broods, each year.

Boreal. Refers to the cold, northern areas in the Canadian and Arctic life zones, usually composed of spruce-fir and sphagnum bogs.

Broad-leaved. Woody, deciduous trees, shrubs, or vines. Trees without needles.

Brood. A flight, or generation, of butterflies of a single species.

Caudal. Referring to the hind end; toward the tail.

Cell. The area of the wings between the veins.

Chalaza(ae). A hardened lump on a larva that bears more than 1 seta.

Chitin. An organic compound that is the major component of the hard exoskeleton of insects.

Chrysalis. The hard case in which the larva transforms to the adult. Also referred to as a pupa.

Cleft. The division into 2 parts or branches at the head or tail of the larva.

Club (antenna). The enlarged tip of a butterfly antenna.

Communal. To group together as larvae or adults.

Coniferous. Forest type comprising softwoods, such as pines, spruces, and firs.

Corolla. The petals of a flower fused and unfused. In some flowers the fused petals form a deep tube.

Costa. The upper or leading edge of a butterfly's wing (fig.4).

Costal fold. A flap containing scent scales (androconia) along the leading edge of the forewing of males in some species.

Costal margin. The area along the costa of the forewing or hindwing (fig.4).

Cove hardwoods. An association of hardwood trees in which yellow poplar is a major component. Usually found in rich, moist bottoms of west facing slopes.

Coxa. The first segment of the leg attached to the thorax.

Cremaster. The posterior end of the pupa (chrysalis) that usually contains hooks that fasten it to a pad of silk spun by the larva.

Cryptic. Refers to an organism that blends into its environment either in color or pattern.

Deciduous. Woody plants (trees and shrubs) that drop their leaves during winter.

Desiccate. To dry out.

Detritus. Fragmented material from decaying plants.

Diapause. A period of reduced or halted development during any life stage, usually to pass a period of unfavorable environmental conditions.

Dicotyledons. Any flowering plant that begins development from 2 seed leaves and has branched veins.

Dimorphic. Having 2 distinct forms usually between sexes; however, it may apply to 2 forms of a single sex.

Discal cell. The area enclosed by the wing veins extending from the base to the middle of the wing (fig.4).

Disjunct. An isolated or widely separated population from the normal range of a species.

Distal. The part furthest away from the point of attachment.

Diurnal. Being active during daylight hours.

Dormant. A state of being inactive.

Dorsal (Dorsum). The upper portion or back surface.

Dorsolateral. The upper portion of the side.

Eclose. To emerge from a pupal case.

Ecology. The study of plants and animals and their environment.

Epiphysis. A movable process of the tibia; an extension or spur.

Eriophyid mites. A small mite that infects plant leaves causing leaf galls to form. Common on black cherry.

Ethyl acetate. A chemical compound often used in killing jars.

Extirpate. To eliminate a species from a geographic area.

Eye spots. Refers to the colored rings in a butterfly wing that resemble eyes.

Falcate. The curve or hook of the tip of a butterfly forewing.

Family. A group or related species with many similar characteristics.

Fat body. Globular structure in the abdomen of a butterfly that stores fats and oils for energy.

Fauna. Animal life of a particular region.

Femur. The third segment of an insect's leg from the body.

Forelegs. The first pair of legs near the head of the butterfly.

Forewing. The larger forward wing of each pair.

Form. A color or seasonal variation of a species.

Frass. The excrement, or droppings, of the larva.

Fringe. The long scales along the outer edge of the wing.

Generation. All the individuals of a life cycle of a given population from egg to adult.

Genitalia. The external parts of the reproductive organs of a butterfly used in mating.

Glassine. A translucent envelope used to store butterfly specimens.

Glycoside. An acetal compound that produces a glycose sugar by the action of enzymes.

Gregarious. To group together.

Gynandromorph. An abnormal individual exhibiting characteristics of both sexes in various parts of the body.

Habitat. The area or plant community in which a butterfly lives.

Heaths. A group of plants belonging to the family Ericaceae.

Hemisphere. A half of a sphere; used to describe an egg flattened on the bottom surface.

Hemolymph. The circulatory fluid of an insect.

Herbaceous. Pertaining to herb-like plants without woody stems.

Hibernaculum. The winter nest or shelter of in insect.

Hibernate. A condition of reduced body activity, which conserves energy, to pass the winter season.

Hindwing. The smaller rear wing of each pair.

Host. A plant or other insect fed upon by the larva.

Host race. A group of butterflies within a species that utilizes a different plant host than the rest of the population.

Humeral vein. A short vein near the base of the hindwing in many species of butterflies (fig.5).

Hyaline. A clear (transparent) spot that lacks scales in the wing of a butterfly.

Hybrid. The offspring of 2 different species that breed together.

Imbibe. To drink or sip liquids.

Immigrant(ate). An individual that moves into an area from somewhere else.

Inflorescence. The flower head or cluster of flowers.

Inner margin. The lower edge of the forewing or hindwing (fig.4).

Insecta. The class of invertebrates to which the insects belong.

Instar. Any stage in the development of a larva. Larvae go through 4 to 8 instars depending upon the species.

Interbreed. When 2 closely related separate species or subspecies breed together, producing a hybrid.

Invertebrate. Any animal that does not have a internal skeletal system.

Keel. A flat, narrow projection from the surface of an object (pupa).

Labial palpus(i). The elongated, hairy mouth part that lies on each side of the proboscis.

Larva(ae). The development stage of a butterfly between the egg and the pupa (chrysalis).

Lateral. Along the side.

Longitudinal. Running lengthwise along the body from head to tail.

Marginal. Along the edge of a butterfly's wing (fig.4).

Median. An area toward the center of a butterfly's wing (fig.4).

Mesic. Characterized by a moderate amount of moisture.

Mesophilic. Growing best in an intermediate environment (as one with a moderate temperature).

Middorsal. The middle of the back or upper surface.

Migrate. To fly from one geographic region to another.

Mimicry. To copy another individual or species through appearance or behavior.

Molt. To shed the skin or exoskeleton.

Monocotyledon. Any flowering plant that sprouts from a seed with a single leaf and has parallel veins (grasses and sedges).

Nectar. A sweet liquid that is produced by flowers and used as food by many butterfly species.

Nuptial. Capable of breeding or mating.

Ommatidium(ia). One of the visual elements that make up the compound eye of an insect.

Osmeterium. A fleshy, orange, forked gland that can be everted from the back of a larva's head when alarmed. It gives off a pungent, foul smelling odor. Found in Papilionidae.

Outer margin. The margin of the wings furthest away from the body (fig.4).

Oviposit. The act of laying eggs.

Paradichlorbenzene (PDB). A chemical fumigant.

Parasite. An insect that feeds and lives on another insect, usually killing the host insect.

Patrol. To fly back and forth through an area in search of a mate.

Perch. To station oneself on a leaf, twig, or stem to await the passing of a mate.

Photoperiod. The amount of daylight in any 24-hour period.

Postbasal. The portion of a butterfly wing above the base (fig.4).

Posterior. The rear portion of an insect opposite the head.

Postmedian. The portion of a butterfly wing beyond the center from the base (fig.4).

Powdery bloom. A white powder that covers portions of the pupa in some species.

Predaceous. An insect that kills and eats other insects.

Proboscis. The coiled, straw-like feeding tube of a butterfly.

Proleg. One of the first pair of legs closest to the head; foreleg.

Pronotum. The dorsal surface behind the head of an insect on the prothorax.

Prothorax. The anterior segment of the thorax that bears the first pair of legs.

Prothoracic shield. The dorsal plate on the prothorax of a larva, usually dark in color.

Pteridine pigment. A yellow crystalline factor in the pigment of butterfly wings.

Pubescence. A dense covering of short hairs creating a soft appearance.

Puddle. A gathering of butterflies (often several species), usually males, at wet spots.

Pupa. The development stage of a butterfly between the larva and the adult. Also termed chrysalis.

Pupate. The transformation from the larva to the pupa.

Race. See *host race.*

Radial veins. A group of veins that terminates near the apex or tip of the wing.

Rehydrate. To reabsorb moisture.

Reticulated. Having a network or pattern resembling a web.

Riparian. The area of land adjacent to a stream or river.

Rosette. Refers to a group of leaves in a circle at the base of a plant.

Scent patch. A group of specialized scales (androconia) located in the wing of some butterfly species, also referred to as the stigma.

Scolus(i). The branching spine or seta-bearing horn on a larva.

Secrete. To produce a substance from a gland.

Sedentary. An individual or population of butterflies that remains close to or within its habitat.

Segment. One of several ringlike sections of a larva or a butterfly's abdomen.

Seta(ae). The hairs or scales of a larva or adult butterfly.

Setose. Hairlike bristle.

Sibling race. A closely related population within a species that is genetically isolated, by flight season or habitat.

Silk girdle. The silken strand around the middle of a butterfly pupa used for support.

Species. A group of similar individuals in a taxonomic classification that freely breed with one another.

Spiracle. An oval breathing vent along the side of a larva or butterfly.

Stigma. See *scent patch*.

Striations. A series of fine stripes or lines across a butterfly's wings.

Subapical. The area of the wing below the tip toward the base (fig.4).

Subcostal. The area of the wing below the leading edge, or costa, bounded by the subcostal vein that is unbranched (fig.5).

Subdorsal. An area of the body below the back or upper surface.

Subfamily. A taxonomic classification of insect groups below the family level (a subdivision of the family).

Sublateral. An area of the body below the sides.

Submarginal. That portion of the wing inside the outer edge (fig.4).

Subspecies. A subdivision of the species classification, usually resulting from geographic isolation of like species. Many subspecies interbreed in zones where the 2 populations intermix.

Substrate. Any material on which a larva attaches its pupa.

Superfamily. A taxonomic classification above the family level that contains several families.

Suture. The dividing line, or joint, between 2 segments of a larva's or butterfly's body.

Tarsal claw. The terminal claw(s) at the end of a butterfly's leg.

Tarsus(i). The terminal end of an butterfly's leg, comprising several segments.

Temperate. A region of moderate temperature. Temperate zone is the region between the Tropic of Cancer and the Arctic Circle.

Thecla spot. An orange, red, and black spot on the outer angle of the hindwing in the hairstreaks (Lycaenidae).

Thorax. The middle section of the body to which the wings and legs are attached.

Tibia. The part of the insect's leg that lies between the femur and the tarsus.

Tibial spur. A spur or spine that arises from the tibia.

Tomentose. A thick mat of hairs; a pubescence.

Tornus. The inner angle or anal angle of the forewing of a butterfly.

Transverse. Extended across the wing.

Traverse. To cross the wing.

Treeline. The northern-most limit of trees toward the Arctic.

Tribe. A taxonomic classification that groups several species into a single category.

Trivoltine. Having 3 generations per year.

Trocanter. The second segment of an insect's leg between the coxa and the femur.

Tropical. A tropical environment occurring between the Tropic of Cancer and the Tropic of Capricorn.

Truncate. Having the tip or apex of the wing squared off.

Tubercle. Any small, rounded projection on the body of a larva or pupa.

Ultraviolet. Short wavelengths, most of which are shorter than that of visible light, but longer than x-rays.

Univoltine. Having a single generation per year.

Ventral. The bottom or lower surface.

Xeric. A dry environment; desertlike.

References

Acciavatti, R. E., T. J. Allen, C. Stuart. 1992. The West Virginia tiger beetles (Coleoptera: Cicindelidae). *Cicindela* 24(3, 4):45–78.

Burns, John M. 1964. Evolution of skipper butterflies in the genus *Erynnis*. *Univ. Calif. Publ. Entomology* 37:1–216.

Calhoun, J. V., T. J. Allen, and D. C. Iftner. 1989. Temporary breeding populations of *Phoebus sennae eubule* (L.) (Pieridae) in Ohio and West Virginia. *J. Res. Lepid.* 28(1–2):123–25.

Clark, A. H. 1926. Carnivorous butterflies. *Smithsonian Institution Publ.* 2856:439–508.

———. 1936. The gold-banded skipper *(Rhabdoides cellus)*. *Smithsonian Miscellaneous Collection* 95(7):1–50.

Clench, H. K. 1972. *Celastrina ebenina*, a new species of Lycaenidae (Lepidoptera) from the eastern United States. *Ann Carnegie Mus.* 44:33–44.

Core, E. 1966. *Vegetation of West Virginia*. Parsons, W.Va.: McClain Printing.

dos Passos, C. F., and A. B. Klots. 1969. The systematics of *Anthocharis midea* Hübner (Lepidoptera: Pieridae). *Entomol. Amer.* 45:1–34.

Drees, B. M., and L. Butler. 1978. Rhopalocera of West Virginia. *Journ. Lepid. Soc.* 32(3):198–206

Edwards, W. H. 1866. Description of certain species of diurnal Lepidoptera found within the limits of the United States and British America. *Proc. Ent. Soc. Philadelphia* 6(5):200–208.

———. 1868, 1884, 1897. *The butterflies of North America*. Vols. 1, 2, 3. Boston, Mass. Houghton Mifflin.

Evans, W. H. 1951–1955. *A catalogue of the American Hesperiidae in the British Museum*. Vols. 1–4. London: British Museum (Natural History).

Fenneman. 1938. *Physiography of eastern United States*. New York: McGraw-Hill.

Gillespie, W. H., and E. C. Murriner. 1991. *Forest resources of West Virginia, 1990*. Charleston: West Virginia Division of Forestry.

Hagen, R. H., R. C. Lederhouse, J. L. Bossart, and J. M. Scriber. 1991. *Papilio canadensis* and *P. glaucus* (Papilionidae) are distinct species. *J. Lepid. Soc.* 45(4):245–58.

Harris, L., Jr. 1972. *Butterflies of Georgia*. Norman: University of Oklahoma Press.

Heitzman, J. R. 1963. The complete life history of *Staphylus hayhurstii*. *J. Res. Lepid.* 2(2):170–72.

————. 1964. The early stages of *Euphyes vestris. J. Res. Lepid.* 3:151–53.

————. 1974. *Atrytonopsis hianna* biology and life history in the Ozarks. *J. Res. Lepid.* 13:239–45.

Howe, W. H. ed. 1975. *The butterflies of North America.* Garden City, N.Y.: Doubleday.

Iftner, D. C., J. A. Shuey, and J. V. Calhoun. 1992. *Butterflies and skippers of Ohio.* Columbus: Ohio State University. Research Report No. 3.

Lindsey, A. W., E. L. Bell, and R. C. Williams. 1931. The Hesperioidea of North America. *J. Sci. Lab.,* Denison Univ., 26:1–142.

Luebke, H. J., J. M. Scriber, and B. S. Yandell. 1988. Use of multivariate discriminant analysis of male wing morphometrics to delineate a hybrid zone for *Papilio glaucus glaucus* and *P. g. canadensis* in Wisconsin. *Amer. Midl. Nat.* 119(2):366–79.

MacNeill, D. C. 1975. Hesperiidae. In *The butterflies of North America,* edited by W. H. Howe, pp. 423–578. New York: Doubleday.

McGuire, W. W. 1982. New oviposition and larval hostplant records for North American *Hesperia* (Rhopalocera: Hesperiidae). *Bull. Allyn. Mus.* 72:1–6.

Miller, L. D., and F. M. Brown. 1981. A catalogue/checklist of the butterflies of America north of Mexico. *Mem. Lepid. Soc.,* no. 2.

Miller, M. E. 1977. Snow in West Virginia. Nat. Oceanic and Atmospheric Adm.-Eastern Reg. Hdqtrs. Cleveland, Ohio: Weather Station Forecast Office. NOAA Tech. Memo. NWS ER-63.

North American Butterfly Association (NABA). 1994. Collated list of English names for North American butterflies. *Amer Butterflies* 2(2):28–35.

Oliver, C. G. 1979. Experimental hybridization between *Phyciodes tharos* and *P. batesii* (Nymphalidae). *J. Lepid. Soc.* 24:77–81.

————. 1980. Phenotypic differentiation and hybrid breakdown within *Phyciodes* "tharos" (Lepidoptera: Nymphalidae) in northeastern United States. *Ann. Ent. Soc. Amer.* 73:715–21.

Opler, P. A., and C. O. Krizek. 1984. Butterflies east of the Great Plains. Baltimore, Md.: Johns Hopkins University Press.

Opler, P. A., C. O. Krizek, and V. Malikul. 1992. *A field guide to eastern Butterflies.* Boston, Mass.: Houghton Mifflin.

Pratt, G. F., D. M. Wright, and H. Pavulaan. 1994. The various taxa and hosts of the North American *Celastrina* (Lepidoptera: Lycaenidae). *Proc. Entomol. Soc. Wash.* 96(3):566–78.

Pyle, R. M. 1981. *The Audubon Society field guide to North American butterflies.* New York: Alfred A. Knopf.

Rutowski, R. L. 1980. Courtship solicitation by females of the checkered white butterfly, *Pieris protodice. Behav. Ecol. Sociobiol.* 7:113–17.

Saunders, W. 1870. On the larva of *Thecla inorata. G. & R. Canad. Ent.* 2(5):61–64.

Schull, Ernest M. 1987. *The butterflies of Indiana.* Indiana Academy of Science. Bloomington and Indianapolis: Indiana University Press.

Scott, J. A. 1975. Mate-locating behavior in western North American butterflies. *J. Res. Lepid.* 14:1–40.

————. 1986. *The butterflies of North America, a natural history and field guide.* Stanford, Calif.: Stanford University Press.

Shapiro, A. M. 1966. *Butterflies of the Delaware Valley.* Philadelphia: Amer. Entomol. Soc., Special Publ.

————. 1974. Butterflies and skippers of New York State. *Search Agriculture* 4(3):1–60.

Shuey, J. A., and J. W. Peacock. 1989. Host plant exploitation in an oligophagous population of *Pieris virginiensis* (Lepidoptera: Pieridae). *Am. Midl. Naturalist* 122(2):255–61.

Silberglied, R. E., and O. R. Taylor. 1973. Ultraviolet differences between the sulphur butterflies, *Colias eurytheme* and *C. philodice,* and a possible isolating mechanism. *Nature* 241:406–408.

Strausbaugh, P. D., and E. L. Core. 1977. Flora of West Virginia. 2d ed. Grantsville, W.Va.: Seneca Books, Inc.

West, D. A., W. M. Snellings, and T. A. Herbek. 1972. Pupal color dimorphism and its environmental control in *Papilio polyxenes asterius.* Stoll (Lepidoptera: Papilionidae). *J. NY Ent. Soc.* 80:205–11.

West Virginia Division of Natural Resources. 1973. Inventory of wildlife resources of West Virginia. Charleston: West Virginia Department of Natural Resources.

Wright, W. B., Jr. 1981. *Erora laeta* (Lycaenidae), observations and breeding experiments. Unpublished report. WVDNR, Operation Center, Elkins, W.Va. (photocopy).

Young, A. M. 1980. Some observations of the natural history and behavior of the Camberwell Beauty (Mourning Cloak) butterfly *Nymphalis antiopa* (Linnaeus) (Lepidoptera: Nymphalidae) in the United States. *Ent. Gazette* 31:7–18.

Acknowledgments

This book is an accumulation of many years of observations and collection data that began with the publication of the *Rhopalocera of West Virginia* by Drees and Butler (1978), which listed 111 species for the state. Their work was followed with surveys conducted by Paul Opler for his book *Butterflies East of the Great Plains* (Opler and Krizek 1984). Nearly a decade of further surveys and observations, along with the information from these two books, form the basis of this book.

I would be remiss if I didn't first acknowledge the one person who has spent endless hours reviewing, editing, typing, and assembling the manuscript for this book. Without the assistance of Karen Eye, the production of this publication would have been very difficult, if not impossible.

Several people spent many hours reviewing and editing each section of the manuscript and provided many helpful suggestions. David Wright reviewed the *Celastrina* species accounts. Kathleen Carothers Leo and Scott Butterworth, West Virginia Division of Natural Resources, with whom I work daily, made the first reviews of the technical sections before they were reviewed and commented upon by Linda Butler, West Virginia University, and Dale Schweitzer, The Nature Conservancy. The final review of the manuscript was completed by Paul A. Opler, National Biological Survey. To these people I am grateful for their assistance and suggestions.

Many collectors and observers provided information compiled for this book, along with records from school collections, the West Virginia collection in Charleston, museums, and universities. Special thanks go to all those who assisted in this effort: James Amrine, James Arnold, Dean Atkins, Rodney Bartgis, Richard Boscoe, Fred Bower, Linda Butler, John Calhoun, Shawn Clark, George Constanz, Sam Coppedge, James Crum, Joshua Crum, Bastiaan Drees, James Evans, Frank Fee, Robert Gardiner, Ronald Gatrelle, Brian

Hagenbuch, Robert Hardbarger, William Hartgroves, Mark Holman, Richard Smith, Jr., Michael Lengwiler, Vincent Lucas, Thomas Manley, Brian McDonald, Donna Mitchell, John Nordin, Sam Norris, John Northeimer, Charles Oliver, Paul Opler, David Parshall, Harry Pavulaan, John Prescott (deceased), June Preston, Robert Raguso, Joe Rieffenberger, Bill Roody, Dale Schweitzer, John Shuey, David Smith, Craig Stihler, Jason Weintraub, and James Woodrum (deceased).

Others provided specimens for use in the plates: David Parshall provided the *Phyciodes batesii,* Robert Gardener the *Erynnis persius,* and Kirk Zufelt the *Incisalia irus.* Photos of caterpillars (larvae) were loaned by the following: Greg Ballmer (plate 33, *Atlides halesus*), Marc Minno (plate 40, *Erynnis horatius*), John Rawlins (plate 33, *Satyrium calanus falacer*), Térèse Arcand (plate 37, *Nymphalis vau-album*), and David Wright (plate 33, *Lycaena epixanthe*). To all these people I am grateful for their assistance.

Special thanks are also extended to David Wright for his assistance in obtaining various Lycaenidae larvae (*Satyrium edwardsii, Satyrium liparaps,* and *Incisalia irus*), to Ronald Gatrelle for providing *Phyciodes batesii* and *Chlosyne gorgone* larvae, and to Earl Hoke for the *Nymphalia milberti* larvae used in the photographs. I would also like to thank Mark Scriber for his review of *Papilio glaucus* and *P. canadensis* hybrid specimens from West Virginia.

Several people also assisted with the production of range maps, figures, and plates presented in this guide: Christin Hudgins produced the majority of the range maps; Janet Clayton, Rebecca Collins, Anne Johansen, and Randy Tucker assisted with maps and figures; and Robert Campbell assisted with the photographing of several plates. To all these folks, I am indebted.

I would also like to acknowledge the West Virginia Division of Natural Resources for giving me the time to do field surveys and to work on the production of this manuscript.

Lastly, I would like to thank my wife for her love and patience while I chased after butterflies.

Index

Numbers in boldface refer to pages on which butterfly plates appear.